Black Lives Matter vs. All Lives Matter

Black Lives Matter vs. All Lives Matter

A Multidisciplinary Primer

Edited by
Abdul Karim Bangura

LEXINGTON BOOKS
Lanham • Boulder • New York • London

Published by Lexington Books
An imprint of The Rowman & Littlefield Publishing Group, Inc.
4501 Forbes Boulevard, Suite 200, Lanham, Maryland 20706
www.rowman.com

6 Tinworth Street, London SE11 5AL, United Kingdom

Copyright © 2021 by The Rowman & Littlefield Publishing Group, Inc.

All rights reserved. No part of this book may be reproduced in any form or by any electronic or mechanical means, including information storage and retrieval systems, without written permission from the publisher, except by a reviewer who may quote passages in a review.

British Library Cataloguing in Publication Information Available

Library of Congress Cataloging-in-Publication Data

Names: Bangura, Abdul Karim, 1953- editor.
Title: Black lives matter vs. all lives matter : a multidisciplinary primer / edited by Abdul Karim Bangura.
Description: Lanham : Lexington Books, [2021] | Includes bibliographical references and index.
Identifiers: LCCN 2021032424 (print) | LCCN 2021032425 (ebook) |
  ISBN 9781793640666 (cloth) | ISBN 9781793640673 (ebook) |
  ISBN 9781793640680 (pbk)
Subjects: LCSH: Black lives matter movement. | Life—Moral and ethical aspects. | Blacks—Social conditions. | Black lives matter movement—United States. | Life—Moral and ethical aspects—United States. | Blacks—United States—Social conditions.
Classification: LCC HT1581 .B53 2021 (print) | LCC HT1581 (ebook) | DDC 323.1196—dc23
LC record available at https://lccn.loc.gov/2021032424
LC ebook record available at https://lccn.loc.gov/2021032425

To humankind across the globe that must endure and triumph over the many contemporary challenges!

Contents

Preface ix
Abdul Karim Bangura

Acknowledgments xv

1 General Introduction 1
  Abdul Karim Bangura

2 Religious Perspective 17
  Simon Gisege Omare

3 Literary Perspective 41
  Saidu Bangura

4 Mathematical Perspective 61
  Abdul Karim Bangura

5 Public Administration/Policy Perspective 75
  Rachael M. Rudolph

6 Linguistic Perspective 107
  Lilian Achieng' Magonya and Pamela Anyango Oloo

7 Sociological Perspective 129
  Benson Waiganjo Kanyingi

8 Gender and Sexuality Perspective 153
  Cecy Edijala Balogun

9 Economic Perspective 181
  Abdul Amin Kamara

10	Psychological Perspective *Lilian Anyango Olick*	197
11	Business Perspective *Olumuyiwa Adekunle Kehinde*	215
12	Political Perspective *Omosefe Oyekanmi*	247
13	Juvenile Justice Perspective *Gerald K. Fosten*	273
14	General Conclusion *Abdul Karim Bangura*	299
Bibliography		321
Index		353
About the Contributors		357

Preface
Abdul Karim Bangura

In the wake of the murder of forty-six-year-old African American George Floyd in Minneapolis, Minnesota, on May 25, 2020, which sparked protests in many cities across the United States and in some foreign countries, the debate between proponents of Black Lives Matter and All Lives Matter has been reignited. It behooves me to quickly mention here that while these two slogans with their attendant movements are the major ones in the debate, there are three others that are less discussed and known. They are (1) Blue Lives Matter, a movement that supports police officers and their sacrifices across the United States; (2) White Student Union Facebook Groups, a movement that represents the interests of white students on university and college campuses across the country; and (3) White Lives Matter, a movement that characterizes itself as "dedicated to promotion of the white race and taking positive action as a united voice against issues facing our race" (Southern Poverty Law Center, 2016, p. 1).

On the one hand, some advocates of Black Lives Matter call for the use of "non-violent civil disobedience" and others do not eschew violence as the method to protest against police brutality and other racially motivated violence against black people. On the other hand, advocates of All Lives Matter insist that their slogan is inclusive of all people, not just blacks. Proponents of both positions transcend race, albeit the debate has been based on emotionalism. This book brings together thinkers from across the globe to go beyond the sentimentalism and offer analyses from across the scholarly disciplines for a more systematic understanding of the issue and suggest policy prescriptions.

Indeed, there exists a plethora of books on either Black Lives Matter or All Lives Matter, with each touting its ideology and disparaging the other. In essence, authors of both ideologies seem to talk past each other. It was not until 2018 that two authors, Amanda Nell Edgar and Andre E. Johnson, collaborated to publish a book juxtaposing both ideologies. The book is titled *The Struggle over Black Lives Matter and All Lives Matter* under the Lexington Books' Rhetoric, Race, and Religion series. Based on the book's description, the coauthors, Edgar being an assistant professor and Johnson being an associate professor of Communication at the University of Memphis in Tennessee, can be said to employ their discipline's perspective to investigate the multiplex nexus between Black Lives Matter and All Lives Matter as it evolves on social media and in offline interpersonal connections. The authors examine cultural influences such family history, fear, religion, postracialism, and workplace pressure to delineate the denotations of these ideological factions from the points of view of average citizens.

Consequently, the book has at least two major limitations. The first limitation is that its explainability (i.e., the extent to which the feature values of an instance are related to its model prediction in such a way that humans can understand them; basically, it is the understanding to the question "why is this happening?") is confined to communication principles pertaining to social media and offline interpersonal relationships. The second limitation is that due to the time it was written, the book does not cover the events that took place and continued to take place in the post-George Floyd timeframe. The current book therefore trumps these shortcomings because of its systematic multidisciplinary analyses and coverage of past and more recent events.

Thus, to begin with, the book is unique because it is the second to broach the debate between the proponents of Black Lives Matter and All Lives Matter, but it is the most comprehensive due to its multidisciplinary nature and timeframe covered. Indeed, a multidisciplinary investigation leads to a better understanding and communication of the phenomenon. Next, the contributors are well qualified because they are seasoned academics from across the globe, with a few doctoral degree candidates collaborating with their academic mentors. In addition, all of them are well published in their disciplines.

Chapter 1 "General Introduction" by Abdul Karim Bangura is the general introduction. It entails the explanatory section at the beginning of the book. It begins with the general tenets of the slogans Black Lives Matter and All Lives Matter. Next, it discusses the ideological propositions of the two slogans. Thereafter, the perspectives of some of the major proponents of the slogans are presented. Thereupon, the criticisms of the competing perspectives are proffered.

Chapter 2 "Religious Perspective" by Simon Gisege Omare examines how at the heart of George Floyd's death is the issue of undermining the dignity of a human being through racial prejudice. The chapter argues that the dualistic dichotomy of the emerging debate between Black Lives Matter and All Lives Matter does not offer a coherent view of humanity that will help to address this problem. The chapter also attempts to offer an alternative worldview, which argues that within the Judeo-Christian, understanding of each and every human being is created in the image, and likeness of God can be found an inclusive motif for equal dignity of all human beings within a multiracial twenty-first-century society.

Chapter 3 "Literary Perspective" by Saidu Bangura looks at the politics of race, identity, gender, colonialism, and slavery as they affect black women in the Motherland, Africa, and in the Diaspora, the United States, within the context of Black Lives Matter versus All Lives Matter. The chapter seeks to connect the multiple painful stories of black women as they struggle to undo the barriers set for them by their male counterparts, blacks as well as whites, and the society in which they live through the works of three women novelists and one playwright: Tsitsi Dangarembga, Toni Morrison, Alice Walker, and Ama Ata Aidoo. Themes from these writers are juxtaposed with those presented by male and other female writers.

Chapter 4 "Mathematical Perspective" by Abdul Karim Bangura entails a quantitative analysis of the coverages the Black Lives Matter and All Lives Matter movements have received on the internet and in the major newspapers and television networks in the United States. Thus, the mathematical analysis comprises both univariate analysis, whereby each variable (i.e. each movement) in the data set collected is explored separately, and bivariate analysis, whereby two variables (i.e., both movements) are examined simultaneously for the purpose of determining the empirical relationship between them.

Chapter 5 "Public Administration/Policy Perspective" by Rachael M. Rudolph investigates debates among the Black Lives Matter and All Lives Matter movements on police reform that first emerged during the Ferguson protests in 2014. The chapter shows how the debates have taken center stage once again with the protests sweeping the United States and around the globe following the death of George Floyd. This chapter also examines these policy debates at the local, state, and federal levels of government and across the various political divisions, from the Anarchists, socialists, and far-right non-mainstream political groups to the traditional, mainstream political groups in American politics. By placing the debates within the complex sociopolitical environment and identifying the points of convergence and divergence, we are better able to explain the successes of the 2020 police reforms.

Chapter 6 "Linguistic Perspective" by Lilian Achieng' Magonya and Pamela Anyango Oloo points out that cognitive linguists advance the thesis that human cognition and categorization are interlaced. Thus, the chapter posits that, evidently, this equally applies to racism as an aspect of human cognition which historically has profiled people of color based on dehumanizing stereotypes. In view of this, the chapter infuses arguments from visual semiotics and cognitive linguistics to explore the interface between semiotics of color and the body pictorial metaphor in Black Lives Matter posters aimed at denouncing racism and the emergent divergent discourse arising from the counter All Lives matter in the context of contested signs.

Chapter 7 "Sociological Perspective" by Benson Waiganjo Kanyingi addresses the topic of Black Lives Matter versus All Lives Matter using the intersectionality theoretical model. It states that injustices are felt by people differently in regard to race, classism, ability, and gender and, therefore, the call for All Lives Matter is one for equality since injustices cut across races. Black Lives Matters, however, is a result of legitimate concerns on specific problems happening to African Americans that are unique to them, which can be traced historically to slavery, lynching, and segregation. The chapter also interrogates the role socializing agents in United States (media representatives, schools, legal and economic systems, etc.—agents of white power) play as systems of racial ignorance that continuously work to undermine genuine aspects of black freedom.

Chapter 8 "Gender and Sexuality Perspective" by Cecy Edijala Balogun looks at how the rising spate of racial discrimination has been the focus of the international community in recent times, resulting in the debate between proponents of Black Lives Matter and All Lives Matter ideologies. The chapter argues that racial discrimination affects diverse segments of a society in different dimensions. It adds that women suffer from racial discrimination from a double perspective based on their gender and race or ethnicity. This chapter therefore addresses racism from a gender and sexuality perspective, focusing on the forms and context of racial discrimination against women, the implication on their performance in the global space, and the efforts being made to address the issue within the context of the Black Lives Matter and All Lives Matter ideologies.

Chapter 9 "Economic Perspective" by Abdul Amin Kamara examines from an economic perspective the racism that emerged after the abolition of the slave trade, the ushering of colonialism, and then the postcolonial era (in-dependence Africa) coming down to the previous and recent Floydian uprisings globally in terms of how they affect the state of affairs economically in the past and now, and in the future. The chapter critically scrutinizes the "powernomics" concept that most black people ignore globally and rely on miracles to happen in black communities in the Motherland (Africa) and in the Diaspora within the contours of Black Lives Matters versus All Lives Matters. This chapter also seeks to connect several scenarios to demonstrate that racism is based predominantly on economics.

Chapter 10 "Psychological Perspective" by Lilian Anyango Olick probes how the continued murders of blacks are the result of the failure of the United States to fight the effects of the past five decades of continued systemic racism, with the death of George Floyd being the most recent. The chapter posits that for blacks, these events are repetitive and traumatic and, as such, represent a severe ongoing threat to everyone's mental health. This chapter then examines the impact of racial unrest on blacks in America and features the need for improving mental health support for this group. It also delineates a sociocultural model to the psychology of racism that integrates diverse programs of theory and the concept of racism as a psychological defense mechanism within the context of the debate between advocates of the Black Lives Matters and All Lives Matter ideologies.

Chapter 11 "Business Perspective" by Olumuyiwa Adekunle Kehinde advances the idea that human beings cannot set apart their work "selves" from their community "selves." It also points out that the United States like many other nations has been preaching diversity and equality, but systemic racism and white supremacy and privilege in corporations around the globe persist. Now, the Black Lives Matter and All Lives Matter movements have magnified their voices to ensure reduction or eradication of historic white privilege. This chapter thus investigates how these movements are motivating the needs for distinct actions among business owners and corporations to rethink and support true equality in workplaces and communities. Perceptions of individuals, corporations, and chief executive officers (CEOs) concerning why Black Lives Matter or All Lives Matter within and outside workplaces will be examined in this chapter.

Chapter 12 "Political Perspective" by Omosefe Oyekanmi observes that as the brutal murder of George Floyd sparks up global debates on the disvalue of black lives, the devastating effect of foreign intrusion into African affairs for selfish interest and political domination, at the detriment of ethnic violence in Africa, has also come to the fore. With an objective to unmask the complex causes of Africa's contemporary crises, this chapter examines Western political exploitation and subjugation in Africa and its counter-effect in inducing ethnic conflict and war vis-à-vis the context of Black Lives Matters versus All Lives Matter. Hinged on the 1948 Human Rights Declaration, which values the human life as sacrosanct, regardless of race, color, or sex, the chapter therefore situates the debate on the premise that all human lives matter and none should be sacrificed for another.

Chapter 13 "Juvenile Justice Perspective" by Gerald K. Fosten utilizes the history of youth services; current theories of adolescent development; and the impact of community disadvantage, child abuse, and neglect on behavior to examine the treatment of black bodies—in particular, black males—as they matriculate into adulthood. Deaths of Treyvon Martin, Tamir Rice, Jordan Edwards, and other black youths at the hands of institutionalized policing reveal patterns of systemic institutionalized behavior that oftentimes manifests in the overuse of force and deaths of Black youths. Parents of black youths having "the talk" with their black children are challenged to protect their children from societal norms that criminalize black youths in their earliest stages of development. The chapter therefore also investigates the challenges of black youths as they attempt to exist in a societal construct that places the full weight of the criminal justice system on their necks. The chapter concludes that if effective change is to be the outcome, proponents of Black Lives Matter and All Lives Matter must address juvenile justice policies and behaviors.

Chapter 14 "General Conclusion" by Abdul Karim Bangura reveals that after a reading of the preceding chapters, many times during the editing process, the general conclusion reached is that the underlying notion in all of them is the Ancient Kemetian/Egyptian *neb ānkh iw neter khe-t* [every life is sacred], a principle that also exists in the tenets of the Abrahamic faiths—that is, Judaism, Christianity, and Islam—as the precept to guide human relations across the world. The chapter then proceeds to elaborate on the Kemetain notion and its renderings in the three Abrahamic faiths.

To guarantee unity and linkage throughout the book, each chapter entails at least six sections. The first section introduces the topic covered; the second section discusses the conceptual framework upon which the chapter is systematically grounded; the third, fourth, and fifth sections entail pertinent case studies or issues pertaining to the topic; and the sixth section draws a conclusion and offers recommendations based on the findings.

In sum, the book is suitable for the general public and as a main or supplementary text for undergraduate and graduate students taking courses in the humanities and sciences. It is also useful to professors teaching about and scholars doing research in these fields. In addition, policy makers in these areas would be interested in the valuable information that the book provides. Furthermore, relevant political activists and advocacy groups would be interested in the book to pursue their objectives.

REFERENCES

Edgar, A. N. and Johnson, A. E. (2018). *The Struggle over Black Lives Matter and All Lives Matter*. Lanham, MD: Lexington Books.

Southern Poverty Law Center. (2016). White Lives Matter. Retrieved on August 21, 2020, from https://www.splcenter.org/fighting-hate/extremist-files/group/white-lives-matter

Acknowledgments

We, and hopefully many readers, owe gratitude to the following:

The Creator, for providing us the fortitude to do this work during this very challenging time.

The Ancestors, for providing us guidance, protection, and the willingness to seek verities.

Mwalimu Emmanuel D. Babatunde and Mwalimu Kelbogile T. Setiloane, for providing us intellectual and spiritual support for this and other projects.

My wonderful daughter, Isatu Ramatu Bangura, for designing the radiant image on the cover of the book.

The anonymous reviewers, for their suggestive evaluations. Asking difficult questions leads to better answers and clarifications.

Our immediate and global families, for their prayers and support.

Chapter 1

General Introduction

Abdul Karim Bangura

This chapter is the explanatory section of the book. It starts with the general tenets of the slogans Black Lives Matter and All Lives Matter. Next, it talks about the ideological propositions of the two slogans. After that, the perspectives of some of the major proponents of the slogans are discussed. Thereupon, the criticisms of the competing perspectives are deliberated. The chapter ends with a conclusion that complements the discussions of the preceding aspects. Before doing all this, however, it makes sense to first delineate what the two slogans represent and provide brief backgrounds of the two movements for those readers who may not be familiar with them.

To begin with, as I state in the preface of this book, on the one hand, some proponents of Black Lives Matter advocate the use of "non-violent civil disobedience" and others do not eschew violence as an approach to protest against police brutality and other racially motivated violence against blacks. On the other hand, advocates of All Lives Matter insist that their slogan is inclusive of all people, not just blacks. As we will later see in this chapter, however, proponents of Black Lives Matter perceive the slogan of All Lives Matter not as a call for inclusiveness but as a criticism of the Black Lives Matter movement.

BRIEF BACKGROUND OF THE BLACK LIVES MATTER MOVEMENT

For starters, Black Lives Matter was launched on July 13, 2013, as a social movement to advocate and protest against racial discrimination worldwide. The founders are Alicia Garza, an African American civil rights activist and writer; Patrisse Cullors, an African American activist and artist; and Opal

Tometi, an African American human rights activist, community organizer, strategist, and writer. Other key members include DeRay Mckesson, an African American civil rights activist, former school administrator, and podcaster; Johnetta "Netta" Elzie, an African American civil rights activist and newsletter editor; Kareem Jackson, also known by his stage name Tef Poe, an African American activist, rapper, and musician; and Erica Garner-Snipes, an African American activist and daughter of Eric Garner who was killed in 2014 by a New York City police officer. The organization is largely located in the United States but also has operations in many other countries, including Australia, Canada, Denmark, France, Germany, Japan, New Zealand, and the United Kingdom (Black Lives Matter, 2020; Maloney, 2015; Taibbi, 2017; Salomon, 2015).

Next, Black Lives Matter started organizing large demonstrations in 2014 and has continued to do so to the present day. It is approximated that in the year 2020 alone, about twenty-six million people from every racial and ethnic group in the United States comprising members and nonmembers of the organization played a role in these demonstrations. Thus, it has emerged as one of the largest social movements in American history. It calls for defunding the police and investing the money in black communities and "alternative emergency response models" to replace those of the police. Its popularity increased in 2019 and 2020 after experiencing a significant decline in 2018 (Buchanan et al., 2020; DefundThePolice.org, 2020; Cohn and Quealy, 2020; Parker et al., 2020).

Also, since Black Lives Matter was launched with its hashtag #BlackLivesMatter in 2013, it has been featured in various cultural spheres that include literature, film, song, television, and the visual arts. Many media organizations are also presenting materials dealing with the organization and racial injustice. In 2020, there was an increase in the popularity of books and television shows that portrayed the organization (Day, 2015; Al-Heeti, 2020).

Brief Background of the All Lives Matter Movement

To start with, All Lives Matter was also launched in 2014 as a response to the national attention Black Lives Matter was receiving. All Lives Matter is not a formal group or network and is based on the premise that Black Lives Matter is a divisive assertion maintaining that *"only* Black Lives Matter" (Agozino, 2018). All Lives Matter does not even have a website; it exists as a hashtag and a catchphrase. On various occasions, All Lives Matter has received support from some well-known people in the United States, including athletes, actors, musicians, and politicians from both the Democratic and the Republican Party, and from every race and ethnicity (Participedia, 2020).

Next, the catchphrase All Lives Matter appears to resonate with more Americans compared to Black Lives Matter. For instance, a Rasmussen Reports' poll conducted via telephone in August of 2015 revealed that the slogan "All Lives Matter" was perceived by 78 percent of American voters to be closest to their own personal belief compared to the slogan "Black Lives Matter" or none of the two. The slogan "Black Lives Matter" was said to be closest to the perspective of 11 percent of voters and 9 percent said neither catchphrase is closest to their beliefs (Rasmussen Reports, 2015).

In addition, individuals who employ the All Lives Matter catchphrase are self-selecting. They use social media and participate in protests. While they do not organize protest rallies themselves, they do make their slogan heard and seen at relevant rallies (Participedia, 2020).

GENERAL TENETS OF BLACK LIVES MATTER AND ALL LIVES MATTER

In this section, I discuss the common precepts of Black Lives Matter and All Lives Matter. They are presented separately for the sake of clarity.

General Tenets of Black Lives Matter

Black Lives Matter advocates proffer a couple of beliefs. First, they opine that in order to achieve equity in the United States, reparations should be paid for damages connected to slavery, redlining in housing should be ended, education policy should promote equality, mass incarceration should be abolished, and food insecurity should be eliminated. Added to these initiatives are ending mass surveillance, investing in public education, communities controlling the police, defunding the police, removing police from schools, decriminalizing sex work, halting the building of new jails, acquitting protesters, and eliminating cash bail (Terrell, 2016; McGirt, 2016; Reuters, 2016; M4BL, 2020).

Second, advocates of Black Lives proffer that the most effective way to get their messages across are through direct action tactics and the use of political slogans. In terms of direct action tactics, advocates believe that to get people to address the movement's concerns, the actions must make people uncomfortable. The actions include rallies, protests, and die-ins (Tucker and Hegg, 2015; The Rachel Maddow Show, 2015; Gottfried and Eccher, 2015). As it pertains to the utilization of political slogans, catchphrases attributed to blacks murdered by police are given credence. Among these slogans are "Black Lives Matter," "I can't breathe," and "Hands up, don't shoot" (USDOJ, 2015; Kim and Jackson, 2014).

General Tenets of All Lives Matter

Advocates of All Lives Matter base their precepts on scriptures in the Holy Bible. The Gospel Light Society, for instance, proposes the following tenets: (a) all lives matter to God, no matter what stand one takes on issues concerning injustice, police brutality, or race in the United States; (b) since every person is made in the image of God, he or she deserves to be treated with dignity, fairness, honor, and dignity; (c) because every life is a delineation of a soul that deserves rescuing from sin and retribution from sin, every life matters to God; (d) all lives matter to God as the term "word" is employed three times in the verses of John 3:16–17: that is,

> For God so loved the world, that he gave his only begotten Son, that whosoever believeth in him should not perish, but have everlasting life. For God sent not his Son into the world to condemn the world; but that the world through him might be saved.

(e) God cares about and wants to save everyone, no matter the person's ethnicity, race, or socioeconomic status (Gospel Light Society, 2020, p. 1).

Also, Randy McClave culls from the Holy Bible to offer precepts on the slogan in his poem accordingly titled "All Lives Matter." The following are the eleven tenets he tenders: (1) everyone was created by God from the same mold; (2) God colored us with different dyes, but we are all the same; (3) no matter our skin colors, God created us either women or men; (4) either when we are living or dead, God sees all of us the same; (5) we must see one another individually or by our acts and deeds, as opposed to listening to rumors and stories in which bigotry dominates; (6) our blood is colored the same when we bleed; (7) all of us are descendants of Adam and Eve and, thus, it is dreadful to judge people only by their races; (8) we should recognize each one's face instead of hating or killing one another; (9) who we are is not composed by one's skin color; (10) being a killer or a drug czar is not the result of one's skin color; and (11) when we accept the verity that All Lives Matter, we will someday shatter many myths and rumors (McClave, 2020).

IDEOLOGICAL PROPOSITIONS OF BLACK LIVES AND ALL LIVES MATTER

Broached here are the hypothesized principles of Black Lives Matter and All Lives Matter. These are proffered independently for lucidity.

Ideological Propositions of Black Lives Matter

The Black Lives Matter movement has hypothesized "13 guiding principles" to which anyone who chooses to be involved in its activities should adhere. They are as follows:

(1) "Restorative Justice—collectively, lovingly and courageously working vigorously for freedom and justice for Black people and, by extension, all people";
(2) "Empathy—engage comrades with the intent to learn about and connect with their contexts";
(3) "Loving Engagement—embodying and practicing justice, liberation, and peace in our engagements with one another";
(4) "Diversity—acknowledging, respecting and celebrating difference(s) and commonalities";
(5) "Globalism—(being) part of the global Black family and (being) aware of the different ways we are impacted or privileged as Black folk who exist in different parts of the world";
(6) "Queer Affirming—freeing ourselves from the tight grip of heteronormative thinking or, rather, the belief that all in the world are heterosexual unless they disclose otherwise";
(7) "Trans Affirming—embracing and making space for trans brothers and sisters to participate and lead";
(8) "Collective Value—Black lives matter, regardless of actual or perceived sexual identity, gender identity, gender expression, economic status, ability, disability, religious beliefs or disbeliefs, immigration status or location";
(9) "Intergenerational—all people, regardless of age, show up with capacity to lead and learn";
(10) "Black Families—making our spaces family-friendly and enable parents to fully participate with their children";
(11) "Black Villages—disrupting the Western-prescribed nuclear family structure requirement by supporting each other as extended families and 'villages' that collectively care for one another";
(12) "Unapologetically Black—in affirming that Black Lives Matter, we need not qualify our position"; and
(13) "Black Women—building a Black women affirming space free from sexism, misogyny, and male-centeredness" (Black Lives Matter, 2018).

Ideological Propositions of All Lives Matter

Since the All Lives Matter movement does not have its own website, it is difficult to delineate its hypothesized principles. Nonetheless, a careful reading of Domonique Foxworth's article on the slogan makes it possible to identify three ideological propositions that can be attributed to the movement. The first ideological proposition is that people have the right to a trial and should therefore not be killed merely because of their skin color. The second ideological proposition denotes that since every person is a human being first, and the notion of race was a later construction, his or her skin color would not matter if no one told the person that it matters. The third ideological proposition designates that blacks and everyone else, including police officers, should be treated like human beings. Hence, just as it is wrong to kill a black person because of his or her race, it is equally wrong to kill a police officer who has not committed a misdeed (Foxworth, 2016).

PERSPECTIVES OF SOME OF THE MAJOR PROPONENTS

This section entails an examination of the viewpoints of some of the key advocates of Black Lives Matter and All Lives Matter. They are propounded individually for coherence. I must state here, however, that only the perspectives of three key advocates for each movement are presented for the sake of brevity.

Perspectives of Some of the Major Proponents of Black Lives Matter

Beginning with former President Barack Obama, he states that the proponents of Black Lives Matter are not suggesting that only the lives of blacks matter; instead, they are saying that there are specific problems present in black communities that are not happening in other communities. He therefore argues that this is a legitimate issue that must be dealt with seriously and candidly (Tucker and Hegg, 2015). In addition, he makes the following clarification to his definition of Black Lives Matter:

> I know that there's some who have criticized even the phrase "Black Lives Matter" as if the notion is as if other lives don't matter. We get "All Lives Matter" or "Blue Lives Matter." I understand the point they're trying to make. I think it's also important for us to understand that the phrase "Black Lives Matter" simply refers to the notion that there's a specific vulnerability for African Americans that needs to be addressed. It's not meant to suggest that other lives don't matter. It's to suggest that other folks aren't experiencing this particular vulnerability and so we shouldn't get too caught up somehow in this notion that people who are asking for fair treatment are somehow automatically

anti-police or trying to only look out for black lives as opposed to others. I think we have to be careful about playing that game because, obviously, that's not what is intended. (quoted in McDonald, 2018, p. 1)

Next, U.S. Democratic Senator Elizabeth Warren argues that the actions of advocates of Black Lives Matter and their supporters are structured around three kinds of discrimination: (1) "economic" (the condition of a group as regards material prosperity), (2) "policing" (the maintenance of law and order by a police force), and (3) "voting" (to register a vote: that is, a formal indication of a choice between two or more candidates or courses of action, expressed typically through a ballot or a show of hands or by voice). She contends that these discriminations that are at the core of the history of African American civil rights struggles remain unfinished. She adds that after fifty years since President John F. Kennedy and the Rev. Dr. Martin Luther King Jr. spoke out, violence against African Americans continues. She also calls for the "restoration" of the Voting Rights Act and to update rules around voting by including automatic registration, a national voting holiday, and an end to felon disenfranchisement (Bouie, 2015).

In addition, Dr. Angela Davis (professor emerita, political activist, philosopher, author and a founding member of the Black Panther Party) asserts that the reforms for which proponents of Black Lives Matter are advocating can go a long way in addressing the intrinsic racism in policing. She believes that the context that has been shaped by the movement is quite different from what she has witnessed in the past, most probably because the coronavirus/COVID-2019 pandemic provided us the opportunity to see the most brutal instances of state violence. She states that the upshot of the brutality and the ensuing protests organized by the Black Lives Matter movement is that more people across the races are now engaging in self-criticism and corporations are dropping racist brandings. As she also puts it, "For hundreds of years, Black people have passed down this collective yearning for freedom from one generation to the next . . . . We are doing now what should have been done in the aftermath of slavery" (quoted in Mosley and Hagan, 2020, p. 1) Nonetheless, she posits that "before eliminating racism, we must eradicate *racial capitalism*: a term designed to encourage people to think about the ways in which capitalism and racism are interlinked" (quoted in Mosley and Hagan, 2020, p. 1). This is because, according to her, "there is no capitalism without racism" (quoted in Mosely and Hagan, 2020, p. 1).

Perspectives of Some of the Major Proponents of All Lives Matter

First, Dr. Alveda King ("activist, author, former state representative for the Twenty-Eighth District in the Georgia House of Representatives, niece of the Rev. Dr. Martin Luther King Jr., and daughter of civil rights activist A. D. King and Naomi Barber King") broaches the veracity that some blacks have recently been shot in very unjust circumstances and that their lives just like all other lives are sacred to God. Thus, for her, "the answer to violence is not more violence." She goes on to suggest that in order for us to discuss and resolve these problems, peace must prevail. She therefore considers the tearing down of statues and real estate, desecrating parks, and tearing up our communities and nation as unwarranted. Instead, she suggests that we "confess to God, 'hey we got it wrong, we want to get it right, help us' " (quoted in Page, 2020, p. 1). Thereafter, she draws from the Holy Bible and states that "the right side of history is understanding that we are one blood, one race—Acts 17:26" and adds that "we are not color blind. If you're color blind, you need glasses; that's a medical condition. Our ethnicity is a special gift. Every ethnic group has something to offer. We don't kill, disrupt and destroy. We just don't do that" (quoted in Page, 2020, p. 1). She then concludes with the following observation:

> We are a human family. Yes the African American community has been mistreated in America. So has the Irish American. So has the Native American. We must learn to live together as brothers and sisters, and we're not going to perish together as fools. But the Black Lives Matter situation comes from a wounded community, a hurt community, that has really been hurt, and that's why it's there. We need to talk; we need to repent as Americans. (quoted in Page, 2020, p. 1)

Second, U.S. Secretary of Housing and Urban Development Dr. Ben Carson avows that "all lives matter—and all lives include Black lives." He therefore calls upon us to stop succumbing to the whims of individuals who want to divide us into the various special interest groups and start thinking about what works for everyone (Sherfinski, 2015). He agrees that we should be very concerned about what is taking place particularly in the inner cities. He adds that it is a crime that for a young black man, the most likely cause of death is homicide. He believes that it is a serious problem that must be addressed seriously. He nonetheless contends that the backlash one receives from proponents of Black Lives Matter for advocating that All Lives Matter is tantamount to "political correctness going amok" (Rankin, 2015, p. 1). And about those individuals and groups that are calling for defunding or eliminating the police, he says the following:

> We need to look at the whole picture. One of the things that I always like to point out to people is how about we just remove the police for 24 hours. Can you imagine the chaos that would ensue? The vast majority of police are very

good people. Are there are bad apples? Of, course. If you hire a plumber and he does a bad job, do you say all plumbers are bad? Let's go out and kill them? I don't think we do that. We need to be a little more mature, but certainly in cases where police are doing things that are inappropriate, I think we ought to investigate those promptly and justice should be swift (quoted in Rankin, 2015, p. 1).

Third, United States Republican Senator Tim Scott of South Carolina is not bothered by Black Lives Matter activists' objection to his use of the slogan All Lives Matter. For him, "Black lives, White lives, police officers, jurists, all of us, even politicians, all of our lives matter" (quoted in Scott, 2015, p. 1). He admits that racism has historically been a matter in the United States regarded as harmful and needing to be dealt with and overcome. He insists, however, that in order to move forward as a country, unity is needed. He adds that "if we're saying that the country has a provocative history on race, I affirm that fact. But for under the circumstances, to find a way forward, it is truly together. One of the things I've said since I've been an elected official is we are better together" (quoted in Scott, 2015, p. 1).

CRITICISMS OF THE COMPETING PERSPECTIVES

Here, disapprovals of the ideas and activities of Black Lives Matter and All Lives Matter are ventilated. These are tendered one by one for intelligibility.

Criticisms of the Black Lives Matter Perspective

Many criticisms have been leveled against the idea and activities of Black Lives Matter proponents. To start off, Black Lives Matter activists are said to proffer a contradictory message when they utter their slogan and at the same time they say that it is time to kill police officers. The message is illogical in that it generalizes all police officers as being bad while these activists also insist that police should not to generalize all of them as being bad (Foxworth, 2016).

Next, the Black Lives Metter movement is accused of preaching "exclusivity" because its focus is solely on African Americans. Thus, the catchphrase Black Lives Matter itself is said to be immanently racially divisive as it focuses only on injustices against Blacks, as opposed to everyone (Condevillamar, 2020).

Also, the "in-your-face" tactics of Black Lives Matter activists are characterized by veteran civil rights leaders as "disrespectful" and "ineffective." The veterans say that this new crop of activists fail to realize that they must work with political leaders in order to get them to make reforms; instead, all they do is to "disrupt" and "make noise." The veterans also see the Black Lives Matter movement as having a polarizing effect on society, especially because it eschews dissent and its members are quick to disparage white politicians who say that "all lives matter" (Jennings, 2015).

In addition, the Blacks Lives Matter movement has been criticized for making male victims of police brutality the center of attention while marginalizing female victims. A support of this claim is that more protest rallies have been organized for the police murders of Trayvon Martin and Michael Martin compared to those for Rekia Boyd and Kayla Moore (Lindsey, 2015).

Furthermore, financial transparency is another aspect for which the Black Lives Matter movement has been faulted. The crux of the criticism centers on the fact that the organization does not disclose the activities on which it spends the millions of dollars in contributions it has received and how much. This situation has led many observers to accuse the organization of donating money to the Democratic National Committee and other liberal organizations and causes (Loiaconi, 2020).

Moreover, the Black Lives Matter movement is censured for ignoring the issue of intra-racial or black-on-black violence (on this issue, see Hill, 2020). This matter is critical because blacks are likely to be killed hundreds of times more by other blacks than by police officers. For example, for the year 2016 (the year for which complete data are available), the U.S. Federal Bureau of Investigation (FBI) reports that of the 2,870 blacks that were murdered, 2,570 were done by other blacks (FBI, 2016): that is, almost 90 percent. Hence, it behooves me to ask the following poignant question: Should Black Lives Matter only when blacks are killed by police officers?

Criticisms of the All Lives Matter Perspective

A number of criticisms have been made against the notion of All Lives Matter and the pursuits of its advocates. First, the aphorism All Lives Matter is pilloried as "missing the big picture." This conjecture is based on the belief that while it is easy for some people to just say Black Lives Matter, they rather insist on the saying All Lives Matter as a way to delegitimize the former catchphrase. Hence, the use of All Lives Matter appears to show disquietude for the lives of a race of a people who have been methodically deprived of rights and privileges for centuries (Baker, 2020).

Second, the slogan All Lives Matter is perceived to be "disingenuous" based on the premise that until Black Lives Matter, all lives cannot matter. It is also regarded as "disingenuous" because "in White-dominated societies, nearly any demand for equality by people of color is met by a backlash couched in terms of White victimhood . . . . In other words, the underlying sentiment is more about White lives rather than all lives" (Participedia, 2020, p. 1).

Third, some critics say that advocates of the All Lives Matter catchphrase use a color-blind oratory that contradicts and wipes out the actualities of racial inequality. They are said to move the debate and awareness away from the historical and present-day discriminations encountered by blacks, thereby depoliticizing the Black Lives Matter and related movements and attributing racism to individual exploits (Participedia, 2020).

Fourth, the use of the slogan All Lives Matter is characterized as dismissing, ignoring, and denying the suffering of blacks. Stated as a platitude that is close to a banality, it is therefore easy to assert as no sensible individual would hold out against the universal postulate. Thus, as David Theo Goldberg puts it, "All lives matter is a universal moral principle, a Kantian categorical imperative. Other things being equal, all lives matter, equally. Except when they don't. And they don't when other things are taken not to be equal. Like racial standing in a society such as ours" (Goldberg, 2016, p. 1).

And, fifth, the catchphrase All Lives Matters is denoted as "racist": that is, being prejudiced against or antagonistic toward a person or people on the basis of their membership in a particular racial or ethnic group, typically one that is a minority or marginalized—in this case, blacks. As Columbia University's Professor Carla Shedd maintains, the All Lives Matter slogan is an attempt at "erasing the vulnerability of and dehumanization of Black people." Shedd adds that while the intention of evoking the catchphrase is often meant to be about a "shared humanity," it is the opposite (see May and USA Today, 2016).

CONCLUSION

The observations made and resolutions tendered by the Communications Workers of America (CWA) and suggestions offered by Richard Sherman, a cornerback of the Seattle Seahawks football team (Foxworth, 2016), vis-à-vis Black Lives Matter and All Lives Matter make for an enlightened conclusion. The ideas of these two sources are presented sequentially in the following paragraphs for cohesion.

To commence with, the CWA discloses that in the summer of 2020, many of its members and those of its allied organizations began intense activism across the United States around the notion that Black Lives Matter. This is in response to the persistence within the country the deleterious effects of "systemic racism," also referred to as "institutional racism": that is, a form of discrimination that is implanted as common practice within a society or an organization, leading to inequality in spheres such as criminal justice, education, employment, health care, housing, and political power. These effects, according to the CWA, are manifested in many socioeconomic aspects such as (a) "youth unemployment," (b) "household wealth," (c) "public elementary and secondary education," and (d) "post-secondary educational achievement" (CWA, 2020, p. 1).

Next, the CWA points out that the entrenched fears within American communities across the country came to the forefront as many young African American men lost their lives during encounters with law enforcement officers. The conditions that led to the development of the divisions among working-class people were not made by law enforcement officers or people who reside in minority communities. While the majority of law enforcement officers are sincere about serving and protecting the communities, no matter their racial compositions, there is, nonetheless, a shrinking level of trust between officers and the residents they serve (CWA, 2020).

In order to resolve the preceding conundrum for law enforcement officers and minority communities, the CWA suggests that the causes of the unfairness that continues to divide members of the working class along racial and economic lines need to be addressed seriously. For the CWA, doing this requires resisting policies that (a) marginalize minority communities and people of color, (b) privatize education in predominantly African American communities, (c) attack public services in order to stigmatized people who use them and workers who provide them as some politicians do, (d) eliminate jobs in small towns and big cities, and (e) suppress the rights of minorities to vote (CWA, 2020).

In addition, the CWA acknowledges that even the labor movement is afflicted by racial divisions, thereby making it weaker. Thus, in order to strengthen its position, the CWA insists that the issue of racial divisions must be placed at the top of the labor movement's priorities. Concomitantly, the CWA makes the following three resolutions:

> Resolution 1: CWA is committed to equality and believes that the lives of every person matter. As long as powerful elites try to divide us by exploiting and oppressing the African American community, CWA remains dedicated to the principle that "black lives matter" and "all lives matter" (CWA, 2020, p. 1).

> Resolution 2: CWA reaffirms its commitment to support policies and practices designed to dismantle structural racial inequality, within our union, the labor movement, in our interactions with employers, and at all levels of government. CWA will continue to fight for equal opportunity in employment, housing, education, and the funding of public services, and to ensure that all citizens are treated with the due process that is their legal right (CWA, 2020, p. 1).

> Resolution 3: CWA will continue to support policies that provide the men and women who work in law enforcement with the resources they need to do their

critical job of protecting the public. The men and women who work in law enforcement deserve full, transparent, and impartial investigations into allegations of misconduct. At the same time, CWA will work to ensure that law enforcement personnel are not themselves made the victims of racial division which dishonors the profession and endangers the lives of those who work in it (CWA, 2020, p. 1).

Also, Sherman suggests that a coalition of athletes should be established to target the inner-city, the black community and many places that have high gang violence and plead to the residents to stop the futile brutality. He proposes that once we stop the black-on-black violence, we unite as a people, and stop perceiving one another as enemies, then we blacks can advance in a vigorous manner. This attitude, he says, will allow us to tackle issues confronting us in a different manner than it has ever been done previously. He adds that if we fail to do this, we will be battling on two fronts: (1) police violence and (2) black-on-black violence (Foxworth, 2016).

Thereafter, Sherman argues that while there is low funding for education and few jobs in black communities, there also are people who work very hard to support their families. As an example, he points to his own parents for being hard workers who did not make much money but made sure that he and his siblings stayed out of gangs and other diableries while living in the inner-city of Watts, South Central California. He adds that there is also the mentality among us blacks to blame others (i.e., "systemic racism") for many black fathers not being around to help nurture their children. He insists that we blacks must transcend the blaming of systemic racism, move forward, and make a difference (Foxworth, 2016).

Finally, Sherman insists that we blacks must be optimistic about the future of race relations because he believes that things will come together in the United States. He pegs his optimism on the fact that the country has encountered worse situations such as slavery and overcame them. While he admits that this is a different temporal context with different issues, he also points out that powerful people from all races are coming together to address these issues and find solutions for them. He therefore believes that the racial challenges the United States is facing will be resolved because there are good people in the country that will make it possible (Foxworth, 2016).

REFERENCES

Agozino, B. (2018). Black Lives Matter otherwise all lives do not matter. *African Journal of Criminology and Justice Studies* 11(1):1–11. Retrieved on October 28, 2020 from https://www.umes.edu/uploadedFiles/_WEBSITES/AJCJS/Content/AJCJS%20VOL11.%20Agozino.pdf

Al-Heeti, A. (July 7, 2020). Black Lives Matter: Netflix movies, TV shows and books that touch on systemic racism. *CNET*. Retrieved on October 28, 2020 from https://www.cnet.com/news/black-lives-matter-movies-tv-shows-and-books-on-systemic-racism/

Baker, P. K. (June 23, 2020). Why saying "All lives matter" misses the big picture. *CNN*. Retrieved on November 4, 2020 from https://www.cnn.com/2020/06/23/opinions/all-lives-matter-misses-the-big-picture-baker/index.html

Black Lives Matter. (2018). Black Lives Matter 13 guiding principles (a project of Teaching for Change by the DC Area Educator for Social Justice). Retrieved on October 31, 2020 from https://www.dcareaeducators4socialjustice.org/black-lives-matter/13-guiding-principles

Black Lives Matter. (2020). BLM's #WHATMATTERS2020 resources. Retrieved on October 27, 2020 from https://blacklivesmatter.com/

Bouie, J. (September 30, 2015). Elizabeth Warren just gave the best response to Black Lives Matter. *Slate*. Retrieved on November 1, 2020 from https://slate.com/news-and-politics/2015/09/elizabeth-warrens-black-lives-matter-speech-was-the-best-one-yet-its-still-not-enough.html

Buchanan, L., Bui, Q. and Patel, J. K. (July 3, 2020). Black Lives Matter may be the largest movement in U.S. history. *The New York Times*. Retrieved on October 28, 2020 from https://www.nytimes.com/interactive/2020/07/03/us/george-floyd-protests-crowd-size.html

Cohn, N. and Quealy, K. (June 10, 2020). How public opinion has moved on Black Lives Matter. *The New York Times*. Retrieved on October 28, 2020 from https://www.nytimes.com/interactive/2020/06/10/upshot/black-lives-matter-attitudes.html

Communications Workers of America—CWA. (2020). Black Lives Matter, all lives matter: Resolution 75A-15-9. Retrieved on August 30, 2020 from https://cwa-union.org/pages/black_lives_matter_all_lives_matter

Condevillamar, J. (July 2, 2020). Black Lives Matter countermovement and criticism. *The Thunderbolt*. Retrieved on November 4, 2020 from https://millsthunderbolt.com/black-lives-matter-countermovement-and-criticisms/

Day, E. (July 19, 2015). #BlackLivesMatter: The birth of a new civil rights movement. *The Observer*. Retrieved on October 28, 2020 from https://www.theguardian.com/world/2015/jul/19/blacklivesmatter-birth-civil-rights-movement

DefundThePolice.org. (2020). Defund the police. Retrieved on October 28, 2020 from https://defundthepolice.org/

Foxworth, D. (July 26, 2016). Richard Sherman: As human beings, all lives matter. *The Undefeated*. Retrieved on August 30, 2020 from https://theundefeated.com/features/richard-sherman-as-human-beings-all-lives-matter/

Goldberg, D. T. (September 25, 2016). Why "Black Lives Matter" because all lives don't matter in America. *Huftpost*. Retrieved on November 5, 2020 from https://www.huffpost.com/entry/why-black-lives-matter_b_8191424

Gospel Light Society. (2020). All Lives Matter to god. *#alllivesmatter*. Retrieved on October 31, 2020 from http://gospellightsociety.com/glmx/all-lives-matter-to-god/

Gottfried, M. H. and Eccher, M. (October 3, 2015). Black Lives Matter's twin cities marathon protest peaceful. *St. Paul Pioneer Press*. Retrieved on October 30,

2020 from https://www.twincities.com/2015/10/03/black-lives-matters-twin-cities-marathon-protest-peaceful/

Hill, M. (September 4, 2020). You can't talk about Black Lives Matter and ignore black on black crimes. *NJ Spotlight News*. Retrieved on November 5, 2020 from https://www.njspotlight.com/news/video/you-cant-talk-about-black-lives-matter-and-ignore-black-on-black-crime/

Jennings, A. (October 30, 2015). Longtime L.A. civil rights leaders dismayed by the in-your-face tactics of new crop of activists. *Los Angeles Times*. Retrieved on November 4, 2020 from https://www.latimes.com/local/california/la-me-black-lives-matter-20151030-story.html

Kim, G. J.-S. and Jackson, J. (December 18, 2014). "I Can't Breathe": Eric Garner's last words symbolize our predicament. *HuffPost*. Retrieved on October 30, 2020 from https://www.huffpost.com/entry/i-cant-breathe-eric-garne_b_6341634

Lindsey, T. B. (2015). Post-Ferguson: A "Herstorical" approach to Black violability. *Feminist Studies* 41(1):232–237.

Loiaconi, S. (June 15, 2020). As Black Lives Matter donations surge, some want to know where the money goes. *abc6*. Retrieved on November 4, 2020 from https://abc6onyourside.com/news/nation-world/as-black-lives-matter-donations-surge-some-want-to-know-where-the-money-goes

M4BL. (2020). Reparations. Retrieved on October 30, 2020 from https://m4bl.org/policy-platforms/reparations/

Maloney, A. (September 29, 2015). When police turn violent, activists Brittany Packnett and Johnetta Elzie push back. *The New York Times*. Retrieved on October 28, 2020 from https://web.archive.org/web/20161219043331/http://nytlive.nytimes.com/womenintheworld/2015/09/29/when-police-turn-violent-activists-brittany-packnett-and-johnetta-elzie-push-back/

May, A. and USA Today. (July 13, 2016). #AllLivesMatter hashtag is racist, critic say. *The Gazette*. Retrieved on November 6, 2020 from https://gazette.com/news/alllivesmatter-hashtag-is-racist-critics-say/article_ce21318a-a6d4-5dbf-b918-6426ed55b95d.html

McDonald, S. N. (July 14, 2016). President Obama clarifies his definition of "Black Lives Matter." *The Undefeated*. Retrieved on November 1, 2020 from https://theundefeated.com/features/president-obamas-clarifies-his-definition-of-black-lives-matter/

McGirt, E. (August 8, 2016). Race ahead: Why ford foundation is underwriting Black Lives Matter. *Fortune*. Retrieved on October 30, 2020 from https://fortune.com/2016/08/08/raceahead-why-ford-foundation-is-underwriting-black-lives-matter/

Mosley, T. and Hagan, A. (June 19, 2020). "An extraordinary moment": Angela Davis says protests recognize long overdue anti-racist work. *WBUR Here and Now*. Retrieved on November 1, 2020 from https://www.wbur.org/hereandnow/2020/06/19/angela-davis-protests-anti-racism

Page, G. (July 2, 2020). "All lives matter," niece of MLK tells VT radio audience. *The Newport Daily Express*. Retrieved on November 1, 2020 from https://newportvermontdailyexpress.com/content/all-lives-matter-niece-mlk-tells-vt-radio-audience

Parker, K., Horowitz, J. M. and Anderson, M. (June 12, 2020). Majorities across racial, ethnic groups express support for the Black Lives Matter movement. *Pew Research Center's Social and Demographic Trends Project*. Retrieved on October 28, 2020 from https://www.pewsocialtrends.org/2020/06/12/amid-protests-majorities-across-racial-and-ethnic-groups-express-support-for-the-black-lives-matter-movement/

Participedia. (2020). *All Lives Matter*. Retrieved on October 29, 2020 from https://participedia.net/case/5563

Rasmussen Reports. (August 20, 2015). Black Lives Matter or all lives matter? *Rasmussen Reports*. Retrieved on October 29, 2020 from https://www.rasmussenreports.com/public_content/politics/general_politics/august_2015/black_lives_matter_or_all_lives_matter

Reuters. (August 2, 2016). Slavery reparations sought in first Black Lives Matter agenda. *Reuters*. Retrieved on October 30, 2020 from https://www.reuters.com/article/us-usa-politics-race-idUSKCN10C3E1

Salomon, H. (February 24, 2015). Exclusive: Erica Garner slams "Fraudulent Claims" in O'Keefe video, announces foundation. *NewsOne*. Retrieved on October 26, 2020 from https://newsone.com/3093518/erica-garner-sharpton/

Scott, E. (September 3, 2015). Tim Scott defends use of "all lives matter." *CNN Politics*. Retrieved on November 3, 2020 from https://www.cnn.com/2015/09/03/politics/tim-scott-all-lives-matter/index.html

Sherfinski, D. (October 15, 2015). Ben Carson: Of course all lives matter—and all lives include Black lives. *The Washington Times*. Retrieved on November 2, 2020 from https://www.washingtontimes.com/news/2015/oct/15/ben-carson-course-all-lives-matter-and-all-lives-i/

Taibbi, M. (2017). *I Can't Breathe: A Killing on Bay Street*. New York, NY: Spiegel and Grau.

Terrell, K. (August 1, 2016). Black Lives Matter releases policy demands, includes reparations and abolishing the death penalty. *Hello Beautiful*. Retrieved on October 30, 2020 from https://hellobeautiful.com/2891207/black-lives-matter-releases-demands/

The Rachel Maddow Show. (August 10, 2015). Black Lives Matter builds power through protest. Retrieved on October 30, 2020 from https://www.msnbc.com/rachel-maddow/watch/-black-lives-matter--presses-equality-demands-501828675508

Tucker, B. and Hegg, S. (October 22, 2015). Tactics of Black Lives Matter. IN Close. Episode 216. KCTS-TV. Archived from the original on November 2, 2015. Retrieved on October 30, 2020 from https://web.archive.org/web/20151102024356/http://kcts9.org/programs/in-close/tactics-black-lives-matter

United States Department of Justice (USDOJ). (March 4, 2015) Department of justice report regarding the criminal investigation into the shooting death of Michael Brown by Ferguson, Missouri Police Officer Darren Wilson. Retrieved on October 30, 2020 from https://www.justice.gov/sites/default/files/opa/press-releases/attachments/2015/03/04/doj_report_on_shooting_of_michael_brown_1.pdf

United States Federal Bureau of Investigation (FBI). (2020). 2016 crime in the United States. Retrieved on November 5, 2020 from https://ucr.fbi.gov/crime-in-the-u.s/2016/crime-in-the-u.s.-2016/tables/expanded-homicide-data-table-3.xls

Chapter 2

Religious Perspective

Simon Gisege Omare

This chapter uses Social Identity Theory to explain the African worldview of humanity in relation to the dualism of Black Lives Matter versus All Lives Matter from the perspective of Religion: that is, the belief in and worship of a superhuman controlling power, especially a personal God or gods. It explains Social Identity Theory, the African worldview of humanity, African philosophies emphasizing on the value of humanness to one another, and the African worldview of how an individual African life's matters to the whole community. It concludes that the same seeds perpetuating all blacks matter should be geared toward the promotion of all lives matter to promote universal brotherhood and sisterhood. By humanity, I mean, a situation whereby we recognize that all humans are equal and they deserve the same human rights and treatment universally.

First, it is good to note that the dualistic dichotomy of the emerging debate between Black Lives Matter and All Lives Matter does not offer a coherent view of humanity that will help to address this problem. This chapter therefore attempts to offer an alternative worldview, which values all humans; explains the need to value the lives of Blacks; and shows that the same can be used to promote universal brotherhood and sisterhood. Ideas of the African worldview can be found as an inclusive motif for equal dignity of all human beings within a multiracial twenty-first-century society.

Black Lives Matter arose as a result of the social and racial injustice that has been institutionalized and subjected to the black community in the United States. The historical systematic injustice meted against the black communities has a long history in the country since the slave trade and colonialism (Cornelius, 2020). The movement first emerged after the acquittal of the white police George Zimmerman after the killing of Trayvon Martin. In February of 2012, seventeen-year-old African American Trayvon Martin was walking home in Florida after buying Skittles at a convenience store (Coates, 2013). A local resident George Zimmerman reported Martin to police as "suspicious," who then confronted the innocent young man and fatally shot him. Zimmerman claimed the act was in self-defense and was later acquitted. After this, the hashtag #BlackLivesMatter began to appear on social media in support of Martin and in protest against social and systemic racism in the American society and through institutions. This grew into a movement, cofounded by three Black community organizers, Alicia Garza, Patrisse Cullors, and Opal Tometi. Later, the killing of George Floyd in 2020 under police custody sparked further protest against police viciousness and systemic racism. The mission of the Black Lives Matter movement is to eradicate white supremacy and build local power to intervene in violence inflicted on black communities by whites.

On the other hand, All Lives Matter was born out of Black Lives Matter. It arose as a way of discrediting Black Lives Matter. When the Black Lives Matter motto arose, some people interpreted the phrase as confrontational and divisive. They took it to exclude other races. The phrase All Lives Matter sprang up in response, ostensibly to argue all lives are equal because we are all human beings. Hoffman and his colleagues (2016) provide a good basis for understanding the two concepts. They submit that Black Lives Matter never intended to suggest that other lives do not matter. Rather, the implicit message in stating Black Lives Matter is "All lives matter, but our society acts as if Black lives do not matter; therefore, we need to be explicit that Black lives also matter for all lives to matter" (Hoffman et al., 2016, p. 1).

The police brutality has led to a global uproar on the killings of the black people worldwide. Many times, the police have shot at innocent lives and walked away scot-free (African Research Bulletin, 2020). The chapter through an African religious worldview proffers the propositions that (1) all humans are created by the same Supernatural being who is known by different names; (2) God gave all humans red blood; hence, all humans are the same; (3) only God has the right of stopping life, regardless of age, or race; (4) African Americans are part of the African community that is made up of the unborn, the living, and the ancestors; (5) it is the duty of all Africans to act according to the community's teachings that promote humanity; (6) killing of other humans interferes with the cosmological balance; and (7) when we accept the verity that All Lives Matter, we will promote universal brotherhood and sisterhood regardless of color. Before broaching all of these aspects, it makes sense to first provide a conceptual discussion of religion to serve as a backdrop for what ensues.

RELIGION: A CONCEPTUAL DISCUSSION

Religion is a specific fundamental set of beliefs and practices generally agreed upon by a number of persons. The term *religion* can be used interchangeably with the word *faith* or *belief system*. It is a part of culture that is composed of worldviews about supernatural beings, sacred histories involving origins of the cosmos and human beings, and symbols that relate humans to spirituality, among others.

Religion is a single phenomenon that can be seen from several angles. Emile Durkheim (1915) explains that religion is multidimensional; it involves the social, mythical, ethical, ritual, doctrinal, and experiential dimensions. By "social dimension," we mean that religion is something made of by a group of people; there is no religion made up by one person. On "mythical dimension," we imply that all religions are made up by stories of origin; origin of the supreme being(s), cosmos, humans, and various relationships. On "ethical dimension," Durkheim maintains that all religions have rules and regulations governing their people: for example, Sharia for Muslims, Ten commandments for Christians, and Taboos for African religion. On "doctrinal dimension," Durkheim holds that all religions have teachings. On the "ritual dimension," he argues that all religions are made up of acts that are done at a specific time in a specific way, with a specific meaning such as baptism for Christians, Hijra for Muslims, and circumcision for African religion. Lastly, the "experiential dimension" explains that all religions talk about the experiences of specific personalities who matter to them such as Prophet Muhammad in Islam, Jesus in Christianity, and Siddhartha Gautama in Buddhism. This multidimensional characteristic of religion makes it problematic in coming up with a single definition of what religion is and what it is not.

Thus, we have numerous definitions of what religion is. These definitions can be classified into theological, moral, philosophical, psychological, sociological, and etymological categories.

Theological Definitions

Theological definitions of religion are those that insist that religion has to do with God, gods, or other supernatural powers: for example, Thomas Aquinas (1964) defines religion as the "belief in God." What about those religions that don't believe in supernatural beings such as Confucianism?

Moral Definitions

These are the kind of definitions that emphasize that religion has to do with how believers ought to conduct their lives. Definitions like "religion is leading a good life" imply that religion is a code of conduct whose source and authority is unquestioned.

Philosophical Definitions

Philosophical definitions denote religion in terms of an abstract, impersonal concept. For example, Paul Tillich (1886–1965) defined religion as a system of beliefs and practices directed toward the *ultimate concern* meaning and power.

Psychological Definitions

These definitions emphasize the place of emotions, beliefs, and other psychological states of a person in relation to the religious object. For instance, Sigmund Freud (1856–1939) defines religion as a "universal obsessive neurosis."

Sociological Definitions

These are those definitions that view religion as a group consciousness embodying cultural norms, thereby regarding religion as a product of society. An example of such a definition is the one by Karl Marx, which posits that "Religion is the opium of the masses."

Etymological Definitions

These definitions are whereby one uses foreign terms to define a religion. For example, the root meaning of the word *religion* is derived from the Latin word *religio*, which means a duty for someone to do (Mugambi, 1990, p. 3).

Clearly, there is no universal definition of religion. All definitions of religion given have various limitations or problems, which can be categorized as vague, narrow, compartmentalized, prejudiced, and true or false limitation. On "vagueness," it is argued that many definitions of religion are extremely unclear and, therefore, do not distinguish the subject matter of religion from other field.

On "narrowness," some definitions restrict the subject matter of religion to specific elements, thereby excluding other components of religion. For example, a definition like "religion is a feeling of total dependence" is indeed limited because religion is more than this. Other than dependence, worship may be an expression of wonder and gratitude.

On "prejudice," we can argue that evaluative definitions do not present an objective picture of what religion is actually about. A definition like "religion is the opium of the masses" is already a prejudiced definition because it is biased against religion. Lastly, on the "true or false limitation," problem arises when all religions are defined in terms of one religion, which posits itself as the true religion. Definitions in this category include, for instance, the ones that posits that "religion is belief in Jesus" or "the only religion in the sight of God is Islam."

Despite these limitations, the available definitions indicate that religion cannot be conceptualized convincingly, but most definitions try to describe the characteristics that are associated with "religious" activities. There are different definitions of religion due to variant aims and purposes behind these expressions. Variant scholarly interests produce different and sometimes conflicting ways of looking and thereby defining religion.

This chapter is concerned with African religion, which is the indigenous faith of Africans that was handed from one generation to another by word of mouth until recent attempts at documentation. The title "African religion" presents an assumed unitary portrait of the religions of the African. I make a proposition that many features of the religion and its practice are similar across Africa, as it would be erroneous to assume that all African religions are 100 percent the same. In defining the concept of African religion, Awolalu and Dopamu (2005) describe it as the indigenous religion of Africans that has been handed down from by the ancestors to the past and now the present generation of Africans. It is not a fossil religion (a thing of the past) but a religion that Africans today have made theirs by living it and practicing it. The religion has no written literature, yet it is "written" everywhere for those who care to see and read about it. It is largely written in the people's myths and folktales, in their songs and dances, in their liturgies and shrines, and in their proverbs and pithy sayings. It is a religion whose historical founder is neither known nor worshiped. It is a religion that has no zeal for membership drive, yet it offers persistent fascination for Africans, young or old.

METHODOLOGICAL AND THEORETICAL APPROACHES

To begin with, this chapter employs qualitative methodology: that is, the emphasis is on words instead of numerical values. The data informing the chapter were collected through interviews and focus-group discussions from purposively sampled respondents in Africa and analyzing literature reviews on the African worldview on humanity.

Black Lives Matter, as stated earlier, can be explained by Social Identity Theory (McLeod, 2019). This theory was coined by Henri Tajfel when he was making a contribution to psychology. This theory emerged out of

Tajfel's early work, which attempted to apply cognitive grouping and gestalt phenomena to social groups. Social identity is a person's sense of who he or she is based on his or her group membership(s). Tajfel explains that the groups that people belonged to were an important source of pride and self-esteem (Tajfel, 1978).

Social Identity Theory begins with the premise that individuals define their own identities with regard to social groups and that such identifications work to protect and bolster self-identity (Tajfel, 1978; Tajfel & Turner, 1979). Tajfel (1978) further explains that groups give us a sense of social identity: a sense of belonging to the social world.

The central argument of this theory is that, generally members of a particular group always seek to find negative aspects of another group, thereby enhancing their self-image. Practically, humans have divided the world into "them" and "us" based on a process of social categorization (social groups). Tajfel (1978) contends that, in order to increase their self-image, humans enhance the status of the group to which they belong. Therefore, it seems that in the United States, black people have a low self-esteem compared to white people due to the discrimination that happens between them. Due to their low self-esteem, other races discriminate against blacks and treat them just like animals. We take the example of extrajudicial killings of black people by the police and vigilantes such as George Zimmerman.

The Black Lives Matter movement has a strong basis for analysis using Social Identity Theory in that the founders of the movement are fighting for their rights as well as reminding everyone that black people are not less human than the other races of the world. Because of the killings and discrimination against them, the social identity of blacks is threatened. This chapter, as hinted earlier, intends to explain the African worldview on humanity with an image in mind that all people of the world are humans, regardless of their race; hence, All Lives Matter. This comes into mind because throughout history intolerant views between cultures have led to racism; in its extreme forms, racism may result in genocide, such as occurred in Germany with the Jews, in Rwanda between the Hutus and Tutsis, and, more recently, in the former Yugoslavia, between the Bosnians and Serbs. In order to understand the value of humanness, the next section of this chapter explains the African worldview of humanity.

THE AFRICAN WORLDVIEW OF HUMANITY

I remember when I was young, having been born in the rural area, I had no exposure to television, Western education or Christianity. I never knew that there existed people with different skin colors. I remember the first time I saw a person with a different color. We were playing our childhood games, then a vehicle stopped near our playing ground and two white persons alighted: a man and a woman. We were scared and fled for our lives. First, we had never seen a vehicle; second, we had never seen white people. We stood at a distance and took a lot of time observing them with curiosity until one of the persons whom we knew in the village started talking to them; that is when we started moving closer with fear. Thanks to the white persons who were friendly to us. They gave us sweets; something we had never tasted before. Our first encounter with the visitors developed several questions of curiosity in our minds. First, what kind of beings were these? What made them different from us? What kind of animal were they riding in? Do they have blood? What kind of language do they use? Why was their dressing different? How does their world look like? This made us prompt the same questions to our parents who made several attempts to explain. Answers provided for such questions by and large depend on the worldview of the individual, a group, or a culture.

Each ethnic group and religious group has its own worldview. In Africa, we have several ethnic groups. Each ethnic group has a worldview; however, on doing analysis, I discovered that almost all ethnic groups have the same worldview on reality; only minor elements differ. In this chapter, I use the term *African worldview* to generalize the African thinking. Purposely, I define the African worldview as the general perception of people living in the African continent about reality. Worldviews answer peculiar questions of life such as what is the origin of the world, humanity, relations, religion, God, and behavior, among others. In a sum, worldviews answer six major questions: (1) Where do we come from? (2) Where are we? (3) Where are we going? (4) What is good or evil? (5) How shall we act? (6) What is true or false? Before I make my argument on All Lives Matter from an African religious perspective, it is crucial to explain the African worldview on life for humans.

The African worldview on humans in relation to All Lives Matter tries to answer the foregoing six questions on worldview. It is crucial to bear in mind that the idea of having people of different races was not in Africa before the advent of the "colored" visitors. Therefore, I choose to use the known to address the unknown. Data answering these questions were collected from oral traditions since our African people had no capacity to read and write in the Western languages. Oral traditions that fed us with data include myths, legends, proverbs, tales, wise sayings, and stories. The six questions of worldview summarize the overall African worldview on humans as discussed in the following subsections.

What Is the Origin of Human Lives?

The first question of "Where do we come from?" is addressed by myths of origin. About 90 percent of the African myths I encountered explained that *all* human beings came from the Supreme Being who is known by different names by each ethnic group but bear the same characteristics as the Christian God. All these indigenous African worldviews did not indicate the exact date when humans came into being.

We have different African myths explaining humans' origins: some originated from the sky while others came from unique natural phenomena surrounding them such as mountains, lakes, and forests. Nonetheless, the common explanation is that human beings were created by God (O'Donovan, 1996). The Akamba people of Kenya explain that God created and lowered the first pair of humankind from the cloud landing on a rock Nzauwi (Mbiti, 2012). The Luhya of western Kenya explicate that the first man and woman were created by God and put on top of Mount Elgon. The Kikuyu of central Kenya give the explanation that their first ancestors were created by God, put on top of Mount Kenya, and they walked down from the mountain (considered to be Heaven) (Mbiti, 1976). The Shona say that the first human beings descended from God (Merwe, 1957). In a nutshell, myths that the first human beings came from the sky are reported among the Ashanti, Azande, Vugusu, Banyoro, Bemba, Elgeyo, Illa, Lugbara, Luo, Turkana, and Maasai (Baumann, 1964).

All of the African myths about God described the Creator with various characteristics apart from being the source of life. The idea of God as the source of life can be seen through the African names. The Abagusii people of western Kenya name God *Engoro*, which literally can be translated as "the heart," referring to "one that supports all life" (Omare, 2015). The Ashanti call Him *Bore-bore*, meaning "the first creator of all things" (Shebesta, 1936). "The Igbo of Nigeria" call God *Chukwu*, meaning "Source Being," which connotes "the Great One from whom being originates." They also name Him *Chineke*, meaning "The Source Being Who creates all things." The Edo people of Nigeria know God as *Osanobua* or *Osanobwa*, which means "the source of all beings who carries and sustains the world or universe" (Mbiti, 2012). The Illa call him *Ushatwakwe*, meaning "Master of His things" (Smith, 1920). Among the Nupe of Nigeria, God is called *Soko*, which means "the creator or supreme deity that resides in heaven" (Ezekwugo, 1987). Is the God of the blacks the Supreme Being of other races? Based on the African worldview, the characteristics of the Supreme Being in Africa are the same to the nature of the Deity as described by Islam and Christianity. The foregoing examples from Africa indicate that all humans came from the same God and all humans matter in His eyes;

therefore, no one should assume to be in charge of deciding who should live and not, except God.

These mythical explanations of the origins of human beings in Africa vary as to the nature of creation, such as where, from what material, the how and even the why of creation of the human being. It is good to note that human beings are always accorded the highest place in the hierarchy of created reality. Most myths indicate that human beings are considered the "completion or perfection of God's work of creation, since nothing else better than man was created afterwards—same to Christianity and Islam" (Mbiti, 1975, p. 6). It is crucial to note that there is no myth that explains that we have a God for different races. This implies that whether white or black, we belong to the same God and the same great grandparents. The only distinction that comes out clear is that there is a difference between humans and other animals (Gehman, 2000); hence, the Bantu name *bantu*, which is used to refer to human beings, means "human being per excellence" (King, 1970). It can be argued that the African worldview explains that all lives come from God, regardless of the ethnicity, tribe, and race. If God created all lives, He is the one who stops it; therefore, life is holy. Destroying life can be considered as murder, and despising another person based on the color of the skin can be considered as despising God's creation.

Where Are Humans?

The answer to this question involves what one perceives the world (*cosmos*) to be. Is it real or is it an illusion? Responses to this question provide answers to the functions and the structures of the world. The term *world* here is taken to mean everything that exists around us in the physical universe, such as living and non-living things, life, society, and culture. For the African, the universe was created by the Supreme Being. Many hold the view that nothing existed before the creation of the universe. The Supreme Being therefore created the universe but uses the created to continue his creative acts. This Supreme Being also continues to sustain the universe by using natural laws.

The universe is actually made up of visible and invisible components as well as material and spiritual realities, which are linked together (Mbiti, 1975). In most African traditional cultures, there seems to be no distinction between man and the rest of creation. There is no dichotomy in the human nature between the material and the immaterial. Therefore, the soul is capable of leaving the body, since it is not viewed as encased by the human body. Of great relevance is the view that there is an inherent order in the universe (Mudimbe, 1994).

The African society is holistic. The term *holistic* derives from the word whole. It implies a dynamic state of being in which composite parts are organically working together. It means being integral. Human beings are expected to maintain cosmic harmony (Kinoti, 2003). Cosmic harmony implies the smooth functioning of the entire natural order, including the animate and the inanimate, the visible as well as the invisible realms.

The anthropocentric nature of the African worldview means that the universe exists and has its purpose for the human being. The human being on the other hand exists to maintain harmony in the universe as Mbiti puts it as follows:

> Man puts himself at the centre of the universe . . . he consequently sees the universe from that perspective. It is as if the whole world exists for man's sake. Therefore African peoples look for the usefulness (or otherwise) of the universe to man. This means both what the world can do for man and how man can use the world for his own good. (1990, p. 7)

The preceding proposition implies that the centrality of the human being in relation to the universe has a priestly functionality whereby the human being links the universe with God the Creator (Mugambi, 1976). This gives reason to the myths discussed earlier and the mention of specific points where they entered the universe. The specific environments are supposed to be cherished and taken care of. Therefore, the human being is taken as the priests of the universe. As priests, humans have turned part of the universe into sacred objects using part of it for sacrifices and offerings to the divinities and the Supreme Being as a way of expressing appreciation to the Creator (Magesa, 1977).

In the African worldview, the cosmos is made up of various elements: humans, spirits, ancestors, plants, animals, rocks, mountains, and so on. Human beings are expected to relate well with all these elements; failure to do so could lead to peculiar diseases, curses, and droughts, among other misfortunes. Since human beings are part of the cosmos, eliminating their lives may affect the state of equilibrium of the cosmos. To the Akan of Ghana, just like other African peoples, whatever happens to the human being has a religious interpretation (Ackah, 1988). To them, behind the physical is the spiritual; behind the seen, there is the unseen. Every event here on earth is traceable to a supernatural source in the spirit realm. From the same source, therefore, lies the ultimate succor. Destruction of any human life is likely to interfere with cosmic harmony. The African is expected to maintain cosmic harmony and avoid anything that can affect the harmony like injuring any life regardless of the race, age, ethnicity, or tribe.

Where Are We (Humans) Going?

The question interrogates the destiny of humans after the current life and also seeks to explain the purpose and future of life in this world. Is there a future life or life after this world? What kind of life? How different is it from the present life? How is life after death, if there is such a life? The African worldview explains how the life of a human should be after birth, his or her growth, death, and after life. Life in the African worldview is cyclic; once one is born, he or she lives, dies, and gets reborn through reincarnation from ancestor to childhood (Magesa, 1997). In other words, human life goes on and on.

In Africa, it is believed that the universe will not end as shown by the rhythms of time. The spirit of the human person never ceases to exist. After the physical death, a person continues to exist in the memory of the person's friends and offspring through naming and practices such as pouring libations. Such a person is in the state of *personal immortality*, he or she is an ancestor, and has all the rights, powers, and obligations of this state. When such a person is no longer in the memory of the living, having passed into the *Zamani*, a new destiny of *collective immortality* is acquired. The person becomes a spirit who is no longer a member of the human families but joins the family of spirits who have an eternal existence (Mbiti, 1990).

The African worldview holds that from birth to death, a person must go through a rigorous process of spiritual and moral formation, reformation, and transformation. There is a relationship between the spiritual and the physical aspects of life. The circle of human life is characterized by some landmarks that are appreciated and celebrated in African Religion. The cycle of human life in the African perception begins at birth, through puberty, marriage, and ends at death. African religion recognizes each of these occasions as worthy of celebration and specific rituals known as rites of passage are designated to this effect. The general aim of these rites is to celebrate the transition of the individual from one stage to another; for example, the transition of a child to adulthood through puberty rites.

The presence of the rites is an indication that life is holistic. In relation to this, everything is done in relation to the whole life and world. The African worldview does not promise people a better life in the future or in the hereafter; those who have departed do not go anywhere either. Africans do not belief in heaven or hell as portrayed in Christianity and Islam. All humans have equality to life, from unborn children to the elderly. The foregoing gives reason why mourning is done for those who have lost life. However, it is held in the African worldview that life is fully lived by those who die at old age and have undergone through all rites of passage (Magesa, 1997). It is a big loss to Africans when young people die, just like the latest shootings of young Blacks.

What Is Good or Evil Life?

The fourth question "What is good or evil life?" determines the level of moral standards expected of human beings. It helps to give directions and purpose in guiding human actions. The question targets values cherished in each community. This question deals with ethics. African ethics answers questions such as the following: What is moral or immoral? Who or what determines what is moral and immoral? What is right and wrong? How is it determined? How should one behave? What are the implications of human existence for the practical order of things? As one can note, African ethics revolves around the betterment of humanity.

There are two dimensions of human conduct in the African worldview: (1) the personal and (2) the social. The personal conduct deals with the life of the individual while the social conduct deals with the life of society. The traditional African moral worldview puts emphasis on social conduct because the individual exists because others exist. Thus, "because of the great emphasis on one's relationship with other people, morals have been evolved in order to keep society not only alive, but in harmony. Without morals, there would be chaos and confusion" (Mbiti, 1975, p. 7).

While the universe and human beings have an ontological existence, evil does not exist in the African worldview. Evil is seen in terms of negative, harmful, or undesirable effects or consequences of acts of human beings, spirits, ancestors, and deities that affect life negatively. Thus, one is not good or evil but acts in ways that are considered good or evil. There is therefore a marked difference between an act and the actor. Acts that are against the life force or are not in harmony with the community and the universe are considered evil acts. Laurenti Magesa understands these acts as being conceptualized as "wrongdoing," "badness," or "destruction of life," rather than as "sin" or "evil" (Magesa, 1977). He also disagrees with the understanding that a person merely commits an evil act. His view is that "evil do not and cannot exist in the human experience except as perceived in people. It is people who are evil or sinful, whether or not they are aided by invisible forces" (Magesa, 1977, p. 1).

Generally, though, the African worldview submits to the understanding that evil resides in forces and spirits that influence people to do evil. Conversely, some people such as sorcerers manipulate forces for evil ends. All in all, "everything which deviates from the normal order of things, both in the natural and in the social world, is regarded as a manifestation of these evil forces and, hence, as dangerous" (Wagner, 1954, p. 1). Evil therefore serves to disrupt the harmony in the universe and human life. When something bad or evil befalls one or the community, the first reaction is that it is a result of displeasure on the part of the ancestors, spirits, divinities, or even the Supreme Being.

In the African moral fabric, God is the source of moral values and the ancestors are the depositories of morals. Ancestors act like policemen as a human being's act "is determined by the ancestors and is 'stored' in the traditions of the people. Tradition, therefore, indicates what the people must do to live ethically" (Mbiti, 1990, p. 8). It is held that the living dead maintain interest in the morals of their descendants, and they may punish offenders by causing failure in undertakings, sickness, and bad dreams as warnings or deterrents. It is also held that the Supreme Being is ultimately watching over the moral life of the community, society, and humankind. From time to time, the Supreme Being may punish the wider society or give warnings through calamities, epidemics, droughts, wars, and famines, if moral order is severely broken. The fear of the foregoing calamities makes the African to fear doing anything that interferes with human life. It also becomes the duty of the other members of the society to stop any evil against humanity; their failure would be affected by communal misfortunes. The foregoing gives reason to why Africans are always concerned and bitter with any injustices against other humans regardless of the color.

What then is right to do and wrong to avoid? In the African moral worldview, "sociability or relationship in daily living by the individual and the community is the central moral and ethical imperative" (Magesa, 1997, p. 1). The African has existence and behaves morally in the context of the community. What therefore maintains life, peace, and harmony in the community is the moral imperative; it is the right thing to do. On the other hand, anything that does not maintain or is contrary to life, communal peace, and harmony is immoral or not right; it is the wrong thing to avoid. African ethics are in forms of laws, rules, customs, traditions, and taboos. African morality is governed by laws that deal majorly with what destroys or promotes humanness. During research, I found out that in Africa, humans are at the center of morality. The African worldview defines morality in the universe: that is, the understanding of the good or the moral acts that sustain life and the bad or immoral acts that destroy it (Magesa, 1997). The deep sense of right and wrong is manifested in the many customs, rules, laws, traditions, and taboos found in African society. It can be noted that laws governing people in African societies reflect on three spheres: (1) the living, (2) the unborn, and (3) the ancestors. The aim of laws is to maintain and promote a good relationship between the three spheres. For instance, let us take the case of incest. Incest is wrong to the African eye because it affects the identity of the unborn children. If incest took place between a father and a daughter, immediate relatives will be angered; hence, conflict will ensue. Ancestors who are the eye of morality for communities will be annoyed, thereby cursing the living. The same case applies to the murdering of people. By murdering humans, it cuts the continuity of life through birth, it affects other members of the society physically and emotionally, and it affects negatively the ancestors of the deceased as it is their wish for humans to live fully till old age.

How Should Humans Act?

The question asks how we should act upon knowing what is good to do and what is evil to avoid. The question also seeks answers for the action needed to solve practical problems faced by human beings on a day-to-day basis. A plan of action is therefore envisaged in this question.

Going through various traditions there is an indication that whatever actions Africans take are meant to promote life. All skills learned are meant to promote survival: for example, herbal skills and nutrition. There are several taboos in Africa that promote life. All African communities forbid murder or any form of action that can eliminate life. This means that life is sacred; therefore, nobody is allowed to eliminate life. It is good to note that in case one murders another person during war, it is a requirement that the individual is isolated and goes through a tedious process of cleansing. Failure to do so can lead to madness or curses in the family. Africans celebrate the joy of living in ceremonies. They put life into action by dancing, singing life, and ritualizing life; they shout life, the festive life, for the community. Therefore, it is the duty for everyone to continue life: that is, through marriage, one is required to have children. Those who die before disseminating life are considered a curse to some communities. Those who recently died are always welcomed to the community through rituals, for example, pouring libations, sacrifices, and offerings.

Some African communities have divinities in charge of life. One's life can be messed up by actions of his or her relatives who lived before him: for example, thieves. Death is taken to be powerful because it takes away life. Various communities have myths to explain the causes of death. In some communities, people perform rituals to evade death: for example, drowning. Death is an enemy of life. Moral teachings and customs are projected toward the promotion of life. Stopping other people's lives or discriminating against them is a direct indication that one is going against the expectations of the Supreme Being and ancestors.

What Is True and What Is False?

This question inquires on the source of knowledge that is adequate for African communities about humans. It is interested in what should inform the acts of humans. A plan of action, as suggested earlier, must be based on knowledge and correct information. It is only when relevant knowledge is acquired that reliable models of life can be constructed. Knowledge on which action is based serves as a pillar on which the entire worldview is anchored.

In the African worldview, it is the duty of all members of the community to spread their knowledge about humanity to the younger generations. Such knowledge is passed down the generations through stories, myths, and rituals. Older people in such societies play a very important role in this process of learning as O'Donovan points out: "In many traditional African societies the idea of truth is related to the stories and myths about life and human experience which are passed down from one generation to another by the elders or grandparents of the clan" (1996, p. 10). Burnett rightly points out that such myths in tribal societies are not "simply fairytale stories but concrete means used to symbolically convey truth and wisdom" (1995, p. 61). Dreams and visions are also considered important means through which the spirits convey messages to the living.

Tradition forms the rubric of the value system in an African traditional society. In other words, everyone is expected to follow without questions what has been done before, tested and proven effective. In such a context, right and wrong depend on what the society has decided depending on its traditions (Loewen, 2000). It is difficult to understand the concept of "truth" from a typical African perspective. This is especially the case when one uses the Western categories such as correspondence, coherence, and pragmatic theories.

One may, however, find a combination of the correspondence and pragmatic theories of truth in the African worldview (Wiredu, 2004). Among the Ewe and Akan of West Africa, for instance, "truth" is likened to knowledge and wisdom. It is not so much the "workability of an idea that makes it true" but rather, "its power to bring about a better human situation, an improvement of conditions or situations in life" (Wiredu, 2004, p. 1). Truth is thus "the normative truth-statement *Nyadzodzoe* . . . what is generally known by society, represented by the elders, to be true in speech as well as in deed. The truth of a statement is therefore in its identity with what has been known to be the case in such matters" (Dzobo, 1992, p. 1). In such a worldview, a lie may be permissible when one is avoiding creating a bad situation. This may happen in a situation where a positive benefit is the proximate result of telling a lie. Truth is therefore not good in itself or a lie evil in itself. Truth is not absolute. It has utility purposes. Thus, to lie to avoid offence is the true thing to do; consequently, to tell the truth that result in offence is the bad thing to do (Masolo, 1994).

It is perhaps important to point out at this juncture that the lack of the concept of equality in the creation of humans means that in the primal worldview, status is a major issue. The kings, herbalists, and elders are considered special and above the rest. As much as they are considered above others, their call is to serve humanity without discrimination. It is clear that in the African worldview, there are no teachings on superiority or inferiority of races in humanity. All are equal and no human is entitled to interfere with the lives of humans from other races.

AFRICAN PHILOSOPHIES EMPHASIZING THE VALUE OF HUMANNESS TO ONE ANOTHER

Having seen the African worldview on humanity, some contemporary leaders have coined African philosophies to promote the idea of all lives matter in Africa though the ideology of socialism. Among them are *ubuntu, undugu, utu,* and *harambee.*

Ubuntu means "humanity" or "humanness." Ubuntu has its origin from the Zulu of South Africa. The Zulu term *Ubuntu* implies that "a person is a person through other persons." It is the acceptance of the need for mutual recognition or reciprocal regard for others regardless of age, race, or ethnicity. Desmond Tutu (1999) explains that a person with Ubuntu is open and available to others based on proper assurance that comes from knowing that he or she belongs to a greater whole and is diminished when others are humiliated or diminished when others are tortured or oppressed. This implies that in the African worldview, human nature is the result of the balance between personal identity and the human community at large. It can be observed that unhealthy relations are forbidden at all costs. It becomes the responsibility of the community to teach younger generations ethics and ensure that they perform acts that promote Ubuntu.

Undungu is a Swahili word that portrays the oneness of all human beings. The term *Undugu* comes from the term *Ndugu,* which means blood brother or sister. U*ndungu* describes brotherhood and sisterhood that forms a community of solidarity. It is believed that Undugu was inspired by the late Tanzanian President Julius Nyerere's philosophy of *Ujamaa* (Mugambi, 1976). This concept of universal brotherhood and sisterhood gave the African peoples noble motives for community life. Nyerere (1976) considers African socialism (*Ujamaa*) as an attitude of the mind whereby each person feels a certain amount of responsibility for the welfare of the fellow human. Africans are trained and taught to love other humans, including strangers; therefore, it is immoral to feast while your neighbor is facing hunger. It is believed that if you do so, the ancestors will withdraw the source of plenty. The philosophy of Undugu demands that Africans should be concerned with other people's welfare by passing greetings and inquiring about the status of others' families. This goes against the trend found in Western developed countries where one can stay with a neighbor who he or she doesn't know or talk to for several years. It is generally known in Africa that your neighbor is your first security in times of need. This gives reason to why Africans love sharing meals without worry. This can be seen in Chinua Achebe's book *Things Fall Apart* who says the following:

> A man who calls his kinsmen to a feast does not do so to save them from starving. They all have food in their own homes. When we gather together in the

moonlit village ground it is not because of the moon. Every man can see it in his own compound. We come together because it is good for kinsmen to do so (Achebe, 1958, p. 8).

Achebe in his book shows that it is a duty for Africans to share as brothers and sisters. Anyone who doesn't share is seen as an outcast. Behaviors that promote individualistic life are condemned through ridicule. The Undugu philosophy demands that whenever an African is in need, community members must come to his or her aid. Issues like paying fees for needy children, searching for employment, sickness, and arrangement for funerals are a communal affair in Africa as a sign of showing humanness to others. Nyerere saw Africa as one family and the whole world as an extended family. It is in this same spirit that Mugambi says, "Most Africans still think of themselves in the context of this extended relationship."

Another African philosophy that promotes humanness is *Utu*, which means "personhood." Thus, what propels one into solidarity with others and the universe is Utu or humanity. One who has Utu is expected to love others without discrimination and respect life at all costs. The term *Utu is* derived from the Swahili word *mtu*, which means "a person." Eunice Kamaara in her inaugural lecture at Moi University noted that it is without contradiction that indigenous Africans appreciate Utu as the essence of individual human persons but only in community (Kamaara, 2012). Kamaara's words were earlier echoed by John Mbiti (1982) who further explains that in traditional African life, the individual does not and cannot exist alone except corporately. He explains that an individual owes his essence to other people, thereby making him or her a part of a whole. Whatever happens to an individual happens to a whole group and whatever happens to the whole group happens to the individual. We can sum up that the individual can say "I am because we are and since we are therefore I am." From the foregoing, it can be interpreted that all lives matter in the African society; hence, losing or disrespecting one life is a concern for the whole group.

Lastly, *Harambee* is a Swahili word, which means "pulling together" or "working together." It is a slogan that ensured that people work together as a group. The term was introduced by the first President of Kenya Jomo Kenyatta. It was a development strategy in which people supplemented government efforts through voluntary contributions. Jomo Kenyatta made it a national Motto in 1963 when he advanced it as unity in all causes of national integrity and human progress. The Harambee spirit embodies ideals of assistance, joint effort, mutual social responsibility, and community self-reliance. The term recognizes the efforts of all people, regardless of age, race, tribe, and gender, toward communal community projects and the welfare of other members of the community. In cases where a person was unable to meet his or her basic needs, it is the duty of other members to pull resources together to assist the individual.

The African philosophies on humanness and humanity imply that all humans are crucial in the society, regardless of the age, sex, and race. They call for togetherness and showing one another love. Any behavior that could go against what could promote love is taken to be a vice. Each member of the African society is supposed to be an eye of another member. It is common knowledge that an individual's misbehavior can lead to communal curses. For instance, if one mistreats another person in secrecy, the ancestors will revenge on behalf of the person. African brotherhood and sisterhood go beyond human boundaries to embrace the entire creation, to include other animals, the environment, and the earth. Human beings are here reminded that they have a close affinity to other animals and other living things. This explains why some African communities use animals, birds, insects, and objects as totems. They often refer to them as their relatives. Every member of the community must have this understanding when using any resource in the world.

In all, what emerges from these philosophies is that in Africa, an individual's life, whether young or old, matters to the community to which s/he belongs. Therefore, showing disrespect for blacks is going against the African religious teachings, ancestors and the Supreme Being, and this irritates the whole African community. Messing one African annoys the whole of Africa and it becomes the responsibility of other Africans to defend their own. Failure to handle the foregoing situation can lead to intercontinental conflict. The following section explains the African worldview on how an African individual matters to the whole of Africa.

AN INDIVIDUAL AFRICAN LIFE'S MATTERS TO THE WHOLE COMMUNITY

In the African worldview, all that which Africans do must be in relation to the community. The relationship between humans and their communal beings is supposed to be stable; if disrupted, then the society's equilibrium is destabilized. In essence, it is a mandate given to all individual Africans to make their personal contribution to the life force of their families, clans, tribes, and the universe. In essence, it is the responsibility of the African community to take care of the needs of the individual. So who is an individual? In the African worldview, an individual *is not* a person until the community has accepted him or her. The community gives the individual identity through rites of passage. During these ceremonies, the candidates are taught the concept of humanity and how to regard humankind universally. In order to achieve the foregoing, all community members are trained on how to promote communal cohesion and how to avoid all forms of conflicts: inter human conflicts, human to human conflicts, human to ancestor conflicts, human to spirits conflicts, and human to unborn conflicts. Africans fear a broken relationship among people of the same group. A broken relationship can be termed *evil*. Everything is done to maintain harmony in the society. The community sets parameters of the norms in life.

The community in the African worldview is defined in terms of common participation in life, history, and destiny. The community includes the unborn, the living, the dead, and the spirits (those who inhabit the spiritual world). In traditional African thought, it is almost impossible to think of a human being in isolation. A human is seen as a member of the community of beings and all what he or she does must be in relation to the community. John Mbiti's (1990) statement that "I am because we are" reflects the idea of African community. The community is therefore determined by common participation in life and destiny communal set-up. The community defines the person as a person. A person is not some isolated static quality of rationality, will, or memory; thus, Mbiti's explanation of "I am because we are."

When talking about All Lives Matter from an African context, as mentioned earlier, it is good to note that by community, in Africa, it is meant the living, the living dead, and the unborn. Apart from the living humans, the belief in reincarnation provides the African community with a link with the past through the ancestors and a link with the future through the unborn. It seems that the fear of reincarnation after death becomes the basis for morality in Africa. This means that life without ancestral focus is empty and meaningless in the community. Therefore, the yet-to-be-born, the living, and the dead form a traditional African family. Based on the foregoing, we can say that life in Africa is shared and responsibilities are never a personal affair but a communitarian concern. No one lives for oneself alone and the misconduct of an individual affects all. Responsibility, participation, and cooperation are the usual community forms. Dialogue is used to overcome disagreements among members and hostility from neighbors.

An individual's life matters to the whole African community. Africans affirm and celebrate each individual's life through varied practices such as rituals, festivals, rites, and ceremonies as it unfolds itself in different stages in the life of an individual and community. John S. Mbiti rightly puts it as follows: "They want to celebrate the joy of living. They do not sit down meditating upon life. Instead, they put it into action: they dance life, they sing life, they ritualise life, they drum life, they shout life, they ceremonise life, they festivise life, for the individual and for the community" (Mbiti, 1997, pp. 200–201).

Mbiti explains that any life matters in the life of Africans and it is taken as a gift from God. Such a crucial gift calls for celebrations. Most of these celebrations start from conception to birth, naming, initiation, marriage, death, and after life. All of the foregoing stages call for communal cerebration. In case a person dies before old age, it was not taken lightly. All members of the community had to investigate why the spiritual world allowed the demise. It called for the involvement of religious specialists who investigated the cause and remedies for the same happening in the future.

According to Mugambi (1976), a person who does not have the good will of his society may, according to the African traditional belief, suffer physically, even to the point of death. Mugambi explains that this belief ensures that individual members of the community do not segregate themselves because if they fall out of favor with the community, the consequences may be fatal. Thus, a person is to maintain good relationships with members of his kinship group. The foregoing explains why Africans who moved from Africa to other continents always keep in touch with their people and participate in communal events through sending cash.

From the preceding observations, one may ask, If All Lives Matter to Africans, why do we have a series of interethnic wars? If one kills during war, is it an indication of not valuing other people's lives? According to Daniel Kasomo (2009), the African system of intergroup coexistence was very intact in the traditional set-up. He blames the colonial government for the current situation that shattered the African system of administration by creating institutions, which conflicted not only with African traditions but also with African mentality (see also Colson, 1969; Brewer and Campel, 1976; Bozeman, 1976; Francis, 1976; Ogot, 1986). To impose these changes, a new society was created and new group structures and a new system of governance were established. Traditional African moral principles, social norms, and religious beliefs and practices were affected by these new systems. Nevertheless, as much as there is interference, the roots of African culture are deeply anchored in the heart of Africans.

Despite the diversity in ethos and religious traditions, all Africans share common characteristics like the promotion of mutual respect for one's neighbors, regardless of their race, ethnicity, creed, culture, sex, and age. In African traditional society, religion was and is the guardian of tradition, the dispenser of morality, the standard of reference, and the teacher of wisdom. Religion also had a creative, cognitive, and dynamic function as energizer and life-giver. Religion holds the society in its fixed pattern. It is the key to society's historical and cultural embeddedness. One can hardly understand the structures of African society unless he or she understands its religion.

In sum, the communal approach to life facilitates holistic life. There is integration, interconnectedness, and mutual dependence of all things in the universe to one another. Everything coexists in harmony. Africans share life intensely in common. There are communal farmlands, economic trees, streams, barns, and markets. There are also communal shrines, squares, masquerades, ritual objects, and festivals for recreational activity, social, economic, and religious purposes. In the African worldview, the individual does not and cannot exist alone, but cooperatively. It is what the community does to the individual that matters most, not the individual's view of himself or herself.

CONCLUSION AND RECOMMENDATIONS

The African worldview is clear that All Lives Matter, regardless of age, sex, or race. The worldview regards universal humanity as it maintains that all human beings deserve to live a free life without being discriminated. The chapter is guided by Social Identity Theory. According to the theory, it is normal for group members of a particular group to always seek to find negative aspects of another group, thereby enhancing their self-image. Practically, humans have divided this world into "them" versus "us" based on a process of social categorization (social groups). As much as social categorization can be healthy to a community, it may also impact the society negatively. Using the case of Black Lives Matter as a social category, it can be argued that failure to contain brutality against Africans may lead to more violent aggression against the abusers from the African community, which may, in turn, lead to more damages, physically and socially, in the places of belligerence.

From the African cases studied in in this chapter, the African worldview is very clear that all Africans belong to their community (Africa) and the same community values them. Hurting one of them hurts the whole of Africa. This implies that all blacks living outside Africa deserve the best. Dehumanizing them is abusing Africa as a community. This calls for borrowing ideas from the African worldview and also calls for the relevant authorities to ensure that all are treated equally. Senghor (1959) provides a vision for the African sense of community that it goes beyond the base of African society. To Senghor, the African sense of community goes beyond the social boundaries of the clan, tribe, or nation. If the same sense of community can be applied successfully, it can promote the sense of brotherhood and sisterhood. The same can be copied from some African leaders who coined ideologies that promote universal brotherhood such as the philosophies of *Ubuntu*, *Undugu*, *Utu*, and *Harambee* as explained earlier. In response to the foregoing, the chapter maintains that the same seeds perpetuating Blacks Lives Matter should be geared to the promotion of All Lives Matter to promote universal brotherhood and sisterhood. This can be achieved by spreading the message of love for all humanity regardless of race, ethnicity, and nationality by borrowing the principles of African worldview on humanness.

REFERENCES

Achebe, C. (1958). *Things Fall Apart*. Lagos, Nigeria: William Heinemann ltd.
Ackah, C. A. (1988). *Akan Ethics: A Study of the Moral Ideas and the Moral Behaviour of the Akan Tribes of Ghana*. Accra, Ghana: Ghana University Press.
African Research Bulletin (July 20, 2020). Kenya: Police brutality protests. Retrieved on January 20, 2021 from www.doi.org/10.1111/j.1467-825X.2020.09528.x
Aquinas, T. (1964). *Summa Theologiae*. trans. Blackfriars. Vol. 39: *Religion and Worship*. New York, NY: McGraw Hill.
Awolalu, J. O. & Dopamu, P. A (2005). *West African Traditional Religion*. Lagos, Nigeria: Macmillan Publishers, pp. 26–27.
Battle, M. (2000). A theology of community: The ubuntu theology of Desmond Tutu. *Interpretation* 54(2):173–182.
Baumann, H. (1964). *Schofung und Urszeit des Menschen in Mythus der afrikanishen Volker*. Berlin, Germany: Dietrich Reimer.
Bozeman, A. B. (1976). *Conflict in Africa: Concepts and Realities*. Princeton, NJ: Princeton University Press.
Brewer, M. B. & Campel, D. T. (1976). *Ethnocentrisim and Intergroup Attitudes: East African Evidence*. New York, NY: John Wiley and Sons.
Bujo, B. (2006). *African Theology in its Social Context*. Eugene, OR: Wipf and Stock Publishers.
Coates, T. N. (July 15, 2013). Trayvon Martin and the irony of American justice. *The Atlantic*. Retrieved on January 15, 2021 from www.theatlantic.com/national/archive/2013/07/trayvon-martin-and-the-irony-of-american-justice/277782/
Colson, E. (1969). African society at the time of the scramble. In Gann, L. & Duignan, P. (eds.). *Colonialism in Africa 1870–1960*. Cambridge, UK: Cambridge University.
Cone, J. H. (July 1, 1975). The story context of Black theology. Retrieved on February 17, 2021 from www://doi.org/10.1177/004057367503200203
Cornelius, N. (September 4, 2020). From slavery and colonialism to Black Lives Matter: New mood music or more fundamental change? Retrieved on February 10, 2021 from www://doi.org/10.1108/EDI-07-2020-0199
Durkheim, E. (1915). *The Elementary Forms of The Religious Life*. London, UK: George Alien Unwin.
Dzobo, N. K. (1992). Knowledge and truth: Ewe and Akan conceptions. In Gyekye, K. and Wiredu, K. (eds.). *Person and Community: Ghanaian Philosophical Studies*. Washington, DC: The Council for Research in Values and Philosophy.
Ezekwugo, C. U. M. (1987). *Chi, the True God in Igbo Religion*. Muvattupuzha Kerala, India: Mar Matthew Press.
Francis, E. K. (1976). *Inter-Ethnic Relations: An Essay in Sociological Theory*. New York, NY: Elsevier.
Gehman, R. J. (1999). *Who Are the Living Dead? A Theology of Death, Life after Death, and the Living Dead*. Nairobi, Kenya: Evangel Publishing House.
Gehman, R. J. (2000). *African Traditional Religion in Biblical Perspective*. Nairobi, Kenya: East African Educational Publishers.

Hoffman, L., Granger, N., Vallejos, L. & Moats, M. (June 1, 2016). An existential–humanistic perspective on Black Lives Matter and contemporary protest movements. Retrieved on January 20, 2021 from www:/doi.org/10.1177/0022167816652273

Kamaara, E. K. (2012). *(Re)constructing Gender: A Holistic Strategy to Controlling HIV/AIDS in Kenya. Moi University Inaugural Lecture 15 Series No. 2012.* Eldoret, Kenya: Moi University Press.

Kasomo, D. (2009). An investigation of sin and evil in African cosmology. *International Journal of Sociology and Anthropology* 1(8):145–155.

Kinoti, H. W. (2003). The integrity of creation: An African perspective. In Theuri, M. M. and Grace, W. (eds.). *Quests for Integrity in Africa.* Nairobi, Kenya: Acton Publishers.

Krige, J. D. & Krige, E. J. (1954). The Lovedu of Transvaal. In Forde, D. (ed.). *African Worlds: Studies in the Cosmological Ideas and Social Values of African Peoples.* London, UK: Oxford University Press.

Magesa, L. (1977). *African Religion.* New York, NY: Maryknoll.

Magesa, L. (1997). *African Religion: The Moral Tradition of Abundant Life*, New York, NY: Orbis Books, Maryknoll.

Masolo, D. A. (1994). *African Philosophy in Search of Identity.* Bloomington, IN: Indiana University Press.

Mbiti, J. S. (1975a). *The Prayers of African Religion.* New York, NY: Orbis Books.

Mbiti, J. S. (1975b). *African Religions and Philosophy, 15: Introduction to African Religion*, 2nd ed., Nairobi, Kenya: East African Educational Publishers Ltd.

Mbiti, J. S. (1982). *African Religions and Philosophy.* London, UK: Heinemann.

Mbiti, J. S. (1990). *African Religions and Philosophy*, 2nd ed. New York, NY: Heinemann.

Mbiti, J. S. (2012). *Concepts of God in Africa.* Nairobi, Kenya: Acton Publishers.

McLeod, S. A. (2019). Social identity theory. *Simply Psychology.* Retrieved on October 7, 2020 from www.simplypsychology.org/social-identity-theory.html

Merwe, W. J. (1957). *The Shona Idea of God.* Fort Victoria, Zimbabwe: Morgenster Mission Press.

Mudimbe, V. Y. (1994). *Invention of Africa: Gnosis, Philosophy, and the Order of Knowledge.* Bloomington, IN: Indiana University Press.

Mugambi, J. & Kirima, N. (1976). *The African Religious Heritage* (a textbook based on Syllabus 224 of the East African Certificate Education). Nairobi, Kenya: Oxford University Press.

Mugambi, J. N. K. & Magesa, L., eds. (1990). *The Church in African Christianity: Innovative Essays in Ecclesiology.* Nairobi, Kenya: Initiatives.Nyerere, J. K. (1971). *Ujamaa: The Basis of African Socialism.* Dar es Salaam, Tanzania: Jihad Productions.

Nyerere, J. K. (1976). *Socialism and Rural Development.* Dar es Salaam, Tanzania: Government Printer.

O'Donovan, W. (1996). *Biblical Christianity in African Perspective.* Carlisle, PA: Paternoster.

Ogot, B. A. (1986). *Kenya before 1900.* Nairobi, Kenya: East African Publishing House.

Olanrewaju, A. (December 9, 2020). In the wake of tumultuous #EndSARS demonstrations, Nigerian artists tell a story of hope and determination through photos—CNN Style. Retrieved on December 12, 2020, from https://edition.cnn.com/style/article/new-nigeria-studios-end-sars-protest-photo-exhibit/index.html

Omare, S. G. (2015). *Witchcraft Scapegoat: Abagusii Beliefs and Violence against "Witches."* Saarbrücken, Germany: Lambert Academic Publishing.

Opoku, K. A. (1978). *West African Traditional Religion.* Islamabad, Pakistan: FEP International Private Limited.

Parrinder, E. G. (1970). *African Traditional Religion.* Boulder, CO: Greenwood Press.

Richmond, Y. & Gestrin, P. (1988). *Into Africa: Intercultural Insights.* Boston, MA: Nicholas Brealey Publishing.

Sakpa, D. (September 7, 2020). In Africa, concerns rising over police brutality. Retrieved on December 11, 2020 from www.dw.com/en/in-africa-concerns-over-rising-police-brutality/a-54845922

Senghor, L. S. (1959). *African Socialism.* New York, NY: Mercer Cook.

Shebesta, P. I. (1936). *My Pygmy and Negro Hosts.* London, UK: Hutchinson and Company.

Smith, E. & Dale, A. M. (1920). *The Illa-Speaking Peoples of Northern Rhodesia.* London, UK: Macmillan.

Strong, K. (December 21, 2017). Do African lives matter to Black Lives Matter? Youth uprisings and the borders of solidarity. Retrieved on December 25, 2020 from www.doi.org/10.1177/0042085917747097

Tajfel, H. (1970). Experiments in intergroup discrimination. *Scientific American* 223:96–102.

Tajfel, H. (1978). The achievement of inter-group differentiation. In Tajfel, H. (ed.). *Differentiation between Social Groups.* London, UK: Academic Press.

Tajfel, H. & Turner, J. C. (1979). An integrative theory of inter-group conflict. In Austin, W. G. and Worchel, S. (eds.). *The Social Psychology of Inter-group Relations.* Monterey, CA: Brooks/Cole.

Tutu, D. (1999). *No Future Without Forgiveness.* New York, NY: Image Books.

Wagner, G. (1954). The Abaluyia of Kavirondo. In Forde, D. (ed.). *Africa Worlds: Studies in the Cosmological and Social Values of African Peoples.* London, UK: Oxford University Press.

Wiredu, K. (2004). Truth and an African language. In Brown, L. M. (ed.). *African Philosophy: New and Traditional Perspectives.* New York, NY: Oxford University Press.

Chapter 3

Literary Perspective

Saidu Bangura

While the debate over Black Lives Matter versus All Lives Matter would want to tempt us to believe that it is only about the politics of race and its contours versus that of humanity, we take a different approach to this issue. In this chapter, I consider the presentation of women in African literature by both female as well as male African writers within the sociocultural milieu of the African woman. Thus, this chapter looks at the debate—Black Lives Matter versus All Lives Matter—from an African standpoint within a three-dimensional perspective: (1) society, (2) culture, and (3) women. To what extent has African literature looked at these three issues to demystify the myth that surrounds African women as they live side-by-side with their male partners in cultural societies that tend to favor the position of the man? In order to answer this question, the chapter puts into context the six burdens/conditions, "mountains on women's backs" (to be fully discussed later), which African women must meet and overcome in their struggles against male, societal, and cultural domination (Ogundipe-Leslie, 1983; cited by Kamara, 2001, p. 216).

This chapter is an analysis of the presentation of women in African literature taking the six burdens African women carry into consideration in the four books—*Things Fall Apart*, *Nervous Conditions*, *So Long a Letter*, and *The Lion and The Jewel*—under review. To contextualize the role women play in African family, societal, and cultural settings, the chapter further investigates the way women are perceived and considered, juxtaposed with the way they see themselves, within these settings, in a bid to determine whether their struggles (through womanist and feminist lenses) are producing meaningful effects. The study becomes a comparative analysis of the way women are presented by both male and female African novelists and playwrights taking cognizance of those traditional beliefs, the six conditions, which tend to stifle women's place (liberation) in society as against their male counterpart in a typical African cultural setting. The chapter then looks at the politics of gender identity, religion, and colonialism as they affect black women in the Motherland, Africa, within the context of the Black Lives Matter versus All Lives Matter debate. The study connects the multiple painful stories of African women as they struggle to undo the barriers set for them by their male counterparts, and the society they live in through the works of three African (one male and two female) novelists and one male playwright. Themes from these writers will be juxtaposed to add voice to the debate around Black Lives Matter versus All Lives Matter. Why do we include African issues in the Black Lives Matter versus All Lives Matter debate? The marginalization of the woman in a typical African society is also another form of Black Lives Matter versus All Lives Matter as we will see in the works analyzed further. Gender relations in the books under review can be seen along the lines of the Black Lives Matter versus All Lives Matter debate.

Literature, oral, or written, fiction or nonfiction, has always played an indispensable role in the way we see and understand the world and our immediate surroundings, our culture, our neighbors, and societies in general. In fact, our general perception of the universe and humanity is intrinsically tied to the way we have been told stories and the way we have perceived them. Oral literature is handed to us through tales told from generation to generation by our grandparents, parents or elderly relatives, or older members of our communities or societies. Whereas oral literature can be made and remade and hence lose some of its authenticity, written literature came into being to preserve how man has lived and how human interactions have ensured human understanding and cooperation. All forms of literature have molded our view of the world. Some of these stories have elicited heated debates given not only the controversies that surround them, but the way they have been told, retold, and analyzed and reanalyzed. In essence, these stories have equally shaped our cultural beliefs in one way or another. In short, all forms of literature should be a window to society, especially the complex network of how we relate and interact with one another. The family then becomes the mirror through which social cohesion and change are manifested. It is also a vehicle that transports the culture of a people/nation. We hope to show how these aspects are brought to light in the books we analyze further in the chapter written by African writers who grapple with the way people live their lives in their societies and the way they deal with certain issues.

LITERATURE: A CONCEPTUAL DISCUSSION

For starters, the study of literature began in Ancient Kemet/Egypt from the Early Dynastic Period (c. 6000–c. 3150 BCE) in the form of "Offering Lists and autobiographies" (Mark, 2016) and has continued to the present day. As such, it is only to be expected that there is not a single generally accepted definition for the discipline today. This truism is captured very well by Irena R. Makaryk when she writes the following:

> Of all the definitions contained in this volume, the one for literature is easily the most fluid. As the collective term for the many divergent objects of study for most critics and scholars . . . literature evolves as criticism evolves, and each critical school, as it defines its practice, recreates literature in its own image. That its definition is under constant revision would suggest that the objects it identifies are linked by relationships that are contingent upon historical circumstances or changing critical standards. (Makaryk, 1993, p. 581)

Thus, Makaryk, for example, defines literature as follows: "Derived from the Latin *literatura*, literature originally denoted either the ability to form letters or, more commonly, the quality of being widely read" (1993, p. 581). Laurence Perrine denotes literature as the study of "the principal forms of fiction (literature in the form of prose, especially short stories and novels, that describes imaginary events and people), poetry (literary work in which special intensity is given to the expression of feelings and ideas by the use of distinctive style and rhythm), and drama (a play for theater, radio, or television)" (Perrine, 1993, p. v; the definitions in parentheses are mine). With a focus on African American literature, Henry Louis Gates Jr. and Nellie Y. McKay characterize it as a "*vernacular*," which they describe as "the church songs, blues, ballads, sermons, stories, and, in our own era, rap songs that are part of the oral, not necessarily the literate (or written-down) tradition of black expression" (1997, p. 1). And, while paying particular attention to children's literature, John W. Griffith and Charles H. Frey express that this form of writing "constitutes our real mythology, the collection of episodes and characters and phrases in which many of our culture's widely held attitudes are best embodied" (1981, p. v). Given these definitions, I offer the following general denotation for how literature is conceptualized in this chapter: that is, written works, especially those considered of superior or lasting artistic merit.

Next, the study of literature is usually classified into two categories: (1) *fiction*, which, as aforementioned, refers to literature in the form of prose, especially short stories and novels, that describes imaginary events and people; and (2) *nonfiction*, which symbolizes prose writing that is based on facts, real events, and real people, such as biography or history. The California Department of Education (CDE) provides a listing with brief definitions of eighteen genres of fiction and five genres of nonfiction literature. The fiction genres are as follows (CDE, 2020, p. 1):

(1) "Drama—stories composed in verse or prose, usually for theatrical performance, where conflicts and emotion are expressed through dialogue and action."
(2) "Fable—narration demonstrating a useful truth, especially in which animals speak as humans; legendary, supernatural tale."
(3) "Fairy Tale—story about fairies or other magical creatures, usually for children."
(4) "Fantasy—fiction with strange or other worldly settings or characters; fiction which invites suspension of reality."
(5) "Fiction—narrative literary works whose content is produced by the imagination and is not necessarily based on fact."
(6) "Fiction in Verse—full-length novels with plot, subplot(s), theme(s), major and minor characters, in which the narrative is presented in (usually blank) verse form."
(7) "Folklore—the songs, stories, myths, and proverbs of a people or "folk" as handed down by word of mouth."
(8) "Historical Fiction—story with fictional characters and events in a historical setting."
(9) "Horror—fiction in which events evoke a feeling of dread in both the characters and the reader."
(10) "Humor—fiction full of fun, fancy, and excitement, meant to entertain; but can be contained in all genres."
(11) "Legend—story, sometimes of a national or folk hero, which has a basis in fact but also includes imaginative material."
(12) "Mystery—fiction dealing with the solution of a crime or the unraveling of secrets."
(13) "Mythology—legend or traditional narrative, often based in part on historical events, that reveals human behavior and natural phenomena by its symbolism; often pertaining to the actions of the gods."
(14) "Poetry—verse and rhythmic writing with imagery that creates emotional responses."
(15) "Realistic Fiction—story that can actually happen and is true to life."
(16) "Science Fiction—story based on impact of actual, imagined, or potential science, usually set in the future or on other planets."
(17) "Short Story—fiction of such brevity that it supports no subplots."
(18) "Tall Tale—humorous story with blatant exaggerations, swaggering heroes who do the impossible with nonchalance."

The following are the nonfiction genres (CDE, 2020, p. 1):

(1) "Biography/Autobiography—narrative of a person's life, a true story about a real person."

(2) "Essay—a short literary composition that reflects the author's outlook or point."
(3) "Narrative Nonfiction—factual information presented in a format which tells a story."
(4) "Nonfiction—informational text dealing with an actual, real-life subject."
(5) "Speech—public address or discourse."

Together, the preceding genres give the person studying literature the ability to discern how readers of literary works improve their vocabulary, reading comprehension and reading ability, and also increase their language development.

THE PRESENTATION OF WOMEN IN LITERATURE: A VIEW FROM THE GARDEN OF EDEN

Taking the aforementioned into consideration, let us briefly look at the story of the first man, Adam, and his wife, Eve in Eden (The Fall story as told by John Milton in *Paradise Lost*). While some (cultural and religious beliefs) have equated this story of the history of humanity to the entry of sin and suffering through these two people, Milton's story attempts to provide a solution to the theological problem of evil: the reconciliation of the existence of evil with a perfectly good, omniscient, and omnipotent Creator, and the workings of human free will that lead to disobedience. If Eve and Adam had not eaten the forbidden fruit, the world would have been freed of sins and suffering, we learn from two of the Abrahamic faiths: Christianity and Islam. John Milton has a different view in *Paradise Lost*. He does not see the eating of the fruit (regardless of the interpretation of this act) as the root cause of Adam and Eve being driven out of Eden. Milton blames neither God, nor the Serpent, nor Adam and Eve. The culprit, Milton points out, is marriage. That is, Adam and Eve fail to maintain a balance in their matrimonial relationship with each other and with God's order. Others have viewed Eden as the battleground and the inception of the fight of supremacy of and between the sexes. Consider John Donne's and Aemeilia Lanyer's blame game as reference points:

For that first marriage was our funeral
One woman at one blow then killed us all.
(John Donne, *The First Anniversary* 104–5).

What weakness offered, Strength might have refused,
Being Lord of all, the greater was his shame.
(Aemeilia Lanyer, *Salve Deus Rex Judaeorum* 779–80).

When we put Adam and Eve's relationship into perspective, we see that when Adam asks for a wife "fit to participate/All rational delight" (PL VIII: 390–1), it was for an equal. Note, however, that Eve is equal to Adam in many aspects but "inferior in the mind/And inward faculties" (PL VIII: 541–2). This basically points to the fact that in Eden there are no equals and there is a hierarchical structure to be respected: the Creator—Angels—Man (Adam first, then Eve)—the animals; and the woman is not seen as being on a par with her male counterpart even though she was created from his ribs, and not from the head or from under his feet. Note how Eve refers to Adam:

My Author and Disposer, what thou bidd'st
Unargu'd I obey; so God ordains,
God is thy law, thou mine: to know no more
Is woman's happiest knowledge and her praise.
(PL IV: 635–8)

You will agree with me that Eve's position in Eden set the pace for the submissive and ensuing place of the woman in society. You will also agree with me that both the Serpent and Eve in *Paradise Lost* have one thing in common; both seem to admire the power of knowledge and consciousness. Besides referring to the Tree as "O Sacred, Wise, and Wisdom-giving plant/Mother of Science" (PL IX 679–80), the Serpent tells Eve:

He knows that in the day
Ye eat thereof, your eyes that seem so clear,
Yet are but dim, shall perfectly ~be then
Op'n'd and clear'd, and ye shall be as Gods. Knowing both Good and Evil as they know.
(PL IX: 705–9)

On this note, we can consider Eden as an educational center. Genna Murphy (2007) observes that

> *Paradise Lost* itself is full of teachers, pupils, knowledge, and guidelines for the passing or receiving of wisdom, and the climax of the poem and the Fall involves the Tree of Knowledge and the pursuit of higher wisdom. (Murphy, 2007, p. 35)

However, the education meant for the man is not the same as that designed for the woman. In Eden, the Creator talks directly to Adam or sends teachers (Raphael and Michael) to teach, instruct, or warn Adam excluding Eve from most of these lectures or sessions. Adam passes on information and knowledge to his wife on his own volition or as his wife prefers. Eve does not receive direct lessons from God. She takes lessons from Adam whom she describes as "My Guide/And Head" (PL IV: 442–43) or has to eavesdrop on some occasions (PLVIII: 48–52), "And from the parting Angel overheard/As in a shady nook I stood behind" (PL IX: 276–77) to get direct lessons from Adam's teachers. Because Eve is excluded from most of the discourses on education and knowledge, she develops a deep yearning for the pursuit of wisdom. And as the poem develops, Eve becomes completely different from the domestic and obedient woman. This other Eve is very ambitious and eager to know. She wants to cross the confines of domesticity and inferiority. To free herself from this oppression, she must be independent. She therefore asks to be alone in executing her gardening function (PL IX: 214–15; PL IX: 205–384). Eve, who once refers to Adam as "My Guide/And Head," "My Author and Disposer, what thou bidd'st/Unargu'd I obey," not only separates herself from her husband but also eats of the Tree of Knowledge so that she can gain wisdom.

Considering this reference to Eve as a backdrop, let us look at how African literature has portrayed women in society and what space has been reserved for women culturally speaking. To what extent has African literature looked at society and culture to demystifying the myth that surrounds (African) women as they live side by side with their male partners in cultural societies that tend to favor the position of the man? In answering this question, we put into perspective the six conditions, "mountains on women's backs," which African women must meet and overcome in their struggles against male, societal, and cultural domination (Ogundipe-Leslie, 1983; cited in Kamara, 2001).

According to Ogundipe-Leslie (1983; cited in Kamara, 2001), African women have six burdens that weigh them down:

(1) oppression from outside forces (foreign intrusion, colonial domination, etc.); (2) heritage of tradition (feudal, slave-based, communal); (3) her own backwardness, a product of colonization and its concomitant poverty, ignorance, etc.; (4) her men, weaned on centuries of male domination who will not willingly relinquish their power and privilege; (5) her race, because the international economic order is divided along race lines; and (6) herself. (Ogundipe-Leslie, 1983; cited in Kamara, 2001, p. 216)

Our concern then becomes the presentation of women in African literature taking the six burdens African women carry into consideration in the four books under review. To contextualize the role women play in African family, societal, and cultural settings, the chapter further investigates the way women are perceived and considered, juxtaposed with the way they see themselves, within these settings, in a bid to determine whether their struggles (through womanist and feminist lenses) are producing meaningful effects. The chapter becomes a comparative analysis of the way women are presented by both male and female African novelists and playwrights taking cognizance of those traditional beliefs, the six conditions, which tend to stifle women's place (liberation) in society as against their male counterpart in a typical African cultural milieu. Let us contextualize Ogundipe-Leslie's wisdom, especially the second burden ("heritage of tradition"), with the poem, "Ode to my Cultural Heritage" by Hassan Sisay. The significance of the repetition of the expressions ("I was born a woman," "I was born a woman," and "But tradition says") cannot be overemphasized even if some readers might want to consider them clichés. What is important to highlight here is the fact traditional African societies give too much importance to the male figure just as foreign forces such as religion and culture have done for centuries. This pro-male attitude has helped to underdevelop African potentials.

GENDER IN AFRICAN LITERATURE: WOMEN AND SOCIETIES

Chinua Achebe's *Things Fall Apart* is set in nineteenth-century Nigeria with a retrospective perspective surrounding the coming of the Europeans with their civilizing and Christianizing missions for Africans and what happened after their arrival. We need to state here that we are looking at a society that is changing both from within and from without. This change is announced right at the beginning of the story, long before the coming of the Whiteman. It is announced in the first three paragraphs of the book, as Achebe presents the protagonist of the story, Okonkwo, who is the embodiment of the tradition and society:

> Okonkwo was well known throughout the nine villages and even beyond. His fame rested on solid personal achievements. As a young man of eighteen he had brought honour to his village by throwing Amalinze the Cat. Amalinze was the great wrestler who for seven years was unbeaten, from Umuofia to Mbaino. He was called the Cat because his back would never touch the earth. It was this man that Okonkwo threw in a fight which the old men agreed was one of the fiercest since the founder of their town engaged a spirit of the wild for seven days and seven nights. (1959, p. 1)

Achebe adds:

> The drums beat and the flutes sang and the spectators held their breath. Amalinze was a wily craftsman, but Okonkwo was as slippery as a fish in water. Every

nerve and every muscle stood out on their arms, on their backs and their thighs, and one almost heard them stretching to breaking point. In the end Okonkwo threw the Cat. (1959, p. 1)

Achebe continues:

That was many years ago, twenty years or more, and during this time Okonkwo's fame had grown like a bush-fire in the harmattan. He was tall and huge, and his bushy eyebrows and wide nose gave him a very severe look. He breathed heavily, and it was said that, when he slept, his wives and children in their houses could hear him breathe. When he walked, his heels hardly touched the ground and he seemed to walk on springs, as if he was going to pounce on somebody. And he did pounce on people quite often. He had a slight stammer and whenever he was angry and could not get his words out quickly enough, he would use his fists. He had no patience with unsuccessful men. He had had no patience with his father. (1959, p. 1)

While change, as presented here, sets the pace for our appreciation of Okonkwo as the personification of the cultural values of his society, this first page should also serve as the basis of the general understanding of the text. Apart from this theme, Achebe deals with other issues in the book. He presents Africa as: peaceful; African societies have defined parameters of right conduct on both the individual and collective levels; the ethics of the society is "live and let live"; the society encourages one to work hard in order to succeed as individual achievement has a prize; the weak are protected from being trampled upon by the strong; there is societal organization as demonstrated by the week of peace when all and sundry should find time to make peace with his neighbor; there is a distinction between just and unjust wars; there is an admirable civilization and culture; there is formidable system of computing time of the day, of the week, season, and of the year, among other themes.

However, where does Achebe go wrong in his defense of African civilization, culture, and way of life? Women and their symbolic importance in society: men are held in high-esteem; men are seen and heard; men consider women (like they do their children) as part of their property; women are beaten and sent off to their relatives as the man deems fit; the number of women and children a man has, just as his barns of yam or harvest, determines his level of success; an unsuccessful man is considered a woman. Yet, when a man has problems, when things go wrong "Mother is supreme." And still, the person who solves all mystic problems is a woman, Chielo, the priestess of Agbala. So, is "mother" or "guardian" not a "woman"? If mother means "refuge," "sympathy," "love," "care," "hope," "protection," and "solace";

then the "other" woman equally is. Both mother and woman form part of the economic unit of the society: both add to the prosperity of the family—they bear children and men pay bride price for their wives, and hence add to the economic well-being of the family and the society.

Achebe's presentation of women in *Things Fall Apart* can be seen in the light of the Black Lives Matter versus All Lives Matter, given the fact that in his attempt to present where the rain began to beat the African sociocultural milieu and sociohistorical reality, Achebe tells us for whom things were never together: women (Stratton, 1994, p. 24ff). While the dignity and respect of the African man is glorified and restored, that of the African woman is demeaned and shattered. The woman is not part of the African civilization that is presented in *Things Fall Apart*. For Stratton (1994), the presentation of women is not much less of a concern compared to the representation of "the District Commissioner whose own version of the story of imperial conquest is to be told in a book entitled *The Pacification of the Primitive Tribes of the Lower Niger*" (Stratton, 1994, p. 24). Stratton (1994) sees this diminution of Africans and their culture as "primitive savages" and the destruction of their "sophisticated culture" to be classified as mere "pacification" as an affront (Stratton, 1994, p. 24) just as the presentation of the women in *Things Fall Apart*.

Tsitsi Dangarembga's *Nervous Conditions*, whose title is taken from the introduction of Fanon's *Wretched of the Earth*—"the status of native is a nervous condition"—is set in Rhodesia (now Zimbabwe) during the colonial period and narrates the coming of age of a rural girl and hence juxtaposes her dreams of becoming free of the burdens of being a girl in her village through education that was meant only for boys and the devastations of colonialism. Tambu, the protagonist, comes face to face with the price of the education she longs for as she explains the ordeals of being a woman. Consider the opening and closing paragraphs of the novel:

> I was not sorry when my brother died. Nor am I apologizing for my callousness, as you may define it, my lack of feeling. For it is not that at all. I feel many things these days, much more than I was able to feel in the days when I was young and my brother died, and there are reasons for this more than the mere consequence of age. Therefore, I shall not apologise but begin by recalling the facts as I remember them that led up to my brother's death, the events that put me in a position to write this account. For though the event of my brother's passing and the events of my story cannot be separated, my story is not after all about death, but about my escape and Lucia's; about my mother's and Maiguru's entrapment; and about Nyasha's rebellion—Nyasha, far-minded and isolated, my uncle's daughter, whose rebellion may not in the end have been successful. (Dangarembga, 1989, p. 1)

Dangaremgba adds:

> Quietly, unobtrusively and extremely fitfully, something in my mind began to assert itself, to question things and refuse to be brainwashed, bringing me to this time when I can set down this story ... my story, the story of four women whom I loved, and our men, this story is how it all began. (Dangarembga, 1989, p. 204)

The attentive reader would connect the links Tambu makes in these two excerpts: how she was able to escape ignorance and illiteracy at the death of her brother and hence becomes educated and how that education lifted her to the stage of the breadwinner for her family, a role normally played by men. It equally pinpoints the fact that she could only be given an opportunity to go to school when her brother died; the story she tells here is not only the story of a single girl/woman but also the story of four women and that long process of emancipation. But that emancipation comes with a price: the nervousness of being a girl/woman in colonial rural Rhodesia, now Zimbabwe, in Africa. Both the colonial system and local tradition gave premium to boys/men: the society is patriarchal. This idea is well-designed in this novel as the Shona traditional codes of conduct or modes of doing things are presented. Note how Tambu captures the patrilinear Shona system in the task she has been given of carrying the water dish for the elders to wash their hands:

> I had to carry the water-dish in which people would wash their hands. I did not like doing this because you had to be very sure of the relative status of everybody present or else it was easy to make mistakes, especially when there were so many people. Today it was doubly tricky because although Babamukuru was the guest of honour, there were male relatives present of higher status than he. Making a considered and perhaps biased decision, I knelt first in front of Babamukuru, which was a mistake because he wanted me to let his uncle Isaiah, our eldest surviving grandfather, wash first. I knelt and rose and knelt and rose in front of my male relatives in descending order of seniority, and lastly in front of my grandmothers and aunts, offering them the water-dish and towel. (Dangarembga, 1989, pp. 40–41)

As she moves from her rural homestead, things begin to change for her:

> All the things that I wanted were tying themselves into a neat package which presented itself to me with a flourish. There should have been trumpets .... I Tambudzai, so recently a peasant, was I not entering, as I had promised myself I would, a world where burdens lightened with every step, soon to disappear altogether? I had an idea that this would happen as I passed through the school gates, those gates that would declare me a young lady, a member of the Young Ladies College of the Sacred Heart. (Dangarembga, 1989, p. 191)

Her reincarnation, which she has been announced earlier in the novel, is better presented on pages 92–93 (see Dangarembga, 1989, pp. 92–93) where she visualizes the change, which will guarantee her success as an educated young woman who has defied her natural surroundings by venturing into a world reserved only for the boy-child/men. Education then becomes her passport to a brighter future. But let us pause and ask a very important question: Is everybody happy with the removal of Tambu from the homestead to get education? Or is everybody pleased with the ways of modernity and the new culture it forces people to emulate? It does not seem so. Her mother does not only complain that her daughter now speaks English, but she rejects a Christian wedding at her age given the fact that they have been deemed sinners:

> Tell me, my daughter, what will I, your mother say to you when you come home a stranger full of white ways and ideas? It will be English, English all the time. He-e, Mummy this, he- e, Mummy that. Like that cousin of yours . . . . To wear a veil, at my age, to wear a veil! (Dangarembga, 1989, p. 184).

However, Tambu who has been very obedient realizes that the colonial life she is living is not all too good. She comes to terms with reality toward the end of the story and realizes that her mother has been right—she had been unnatural within her sociocultural milieu by not only listening to her parents but to her uncle, but also by laughing at her parents at the request of her uncle (see Dangarembga, 1989, p. 165). This forms part of the nervousness of girls/women that the novel depicts.

If Achebe's *Things Fall Apart* presents a precolonial Africa with all its glory and cultural sophistication around the menfolk and presents the womenfolk as servants of the former, Dangarembga's *Nervous Conditions* gives us a clue how to dismantle the barrier or burdens set for the women: education. Tambu breaks the confines of her predestined role as a woman/servant of the menfolk in her Shona culture, thanks to education.

Wole Soyinka's (1963) *The Lion and The Jewel* is set in a traditional African community, Ilujinle, Nigeria, in the firm grip of gender inequality and male chauvinism to an extent that older African traditional women condescend to this sociocultural milieu and female deprivation to the point of scheming plots with men or simply collaborate with them in order to have the younger generation of women physically, intellectually, psychologically, and sexually join the bandwagon of having more women in the backyard to do the whims and caprices of men. And the men who strongly believe in such a way of life will stop at nothing to achieve their goals. This scheme is so tactfully employed in this satirical play where we see a defeat of not only genuine love as represented by the village schoolteacher by the traditional polygamous life and sexual thirst represented by the "Bale" (though with a little taste of modern techniques: the photographer, and the images in the magazine) but also the role elderly women play to deprive younger women of enlightenment and social and economic elevation. This role is so skillfully embodied in the character of Sadiku, the symbolic representation of the traditional African woman, for the success of the old traditional way of life and leaves Sidi, the village belle, *the jewel* of Ilujinle, with no escape route but to fall prey to Baroka, *the lion* of Ilujinle, and thus the age-long entrapment of the female-kind in the hands of men like Baroka in African traditional rural societies.

The play is centered on Sidi, the beauty of Ilujinle, hopelessly caught between two powerful and opposing forces, the traditional way of life as against educated men and their new way of life, modern civilization. She does not have strong will-power to withstand both forces and find a way out of the dilemma she faces. Her encounters with Sadiku and her orchestrated guidance leads to her consequent entanglement in the traditional way of life, which she thought she has hopelessly defeated with her images in the magazine, which have spread as far as Lagos, the symbol of the new world.

The play opens with an encounter between Sidi and Lakunle, the village schoolteacher, one of the contenders for the village belle, whose undying love for Sidi makes him vehemently condemn her carrying things on her head and her exposing her shoulders for "good-for-nothing shameless men" (Soyinka, 1963, p. 3) to see. Despite Lakunle's declarations of love and constant asking of Sidi's hand in marriage, she, as a die-hard traditionalist, will only accept if he agrees to pay the bride price. Lakunle detests this bride price custom to the extent that he calls it a "savage custom," "an ignoble custom, infamous, ignominious" and "shaming our heritage before the world" (Soyinka, 1963, p. 7). For him, to pay the bride price is like buying something from a shop: she would become his mere property (Soyinka, 1963, p. 8). He declares his reasons of marrying a woman to Sidi, quite contrary to tradition. For Lakunle, marrying a woman equals companionship and never to do household chores and bear too many children (Soyinka, 1963, pp. 7–8).

Because Lakunle does not see himself part of customs such as paying a dowry, Sidi urges him to go to other places where women "would understand" his thoughts of "future wonders" and she clearly denounces his love manifestations. For her, he has no place in their community if marrying a woman only for the sake of love and true companionship with all its fêted modern flavors—sitting, eating, working together, and walking side by side—means not paying the bride price. Her position becomes stronger when her photos are brought by the photographer and the impact they have on people like the Bale. The Bale's encounter with Lakunle complicates matters for both Sidi and Lakunle. Baroka, gazing at the beauty of the images, declares: "It is five full months since last I took a wife . . . five full months" (Soyinka, 1963, p. 18) as if taking wives were picking things from a store. How can the

Bale achieve his objective of adding one more wife to his harem? How can he get this belle whose beauty and fame he has helped to make? Would his endeavors go in vain?

The answer to these questions is Sadiku, the woman with "the sharpest tongue," and his constant "match-maker without the prompting" and "go-between" when it comes to women (Soyinka, 1963, pp. 43–44). It is traditionally natural and common that the senior wife in a harem always acts as the go-between for the junior wives or marries them for his husband. So, Sadiku steps in for her husband. She tells Sidi her husband's intensions. Sidi emphatically refuses even with Sadiku's heap of benefits she stands to gain from this relationship as the last and youngest wife in the Bale's harem partly due to the teachings of Lakunle and partly due to the fame and beauty the images have exposed of her (Soyinka, 1963, pp. 20–23). This apart, Sidi tells us that she is "young and brimming," "the twinkle of a jewel," and hence cannot marry an old man like the Bale who is "spent" and the "hind quarter of a lion" (Soyinka, 1963, pp. 21–23).

Sadiku, who does not feel pleased with Sidi's refusal, tells her the second plan: the invitation to supper. Sidi, well-acquainted with the Bale's tricks and tales of supper, turns down the invitation: "Tell your lord that Sidi does not sup with married men" (Soyinka, 1963, p. 23). As usual she defends her husband but her defense fell on deaf ears.

Sadiku's bad news from Sidi does not stop Baroka from making known his final plan for Sidi, that he has lost his manhood, to Sadiku knowing fully well the weakness of women, their tongue; that it will be revealed, she will not keep it a secret. Should Sidi or any other woman hear of it, she will want to mock him. Sadiku's celebration of the victory of women over men, in the sequence of Baroka's declaring his "loss of manhood," whether a conscious plan to lure Sidi to attempt provoking Baroka or mere boastfulness of her own personal triumph over men from Okiki to Baroka, has very negative consequences on Sidi. Although Sidi has her reservation on the validity of such news yet, she cannot withstand the tempting whisper of Sadiku, and then comes her sudden change of mind with regard to the invitation to the supper, to which she plans to "mock the devil" (Soyinka, 1963, p. 34).

This "way to mock the devil" (Soyinka, 1963, p. 34).turns out to be the way to become the favorite of Baroka and the proof that, indeed, Africa's traditions, for as long as we have uncompromising traditionalists like Sadiku, will remain intact; men will always scheme plans to triumph over women and this time not without the help of modern technology, the camera ("the one-eyed box") and the beauty magazine ("the book"). But, as we have seen, even with the help of the stranger with the modern technology of exposing a woman's beauty, and the "weak" attempt of Lakunle to win Sidi's hand in western and Christian style marriage without respecting the traditions and customs of Ilujinle, Baroka will not have succeeded in adding the village belle to his fold if he does not have a queen like Sadiku, who will do everything in her power to win more women for her husband. And as the embodiment of traditional African women, she will not sit by and see her beliefs, culture, customs, and traditions be torn apart and turned upside down by strange traditions. Therefore, Soyinka silenced most of the women except the girls who are given the gossiping and informant roles so that Sadiku can be seen and heard in her move to restrain this weak civilizing mission of Lakunle, the village teacher.

Mariama Bâ's *So Long a Letter* is set in post-independent Senegal with a multidimensional critical message about the position of women in postcolonial Africa. The novel deals with the problems of polygamy. This becomes more complex as it is supported by both Islam, the dominant religion, and the traditional African setting. The two protagonists, Ramatoulaye and Aissatou, are educated and got married to two educated men as well—Modou, a lawyer and Mawdo, a medical doctor. Theirs is not the problem of lack of education; their problem is created by the fact that the society is male-dominated and is polygamous. When challenged by this age-long tradition, Ramatoulaye and Aissatou present their perspectives for their emancipation and consequently that of other African women. For Ramatoulaye, one of the burdens that women carry in Africa is summarized thus:

> And to think that I loved this man passionately, to think that I gave him thirty years of my life, to think that twelve times over I carried his child. The addition of a rival to my life was not enough for him. In loving someone else, he burned his past, both morally and materially. He dared to commit such an act of disavowal. (Bâ, 1981, p. 12)

While this position would convince the reader that Ramatoulaye has taken a decision to leave Modou, we see a strong woman who waits for her husband to come home and help in raising their twelve children. Since the husband does not come, she stays at home and takes care of her children. At the death of Modou, Ramatoulaye mourns her husband as the tradition and the culture demand. She presents the following picture as what she thinks is the solution to the predicament of many African women:

> If only each partner could move sincerely towards the other! If each could only melt into the other! If each would only accept the other's successes and failures!
>
> ...
>
> The success of the family is born of a couple's harmony, as the harmony of multiple instruments creates a pleasant symphony.

The nation is made up of all the families, rich or poor, united or separated, aware or unaware. The success of a nation therefore depends inevitably on the family. (Bâ, 1981, p. 89)

Ramatoulaye, therefore, represents the concept of womanism, a concept based on love and equal responsibility for both couple.

On the other hand, her friend, Aissatou, proposes another solution: feminism. Not being able to face and accept polygamy, she leaves this letter for her husband:

Mawdo,
Princes master their feelings to fulfill their duties. "Others" bend their heads and, in silence, accept a destiny that oppresses them.

That briefly put is the internal ordering of our society, with its absurd divisions. I will not yield to it. I cannot accept what you are offering me today in place of the happiness we once had. You want to draw a line between heartfelt love and physical love. . .

Your reasoning, which makes a distinction, is unacceptable to me: on my side, me, "your life, your love, your choice" on the other side, "young Nabou," to be tolerated for reasons of duty.

I am stripping myself of your love, your name. Clothed in my dignity, the only worthy garment, I go my way.
Goodbye,
Aissatou.
(Bâ, 1981, p. 32)

With this letter, Aissatou leaves Mawdo, and travels to France in pursuit of education where she might probably join the feminist movement, which does not have a space in Senegal, Africa.

CONCLUSIONS AND SUGGESTIONS

How can African women remove the six mountains on their backs? The emancipation of the woman depends on how well she can dismantle, demystify, off-load, and escape the complex network in the society in which she lives as follows:

(a) The woman must face, recognize, and "fight" (metaphorically) against the OUTSIDE FORCES—colonialism, religion, and other cultural forces that seem to oppress her. Novelists and playwrights must put the woman at the center of their works to show how these outside cultural forces are

violently preventing the woman from achieving a space of respect within the sociocultural milieu of her society or reaching the top echelons of society.
(b) The woman inherits beliefs, traditions, and customs that she cannot go against. She is obliged to obey and uphold them and in the interest of continuity she must pass them on to her generation yet unborn. How do these customs help in her strides to move on with changing times? She needs to sift some of these customs and traditions otherwise her future generation will inherit her predicaments. These beliefs, traditions, and customs must be subjects of scholarly study to improve on the good ones and phase off/eliminate those that are harmful to the peace and progress of not only women but also the general membership of society.
(c) As a product of colonialism, ignorance, poverty, and consequently neo-colonialism, the African woman must demystify and unmask her own backwardness caused by her refusal of education by both colonial and religious forces. She now needs to embrace education. Education of the girl-child should be a top priority if families, nations, and cultures must enjoy the fruits of gender equity and equality. Both Dangarembga and Bâ use education as instrument for the emancipation of the girl-child and woman.
(d) Male domination and selfishness are the worst challenges that the woman faces in Africa: How can she convince her male counterpart to relinquish or to share some of his powers and privileges with her? Policy makers and legislators must ensure the sharing of political and institutional powers to ensure progress and equity of the sexes in society.
(e) Herself vis-à-vis the choices she must make—whether to accept the society and its principles laid down by men or make new rules or her own rules of the game. Women's participation in all aspects of society is very crucial. Women are needed to become the champions of major sociocultural, socioeconomic, and sociopolitical changes that are urgently needed in altering the narratives of the African continent.
(f) Polygamy—the complex sexist feature of traditional Africa supported by the literal interpretation of the Al-Quran. While this is one of the thorny issues in traditional societies, we urge both men and women to negotiate the way forward in modernizing the practice through legislation and religious education.

Considering the aforementioned aspects, we need people like Daouda Dieng who "insist on changing the rules of the game and injecting new life into it" (Bâ, 1981, p. 61). We can only have a new and positive Africa if we have the full participation of the women in every aspect of our societies to go with Dauoda Dieng's philosophy of a new Africa:

Women are no longer decorative accessories, objects to be moved about, companions to be flattered or calmed with promises. Women are the nation's primary fundamental root, from which all else grows and blossoms. Women must be encouraged to take a keener interest in the destiny of the *continent* (italics are mine, Bâ, 1981, pp. 61–62).

Considering the debate on Black Lives Matter versus All Lives Matter, and given the preceding analysis of the presentation of women in African literature, the suggestions I have proffered for policy makers in Africa, and putting into perspective Daouda Dieng's philosophy of a new Africa, I conclude this chapter with the following poem I wrote:

The Sunrise of a New Dawn
For Amina and Anne-Marie (my twin daughters)

Out of the gloom of her relegation
out of the abyss of hopeless darkness
out of primordial denial of her place—
even in Eden where she was meant to be
equal in essence, even there we are told
she was weak, the door to our funeral
and expulsion, and she must submit
and obey unarguably—so God ordains:
the woman is rising to a new dawn!

Out of her pains as a daughter, woman
wife, mother, in the South as in the North—
out of her sufferings, her griefs, her sorrows,
her courage, her resilience, her benevolence,
her struggles, her sacrifices, her productivity,
her defiance on the laws that subjugate her
that deny her a place in what she builds:
the sunrise of a new day is dawning on her—
the woman is rising to a new dawn, a new day!

Out of the shadows of her historical trajectory
out of the wickedness of cultural violence on her
out of the contours of male domination over her
out of the ocean of tears she has wallowed in
out of burgeoning modern injustice on the woman
out of the pile of rot she had to make clean, pure
out of the hell she has gone through for humanity—

the sunrise of a new dawn is smiling on the woman,
the woman is rising to a new dawn, to a new day!

Saidu Bangura, Praia, November 8, 2020

REFERENCES

Achebe, C. (1959). *Things Fall Apart.* London, UK: Heinemann Publisher.
Bâ, M. (1981). *So Long a Letter.* Oxford, UK: Heinemann Publisher.
Bangura, S. (November 8, 2020). The sunrise of a new dawn: A poem written by me.
California Department of Education (CDE). (April 9, 2020). Literary genres. Retrieved on January 20, 2021 from https://www.cde.ca.gov/ci/cr/rl/litrlgenres.asp.
Dangarembga, T. (1988). *Nervous Conditions.* New York, NY: Seal Press.
Donne, John. (2021). The first anniversary: A poem. *Poetry Foundation.* Retrieved on January 20, 2021 from https://www.poetryfoundation.org/poems/50336/the-anniversary-56d22d56d635f
Gates Jr., H. L. and McKay, N. Y., general editors. (1997). *The Norton Anthology of African American Literature.* New York, NY: W. W. Norton and Company.
Griffith, J. W. and Frey, C. H. (1981). *Classics of Children's Literature.* New York, NY: Macmillan Publishing Company, Inc.
Kamara, G. (2001). The feminist struggle in the Senegalese novel: Mariama Ba and Sembene Ousmane. *Journal of Black Studies* 32(2):212–228.
Lanyer, A. (2021). Salve Deus Rex Judaeorum: A poem. *Press Books.* Retrieved on January 20, 2021 from https://earlybritishlit.pressbooks.com/chapter/aemilia-lanyar-salve-deus-rex-judaeorum/
Makaryk, I. R., general editor and compiler. (1993). *Encyclopedia of Contemporary Literary Theory: Approaches, Scholars, Terms.* Toronto, Canada: University of Toronto Press.
Mark, J. J. (November 14, 2016). Ancient Egyptian literature. *Ancient History Encyclopedia.* Retrieved on January 19, 2021 from https://www.ancient.eu/Egyptian_Literature/
Milton, J. (1989). *Paradise Lost.* London, UK: Penguin Classics.
Murphy, G. (2007). E(a)vesdropping in *Paradise Lost*: Knowledge and disobedience. MA Thesis, Acadia University. Library and Archives Canada.
Ogundipe-Leslie, O. (1983). African women, culture and another development. *Journal of African Marxist* 5:77–92.
Perrine, L. (1993). *Literature: Structure, Sound, and Sense* (6th ed.). San Diego, CA: Harcourt Brace Jovanovich College Publishers.
Sisay, H. (2012). Ode to my cultural heritage: A poem. Retrieved on February 21, 2021 from http://thepatrioticvanguard.com/ode-to-my-cultural-heritage
Soyinka, W. (1963). *The Lion and the Jewel.* Oxford, UK: Oxford University Press.
Strutton, F. (1994). *Contemporary African Literature and the Politics of Gender.* New York, NY: Routledge.

Chapter 4

Mathematical Perspective

Abdul Karim Bangura

This chapter encompasses a mathematical analysis of how the internet, major newspapers, and major television networks in the United States have presented issues pertaining to the Black Lives Matter and All Lives Matter movements. Mathematical analysis, as I have defined the notion elsewhere, involves "the systematic study of *change, quantity, relation, space, structure*, and other topics dealing with *entity, form*, and *pattern*" (Bangura, 2020, p. 15). The italicized terms are commonly defined as follows: (a) *change* is the act or instance of making or becoming different; (b) *quantity* means a value or component that may be expressed in numbers; (c) *relation* denotes a thing's effect on or relevance to another; (d) *space* refers to a continuous area or expanse which is free, available, or unoccupied; (e) *structure* stands for the arrangement of and relations among the parts or elements of something complex; (f) *entity* designates a thing with distinct and independent existence; (g) *form* signifies the visible shape or configuration of something; and (h) *pattern* shows an arrangement of lines or shapes.

Thus, the major question probed in this chapter is: How have the internet, major newspapers, and major television networks in the United States represented issues pertaining to the Black Lives Matter and All Lives Matter movements? This question and its investigation are essential because the exercise will allow us to know which of these movements has received the most attention from these media and, therefore, deemed to be more privileged or more active. Accordingly, the major proposition here is that the movement that has been more privileged or more active received the most attention from the three media.

As a mathematical analysis of the topic broached in this chapter, the methodological approach employed is quantitative. This means that the amounts of coverages the three media have given to the two movements are measured in terms of their numerical values rather than their quality. Thus, the mathematical exploration comprises both univariate analysis, whereby each variable (i.e., each movement) as represented in the data set collected are explored separately; and bivariate analysis, whereby two variables (i.e., both movements) as represented are examined simultaneously for the purpose of determining the empirical relationship between them. I must also mention here that while univariate analysis is applicable for data from the three media, only the data from the newspapers and television networks are applicable for bivariate analysis because the data from the internet cover only one valid case for each variable.

At the univariate level, five statistical measures are employed. The first measure is the *total number of cases in a population* (n), which simply involves counting the individual cases in a sample and providing the sum for them: that is, $X_1 + X_2 + X_3 + \ldots + X_n$.

The second measure is the *percentage* (% or p), which is calculated by determining a rate, number, or amount in each hundred. The following is the formula for the *percentage*:

$$\% = \frac{X}{100}$$

where X = rate, number, or amount.

The third measure is the *mean* ($\bar{X}$ or m), which is calculated by adding up all the numbers and then dividing the sum by how many numbers there are. The formula for the *mean* is as follows:

$$\bar{X} = \Sigma(X_1) / n$$

where Σ = summation notation or sum of all values, X_1 = all of the X values, and n = number of items in the sample.

The fourth measure is the *standard deviation* (σ or sd), which is calculated by indicating the extent of the amount by which a single measurement differs from a fixed value such as the mean for a group as a whole. This is the formula for the *standard deviation*:

$$\sigma = \sqrt{\Sigma(X_i - \mu)^2 / N}$$

where X_i = each value from the population, μ = population mean, and N = size of the population.

The fifth measure is the *range* (Range(x)), which is calculated by determining the difference between the highest/maximum(X) and lowest/minimum(X) values of a variable. The formula for the *range* is the following:

$$\text{Range}(X) = \text{Maximum}(X) - \text{Minimum}(X)$$

For the bivariate level, the *paired sample t-test* (*t*) measure is used. The technique involves determining whether the mean difference between two sets of observations is zero. This measure's formula is as follows:

$$t = \frac{m}{s\sqrt{n}}$$

where *m* = mean and *s* = standard deviation of *d* = difference, respectively; *n* = size of *d*.

Also, the data collected for the analysis were computed by using the Matrix Laboratory (MATLAB) software. And, according to its manufacturer, "MATLAB is a programming platform designed specifically for engineers and scientists. The heart of MATLAB is the MATLAB language, a matrix-based language allowing the most natural expression of computational mathematics" (MATLAB, 2020, p. 1).

In addition, concentrated searches were done on December 24, 2020, to tease out the needed data from the internet and the websites of the newspapers and television networks studied. This means that the phrases Black Lives Matter and All Lives Matter were placed within quotation marks so that only those results with the exact phrasings would emerge.

In order to conduct the analysis with lucidity, the rest of the chapter is divided into three major sections entailing examinations of the three media separately. The chapter then ends with a conclusion and recommendations for policy makers and future research on the topic. Before doing all this, however, it behooves me to first tender a conceptual disquisition of mathematics, which is the major notion that underlies this chapter.

Mathematics: A Conceptual Discussion

The study of mathematics is normally divided into three areas. The first area is basic mathematics, which commonly entails counting, addition, subtraction, multiplication, and division, and typically taught in secondary education or in the first year of college and university. The following are the topics covered in basic mathematics with their foci:

(a) Discrete mathematics focuses on objects that can assume only distinct, separated values.
(b) Calculus focuses on the finding and properties of derivatives and integrals of functions generated by using methods originally based on the summation of infinitesimal differences.

(c) Geometry focuses on the properties and relations of points, lines, surfaces, solids, and higher dimensional analogs.
(d) Trigonometry focuses on the relations of the sides and angles of triangles and with the relevant functions of any angles.
(e) Logic focuses on the systematic use of symbolic and mathematical techniques to determine the forms of valid deductive arguments.

The second area is pure mathematics, which is the abstract science of number, quantity, and space studied in its own right. The subject matters studied in pure mathematics with their foci are as follows:

(a) Algebra focuses on letters and other general symbols used to represent numbers and quantities in formulae and equations.
(b) Calculus and analysis focuses on the calculation of derivatives, integrals and limits of functions of real numbers, and especially immediate rates of change.
(c) Geometry and topology focuses on the initial study of spatial figures such as circles and cubes and then generalized considerably; also studied is the development from geometry by looking at those properties that do not change even when the figures are deformed by stretching and bending, such as dimension.
(d) Combinatorics focuses on amalgamations of objects belonging to a finite set in accordance with certain constraints, such as those of Graph Theory: that is, the mathematical postulate of the properties and applications of diagrams showing the relations among variable quantities, typically between two variables, each measured along one of a pair of axes at right angles.
(e) Logic at this level focuses on the formalization of valid reasoning, particularly how it attempts to define what constitutes a proof.
(f) Number Theory focuses on the properties and relationships of numerals, especially the positive integers.

The third area is applied mathematics, which is the abstract science of number, quantity, and space applied to other disciplines such as physics and engineering. The subjects learned in applied mathematics with their foci are the following:

(a) Dynamical systems and differential equations focuses on statements for which the values of two mathematical expressions are equal (indicated by the sign =) involving unknown functions and their derivatives, and also a fixed rule that describes the time dependence of a point in a geometrical space.

(b) Mathematical physics focuses on problems in the field of physics (the branch of science concerned with the nature and properties of matter and energy; the subject matter of physics, distinguished from that of chemistry and biology, includes mechanics, heat, light and other radiation, sound, electricity, magnetism, and the structure of atoms) by utilizing mathematical techniques capable for such applications and for the formulation of physical postulates.
(c) Theory of computation focuses on algorithms and data structures, and the algorithmic techniques for solving problems in science, technology, engineering, and mathematics (STEM).
(d) Information theory and signal processing focuses on the quantification of mathematical quantity expressing the probability of occurrence of a particular sequence of symbols, impulses, and so on, as contrasted with that of alternative sequences, and the examination, explanation, and manipulation of signals.
(e) Probability and statistics focuses on the giving of a definite structure and investigation of the mathematics of uncertain events or knowledge and collecting and analyzing data.
(f) Game theory focuses on the analysis of strategies for dealing with competitive situations whereby the outcome of a participant's choice of action depends critically on the actions of other participants.
(g) Operations research focuses on the application of scientific principles to business management, providing a quantitative basis for complex decisions.

Yet, despite the numerous aforementioned advances that have been made in the field of mathematics, the subject has become more concealed to the non-mathematician. Keith Devlin captures this truism quite well when he states the following:

> As the role of mathematics has grown more and more significant over the past century, it has become more and more hidden from view, forming an invisible universe that supports much of our lives. Just as our everyday action is governed by the invisible forces of nature (such as gravity), we now live in the invisible universe created by mathematics, subject to invisible mathematical laws. (Devlin, 2000, p. 12)

Thus, one objective of this chapter is to show the reader how mathematics can be used to see an aspect of the invisible structure that underlies the coverage of the Black Lives Matter and All Lives Matter movements in the media—specifically, the internet, and major newspapers and major television networks in the United States.

COVERAGE OF THE MOVEMENTS ON THE INTERNET

The internet refers to a "global computer network" providing a variety of information and communication facilities, consisting of interconnected networks using standardized communication protocols. According to Robert Kahn, by making it possible for numerous networks of computers across the globe to connect with one another, the internet medium has revolutionized communications. Often dubbed as a "meta-network" or, as Kahn calls it, "a network of networks," the internet was developed in the United States in the 1970s. It was not until the early 1990s, however, that the medium was seen by the general public. But, by 2020, more than half of the world's population—that is, 4.5 billion people—was determined to have access to the medium (Kahn, 2020).

Also, Kahn points out that the internet is accessible to anyone who connects to any of its integral networks because the medium makes available very powerful and universal capabilities that can be employed for any purpose that is contingent on information. Thus, people can work cooperatively at many differences places as the medium can facilitate human communication through audio and video transmissions, "chat rooms," electronic mail (e-mail), newsgroups or listservs, and social media. In addition, the medium provides ingress to digital information via many applications such as the World Wide Web (WWW). As a result, e-businesses and their traditional subsidiaries have found the internet to be a very efficient medium to conduct most of their sales and services (Kahn, 2020).

Thus, the question that arises and examined here is the following: How much coverage has the Black Lives Matter and All Lives Matter movements received on the internet? The rest of this section provides an answer to this question.

Univariate Analysis

The data used for the analysis in this subsection were gleaned from the internet using the Google search engine. And, according to Caroline Forsey, Google is "the most popular search engine with more than 70% of the search market share" (2020, p. 1).

As can be seen in table 4.1, the overwhelming majority of the results—98,700,000 or 96.08 percent yielded in 0.99 seconds—were about the Black Lives Matter movement. The All Lives Matter movement had 4,030,000 or 3.92 percent results yielded in 0.78 seconds. In sum, the Black Lives Matter movement was much more privileged or active to receive such profuse attention on the internet.

Table 4.1 Coverage of the Movements on the Internet

Movement	n	%
Black Lives Matter	98,700,000 (results in 0.99 seconds)	96.08
All Lives Matter	4,030,000 (results in 0.78 seconds)	3.92
Total	102,730,000	100.00

Source: Self-generated by the author from data retrieved from the internet.

COVERAGE OF THE MOVEMENTS IN MAJOR NEWSPAPERS

Newspapers are printed publications (usually issued daily or weekly) consisting of folded unstapled sheets and containing news, feature articles, advertisements, and correspondence. As the editors of the *Encyclopedia Britannica* (2020) inform us, the predecessors of contemporary newspapers "include ancient Rome's *Acta diurna* ('daily acts')." The publication featured reports of political and social occurrences. Manuscript newsletters were also distributed during the late Middle Ages by many international traders such as the Fugger family of Augsburg, Bavaria, in South Germany.

The editors add that in England, printed news pamphlets and books entailed one topical occurrence like a public celebration, disaster, or battle. An early example is an eyewitness description of the Battle of Flodden of 1513 in which the English defeated the Scots. Other precursor news publications included the ballads and broadsides and the town crier (Editors of the *Encyclopedia Britannica*, 2020).

Concomitantly, the following question is probed in this section: How much coverage has the Black Lives Matter and All Lives Matter movements received in major U.S. newspapers? The two subsections that follow entail an answer to the question.

Univariate Analysis

For the analysis in this and the ensuing subsection, the data employed were retrieved from the websites of the five largest daily U.S. newspapers in order of circulation in 2020. As the public relations firm Agility (2020) proffers, these newspapers are (1) the *New York Post*, (2) *The Wall Street Journal*, (3) *The New York Times*, (4) the *Chicago Tribune*, and (5) *The Washington Post*.

Table 4.2 reveals that all of the newspapers have immensely larger results for the Black Lives Matter movement than the All Lives Matter movement. The totals, percentages, and means reflect this enormous difference in coverage. Nonetheless, the very large ranges and standard deviations for both movements point to significant variations among the newspapers.

Table 4.2 Coverage of the Movements in the Newspapers

Newspapers & Statistics	Black Lives Matter	All Lives Matter	Total
New York Post	4,693	10,000	14,693
The Wall Street Journal	580	13	593
The New York Times	3,374	122	3,500
Chicago Tribune	177	8	185
The Washington Post	6,285	352	6,637
Total	15,113	10,493	25,608
%	59.02	40.98	100
Mean	3,022.60	2,099.00	N/A
Standard Deviation	2,627.91	4,418.99	N/A
Range	6,108	9,992	N/A

Note: N/A = Not applicable.
Source: Self-generated by the author from data retrieved from the newspapers' websites.

Table 4.3 Paired Samples Test of the Coverage of the Movements in the Newspapers

Black Lives Matter & All Lives Matter Correlated Black Lives Matter-All Lives Matter Paired Statistics	Statistical Result
Correlation	0.38 (significance = 0.52)
Mean	923.60
Standard Deviation	4,184.83
Standard Error Mean	1,871.51
95% Confidence Interval of the Difference: Lower	−4,272.55
95% Confidence Interval of the Difference: Upper	6,119.75
t Statistic	0.49
Degrees of Freedom	4
Significance (2-tailed)	0.65

Source: Self-generated by the author from data retrieved from the newspapers' websites

Bivariate Analysis

From table 4.3, it can be discerned that while there is no statistically significant correlation (i.e., the interdependence of variable quantities) among the newspaper coverages of the two movements, there is also no statistically significant difference among them vis-à-vis the disparity of coverage at the 0.05 significance level. So, here again, the newspapers' variations indicate a privileging of or greater activity by the Black Lives Matter movement.

COVERAGE OF THE MOVEMENTS ON MAJOR TELEVISION NETWORKS

Television networks comprise organizations that transmit television programs. And, television denotes a system for transmitting visual images and sound that are reproduced on screens, chiefly used to broadcast programs for entertainment, information, and education.

The Definitions.net dictionary and translator describes television networks as ventures that relay content over terrestrial television: that is, the use of a network of transmission towers to relay a signal across a country via radio waves. These ventures utilize "analog" (i.e., relating to or using signals or information represented by a continuously variable physical quantity such as spatial position and voltage) or "digital" (i.e., expressed as series of the digits 0 and 1, typically represented by values of a physical quantity such as voltage or magnetic polarization) television signals to transmit television content. Hence, whereas an analog system limits television broadcasting to a single television channel, a digital system allows for broadcasting through many sub-channels. The standards for these broadcasting systems are set by governments, and they differ from country to country (Definitions.net, 2020).

In addition, the dictionary and translator states the following salient clarification, requirements, and example for operating a television station in the United States:

> The term "television station" is normally applied to terrestrial television stations, and not to cable television or satellite television broadcasting. Television stations usually require a broadcast license from a government agency which sets the requirements and limitations on the station. In the United States, for example, a television license defines the broadcast range, or geographic area, that the station is limited to, allocates the broadcast frequency of the radio spectrum for that station's transmissions, sets limits on what types of television programs can be programmed for broadcast, and requires a station to broadcast a minimum amount of certain programs types, such as public affairs messages, among other conditions. (Definitions.net, 2020, p. 1)

Accordingly, the question that emerges at this juncture and explored in this section is as follows: How much coverage has the Black Lives Matter and All Lives Matter movements received on major United States television networks? What ensues in the rest of this section encompasses an answer to the question.

Univariate Analysis

The data utilized for the exploration in this and the next subsection were gathered from the websites of the five most watched television networks in the United States in 2020. These networks, as the All Top Everything (2020) and Amy Watson (2020) of Statista report, in order of ranking, are (1) Columbia Broadcasting System (CBS) with 7.14 million viewers on average; (2) National Broadcasting Company (NBC) with 6.33 million viewers on average; (3) American Broadcasting Company (ABC) with 5.19 million

Table 4.4 Coverage of the Movements in the Television Networks

Newspapers & Statistics	Black Lives Matter	All Lives Matter	Total
Columbia Broadcasting System	1,050	2	1,052
National Broadcasting Company	7,590	215	7,805
American Broadcasting Company	14 3,594	56,555	200,149
Fox Broadcasting	21	3	24
Fox News Channel	32,000	45,700	77,700
Total	184,255	102,475	286,730
%	64.26	35.74	100
Mean	36,851.00	20,495.00	N/A
Standard Deviation	6,105.28	28,255.78	N/A
Range	143,573	56,553	N/A

Note: N/A = Not applicable.
Source: Self-generated by the author from data retrieved from the networks' websites.

Table 4.5 Paired Samples Test of the Coverage of the Movements in the Television Networks

Black Lives Matter & All Lives Matter Correlated Black Lives Matter-All Lives Matter Paired Statistics	Statistical Result
Correlation	0.84 (significance = 0.073)
Mean	16,356.00
Standard Deviation	40,253.49
Standard Error Mean	18,001.91
95% Confidence Interval of the Difference: Lower	−33,625.31
95% Confidence Interval of the Difference: Upper	66,337.31
t Statistic	0.91
Degrees of Freedom	4
Significance (2-tailed)	0.42

Source: Self-generated by the author from data retrieved from the networks' websites.

viewers on average; (4) Fox Broadcasting (FOX) with 4.62 million viewers on average; and (5) Fox News Channel (Fox News) with 2.50 million viewers on average.

Table 4.4 shows that there is a significant difference between the amount of coverage the Black Lives Matter movement received from the television networks than that for the All Lives Matter movement, as manifested by the totals, percentages, and means of the results. The standard deviations and the ranges, however, indicate that there were great variations among the coverages by the networks.

Bivariate Analysis

It can be observed in table 4.5 that the correlation between the two variables, while quite reasonable ($p = 0.07$), is not statistically significant at the 0.05

level. This is because as the paired samples results reveal, the difference between the scores for the two movements is also not statistically significant at the 0.05 level. Once more, it is abundantly clear that even though there are differences among the amounts of coverages given to the Black Lives Matter and All Lives Matter movements by the television networks, the coverages privileged or the Black Lives Matter movement was just more active.

CONCLUSION AND RECOMMENDATIONS

As demonstrated in the preceding sections, results from all three media investigated—that is, the internet, major newspapers, and major television networks in the United States—reflect a more privileging of or more activities by the Black Lives Matter movement compared to the All Lives Matter movement. Is this outcome the result of the peaceful nature of the activities of the All Lives Matter movement compared to the many activities by the Black Lives Matter movement that have been quite violent?

The preceding question is pertinent because as I delineate in our book in progress to be titled *Corohysteria: A Consequence of COVID-2019*, there are at least five reasons for why the media pay more attention to certain events than others. These reasons are quite applicable as implications for the findings in this chapter. First, many journalists have a knack for *yellow journalism*—that is, reporting that is based upon sensationalism and unrefined magnification. This proclivity makes many journalists to use exciting or shocking stories or language at the expense of accuracy in order to provoke public interest or excitement. It also makes them to be offensively coarse when reporting the news.

Second, the media are highly competitive. Thus, they have a strong desire to be more successful than others in the industry. This disposition leads journalists to rush and be the first to tell a story, even before getting complete data.

Third, the media have agendas that they promote. They have plans of things to be done or problems to be addressed. They also have underlying intentions or motives. Consequently, journalists are vigorous in furthering, supporting, or actively encouraging the progress of their plans, intentions, or motives.

Fourth, many journalists are inclined to see the world through the standpoints of their employers. This natural survival tendency of journalists to keep their jobs makes them to neglect the fact that while their employers hire them, they do not own them.

Fifth, many journalists are not the most knowledgeable individuals when it comes to numbers because most of the students who major in journalism and other communication areas in the United States, and most probably the other countries across the globe, are those with the lowest grade point averages (GPAs) and standardized aptitude test (SAT) scores as compared to those who major in the sciences with higher GPAs and SAT scores. Also, communication programs have very weak mathematics requirements in their curricula.

In light of the foregoing shortcomings, I offer two suggestions here. First, policy makers must transcend the mainstream media and consult alternative media and firsthand accounts when making decisions pertaining to the Black Lives Matter and All Lives Matter movements. Second, future researchers should conduct a content analysis of the reports on the two movements in the media. Content analysis is a technique employed "to make replicable and valid inferences by interpreting and coding textual material. By systematically evaluating texts (e.g., documents, oral communication, and graphics), qualitative data can be converted into quantitative data" (Pfarrer, 2020, p. 1). Thus, the approach will allow researchers to systematically analyze the subject matters of the texts from the media.

REFERENCES

Agility. (August 2020). Top 10 U.S. newspapers by circulation. *PR Solutions*. Retrieved on December 24, 2020 from https://www.agilitypr.com/resources/top-media-outlets/top-10-daily-american-newspapers/

All Top Everything. (2020). The 10 most watched TV networks in the USA 2020. *The Best of Everything*. Retrieved on December 24, 2020 from https://www.alltopeverything.com/top-10-most-watched-tv-networks-in-the-usa/

Bangura, A. K. (2020). *The African Mother Tongue and Mathematical Ideas: A Diopian Pluridisciplinary Approach*. Wilmington, DE: Vernon Press.

Definitions.net. (2020). Television station. *Definitions & Translations*. Retrieved on December 24, 2020 from https://www.definitions.net/definition/television+station

Devlin, K. (2000). *The Language of Mathematics: Making the Invisible Visible*. New York, NY: W. H. Freeman Henry Holt and Company.

Editors of the *Encyclopedia Britannica*. (2020). Newspaper. *Encyclopedia Britannica*. Retrieved on December 24, 2020 from https://www.britannica.com/biography/Nikolay-Rimsky-Korsakov

Forsey, C. (2020). The top 7 search engines, ranked by popularity. *Hub Spot*. Retrieved on December 24, 2020 from https://blog.hubspot.com/marketing/top-search-engines

Kahn, R. (2020). Internet computer network. *Encyclopedia Britannica*. Retrieved on December 24, 2020 from https://www.britannica.com/technology/Internet

MATLAB. (2020). What is MATLAB? *Math Works*. Retrieved on December 26, 2020 from https://www.mathworks.com/discovery/what-is-matlab.html

Pfarrer, M. (2020). Content analysis. Resource by the Department of Management at the Terry College of Business, University of Georgia. Retrieved on December 28, 2020 from https://www.terry.uga.edu/contentanalysis/index.php

Watson, A. (January 13, 2020). Leading ad supported broadcast and cable networks in the United States in 2019, by average number of viewers. *Statista*. Retrieved on December 28, 2020 from https://www.statista.com/statistics/530119/tv-networks-viewers-usa/

Chapter 5

Public Administration/Policy Perspective

Rachael M. Rudolph

In chapter 1, Abdul Karim Bangura provided a brief background on both Black Lives Matter (BLM) and All Lives Matter (ALM), as well as their general tenets, ideological propositions, and some of the perspectives of their major proponents and opponents. The BLM movement began with a hashtag on social media in 2012 following the death of Trayvon Martin in Sanford, Florida (Ray, 2020; Ruffin, 2020). In 2013, it became a nationwide phenomenon following a range of collective action taken to bring attention to a variety of incidents of police violence targeting the black community in the United States. From Ferguson to Baltimore, national and international activists from all walks of life, irrespective of race, religion, ethnicity, or creed, joined the BLM activists in calling for police reform.

While recognizing the need for police reform, ALM voices began to emerge within the national and international coalition of activists. Those voices called for the need to move the discourse from what some perceived as the exclusive focus on the black community to emphasize injustices experienced by all living in heavily policed communities. They argued that while the black community is disproportionately targeted by the police, policy change necessitates an expansion of the concept of intersectionality adopted by BLM activists. Many of the BLM activists (black and white alike) viewed these voices as an attempt to divert attention from the movement and to contain the momentum that had been created resulting from coordinated national and international collective action.

Although divisions emerged within the BLM movement and among other national and international cliques coordinating with the BLM activists, the momentum for police reform was maintained and policy action was undertaken by political leaders in the post-Ferguson period. Their impact is underscored by the fact that the policing literature is denoted temporally by the pre-and-post Ferguson periods. Police reform in the pre-Ferguson period focused primarily on addressing officer misconduct from an instrumentalist approach, while the post-Ferguson period shifted the emphasis to address the legitimacy problem resulting from perceptions about police misconduct and the breakdown in police-community relations. Another shift occurred following the 2020 BLM uprisings, ushering in greater emphasis on governance and power relations.

The existing literature on BLM mainly focuses on race and identity (Holt and Sweitzer, 2018), messaging (Bonilla and Tillery, 2020; Hordge-Freeman and Loblack, 2020), and support for the collective (Holt and Sweitzer, 2020; Hordge-Freeman and Loblack, 2020). ALM is only mentioned by some scholars (Holt and Sweitzer, 2020; Umamaheswar, 2020). Police reform within the context of the BLM and ALM literature is focused on by few scholars. A larger body of literature on police reform does exist, but much of it tends to examine reforms either before or immediately after the Ferguson protests in 2014. There are two exceptions, however.

Price and Payton (2017) highlight the role of biases in police practices and the need for the federal government to play a greater role in addressing systemic biases in police departments and among police officers, limiting police use of lethal force, and implementing police reform. Simonson (2020) utilizes the case of BLM as a social movement to highlight the centrality of power relations in the debate on police reform and to make a case for a new theoretical framework to be used for analysis. Building on these two scholars, this chapter examines the federal government's national dialogue on police reform following the uprisings through a review of executive and legislative actions. The executive branch produced several executive orders, while the legislative branch proposed thirty-four bills. Only one of those bills, which was indirectly related, namely the bill for the establishment of a Commission on the Social Status of Black Men and Boys Act, became public law. Nonetheless, the totality of these documents shed light on the nature of dialogue on police reform at the federal level; and that dialogue is important to understand if America, as a nation, is going to move forward on police reform at the domestic level and to mitigate the impact the issue has on its foreign policy endeavors, particularly in the area bilateral and multilateral engagement on non-traditional security cooperation.

As highlighted in the review of the competing perspectives on approaches to police reform in the next section, there has not been a study (at least at the time of this publication) on the nature of the federal dialogue and how it relates to the approaches to police reform and their corresponding debates following the 2020 uprisings. In fact, there has not heretofore been a systematic study of all executive and congressional actions within a given period on the topic. This chapter, therefore, makes a valuable contribution to the literature.

It also makes a practical contribution to the debate because of police reform being an issue that the Biden administration will take up over the next four years, as it has both domestic and foreign policy ramifications.

Section 2 provides readers with a brief review of the policing literature, paying specific attention to the three dominant approaches to police reform, namely the instrumental, legitimacy, and governance approaches; outlines the major focus and assumptions for each approach; and highlights the major debates across the approaches and existing literature. These approaches are used as an interpretive lens for the federal government's national narrative on police reform. The key set of questions raised is as follows: How does the national narrative correspond to the policing approaches? Is the instrumental approach more prevalent in the national discourse, as is highlighted in the existing policing literature? Or does the federal government's narrative follow in the trajectory of the activists; that is, does it shift to focusing on governance and power relations following the uprisings? Why does the narrative matter? Finally, what are the implications for the country as it moves forward with police reform? The mixed-method qualitative methodology adopted to answer these questions is outlined in section 3, while section 4 provides an interpretative accounting of the federal narrative. The chapter concludes with a discussion on why the narrative is important for both national security and foreign policy and provides recommendations for academics, activists, and policymakers.

APPROACHES TO POLICE REFORM: INSTRUMENTAL, LEGITIMACY, AND GOVERNANCE

As noted earlier, the post-Ferguson period represents a significant turning point in police reform. It denotes a shift away from focusing almost exclusively on the instrumental approaches designed to target individual behavior and structural changes in policing toward approaches emphasizing specific behavioral and institutional changes that address both governance and police-community relations. Another shift in police reform occurs following the 2020 BLM uprisings (Simonson, 2020). Embedded in these approaches are debates about the type of reform (instrumental, legitimacy, and governance), nature of reform (top-down or bottom-up), and pace in which reform should be pursed (incremental or transformational).

Simonson (2020) provides a taxonomy of the existing literature on police reform based on the focus of and call for reform, namely the instrumentalist approach, legitimacy approach, and governance approach. Now, as noted in the introduction, she does this for the purpose of arguing that the existing literature fails to examine reform from a power lens' perspective.

Her approach is arguably rooted in the governance approach, given that it attempts to explain how calls for a shift in the distribution of power by social movements like BLM is different from the focus of and calls for reform in the past, including those in the immediate aftermath of the Ferguson protests. Adopting her taxonomy but going a step further by adding the key debates in each category from selected scholarship covering police reform from the 1960s to 2021, this section provides readers with a brief overview of the main foci, debates, and assumptions of each approach. It concludes with a discussion on the nature of reform and the pace in which reform is to be pursued. The discussion on the types, nature and pace of reform provides the foundation for the interpretive lens used to analyze the federal government's narrative on police reform.

The Instrumental Approach

The instrumental approach examines the behavior of law enforcement personnel, procedural policies (including police strategies and tactics), organizational policies (including police culture), and structural policies (i.e., management) from rationalist and institutionalist perspectives. Rationalists and institutionalists debate over whether change in police officers' behavior (shaped by beliefs, biases, and perceptions of justice—law and order) and policing procedures (i.e., policies, strategies, and tactics) or change in organizational and structural policies will bring about sufficient reform (Williams, 2003; Scott, 2009; Mummolo, 2018; Simmons, 2018).

Rationalists posit that change in beliefs, biases, perceptions and misperceptions, and policing policies, strategies and tactics will enhance law enforcement's performance, facilitate trust in policed communities, and maintain law and order. The most common reforms proposed by them for addressing officer behavior include education and training and judicial prosecution for misconduct that is criminal in nature at the state and federal levels (Simmons, 2008; Scott, 2009; Price and Payton, 2017; Mummolo, 2018; Robinson, 2020; Zimring, 2020). Procedural reforms include enhancing recruitment and adopting screening programs for biases of personnel (Scott, 2009; Robinson, 2020); adopting better internal mechanisms to investigate and penalize officer misconduct (Simmons, 2008; Scott, 2009; Robinson, 2020); standardizing the use of technology to increase managerial oversight and transparency of officer behavior while out in the field (MacDonald et al., 2007; Scott, 2009; Ruane, 2017); enhancing reporting mechanisms, data collection and analyses (Price and Payton, 2017; Ruane 2017; Mummolo, 2018; Robinson, 2020); and changing policing strategies to reduce, modify, or eliminate those that exacerbate tensions between the police and community and enable the police to more efficiently promote law and order (Scott, 2009; McCall, 2019).

Institutionalists posit that a change in behavior is not alone sufficient for police reform; there must be change in both organizational and procedural policies for changes in individual behavior to be both internalized and institutionalized. Scholars highlighting the organizational approach to change place emphasis on policing culture, arguing that a shift in culture enables or predetermines policing strategies, which, in turn, shapes police officers' behavior (Williams, 2003; Scott, 2009; Price and Payton, 2017). A shift in police culture requires commitment by both law enforcement leadership and political leaders, as well as adjustment to (if not a full revising of) existing educational curricula at police academies. Scholars adopting a structural approach posit that structure is the main determinant of police officers' behavior. Thus, there needs to be a shift in the hierarchical, authoritarian structure to one that promotes participatory management or power sharing within the police department and lateral communication networks (Williams, 2003). Police departments rather than political leaders should be responsible for organizing their institutional structures, processes, data, and communication networks because they know best what is needed in the environments where they operate (Scott, 2009). The environment should be a driving factor in determining which procedures, strategies, and tactics to employ and when they should be employed. In the absence of taking the environment into consideration, there is less likely to be a change in police officers' behavior. As will be highlighted in the next section, the legitimacy approach connects to and builds on the institutionalists' focus on the environment by highlighting the problem of police-community relations.

The Legitimacy Approach

The legitimacy approach is primarily concerned with police-community relations, paying particular attention to both individual behavior and procedural practices that lead to a breakdown in trust between the police and community (two key stakeholders in the reform process), perceptions and misperceptions of the stakeholders, failure to include both police offers and policed communities in the reform process, and the environment where officers operate and community members live. This approach is quite different from the previous approach since it seeks to specifically target the lack of trust and declining legitimacy of law enforcement in heavily policed communities. Law enforcement depends heavily on its relationship with the community to carry out its functions. It is simply not capable of providing law and order (without using a heavy hand) in the absence of trust and legitimacy in the communities where officers operate. Thus, the key to change is police-community relations.

Within the selected scholarship, there are four common assumptions shaping the debates on police reform from this approach. First, policed communities are more likely to comply with law when law enforcement is perceived to be legitimate (Simonson, 2020). Legitimacy depends on trust; and trust can be broken because of the policing policies and procedures adopted and both perceptions of and misperceptions about racism existing within law enforcement and the community. Second, perceptions exist about policing practices intentionally targeting members of the community based on race and that there is support for those practices by political leaders for the purpose of maintaining their dominant political and economic positions within existing sociopolitical and socioeconomic hierarchies (MacDonald et al., 2007). These perceptions are shaped by both historical and contemporary mistreatments of blacks and other ethnic minority communities living in neighborhoods affected by problems of poverty, unemployment, racial and ethnic segregation, social disorder, and crime. Interestingly, studies demonstrate there are marked differences in treatment between black and white communities in those areas, with black communities being disproportionately targeted by law enforcement. Third, national and local dimensions contribute to a climate of tension, anger, and fear among communities and police officers (Adegible, 2017). Communities fear the stigmatization of over-policing in their communities and the excessive use of force by police officers. Police officers face danger each day due to the nature and types of crimes committed in the communities they police, and their performance depends on public approval of their existence and behavior. The absence of approval increases fears of them being targeted with violence by criminal perpetrators. Communication about perceptions and misperceptions and environment are critical for and the reason why both community representatives and police officers must be part of the reform process (Simmons, 2018). Finally, the economic, political, and social conditions in highly policed communities contribute to the breakdown of law and order. Police officers are accountable for maintaining law and order, while political leaders are responsible for addressing the underlying factors contributing to the breakdown. Although their functions are different, scholars and activists posit that police officers have a role to play in that they can advocate for and apply pressure on political leaders to address those underlying environmental conditions.

Reforms advocated for from this approach target each of the above assumptions. Given that trust and legitimacy are dependent on the behavior of law enforcement and policing policies and procedures, advocates emphasize the adoption of practices, which policed communities deem fair and just. Community review boards and town halls whereby police officers and community representatives can participate are essential. Likewise, they will help to address the breakdown in communication. Communication among and between each stakeholder is key to overcoming perceptions and misperceptions that both police officers and community members have about each other and policing. It will help to allay some of the existing fears they have as well. Political leaders, police officers, and community representatives should work together to address the underlying problems contributing to crime. Thus, a more holistic approach to policing and a shift to rehabilitative and restorative justice are often highlighted to address the environmental problems.

The Governance Approach

The governance approach focuses on and debates about the role of government in police reform at the federal, state and local levels, the mechanisms available to them for policy formulation, implementation and oversight, and the problems each level faces in reform efforts; the nature of power relations among stakeholders (government, law enforcement and policed communities) and the historical tensions in the distribution of power; and shifting power relations as a result of calls for transformational change in policing (Adegible, 2017; Chanin, 2017; Simmons, 2018; Robinson, 2020; Simonson, 2020; Zimring, 2020).

Scholars, policymakers, and political philosophers have long debated the role of government on key issues areas since the creation of the United States, and policing is one such area where those historical tensions emerge. Some argue the federal government should play a greater role in police reform, while others disagree, arguing that because states are responsible for adjudicating and incarcerating the majority of those imprisoned in America, they should be the primary government stakeholder in reform efforts (Adegible, 2017; Chanin, 2017; Robinson, 2020). The decentralized nature of America's policing model also strengthens the role of state and local governments over that of the federal government. A few adopt the position that federal action or reform impinges on states' rights and individual liberties (Chanin, 2017).

As Chanin highlights in his study, there are traditional historical and ideological tensions at play over the role of government in police reform that harken back to debates on American federalism. For example, Hamiltonians believe in a strong centralized governing administration, while Jeffersonians prefer a strong state/local government and a weak federal government. Madisonians adopt a balance of power position in governance. Wilsonians argue for hierarchical accountability and administrative competency. Political leaders at both levels of government, who are responsible for and play a large role in police reform, fall somewhere along this historical-ideological spectrum, often varying according to the issue being considered. Nonetheless, all of them support the role of government in police reform.

The mechanisms available to government for police reform vary, and often their use depends on national crises stemming from major incidents of police misconduct ranging from corruption to the excessive use of force.

Section 14141 of the Violent Crime and Control Act of 1994 provides the federal government with regulatory power over state and local law enforcement. The mechanisms it has used in the past include conducting investigations, which are usually done in tandem with the appropriate authorities in state governments, memorandums of agreement (MOA), consent decrees, negotiated settlements, and technical assistance letters (Chanin, 2017; Simmons, 2018). MOAs typically contain a package of reforms targeting internal policing policies that enhance public accountability. They are usually accomplished through a negotiated settlement with local and state law enforcement following a Department of Justice (DoJ) investigation. Consent decrees address substantive policing policies, whereas technical letters address a range of technical issues. The latter were often used in the Bush administration while MOAs and negotiated agreements were the preferred course of action during the Obama administration. Presidential administrations have historically preferred them over taking legal action. State governments have the authority to set policy, investigate incidents of wrongdoing, and prosecute officers for criminal misconduct. Citizens have typically played an advisory rather than a direct role in policymaking and decision-making. Many activists have called for the creation of an independent body with power over policies and decisions and the creation of more mechanisms for engagement (Simonson, 2020).

Thus, taking the governance approach a step further, Simonson and others focus on the role of power. Traditionally, power has flowed top-down irrespective of whether reform was initiated by the state or federal government (Chanin, 2017). Government leaders have worked with law enforcement leadership and consulted with experts and community members, but, ultimately, they were the primary decision-makers. Instances where the federal government took a hands-off approach, reform efforts were left to state leaders. In states where political leaders failed to take a leading role, reform efforts were left to law enforcement leadership (Robinson, 2020). Some police departments reached out to the federal government to request assistance (through intervention, investigation, etc.) when state leaders failed to take initiative, while others adopted a go-it-alone approach in the absence of both state and federal government receptivity. The problem in leaving reform to local police departments is their lack of resources, motivation (in the face of internal opposition), and competence in conducting the scientific investigations needed for evaluating the type of reforms needed (Zimring, 2020).

Simonson (2020) is the only scholar outside of BLM scholars focusing exclusively on examining police reform through a power lens. A shift in power relations, which is what BLM and other criminal justice reform activists seek, would bring reform to decision-making at the state and local levels, and include community representatives in positions of power to formulate, implement, and oversee policing and police reform. Again, the problem here is like the one mentioned earlier for reform; that is, local law enforcement leadership lacks the resources and capacity to undertake the reform process alone.

There are two pervading debates across the approaches and within the existing scholarship. The first centers on nature of reform; that is, whether reform should be pursued and implemented top-down or bottom-up. A top-down approach, as was highlighted in this section, has been the traditional method employed by both political and law enforcement leaders. Scholars and activists have long called for a bottom-up approach, whereby it is driven by the demands of the community. Some scholars have argued for an integrative approach that combines top-down and bottom-up reform. The second debate centers on whether reform should be incremental or transformative. An incremental approach to reform entails a gradual process of change, whereas a transformative approach is more revolutionary in nature in that it seeks to radically change behavior, policies, and practices all at once. Some scholars have noted that if transformative behavioral changes, policies, and practices are implemented gradually, then they are in effect incremental in nature. Though incremental change is more stable, there is a chance that momentum for reform can be lost and bureaucratic inertia can set in, thus bringing reform to an end. A revolutionary, transformative change can be destabilizing at the outset, but it harnesses well the momentum for reform and reduces bureaucratic resistance to change. BLM and other criminal justice and police reform activists who took part in the 2020 uprisings have called for radical, transformative change.

METHODOLOGY

Previous scholarship on policing reform tends to focus on specific executive actions (e.g., the DOJ's actions) in response to major national crises (e.g., incidents in Ferguson, Missouri, and Baltimore, Maryland), case studies of law enforcement reform in a specific state (e.g., Maryland, Missouri, New York, and Ohio), or in selected police departments within a state or across different states in order to assess the nature and type of reform (i.e., through the reform approaches highlighted earlier). This chapter is like other case studies in that it is temporally bound, but it deviates from the traditional case study approach by systematically examining federal actions at the executive and legislative levels following the 2020 BLM Uprisings (hereinafter "the uprisings"). It employs a mixed-method qualitative approach to both data collection and analysis to gain understanding of the sense of federal policymakers' understanding of police reform; and to assess their actions in relation to the approaches on and debates about police reform identified in the existing literature. The remainder of this section outlines the data selected for analysis and the analytical process.

For the executive branch, four documents were selected for analysis. They include Executive Order 1329—Safe Policing for Safe Communities; Executive Order 13977—Protecting Law Enforcement Officers, Judges, Prosecutors, and their Families; Executive Order 13896—Commission on Law Enforcement and the Administration of Justice; and the DoJ's final report from the President's Commission on Law Enforcement and the Administration of Justice. E.O. 13896 was signed prior to the uprisings, but it was included because it authorized the President's Commission on Law Enforcement and the Administration of Justice. The later was released in December 2020 and includes references to the uprisings and the issues raised by activists. All executive orders were obtained from the Federal Register, while the Commission's report was obtained from the DoJ.

For the legislative branch, a total of thirty-four bills were selected for analysis from the Library of Congress database. Chapter appendix, titled "Table of Legislative Actions on Police Reform and Other Related Actions," denotes the bill number and its title and date, party of the sponsor (Democrat, Republican, or Bipartisan), action taken, related pieces of legislation, and key issue(s) covered as related to the approaches to police reform. Cluster mapping methodology was adopted to determine which of the bills were central to the discussion on police reform by legislative members. Figure 5.1 depicts the clustering of the bills and table 5.1 provides the total number of legislative ties. The total number of legislative ties was used to determine the centrality of the bills and which of the related bills to include in the analysis.

The bills introduced in 2020 are circled, while those introduced in 2019 do not have a circle. The party of the sponsor is indicated in parentheses. As highlighted in figure 5.1, there are clusters corresponding to the parties. Again, these clusters are determined by the bills related to them by the Library of Congress rather than them being an analytically imposed by the researcher. This party dynamic therefore dictated the examination of the sense of congress by party in the analysis.

As highlighted in the preceding paragraph and table 5.1, the Library of Congress denotes related bills for each piece of legislation. For example, S.4141—Ending Qualified Immunity Act was related to H.R. 7085—Ending Qualified Immunity, H.R. 8979—Qualified Immunity Act, and S.4036—Ending Qualified Immunity. Each of the related pieces of legislation for those bills were examined. In the case of this cluster, they all related to one another; thus, it completed the cluster, as denoted in figure 5.1. The index lists all the related bills for each piece of legislation. This process was performed for all thirty-four bills to determine the cluster and which bills were central to the

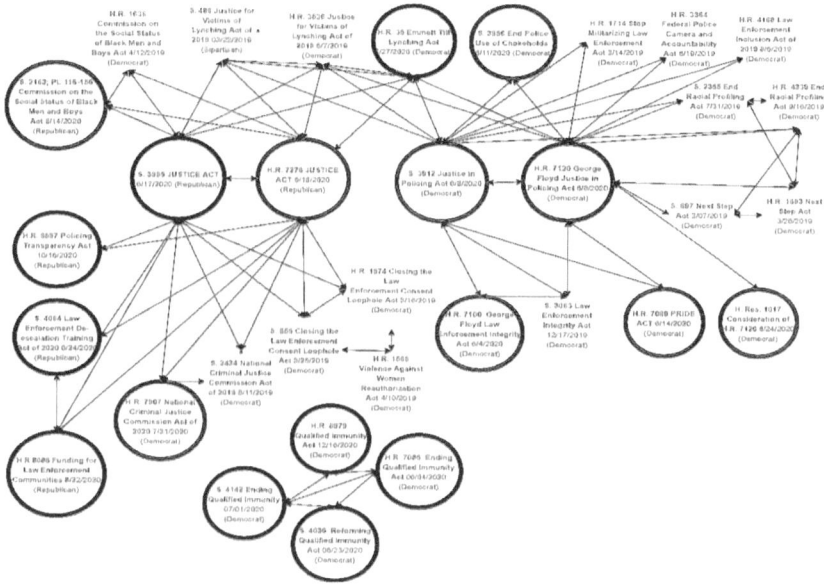

Figure 5.1 Cluster Map of Legislative Actions Following the 2020 BLM Uprisings and their Corresponding Legislative Actions. *Source:* Image by Rachael M. Rudolph.

Table 5.1 Ranking of Legislative Bills According to the Number of Ties to Related Bills

Legislative Bills by Number of Ties								
S. 3985	15	H.R. 1574	4	S.2163; PL 116-156	3	H.R. 7100	2
H.R. 7278	14	H.R. 7907	4	S. 2434	3	H.R. 8597	2
S. 3912	13	S. 697	4	S. 3063	3	H.R. 8979	2
H.R. 7120	12	S. 855	4	S. 4064	3	S. 3956	2
S. 488	7	S. 2355	4	S. 4142	3	S. 4036	2
H.R. 35	6	H.R. 1636	3	H.R. 1585	2	H.Res. 1017	1
H.R. 1893	5	H.R. 7085	3	H.R. 1714	2	S. 1557	1
H.R. 3536	5	H.R. 7089	3	H.R. 3364	2		
H.R. 4339	5	H.R. 8088	3	H.R. 4168	2		

Source: Self-generated by the author, with matrix analysis used to calculate the number of ties.

clusters. The bills with the greatest number of ties are central to the entire cluster map.

Content analysis was used to identify patterns across the documents and within specific clusters to garner understanding of the sense of federal policymakers' perception of and their proposed recommendations for police reform (referred to in the next section as policy preferences). Finally, the latter was examined in relation to the approaches to and debates on police reform, which were outlined in the previous section. Both the sense of the executive and legislative branches of government and their proposed reforms were treated separately at first and then as whole to analytically capture the points of convergence and divergence.

THE FEDERAL GOVERNMENT'S NARRATIVE ON POLICE REFORM

For the federal government, law enforcement is a key stakeholder in the criminal justice system, responsible for upholding law and order and enforcing criminal and public safety laws passed by federal, state, and local policymakers. Law enforcement's primary function is to prevent and reduce crime, as "crime, especially violent crime, denies people their inalienable rights to life, liberty and the pursuit of happiness" (Exec. Order No. 13896, 2019, p. 1). Proper policing is, therefore, paramount for ensuring law and order and maintaining national security. Police misconduct like excessive use-of-force, though recognized as not typically characteristic of law enforcement behavior, was identified by both branches of the federal government as having a negative impact on law enforcement's ability to discharge its duties and having led to a breakdown in police-community relations.

It should come as no surprise then that most executive and legislative documents examined during this period dealt with policymakers' views on proper policing. Very few of them focused on the underlying social problems contributing to crime. The DoJ's report most extensively emphasized and addressed the need for policymakers, community representatives, and businesses to work together to deal with the social problems contributing to crime, which it perceived as placing an undue burden on law enforcement. This section begins by highlighting the preferred policy preferences and discussing them in relation to the approaches to police reform. Then, it turns to assessing the narrative's trajectory in relation to that of the trajectory highlighted in the introduction; that is, the shift from a hybrid instrumentalist-legitimacy-based approach to focusing more on governance and power relations.

Policy Preferences for and Approaches to Police Reform

An examination of key issues in both congressional and executive branch documents and the proposed actions captures policymakers' key preferences for policing reform following the 2020 BLM uprisings. Table 5.2 provides a breakdown of the policy preferences by percentage of those covered in the documents that specifically pertain to police reform.

Table 5.2 The Federal Government's Policy Preferences for Police Reform

Federal Government's Policy Preferences for Police Reform Policy Issue Area	Legislative Branch			Executive Branch	Total % of Legislative and Executive Branch References
	Democrat	Republican	Total % for Congress		
Education and Training: Training on eliminating the practice of racial profiling and teaching about the history of racism in America; training on the use of force, de-escalation tactics and techniques and development of curricula for such training; training on use, handling, and retention of body cameras; training on how to handle behavioral health crises	7%	12%	8%	8%	9%
Recruitment: Priority for and inducements (education and training) to be given to officers who live in the same communities they serve; requiring police officers to live in the communities they serve; greater diversification needed, and personnel should be representative of the communities they serve; national standards for hiring	6%	3%	5%	8%	6%
Internal Mechanisms: Procedures for investigating and responding to complaints; independent investigations for use of force incidents; early warning systems and intervention programs; establishing due process requirements; adoption of models for reduction of misconduct; adoption of a records maintenance system that includes complaints, commendations, etc.; disciplinary measures for officers failing to use or in any way alter body and patrol car cameras; policies and programs to ensure the safety, health, and well-being of police officers	12%	15%	13%	8%	12%

(Continued)

Table 5.2 (Continued)

Federal Government's Policy Preferences for Police Reform Policy Issue Area	Legislative Branch			Executive Branch	Total % of Legislative and Executive Branch References
	Democrat	Republican	Total % for Congress		
Oversight: Accrediting standards and maintain a list of agencies that have been certified; independent investigations; diverse civilian review and complaint boards that have funding, investigatory power, subpoena power, ability to hold hearings; creation of a national registry for misconduct; National Task Force on Law Enforcement oversight; National Criminal Justice Commission; Sentencing Commission; National Use-of-Force database	9%	6%	8%	4%	8%
Transparency and Accountability: Auditing of use of force and other misconduct incidents; Make data publicly available	5%	12%	7%	8%	4%
Judicial Prosecution and Other Legal Actions: Criminalizing sexual activity with an individual under arrest, in detention, or custody while acting under color of the law; lowering the criminal intent standard from willful to knowing or reckless to increase conviction of officers for criminal misconduct; limiting qualified immunity to open the door to civil suits; penalizing for falsification of police incident reports	11%	9%	10%	8%	10%

Policing policies, strategies and tactics: Establish policies and procedures on the use of force and alternative techniques to the use of force; use of body cameras, patrol car cameras; ending racial and religious profiling and other discriminatory practices with community input; requiring police officer intervention when other officers are engaging in misconduct; requiring police officers to give warning before using force; banning no-knock warrants in drug cases and chokeholds; adopting targeted deterrence approaches like evidence-based policing	13%	15%	14%	13%	14%
Technology: Body cameras, cameras installed in patrol cars, and prohibiting the use of facial recognition technology (FRT; until this can be further studied); adoption of video monitoring technology and other technology to help combat crime. Note: There was divergence between congress and the DOJ on FRT, with the latter recommending its potential adoption for use to combat crime	6%	9%	7%	8%	7%
Other: Restricting the purchase and use of military equipment by law enforcement agencies; victim counseling for individuals suffering from police misconduct; enhanced protection of law enforcement officers, judges, and prosecution and their families who are subjected to threat or use of violence because of their public service	6%	0%	4%	4%	4%
Data Collection, Analysis, and Reporting: Collect, provide data, and report on the number of incidents of officer shootings, use-of-force, racial profiling, misconduct (in general), complaints, threats and use of violence by citizens against police officers	12%	6%	10%	13%	12%

(Continued)

Table 5.2 (Continued)

Federal Government's Policy Preferences for Police Reform Policy Issue Area	Legislative Branch			Executive Branch	Total % of Legislative and Executive Branch References
	Democrat	Republican	Total % for Congress		
Grant Funding: Reporting requirements, hiring, and training, using technology, establishing a monitoring requirement, development of new policies and procedures, establishing civilian review boards; and, tying grant funding to change in law enforcement policies and procedures as well as compliance on reporting	13%	9%	12%	8%	12%
Community Engagement: Promote youth interaction and engagement with police officers; community input on policies and procedures; public–private initiatives to improve police-community relations; policies and programs to promote public trust in law enforcement	1%	3%	2%	8%	3%

Source: Self-generated by the author.

In table 5.2, readers will note that there are two shaded columns—one representing the total percentage for congress and the other reflecting the total percentage for the federal government by each policy preference. The total percentage by each policy preference for congress is shaded to capture the areas of convergence and divergence between the two branches of government, while the other column denoting the total across the branches of the federal government permits readers to easily capture the issue areas where there is common ground. A ranking of the policy preferences by category from the highest to lowest percentages (as previously noted) is as follows: (a) Policing policies, strategies, and tactics; (b) internal mechanisms; (c) data collection, analysis, and reporting; (d) grant funding (and tying it to policy changes); (e) judicial prosecution and other legal actions; (f) education and training; (g) oversight; (h) technology; (i) recruitment; (j) transparency and accountability; (k) other; and (l) community engagement.

Percentages by party are provided to capture areas of convergence and divergence, and to highlight the need for a study on how intense politicization over the past four years may have hindered the passing of any substantial police reform at the federal level during this period. There are significant similarities in many of the bills proposed by democrats and republicans, yet they were unable to bridge their differences to pass any substantial police reform. Given the change in composition in congress because of the 2020 elections and support by republicans for congressional action to address policing policies, strategies, tactics, and internal mechanisms; data collection, analysis, and reporting; and tying grant funding to those changes suggest it is possible for substantial policing reform legislation to be passed at the federal level.

Finally, readers will note that there are some key oversight issue areas bolded in table 5.2. They are bolded to highlight the call and support for the establishment of national commissions pertaining to criminal justice and police reform, a national registry, and the collection of widespread data at the national level. One of the most interesting findings after reading and analyzing all congressional bills (listed in chapter appendix) and executive documents (the DOJ's final report in particular) was that there seems to be growing support, and belief in the need, for the federal government to play a greater role. This is significant given the historical tension between the federal and state government on policing issues, as highlighted and discussed in section 2 of this chapter.

Now, when examining policy preferences in relation to the policing approaches outlined in section 2 of this chapter, the instrumental approach to police reform is more salient among policymakers at the federal level than the legitimacy and governance approaches. As will be recalled from section 2, there are two different trends within the instrumental approach—the rationalist approach and the institutional approach. Rationalists believe that change in police officers' behavior, the strategies, and tactics they employ, and change in policies and procedures aimed at institutionalizing changes in their behavior will bring about reform and the bettering of police-community relations. Institutionalists posit that change in organizational and structural policies designed to usher in a new policing culture and participatory management will bring about reform and the bettering of police-community relations.

An examination of the recommended actions for law enforcement agencies in the bills and executive documents finds the rationalist approach to be more salient among policymakers than the institutionalist approach. Most of the recommended courses of action dealt with changing policing policies, procedures, and tactics to alter and institutionalize change in officers' behavior rather than adjusting policing culture or implementing transformative change in the management structure. Very few congressional members highlighted the need to change policing culture from the traditional to the guardian mindset. Traditional policing culture was also emphasized in the executive documents, with the DoJ highlighting that the role of law enforcement is to maintain law and order and enforce the criminal and public safety laws passed by policymakers. Both branches of the federal government reaffirmed the central role of law enforcement leadership in shaping policing policies, procedures, strategies, and tactics and for knowing best how they should be formulated and implemented within local, state, and tribal agencies, but highlighted the need for them to consult with all relevant stakeholders including community members, and for state, local, and federal government officials to play a greater role in oversight. Very few policymakers emphasized or expressed support for the inclusion of community representatives and community-based organizations in the power structure underlying the decision-making process.

Police-community relations and emphases on legitimacy of law enforcement as an institution and trust between police officers and the communities they serve, which are at heart of the legitimacy approach, are noted as important components of reform because of them being central to the ability of law enforcement to maintain law and order and ensure public safety. Federal policymakers overwhelmingly believe that policing policies and practices contribute to perceptions of trust and legitimacy of law enforcement. As was highlighted in the table 5.2, a change in practices and, more specifically, adopting standardized policies and procedures on use-of-force, race-based training and the like is believed to contribute to changing the nature of police-community relations; and regular meetings between law enforcement and members of the community to enhance communication between the two key stakeholders. The DoJ goes a step further in its report than the legislature to recommend additional programs targeting youth-law enforcement engagement, business-law enforcement engagement, and community-law enforcement engagement. Congress emphasized training on race-based relations and the history of racism in America as means for altering perceptions on race-based relations. There were only a few members of congress that supported giving power to members of the community over policing to improve police-community relations. Most policymakers overwhelmingly support a participatory role for an independent body comprising representatives of the community, but not one that transforms the existing, traditional power dynamics of policing.

Highlighted in the aforementioned discussions on the instrumental and legitimacy approaches is growing support for the federal government to play a greater role in the oversight of policing in America. As will be recalled from section 2 in the discussion on the governance approach, policymakers typically fall along a historical-ideological continuum corresponding to the philosophical traditions of American federalism—Hamiltonian tradition (strong role for federal government), Jeffersonian tradition (strong state/local governance and weak federal governance), Madisonian tradition (balance of power position), and Wilsonian tradition (hierarchical accountability and administrative competency). A close reading of the bills and executive documents finds the Madisonian and Wilsonian traditions to be more prevalent in the federal government's narrative than the other two traditions. Nonetheless, there is some variance within the two branches of federal government and among policymakers.

The DoJ specifically highlights its respect for the historical balance of power position between the levels and among the branches of government in policing and emphasizes that only a collective and collaborative effort will bring about reform. While recognizing the traditional and prominent role of law enforcement agencies and personnel, it emphasizes that "[agencies and personnel] do not singularly possess the key to unlocking sound solutions to the myriad of public safety challenges facing our nation" (Department of Justice, 2020, p. 223). Rather, it is an all-of-government or holistic approach that includes community representatives, community-based organizations, and businesses coming together to address the underlying problems contributing to crime and affecting law enforcement's ability to discharge its duties. For policing, the DoJ highlights that federal agencies have a direct role to play such as directing funding, setting policy and direction, and providing other support, while state and local governments have an intermediary role in strengthening and preserving justice. Its recommendations for policing reform are directed at congress, state, and local government, and law enforcement agencies at the federal, state, local, and tribal levels, while congressional bills primarily direct proposed policy changes to the DoJ and law enforcement agencies. There were a few bills that imposed penalties on state and local governments for the failure of law enforcement agencies to enact policing reforms.

Congress, as the lawmaking body, is expected to pass legislation guiding reform and allocate appropriate funding for it to be implemented. In most congressional bills (irrespective of political party), there was overwhelming support for increasing the use of federal grant funding to require changes in policing policies, procedures, strategies, and tactics; require training to facilitate behavioral change at the individual level; and require more in-depth and targeted data collection and analysis. The DoJ is expected to work with law enforcement agencies to develop those policies, procedures, strategies, and tactics; design training curriculum and certification standards for agencies administering training; and collect, analyze, and report to congress on the data collected and make policy recommendations for them to consider. Congressional bills specifically outline the type of data to be collected and on which area congress specifically wants an accounting such as use of force and misconduct, stop and search activities, race-based complaints, and policy and procedural changes made at the state and local level nationwide. Both the DoJ and congress support the establishment of nationwide standards on policing policies, procedures, and so on, pertaining to the areas of policing that are of national concern (i.e., use of force and misconduct) and standardized data reporting at all levels to promote transparency. Transparency in policies, procedures, reporting, and so on is perceived to be key to addressing perceptions and misperceptions existing across America on policing.

Traditionally, the policing literature tends to focus on the role of the DoJ and the legal mechanisms available to it for intervening in and facilitating change on policing. The role of congress and the use of both funding and executive administrative oversight tend to be overlooked as means for influencing police reform. State, local, and tribal law enforcement agencies are heavily dependent on federal funding. Authorization of and specific requirements imposed for receipt of federal funds are powerful tools that, if wielded strategically and with a concrete reform program, could result in significant changes in law enforcement policies, practices, and procedures nationwide. Perhaps this is part of the reason why BLM and other police and criminal justice reform activists have concentrated heavily on the funding issue in their demands. Unfortunately, republicans and democrats were unable to come together to enact substantial police reform in the period under investigation and the executive branch is limited in what it can do in the absence of congress passing the appropriate legislation needed for it to act.

As the literature highlights, an absence of leadership at the federal level leaves the challenge of police reform to the state and local governments. There have been a significant number of reform bills proposed and some passed nationwide. Time and space do not permit a systematic examination of them for this chapter, but it is worthwhile to mention here in the discussion on governance that though there may be ideological support for a greater role to be played by the federal government on police reform, it has been historically left to the state and local levels. This presents a problem, as highlighted in the policing literature, because state and local governments and the respective state, local, and tribal agencies have limited resources and depend on the federal government for the implementation of reform. Implementation of reform has been another issue raised in the literature and by activists.

An examination of past attempts at and actual actions taken on reform and what the national discussion in the present highlights are that policymakers, law enforcement agencies, communities, and activists have been talking about many of the same policing issues since the 1960s. The DoJ report is correct when it states that an all-of-government or holistic approach is needed. However, in the absence of congressional leadership on this issue, policing is likely to continue to remain a problem. The key to overcoming this problem is not only understanding the federal government's narrative but also to find the points of convergence between the two branches of government and the political parties so that more concentrated actions can be taken to facilitate the momentum and to create a power base from which federal policymakers can draw from to formulate, pass, and implement police reform legislation at the national level.

NARRATIVE, COLLECTIVE ACTION, AND POLICY CHANGE AT THE FEDERAL LEVEL

BLM, ALM, and other activists are united in their calls for police reform, and policymakers at the federal, state, and local levels all recognize that it is vital to national security. As was highlighted in the introduction and in the review of the policing literature in section 2, the narratives among activists and academics have transitioned from focusing exclusively on police reform from an instrumental approach in the pre-Ferguson period to an emphasis on legitimacy and police-community relations in the post-Ferguson period, and from a hybrid approach (combining both the instrumental and legitimacy approaches) to concentrating on governance and power relations following the 2020 BLM uprisings. The federal government's narrative encompasses all three approaches despite the preeminence of an instrumental approach in its policy preferences on police reform, thereby making it complex in nature. Yet, it was unable to produce federal legislation on police reform.

Narratives are always complex and exist within a power structure. During and immediately following the Ferguson protests, BLM and other activists called for federal government intervention, directing much of their protest narrative on the need for congress to act by passing legislation to facilitate changes in policing practices and procedures. During the 2020 uprisings, BLM and other activists called for changes in policing practices and procedures but focused their calls on the need for state and local government officials to act, thereby recognizing the error in their strategy adopted in the Ferguson period. A combination of targeted action and localized campaigns designed to facilitate change from the bottom-up contributed to the beginning of a reform process at the state and local level that continues to this day.

The strategy adopted for collective action in the 2020 uprisings is like that which was adopted during the New Deal period, when President Franklin D. Roosevelt attempted to get congress to pass sweeping social welfare legislation. The federal legislature's inability at that time to compromise led activists to take to the streets to facilitate reform at the local and state levels (overwhelmingly in that order). Their actions resulted in policy change from the bottom-up, providing the president the power base he needed to drive his domestic agenda with congress, and placed enormous pressure on congress to pass social welfare legislation at the federal level. A similar strategy was adopted during the Obama administration in the national and international collective action campaigns in support of the transfer of Guantanamo Bay detainees, closing of the Guantanamo Bay prison, and implementing prison reform in the United States (all of which were connected by a shared criminal justice narrative). The collective actions campaigns during that period led to some policy changes and gave President Obama the domestic and international power base he needed to drive his domestic agenda on those issues. Much of the success in these campaigns—from the New Deal under FDR and Guantanamo and prison reform under to Obama to police reform at the local and state government levels following the 2020 uprisings—is recognition of the importance of narratives and the intersectionality of issues that affect people from all walks of life. It is both narratives and issues that connect the diverse geographical, socioeconomic, and sociopolitical cleavages across America.

Although this chapter does not examine proposed policy actions across the states and recognizes the need for a systematic study on that, its emphasis on the federal government's narrative is important because the final phase in facilitating change in policing across America is going to require the formulation, adoption, and implementation of police reform at the federal level. This is going to require a shift in narrative, moving from the exclusive focus on how policing affects black communities to its impact on all living in heavily policed areas. A close reading of the federal legislative and executive actions following the 2020 uprisings highlights that policymakers from both parties do recognize the disenfranchisement of the black community and it being the primary target in heavily policed areas; thus, a shift in narrative is not going to result in that being overlooked or being lost in debate, particularly given the reform undertaken at the state and local levels. Black lives do matter, but the drive for change at the federal level now needs to move beyond how the issues underlying policing affect a specific community to how it impacts everyone; and how it is in the interest of national security to implement police reform at the federal level. This shift can only occur by understanding the narratives of all the key stakeholders, the points of convergence and divergence, and development of a national strategy to facilitate policy change at the federal level that links the changes underway at the state and local levels to those which had been proposed by both republicans and democrats in the immediate aftermath of the 2020 uprisings and the impact that failing to act has on American foreign policy.

CONCLUSION AND RECOMMENDATIONS

Policing and police reform have been topics of national debate since the 1960s. As was highlighted in the literature, mentioned by BLM and ALM activists in their calls for police reform, and demonstrated in this chapter on the federal government's narrative, many of the issues pertaining to policing policies and procedures, police-community relations, and governance have remained constant over time and space. Today, there exists political will at the federal level for federal legislation on national reform, as is evident not only from the narrative highlighted in this chapter but also from the sweeping reforms underway at the state and local levels. The momentum from the latter can be harnessed to bring about substantial police reform at the federal level. Police reform is not only necessary for national well-being but also for American foreign policy.

As the DoJ highlighted in its 2020 report, policing and perceptions of policing have national security ramifications. Law and order break down when communities perceive the body charged with maintaining public safety as illegitimate. Law enforcement is unable to perform its duties in the absence of the people's trust. The people's trust cannot be restored without addressing their concerns about policing. Furthermore, the environment, already plagued by a myriad of social and economic problems and beset by deep political divisions across urban and rural and federal and state divides, becomes even more dangerous when major stakeholders—law enforcement, communities, and political leaders at all levels of government—cannot come together to find solutions to these problems. Solutions to these problems cannot be implemented without leadership at the federal level. Thus, it is a holistic approach that is needed, one that encompasses all the key components of each approach to policing—instrumental, legitimacy and governance—and the adoption of a narrative that transcends divides by focusing on the key issues, namely policing policies and procedures, internal mechanisms, data collection and analysis, funding, governance and oversight, and transparency and their impact not just on the practice of policing but also on police-community relations.

Policing in America also has foreign policy implications. The United States provides a significant amount of funding and training to law enforcement agencies across the globe. Thus, the image of America's policing problem, even if that problem is a product of the misconduct of a few police officers rather than representative of the entire law enforcement community, will impact its ability to advocate for good policing practices to be adopted in countries that have widespread law enforcement problems. It will also impact how America's police officers are received when they engage in international training programs or cooperate with foreign law enforcement agencies to combat major transnational crimes such as arms, drug, and human trafficking.

Given the aforementioned, there are several recommendations for academics, activists, and policymakers. For academics, studies on policing and police reform need to go beyond the simple, single, or comparative case study method to include more systematic analyses of proposed and actual policing reforms adopted to understand better where the breakdown is, particularly given that the issues that activists and policymakers are debating have traversed time and space. Other scholars have noted the need for lawmakers and police departments to engage in more in-depth analysis of the issues facing policing and law enforcement and called for academics to fill the void. Reiterating the point made by some of those scholars cited in this chapter, our findings and methods must be translatable to the public otherwise we will continue talking at rather than to the key stakeholders. In-depth, systematic studies in policing take time and resources; therefore, there should be additional grant funding allocated to this endeavor like there was following September 11, 2001, where federal resources were allocated for grant funding to study different aspects of and widespread methods to combat domestic and international terrorism. For activists, there needs to be more emphasis on the intersectionality of narratives and issues to devise more strategic campaigns to facilitate policy change at the federal level. Police reform is going to require a coalition of activists that go beyond specific collective groupings. For policymakers, the health of nation necessitates action on the issue, and it has, as highlighted earlier, significant foreign policy ramifications. There is a will and need for national standards on policing and greater federal oversight, but to have real and long-lasting reform, there is a need for national commissions on police and criminal justice reform and resources to be allocated for them to study and formulate the recommendations congress needs for police reform. Police reform is essential for the health and image of America.

REFERENCES

Adegible, D. P. (2017). Policing through an American prism. *Yale Law Journal* 126(7):2222–2259.

Bonilla, T. and Tillery Jr., A. B. (2020). Which identity frames boost support for and mobilization in the #BlackLivesMatter movement? An experimental test. *American Political Science Review* 114(4):947–962.

Chanin, J. (2017). Police reform through an administrative lens: Revisiting the Justice Department's pattern or practice initiative. *Administrative Theory & Praxis* 39(4):257–274.

Department of Justice. (December, 2020). *President's Commission on Law Enforcement and the Administration of Justice*. Retrieved on January 15, 2021 from https://www.justice.gov/file/1347866/download

Executive Order No. 13896, 84 F.R. 58595. (2019). Retrieved on January 15, 2021 from https://www.federalregister.gov/documents/2019/11/01/2019-24040/commission-on-law-enforcement-and-the-administration-of-justice

Holt, L. F. and Sweitzer, M. D. (2018). More than a black and white issue: Ethnic identity, social dominance orientation, and support for the black lives matter movement. *Self and Identity*:1–15.

Hordge-Freeman, E. and Loblack, A. (2020). "Cops only see the Brown skin, they could care less where it originated": Afro-Latinx perceptions of the #BlackLivesMatter Movement. *Sociological Perspectives* 64(4):1–18.

MacDonald, J., Stokes, R. J., Ridgeway, G. and Riley, K. J. (2007). Race, neighbourhood context and perceptions of injustice by the police in Cincinnati. *Urban Studies* 44(13):2567–2585.

McCall, A. (2019). Resident assistance, police chief learning, and the persistence of aggressive policing tactics in Black neighborhoods. *Journal of Politics* 81(3):1133–1142.

Mummolo, J. (2018). Modern police tactics, police-citizen interactions, and the prospects for reform. *Journal of Politics* 80(1):1–15.

Price, J. and Payton, E. (2017). Implicit racial bias and police use of lethal force: Justifiable homicide or potential discrimination? *Journal of African American Studies* 21(4):674–683.

Ray, R. (2020). Setting the record straight on the movement for Black Lives. *Ethnic and Racial Studies*:1–9.

Ruane, J. M. (2017). Re(searching) the truth about our criminal justice system: Some challenges. *Sociological Forum* 32:1127–1139.

Ruffin II, H. G. (2020). Working together to survive and thrive: The struggle for Black lives past and present. *Leadership*:1–15.

Scott, M. S. (2009). Progress in American policing? Reviewing the national reviews. *Law & Social Inquiry* 34(1):169–185.

Simmons, K. C. (1998). The politics of policing: Ensuring stakeholder collaboration in the federal reform of local law enforcement agencies. *The Journal of Criminal Law & Criminology* 98(2):489–546.

Simonson, J. (November 16, 2020). Police reform through a power lens. *Social Science Research Network*. Retrieved on January 15, 2021 from https://ssrn.com/abstracts=3731173

Umamaheswar, J. (2020). Policing and racial (in)justice in the media: Newspaper portrayals of the 'Black Lives Matter' movement. *Civic Sociology:*1–13.

Williams, E. J. (2003). Structuring in community policing: Institutionalizing innovative change. *Police Practice & Research* 4(2):119–129.

Zimring, F. E. (2020). Police killings as a problem of governance. *The Annals of the American Academy* 687:114–123.

CHAPTER APPENDIX: TABLE OF LEGISLATIVE ACTIONS ON POLICE REFORM AND OTHER RELATED ACTIONS

U.S. Congress		Proposed Legislative Bill	Date	Party of the Sponsor	Action Taken	Related Bill	Key Issue(s)
House of Representatives	H.R. 35	Emmett Till Antilynching Act	2/27/2020	Democrat	Passed House; Introduced in Senate	H.R. 3536; H.R. 7120; H.R. 7278; S. 488; S. 3912; S. 3985	Criminal justice reform
	H.Res. 1017	Providing for consideration of H.R. 7120	6/24/2020	Democrat	Motion to reconsider	H.R. 7120	Policing practices, accountability, and transparency
	H.R. 1574	Closing the Law Enforcement Consent Loophole	3/16/2019	Democrat	Referred to Committee	H.R. 1585; H.R. 7278; S. 855; S. 2843; S. 2920; S. 3985	Policing practices, accountability, and transparency
	H.R. 1585	Violence against Women Reauthorization Act of 2019	04-10-2019	Democrat	Passed House	H.R.570; H.R.600; H.R. 1574; H.R. 2029; H.R. 2552; H.Res. 281; S. 134; S. 171; S. 336; S. 855; S. 1432; S. 2843	Civil Rights
	H.R. 1636	Commission on the Social Status of Black Men and Boys Act	04-12-2019	Democrat	Referred to Committee	H.R. 7278; S. 2163; S. 3985	Highlights that black men and boys are disproportionately subjected to profiling, incarceration, and longer prison sentences than their white male counterparts
	H.R. 1714	Stop Militarizing Law Enforcement Act	3/14/2019	Democrat	Referred to Committee	H.R. 7120; S. 3912	Policing policies; accountability

(*Continued*)

U.S. Congress	Proposed Legislative Bill	Date	Party of the Sponsor	Action Taken	Related Bill	Key Issue(s)
H.R. 1893	Next Step Act of 2019	3/26/2019	Democrat	Referred to Committee	H.R. 196; H.R. 1076; H.R. 1456; H.R. 1951; H.R. 2232; H.R. 2410; H.R. 2865; H.R. 4339; H.R. 7270; H.R. 8941	Criminal justice reform
H.R. 3364	Federal Police Camera and Accountability Act of 2019	6/19/2019	Democrat	Referred to Committee	H.R. 7120; S. 3912	Policing practices, accountability, and transparency
H.R. 3536	Justice for Victims of Lynching Act of 2019	6/27/2019	Democrat	Referred to Committee	H.R. 35; H.R. 7120; H.R. 7278; S. 488; S. 3912; S. 3985	Criminal justice reform
H.R. 4168	Law Enforcement Inclusion Act of 2019	08-06-2019	Democrat	Referred to Committee	H.R. 7120; S. 3912	Policing policies; accountability
H.R. 4339	End Racial Profiling Act of 2019	9/16/2019	Democrat	Referred to Committee	H.R. 1893; H.R. 7120; S. 697; S. 2355; S. 3912	Policing practices, accountability, and transparency
H.R. 7085	Ending Qualified Immunity Act	06-04-2020	Democrat	Referred to Committee	H.R. 8979; S. 4036; S. 4142	Policing practices, accountability, and transparency
H.R. 7089	PRIDE ACT—Police Reporting Information, Data and Evidence Act of 2020	6/14/2020	Democrat	Referred to Committee	H.R. 1893; H.R. 7120; S. 697; S. 3912	Policing policies, practices, accountability, and transparency
H.R. 7100	George Floyd Law Enforcement Trust and Integrity Act of 2020	06-04-2020	Democrat	Referred to Committee	S. 3063; S. 3912	Policing policies, practices, accountability, and transparency

H.R. 7120	George Floyd Justice in Policing Act	06-08-2020	Democrat	Passed House; Placed on Senate Calendar on 7/20/2020	H.R. 35; H.R. 1714; H.R. 3364; H.R. 3536; H.R. 4168; H.R. 4339; H.R. 7089; H. Res. 1017; S. 488; S. 2355; S. 3063; S. 3912; S. 3956	Policing practices, accountability, and transparency
H.R. 7278	Justice Act	6/18/2020	Republican	Referred to Committee	H.R. 35; H.R. 1574; H.R. 1636; H.R. 3536; H.R. 7907; H.R. 8088; H.R. 8597; S. 488; S. 855; S. 2163; S. 2434; S. 3985; S. 4064	Policing practices, accountability, and transparency
H.R. 7907	National Criminal Justice Commission Act of 2020	7/31/2020	Democrat	Referred to Committee	H.R. 7278; S. 2434; S. 3985	Comprehensive review of the criminal justice system
H.R. 8088	To provide for funding for law enforcement agencies	8/22/2020	Republican	Referred to Committee	H.R. 7278; S. 3985; S. 4064	Policing policies, practices, and accountability
H.R. 8597	Policing Transparency Act	10/16/2020	Republican	Referred to Committee	H.R. 7278; S. 3985	Policing practices, accountability, and transparency
H.R. 8979	Qualified Immunity Abolition Act	12/16/2020	Democrat	Referred to Committee	H.R. 7085; S. 4142	Policing practices, accountability, and transparency
Senate						
S. 488	Justice for Victims of Lynching Act of 2019	3/22/2019	Bipartisan	Passed the Senate; died in the House	H.R. 35; H.R. 3535; H.R. 7278; S. 3912; S. 3985	Civil Rights

(Continued)

U.S. Congress	Proposed Legislative Bill	Date	Party of the Sponsor	Action Taken	Related Bill	Key Issue(s)
S. 697	Next Step Act of 2019	03-07-2019	Democrat	Referred to Committee	H.R. 197; H.R. 1076; H.R. 1456; H.R. 1893 (Identical Bill); H.R. 1951; H.R. 3332; H.R. 2410; H.R. 2865; H.R. 4339; H.R. 7089; H.R. 7270; H.R. 8941; S. 387; S. 597; S. 1068; S. 1080; S. 1557; S. 2355; S. 2850	Policing practices, accountability, and transparency
S. 855	Closing the Law Enforcement Consent Loophole Act of 2019	3/25/2019	Democrat	Referred to Committee	H.R. 1574; H.R. 1585; H.R. 7278; S. 2843; S. 2920; S. 3985	Policing practices
S. 1557	Reverse Mass Incarceration Act of 2019	5/21/2019	Democrat	Referred to Committee	H.R. 1893; H.R. 2865; S. 697	Criminal justice reform
S. 2163; PL-116-156	Commission on the Social Status of Black Men and Boys Act	8/14/2020	Republican	Became Public Law	H.R. 1636; H.R. 7278; S. 3985	Highlights that Black men and boys are disproportionately subjected to profiling, incarceration, and longer prison sentences than their white male counterparts
S. 2355	End Racial Profiling Act of 2019	7/31/2019	Democrat	Referred to Committee	H.R. 1893; H.R. 4339; H.R. 7120; S. 697; S. 3912	Policing practices, accountability, and transparency

Bill	Name	Date	Party	Status	Related Bills	Topic
S. 2434	National Criminal Justice Commission Act of 2019	08-11-2019	Democrat	Referred to Committee	H.R. 7278; H.R. 7907; S. 3985	Criminal justice reform
S. 3063	Law Enforcement Trust and Integrity Act of 2019	12/17/2019	Democrat	Referred to Committee	H.R. 7100; H.R. 7120; S. 3912	Policing practices, accountability, and transparency
S. 3912	Justice in Policing Act of 2020	06-08-2020	Democrat	Referred to Committee	H.R. 35; H.R. 1714; H.R. 3364; H.R. 3536; H.R. 4168; H.R. 4339; H.R. 7089; H.R. 7100; H.R. 7120; S. 488; S. 2355; S. 3063; S. 3956	Policing policies, practices, accountability, and transparency
S. 3956	End Police Use of Chokeholds	06-11-2020	Democrat	Referred to Committee	H.R. 7120; S. 3912	Policing practices, accountability, and transparency
S. 3985	Just and Unifying Solutions to Invigorate Communities Act (JUSTICE Act)	6/17/2020	Republican	Motion to consider	H.R. 35; H.R. 1574; H.R. 1636; H.R. 3536; H.R. 7278; H.R. 7907; H.R. 8088; H.R. 8597; S. 488; S. 855; S. 2163; S. 2434; S. 3985; S. 4064	Policing practices, accountability, and transparency
S. 4036	Reforming Qualified Immunity Act	6/23/2020	Republican	Referred to Committee	H.R. 7085; S. 4142	Policing policies; accountability
S. 4064	Law Enforcement De-escalation Training Act of 2020	6/24/2020	Republican	Referred to Committee	H.R. 7278; H.R. 8088; S. 3985	Policing policies, practices, and accountability
S. 4142	Ending Qualified Immunity Act	07-01-2020	Democrat	Referred to Committee	H.R. 7085; H.R. 8979; S. 4036	Policing policies; accountability

Source: Self-generated by the Author, with all bills obtained from the Library of Congress (www.congress.gov).

Chapter 6

Linguistic Perspective

Lilian Achieng' Magonya and
Pamela Anyango Oloo

This chapter infuses arguments from cognitive linguistics, discourse analysis, visual semiotics, and color symbolism to analyze hand and face pictorial metaphors in Black Lives Matter and All Lives Matter posters sampled from the Shutterstock.com online platform. The posters are designed to condemn all manner of racism committed against people of color. Historically, racial profiling remains a societal problem that has dominated scholarly debates among anthropologists, historians, political scientists, and even linguists. This is because racial discrimination contributes to social class inequalities, with minorities unfairly denied access to good housing in affluent neighborhoods, employment in reputable institutions, education, jobs, political rights, and health care among others (van Dijk, 1993a, b; Wodak and Reisigil, 2001; Rattansi, 2007; Hill, 2008; Nguyen-Phuong-Mai, 2017).

According to Rattansi (2007), early forms of racism can be traced to around the fourth century AD during the Byzantine era when Christians discriminated against Jews who were labeled lewd, gluttonous, and murderers. Later, racial discrimination extended to Spain, India (under the caste system), and America (since slave trade to contemporary times). In other words, racism has existed in America for over five centuries. Theorists such as van Dijk (1993a) and Nguyen-Phuong-Mai (2017) concur that racism is an extended version of stereotypes and prejudice advanced by white supremacists who pigeonhole minorities into racially bias categories, which misrepresent them by downplaying their rich cultural heritage. A case in point is if one black person commits a crime, automatically all blacks are labeled criminals or Christopher Columbus euro-centric perception of the Caribs and Arawaks whom he labeled primitive and uncivilized people, yet they were culturally advanced (Rattansi, 2007). Such models are based on half-truths, exploited by white supremacists to discriminate against minorities.

Discourse analyst Teun van Dijk (1993a, b) has extensively researched on racism in political and elitist discourses. He holds the thesis that any written, spoken, or signed discourse can potentially serve as a platform for producing and reproducing racial prejudices, which naturally occur in everyday parlance of white supremacists when interacting with fellow compatriots. Further, van Dijk (1993a, b) perceives racism as having two tiers, notably the cognitive and social dimensions. On one hand, the cognitive dimension relies on mental representations hosting racially bias mental models of other groups to generate socially shared mental representations capable of polarizing white supremacists and minorities into the "Us" versus "Them" ideological paradigm. On the other hand, the social dimension first entails discriminative practices socially expressed in stereotypes and prejudices at a micro level. And second, the relationship between power and abuse by dominant groups at the macro level. In such a scenario, the elitist class controls various institutions such as the media, academia, and vital state agencies, which enact, legitimate, and propagate their racist ideologies. For van Dijk (1993a, 2005) and Nguyen-Phoung-Mai (2017), the media is powerful tool exploited by the white supremacists to negatively present minorities whereby both the headlines and newspaper contents can have positive constructions about the in-group and negative images about the out-groups especially in articles touching on immigration and cultural diversity.

Textbooks are sources of literature where children learn racist ideologies. In fact, van Dijk (1993a) stresses that racism is learned in institutions and not acquired. He argues that in the 1980s, minorities were virtually nonexistent in Eurocentric literature meaning they were invisible in western literature. With regard to state agencies, immigration departments and the police have traditionally been state instruments for enforcing racist ideologies. A case in point is the unfortunate case of George Floyd, a black American regular shopper at Cup Foods grocery store in Minneapolis, Minnesota, who met his death in the hands of a Derek Chauvin, a white policeman under the false allegation that he had bought cigarettes worth twenty dollars using a counterfeit bill. The aftermath of his death was mass protests across the United State under the theme Black Lives Matter to denounce police brutality against minorities (British Broadcasting Cooperation, 2020). Apparently, the question of racism within security agencies resonates with Hill's (2008) direct quote from a personal communion with Ladson-Billings in January 2004 who commented: "Your race is what you are when the cops pull you over at two o' clock in the morning" (Hill, 2008, p. 13).

Interestingly, such a statement is unsurprisingly familiar with people of color. It is against this background that this chapter draws insights from cognitive linguistics, visual semiotics, and discourse analysis in an attempt to answer the following questions: First, what types of cross-domain mappings exist in the hand pictorial metaphors in the Black Lives Matter/All Lives Matter posters? Second, what are the cross-domain mappings of the face pictorial metaphors in Black Lives Matter/All Lives Matter posters? And finally, how does visual semiotics and related subfields address the question of color symbolism in the posters? The conceptual framework guiding this study will draw insights from Lakoff and Johnson (2003), Forceville (1996), and van Dijk (1987, 1993a, b). Cognitive linguists notably Forceville (1996) and Lakoff (2003) have extensively researched on conceptual metaphors and pictorial metaphors respectively, while van Dijk's (1987, 1993a, b) insights in discourse analysis will complement the cognitive linguistics theorists by infusing insights from language and ideology to account for othering exercised by white supremacists. The subsequent sections of this chapter will focus on the conceptual framework, color symbolism, and case studies on the hand and face pictorial metaphors.

CONCEPTUAL DISCUSSION

In this section, we incorporate the theoretical thinking on metaphors, discourse analysis, and linguistic strategies used by white supremacists in racist discourse. In this paper, conceptual metaphors and metonymic frames are presented in italics.

Lakoff and Johnson (1980, 2003) draw arguments from the Conceptual Metaphor Theory (CMT). Further, Lakoff and Johnson (2003), Rasekh and Ghafel (2011) and Bertucelli (2013) advance the argument that in any human language, metaphors serve as cognitive frames upon which conceptual systems are designed. This means that our thoughts, feelings, and actions are structured metaphorically to creatively express our embodied experience with phenomenon. Metaphors have two manifestations—linguistic and conceptual—as illustrated in the expression "Steal the show or be in the spotlight" as a linguistic metaphor framed under *life is a play* conceptual metaphor (Kövesces, 2006). Seemingly, metaphors partially structure one thing in terms of another and have two domains namely source domain mapped on the target domain as illustrated by *hunger is heated fluid in a container* conceptual metaphor in expressions such as "I was boiling with rage" (Lakoff, 1987 as cited in Croft and Cruse, 2004, p. 197), as indicated in table 6.1.

Lakoff and Johnson (2003) state that there are three types of metaphors: orientational, ontological, and structural metaphors. Orientational metaphors organize concepts using spatial orientation and they vary culturally, for example, *happy is being up* and *sad is being up* conceptual metaphors in expressions such as "I am feeling up today or I am feeling down." Lakoff and Johnson (2003) argue that based on our embodied experience, we assume

Table 6.1 Hunger Is Heated Fluid in a Container Conceptual Metaphor

Source Domain: Heated Fluid	Target Domain: Anger
Container	Body
Heated fluid	Anger
Heat of scale	Scale of anger
Pressure in a container	Experienced pressure
Agitation of boiling fluid	Experienced agitation
Limit of a container's resistance	Limit of a person's ability to suppress anger
Explosion	Loss of control

Source: Self-generated by the authors using Croft and Cruse, 2004, p. 197.

a drooping posture when depressed or sad but have an erect posture when we are in high spirits. Ontological metaphors structure our experiences with events, activities, emotions, or ideas. For example, under *visual fields are containers* conceptual metaphors, there are expressions such as "I have him in sight, He is out of sight now," whereby one's vision is conceptualized as a container and anything appearing within ones line of vision is within sight and others outside it are considered outside. Then, structural metaphors show how one concept is partially perceived as another one. For instance, *love is a journey*, where the duration of one in a relationship is conceptualized as journey. Closely related to metaphors are personification and metonymy. For Lakoff and Johnson (2003), Fang-fang (2009), Sānchez (2012), and Mårup (2016), personification mostly stems from ontological metaphors, which allow non-human entities to be perceived as having human characteristics. This enables us to make sense of our motivations, actions, and characteristics such as "coastal armoring," "sea walls," and other "man-made structures" operating under the *coast is a warrior* conceptual metaphor (Sānchez, 2012). This example demonstrates how a coastline is accorded human qualities of armoring itself like a soldier preparing for war. Metonymy, like metaphors, express our experience with phenomenon in everyday discourse by focusing on the part-whole relationships within concepts and their cross-domain mapping is confined to one domain, unlike metaphors that have two domains such as *the place for institution* and *producer for the product* metonymic expressions are realized in the constructions "Paris is introducing longer skirts this year" and "he bought a Ford" respectively (Kövesces, 2006).

Besides these, there are metonymic cultural and religious symbolisms. A case in point is in Christianity where *the dove stands for the holy spirit* metonymy is grounded on the western culture, which perceives the dove as beautiful, friendly, and graceful. Moreover, its habitat being the sky metonymically represents heaven (Lakoff and Johnson, 2003). Scholars such as Croft and Cruse (2004), Evans and Green (2006), Bertuccelli (2013), Fan (2017), and Negro (2019) have coined the term *metaphonymy* in reference to the metaphor-metonymy interface as in the illustration: "She caught the Prime Minister's ear and persuaded him to accept her plan" (Evans and Green, 2006, p. 230). In this case, *attention is a moving physical entity* is the underlying conceptual metaphor with the ear for attention is its metonymy. From the foregoing, in the analysis of Black Lives Matter posters, we will be cognizant of the fact that body parts such as the hand and face are metonymic as they represent the bodies of people of color, and such bodies effectively communicate social injustices in a Western society.

COLOR SYMBOLISM

Closely related to the issue of metaphonymy is color symbolism (Rasekh and Ghafel, 2011 and Qiang, 2011), where Rasekh and Ghafel in their comparative analysis of color idioms in Persian and English state that color is a subcategory of metaphor. Seemingly, such color terms can be used literally and metaphorically. Further, a single color might have connotative meanings and equally provide insights about a community's cultural identity (De Bortoli and Maroto, 2001; Qiang, 2011; Wang, 2015). Still on color symbolism and culture, Qiang (2011) concurs with Rasekh and Ghafel that language is influenced by culture thesis. Qiang (2011) and Li (2020) observe that the red color (*hong se* in Chinese) is embedded in both the Chinese and other Asiatic cultures and has numerous meanings. For instance, it is perceived as the color of life, happiness, good fortune, and warmth. In matrimony, it denotes happiness, good fortune, joy, prosperity, and celebration, where couples are given money in *hong bao* (red envelopes) to wish them well, when they have children, during holidays and on special occasions. In the political arena, red symbolizes bloodshed during the struggle for independence, passion, and revolution or socialism in both China and Russia. Moreover, in China, red is associated with royalty as kings would dress in red and dignitaries would be treated to a red carpet reception. For Yu (2014), red is considered a sacred color for the Chou Dynasty and even for the Roman Catholic cardinals who wear red hats. In the beauty context, there are Chinese expressions used in reference to women, their clothes or make up using the term red such as *hong-yan* (red face) and *hong zhuang* (red clothes) or *hong feng* (red powder).

With regard to emotions, just like in English and Persian as observed with Steinvall (2007) and Rasekh and Ghafel (2011), under *emotion is heat* conceptual metaphor, the color red is associated with embarrassment and in Chinese and like in most cultures, it equally denotes danger. Interestingly, according to Yu (2014), red is associated with death in the Celtic world. Besides Chinese examples, the English culture also uses colors metaphorically in expressions denoting emotions such as "I am feeling blue" (to suggest that one is either sad or depressed), whereas the German variant *blau sein* (to be blue) means to be intoxicated; "to be tickled pink by a golden opportunity then come out blue" (to be excited about an opportunity only to be disappointed later), "to be green with envy" (jealous), "to see red" (to be suddenly angry), and "to be green on the gills" (to be ill) (De Bortoli, and Maroto (2001); Steinvall (2007); Rasekh and Ghafel (2011); Ghafel and Mirzaie (2014); Yu (2014); Wang, (2015); Moffarej and Rabab'ah (2020). With regard to the black and white colors, on one hand, white is associated with positive attributes such as eternity, virtue, innocence, purity, virginity, heaven, tolerance, and light.

On the other hand, black is perceived negatively in terms such as death, mourning, sin, mystery, hatred, unforgiveness, black magic, and evil. such attributes are framed under *white is good* and *bad is black* conceptual metaphors, though according to De Bortoli and Maroto (2001), Yu (2014) and Wang (2015) in China, Korean, and other Asiatic countries, white has traditionally been the color associated with misfortunes, death, and mourning. Thus, during funerals, mourners wear white garments instead of black unlike in Western cultures. Further, among the Inuit, there are seventeen white color schemes for snow, making the concept "white" relative. A similar observation was made by Rattansi (2007) who argues that in the context of racism, the Irish were once labeled black, while the Nordics were considered more white than other Europeans.

For Ghafel and Mirzaie (2014), the black-white distinction clearly emerges in the following metaphonymy derived from Persian idioms "to have white beard" and "to have white hair" (Grey hair in English) means to be an experienced or wise man/lady. This means that the older people have a wealth of experience on life challenges and they make the best youth counselors as unpacked by conceptual metaphors and metonymic frames designed by Ghafel and Mirzaie (2014, pp. 138–139) in the Persian linguistic metaphor *rĭs sefid/gis sefid* meaning he has gray hair under *wisdom is having grey/white hair* conceptual metaphor. The metaphor comprises *the body part stands for the person* metonymy, *the beard/hair stands for the person* metonymy, *white color of the hair/beard stands for the whole person* metonymy, *old is becoming white on the hair/beard* metaphor, *oldness stands for wisdom* metonymy, all the outlined metaphors and metonymies generate *wisdom is white* conceptual metaphor.

Besides this, Ghafel and Mirzaie (2014) analyze the use of black in the idiom "to have a black mouth" (palatal), which translates as "someone whose imprecation caught others." In the Persian and Jordanian Arabic cultures, black symbolizes a wicked spirit or an unforgiving person under *bad is black* conceptual metaphor (Moffarej and Rabab'ah, 2020). Therefore, an offensive person normally draws other people's attention as conceptualized by Ghafel and Mirzaie (2014, p. 140) in the Persian expression *saeq sijâh* framed under *slandering is having a black mouth* conceptual metaphor. The metaphor comprises the following metaphors and metonymies: *the body part stands for the person* metonymy, *the mouth stands for the person* metonymy, *the black force in the mouth stands for evil speech* metonymy, *bad is black* conceptual metaphor, *manner is color* conceptual metaphor, and finally all these figurative expressions generate *slandering (evil saying) is black* conceptual metaphor.

Color symbolism will be revisited in the next section. The focus here was to discuss the interplay of metaphonymy, color symbolism, and body parts. This section explores insights from Forceville (1996) on pictorial metaphor founded on ideas espoused from Black's (1962) Interactionist Theory. Forceville (1996) argues that images have intentionality, which springs from their denotative and connotative meanings. For instance, the picture of an apple has its basic meaning as a fruit, while its connotative meanings, which are symbolic or metaphorical, yield the following meaning: healthy living, a tasty fruit or the fruit used by the serpent to tempt Eve in the Garden of Eden. Pictorial metaphors are guided by Lakoff and Johnson (2003) ideology on metaphoricity. First, that cross-domain mappings are unidirectional from the source domain to the target domain. Second, the pictorial metaphors can cover a range of either tropes. Third, to understand pictorial metaphors context is important and the metaphors can be expanded to include cultural, aesthetic, and social contexts. In fact, Kövesces (2011) adds for the case of context-based metaphors one needs to examine the immediate cultural context, social context, linguistic context, and our encyclopedia knowledge of the major entities in discourse. Such factors aid in metaphorical comprehension. Fourth, any pictorial metaphor is complemented by a verbal counterpart, which aids in unveiling the speaker's intention.

Having explored the metaphors and metonymy from a cognitive linguistic perspective, we are cognizant of the fact that besides metaphors, it is possible to unearth the racist ideology using arguments from discourse analysts such as van Dijk (2001). The focus here is on exploring the aspects that will explain the "Us" versus "Them" ideological square guided by polarized views advancing the following thesis *Emphasize our good things, emphasize their bad things, mitigate our bad,* and *mitigate their good*. Such an ideology is advanced by white supremacists who use various channels such as the media, academia, and politics in advancing a racist agenda characterized by the following linguistic features as outlined by van Dijk (2001):

(a) Nonverbal structures: a racist picture, derogatory gesture, and negative headline emphasizing negative meanings about "Them."

(b) Sounds: An insolent intonation (speaking too loudly).
(c) Syntax: (De)-emphasizing responsibility fraction by active versus passive constructions. Here active constructions show the actors, while the passive constructions conceal the identities of the culprits. For example, injustices by state organs are downplayed by an article alluding to discrimination without mentioning the actors and who were discriminated against.
(d) Lexicon: Selection of a word that may be more or less negative about "Them" and positive about "Us" (e.g., terrorist versus freedom fighter or present immigrants negatively in expressions by labeling them as illegal or undocumented in political discourse (van Dijk, 2001).
(e) Local (sentence) meaning: being vague/indirect about our racism and detailed/precise about their crimes/misbehavior. According to Nguyen-Phoung-Mai (2017), when a white man kills, he is labeled a lone wolf, whereas murder committed by a black person is generalized to the entire community.
(f) Global discourse meaning: selecting or emphasizing positive topics like aid and tolerance for "Us."
(g) Schemata conventional forms of global discourse organization presence/absence of standard schematic categories, for example, as schemata that emphasizes our Good things and their bad things.
(h) Rhetorical devices: metaphor, metonymy, hyperbole, euphemism, irony focusing on positive/negative information about " Us/Them," for example, using a negative metaphor such as negative invasion of refugees under *refugees are invaders* conceptual metaphor.
(i) Speech acts: accusations to derogate "Them" or defenses to legitimize our discrimination.
(j) Interaction: Interruption of others, closing meeting before others speak, disagreeing with others, non-responding to questions, which are forms of direct interactional discrimination. For example, a white person might interrupt a person of color by telling the "Speak English! This is America" (Hill, 2008).

According to van Dijk (2001) and Wodak and Reisigil (2001), such racist discourse strategies are used by white supremacists to establish dominance and hegemony by controlling minds of minorities. From this conceptual framework, we infuse arguments from cognitive linguistics and discourse analysis in the analysis of Black Lives Matter posters by addressing issues touching on color and the hand and face as metonymic concepts of the body metaphor in the light of racism.

METHODOLOGY

This chapter focused on Black Lives Matter and All Lives Matter posters obtained from shutterstock.com online platform. The site has a total population of 11,848 Black Lives Matter posters and 2,771 All Lives Matter posters. For our analysis, we purposively sampled the most recurrent themes in the Black Lives Matter posters under the hand pictorial metaphors, face pictorial metaphors, and All Lives Matter posters. The hand pictorial metaphors comprised seven posters under the following conceptual metaphors: *Clenched fist is a revolution symbol for denouncing racial oppression; a bleeding black clenched fist holding a barbed wire is a symbol of oppression; a black clenched fist sandwiched between two ends of a broken chain is advocating for the end of racism; black hands hanging loosely from an American flag designed as a wooden stock is a symbol of oppression; black hands clasped like in prayer is a symbol of supplication; raised hands is imploring for the end of racism,* and *joined hands of people of color is unity against racism.*

For the face metaphors, the following five metaphors were considered: *the face is a surface for displaying emotion*s; *the skull underneath the face is a symbol of merciless execution of Black*s; *the head hosting the face is a container of emotions*; *gagging is silencing racial injustice*; and *human interaction is interaction between faces.* Further, under the All Lives Matter posters, only four posters were analyzed under the following conceptual metaphors: *Colored eggs symbolism is appreciating American racial diversity*; *the heart as held by hands of people of color is a container of emotions/a valuable object/metonymically represents a human being; black and white faces facing the All Lives Matter slogan is confronting racism/the face stands for actions it is involved in* and *noting down the major racial issues in America is fighting for equality in a racist society.* In total, seventeen posters were analyzed qualitatively using insights from Lakoff and Johnson (2003), van Dijk (1993a, b, 2001) arguments on racism and ideology and color symbolism from a cognitive linguistics perspective.

CASE STUDY ONE: THE HAND CONCEPTUAL METAPHOR IN THE BLACK LIVES MATTER POSTERS

Cognitive linguists argue that human cognition is embodied and that our cognitive conceptualization of concepts is based on our bodily experiences with them. Škara (2004), Swan (2009), Fang-fang (2009), Bertuccelli (2013), Afreh (2015), Fan (2017), and Mofarrej and Rabab'ah (2020) argue that our

Table 6.2 The Human Body Conceptual Metaphors

Source Domain: Human Body	Target Domain: Concert Object/Body Part
Head	Head of an arrow, head of a page
Face	Face of a watch, face of a dice
Eye	Eye of a potato, eye of a hurricane
Nose	Nose of a car, nose of a plane
Mouth	Mouth of a hole, mouth of river
Neck	Neck of the land, neck of a shirt
Shoulder	Shoulder of a mountain, shoulder of a bottle
Hands	Hands of a watch
Foot	Foot of a page, foot of the mountain
Arm	Arm of the sea, arm of the chair

Source: Self-generated by the authors using Fang-fang, 2009, p. 9.

embodied cognition with the body structures our metonymic perception of various concepts using various body parts as in the following constructions: "the arm of a chair," "the leg of a table," "the face and hands of a clock/watch," "a letter head," "nose of an airplane," "the neck of a bottle," "mouth of a river," "the skin of a banana," or "heart of lettuce/matter." In fact, Fang-fang (2009, p. 9) outlines the cross-domain mapping from the human body source domain to the concrete domain object domain as shown in the following cross-domain mappings outlined in table 6.2.

Besides this, there are basic image schemas under which we conceptualize concepts, for instance, *the body as a container* is based on the in-out schema where the body is conceptualized as a container having both an interior and exterior thus generating expressions such as "to jump out of one's skin." The in-out schema would have "to have in mind or to be out of sight" (Mofarrej and Rabab'ah, 2020).

Moreover, Bertuccelli (2013), Fan (2017), and Al-Amoudi (2018) contend there are hand metonymies in English, Italian, Chinese, and Arabic, where the hand stands for an author, skill, assistance, possession/power, behaviors, actions, capacities, disability, cooperation, value, sequence, sides, quantity, feeling, and objects as in the following expressions: hand of a painter, try one's hand in farming, give someone a hand, to be in someone's hands, right hand man, high handed, my hands are tied, take one's hand in marriage (to wed as an action), first/second hand, on one hand, I would like a job, which pays more, but on the other hand, I enjoy the work, a handful, the warm, dry, luxurious hand of silk and a handset/handbag. Bertuccelli (2013, p. 11) adds that there are similes and phrasal verbs that use hand as in the expressions 'to know something like the back of one's hand" or phrasal verbs like "to hand something down" (to give something to someone) or "hand in something" (to deliver something). škara (2004) further argues that in contemporary times, the body is metonymically viewed as parts, of which the hand equally represents the body. For Dur (2015), the hand not only symbolizes power and possession but has cross culturally diverse meanings.

From a religious viewpoint, the hand of Fatima (Hamsa in Islam) called as the Hand of Mary in Christianity was perceived as the hand of Mary. For Christians, God's hand pictorially begins from the wrists and stretches from heaven to earth to show divine intervention or God's power. During worship, raised hands opened outward or when placed together near the chest symbolize prayer or supplication. In the classroom or restaurants, raised hands denoted the need for attention. Hands on the neck signal sacrifice, hands on top of the other palms register meditation or being a receiver, a hand inside another represents promise of service, and index finger pointing at the audience denotes authority. From the foregoing, Bertucelli (2013), Dur (2015) and Fan (2017) concur that culturally there are various meanings assigned to the hand metaphor and this is part of our embodied experience with hand metaphor as expressed in linguistic expressions. Dur adds that pictorial metaphors explain sophisticated thoughts in novel ways such that the invisible become visible, the unimaginable becomes imaginable hence making thoughts accessible to a particular audience. Likewise, the hand metaphor was used extensively in Black Lives Matter posters under the following conceptual metaphors: *clenched fist is a revolution symbol for denouncing racial oppression; black hands clasped like in prayer is a symbol of supplication; raised hands is imploring for justice against racism*, and *joined hands of people of color is unity against racism*.

First and foremost, there are a number of posters operating under the generic *clenched fist is a revolution symbol for denouncing racial oppression* conceptual metaphor. Several posters are designed under this theme in their usage of the black clenched fist, while others had clenched fists of people of color alongside the Black Lives Matter slogan. According to Dur (2015), clenched fists resonate with political propaganda and symbolize revolution, power, and war. Likewise, the Black Lives Matter campaign is geared toward rallying minorities to fight for their rights in the American society since the power to bring change lies in their hands.

There are two specific conceptual metaphors operating under this generic conceptual metaphor notably *a bleeding black clenched fist holding a barbed wire is a symbol of oppression* and *a black clenched fist sandwiched between two ends of a broken chain is advocating for the end of racism*. Further, *black hands hanging loosely from an American flag designed as a wooden stock is a symbol of oppression; black hands clasped like in prayer is a symbol of supplication; raised hands is imploring for the end of racism*; and *joined hands of people of color is unity against racism* conceptual metaphors are considered under the hand pictorial metaphor theme. First and foremost, under *a bleeding black clenched fist holding a barbed wire is a symbol of racial oppression* metaphor, here the poster has a black clenched fist that is firmly holding a barbed wire, which extends to the wrist. Alongside this, there are two drops of blood dripping from the clenched fist and the poster bears the message reading Black Lives Matter. The barbed wire symbolizes instruments of oppression. Whenever, fencing is done using barbed wire, it deters trespassers from accessing people's compounds. Likewise, the pictorial metaphor in the poster conceptualizes racism as divisive as it pitches whites against blacks along unrealistic racial lines.

Second, we have a *black clenched fist sandwiched between two ends of a broken chain is advocating for the end of black oppression* conceptual metaphor. In this case, there are two black clenched fists sandwiched between broken chains against the backdrop of two Rastafarian flags in two separate portions of the same poster. The pictorial metaphor advocates for the end of racial exploitation as symbolized by the broken chains of racial bondage advanced by its message "Break the racism chain. Black Lives Matter" with one section of the poster written in white and another written in gold and green colors of the Rastafarian flag. Dur (2015) contends that hands can symbolize revolution, and the two black clenched fists sandwiched between broken chains against the backdrop of two Rastafarian flags are advocating for the breaking away from racial bondage just like the case of the barbed wire in the previous poster. For Loadenthal (2013) and Pereira (2014), the Rastafarian ideology emerged in the 1930s among the poor in Kingston slums in Jamaica and embraces black nationalism, which fights racism, oppression, and social class inequalities. Moreover, the Rastafarian flag colors notably red, gold, and green are symbolic; red represents the blood that bleeds the earth and replenishes the land, green represents the African vegetation, and gold symbolizes prosperity of Africa prior to the extraction of gold and diamond during slavery (Pereira, 2014).

In sum, the similarity between the Rastafarian movement and the Black Lives Matter campaigns is centered on social inequalities between minorities and white supremacists who exploit state agencies such as the media and the police to enforce their racial agenda using instruments of torture such as chains and barbed wires as outlined in van Dijk's social dimension of racial ideology (van Dijk, 1993a, 1997, Hill 2008).

Third, *black hands hanging loosely from an American flag designed as a wooden stock is a symbol of oppression* conceptual metaphor, whereby the stock like the barbed wire and chains represents years of racial exploitation associated with slavery and oppression. Fourth, *black hands clasped like in prayer is a symbol of supplication* conceptual metaphor is used in a Black Lives Matter poster where the hand of a black person is clasped as if in prayer. From a religious viewpoint, Dur (2015) holds that such a visual pictorial metaphor of the hand is imploring for divine intervention to solve a prolonged social class struggles that has for centuries gravely affected minorities. Alongside the clenched fist pictorial metaphors, there is the use of *raised hands is imploring for the end of racism* conceptual metaphor where the poster has many raised open hands of people from diverse races and below the raised hands is the message Black Lives Matter. In the classroom or in a pub, raised hands serve as ostensive stimulus geared toward demanding attention either of the teacher or the bar attendant. However, going by Dur (2015), in religious and military domains, raised hands are synonymous with surrendering to a superior power. In other words, by raising both hands during religious services, Christians normally surrender their lives to God who forever has total control of their lives. Likewise, an overpowered enemy will raise both hands to show that they are have surrendered to a stronger power. In the posters, raised open hands symbolize surrender and calls for a truce. This therefore communicates the message that excess police brutality as witnessed in the case of Floyd and other people of color is unnecessary.

Finally, *under joined colored hands is unity against racism* conceptual metaphor, many hands of people of color are joined in together in a circular shape and the accompanying message being Black Lives Matter. Dur (2015), Al-Amoudi (2018), and The National News (2021) suggest that joined hands symbolize cooperation and unity, the fight against racism requires combined effort from all races since they all need each other for socioeconomic development of America. From the discussions on this page, it cannot be overemphasized that the hand as a pictorial metaphor in the Black Lives Matter poster acquires numerous meanings in diverse contexts whether clenched fists, raised hands, and joined hands articulate aspects of racial inequalities geared toward safeguarding the lives of minority groups who are familiar with the state instruments of psychological torture such as stocks, barbed wires, and chains. Seemingly, people of color are now advocating for an end to racism for peaceful coexistence between all races.

CASE STUDY TWO: THE FACE AS A PICTORIAL METAPHOR IN THE BLACK LIVES MATTER POSTERS

Fang-fang (2009) and Mårup (2016) have extensively researched on eye and face metaphors and metonymies. Fang-fang advances the following thesis on face metaphors and face metonymies. As pertains the former, the face can be conceptualized under the following metaphors: *the face is a container* metaphor as in the linguistic expression "She saw the worried misery on this face" (Fang-fang, 2009, p. 12), *the face is a natural physical object* also conceptualized as *emotions are objects contained in the face* as in the expression "she got a red/white face" (Fang-fang, 2009, p. 15), where red and white depict bodily changes, specifically, the speed of blood flow is associated with emotions such as anger and fright respectively. *The face is the surface/place where emotions are displayed*, where emotions and facial expressions are portrayed as objects or even animate beings in the expression "a smile rippled across her wrinkled face and was gone."

Similar emotions can be personified where the *face symbolizes an external surface* or *appearance of a whole person* as in the following example "I saw a few faces in the meeting" (own example), *the face is the surface of a concrete domain* as in "The face of watch/clock" (Fang-fang, 2009, p. 16), *the face is an external image of an abstract domain* as in the expression "the face of this company" or *attitude is face* as in "He managed to show a bold face" (Fang-fang, 2009, p. 19) and *the face stands for actions it is involved in* like confronting issues in the expression "He will face the music this time round" (own example). With regard to face metonymies, he singles out three categories, *part for whole*, for example, "we should give the face a chance" (Fang-fang, 2009, p. 21) where the face represents a whole person, *part for part* as in "shut your face" (Fang-fang, 2009, p. 22) where the face metonymically represents the mouth and *whole for part* using the "Shut your face" example Fang-fang argues that one can view the face as a whole and the mouth as part of the face hence justifying the *whole for part* metonymy. In our analysis, we thematically identified the following face conceptual metaphors: *The face is a surface for displaying emotions*; *the skull underneath the face is a symbol of merciless execution of blacks*; *the head hosting the face is a container of emotions*; and *gagging is silencing racial injustice and human interaction is interaction between faces*.

First and foremost, under the *face is a surface for displaying emotions*, we analyzed three posters. One poster has the face of a black man with welled eyes having tears flowing freely from his eyes down to his cheeks and its accompanying message BLACK LIVES MATTER is written in black and in capital letters. In another poster, there is the image of a black woman with one teardrop trickling down her cheeks, then above her head is the #BLACK LIVES MATTER# message. Fang-fang (2009) and Mårup (2016) hold the thesis that eyes together with other facial features register emotions, for example, bright eyes are associated with happiness, while teary eyes are synonymous with sadness. Hence, in this case, *the eye is a container of emotions* is the underlying conceptual metaphor, as both the black man and woman represent minority groups who have been psychologically traumatized to the point of shedding tears against racial injustices. Further, there is another poster of black man crouching, with his two arms holding his downcast head to equally register the psychological trauma associated with racism. It is important to state that the part-whole metonymic relations are manifested where black or colored faces represent minority groups.

Second, *the skull underneath the face is a symbol of merciless execution of blacks*, in the poster, there is a skull, and above the skull is the word BLACK written in capital letters, then on the frontal part of the skull is the word LIVES written in red and in capital letters, which metonymically represents the need to safeguard the lives of minorities, which has overtly been written on the frontal section of the skull for the audience to see. Then, below the skull is the word MATTER, written in black and also in capital letters. Magonya (2017) observes that images of skulls just like skeletons, owls, and the Grim reaper personify death, which metaphorically represents the merciless execution of people of color. Said differently, this is tantamount to infringing the rights of minority groups.

Third, *the head hosting the face is a container of emotions* metaphor is used in a photo where on the right side of the poster, there is silhouette of a black man's head bearing the words Black Lives Matter written in white across his face, cheeks, and chin. Here, the part-whole metonymies are seen where the head, face, and cheeks of the black man represents his body where Afreh (2015) and Mofarrej and Rabab'ah (2020) argue that any part of a human body can be used to express thoughts or emotions. The black man's sentiments on racisms are echoed in parts of his face hence depicting the *part for part* metonymy, since thoughts are normally registered in the brain but not face, cheeks, and chin. Therefore, the outlined organs metonymically represent the thoughts of a black man who is against racial injustices. Fourth, *gagging is silencing racial injustice* metaphor is seen in a poster having seven gagged faces of colored people comprising three men and four women. Some gags bear inscriptions such as "we," others "can't," others "breathe," and one gagged face has the capitalized message WE CANT BREATHE. According to van Dijk's (2001) ideological square, the use of pronouns such as "we" versus "them" registers polarity between the exploited and exploiters and the capitalizations such as BLACK LIVES MATTER and WE CAN'T BREATHE introduces an amplification effect that shows that the minority groups are raising their voices against racial injustice in the community.

Finally, under *human interaction is interaction between faces* metaphor has four faces of black and white men and women, of which on the left of the poster, there are two faces (one of a black woman and another of a white woman) facing two faces on the right of the poster (one of a black man and another of white man). In between the faces is the message BLACK LIVES MATTER written in capital letters. Seemingly, the talking faces are engaged in an inter-racial dialogue on the injustices affecting minority groups under the Black Lives Matter campaign. Further, espousing Fang-fang's arguments on facing an issue is confronting the issue as conceptualized in the *face stands for the action it is involved in* conceptual metaphor, it can be argued that under *knowing is seeing* conceptual metaphor that the outcome of the inter racial dialogue will raise awareness on the need to safeguard the lives of the oppressed minority groups in America.

CASE STUDY THREE: ALL LIVES MATTER POSTERS

From our observation, there are also posters that advocated for All Lives Matter as captured in the following four cases*: Colored eggs symbolism is appreciating American racial diversity*; *the heart as held by hand of people of color is a container of emotions/a valuable object/metonymically represents a human being in the All Lives Matter campaign*; *black and white faces facing the All Lives Matter campaign slogan is confronting racism/the face stands for actions it is involved in*; and finally, *noting down the major racial issues in America is fighting for equality in a racist society.*

To begin with, in *colored eggs symbolism is appreciating American racial diversity* metaphor, the poster uses pictorial metaphors of twelve dyed eggs arranged in two rows where each row has six dyed eggs arranged per row using the following color pattern: green, blue, red, black, white, and violet. Below the eggs is the "All Lives Matter" slogan, where the letters are written using the following colors, AL in green, LL in blue, IVE in red, SM in black, ATT in white, and ER in violet. According to Richardson (2020) and Alimentarium (2021), since medieval times, eggs have been viewed as symbols of life in Chinese, Egyptian, Persian, Phoenician, and Greek cultures, and they were shared out as gifts to celebrate life during spring. For Christians, during the entire period of lent eggs, it was forbidden to eat eggs, they were only eaten during Easter holidays. Incidentally, during this time, eggs were dyed red to denote the bloodshed synonymous with Christ's crucifixion. Moreover, eggs were shared as gifts to commemorate the resurrection of Christ. With time, different colors were used to dye Easter eggs. According to Alimentarium (2021), the religious symbolism of eggs and Christ's resurrection is tied to the analogy between the egg's structure and tomb where Jesus was laid. In other words, just as graves keeps cadavers covered by the earth.

Likewise, eggs are also custodians of lives and hence they culturally represent the tomb that hosted the body of Jesus before his resurrection, which is metaphorically comparable to the hatching of a chick or new life form. From the Christian background of celebrating lives, All Lives Matter campaigns underscore the importance of celebrating racial diversity to combat racism. Second, under *the heart as held by hands of people of color is a container of emotions/a valuable object* metonymically represents a human being in the All Lives Matter campaigns. Swan (2009), Afreh (2015), and Mofarrej and Rabab'ah (2020) adopt Niemeier's (2003) universal conceptualization of the heart as the custodian/seat of emotions such as love, happiness, sorrow, hatred, cowardice, courage, feelings, laziness, meanness, forgiveness, cultural beliefs, and values. Further universally, the following generic metaphors show the cross-cultural conceptualizations of the heart: *heart as metonymy of a person*, where the heart of the person in love stands for the person as in the expression "I have given you all my heart" (Afreh, 2015, p. 45), *heart is a living organism* as in "All hearts throb for her" (Afreh, 2015, p. 44), *the heart is a valuable object* in "To win someone's heart" (Afreh, 2015, p. 44), *the heat is a container for emotions* in "From the bottom of my heart" (Mofarrej and Rabab'ah, 2020, p. 72) and *the heart is the seat of values of morality and spirituality* in "Such as a pure heart" (Swan, 2009, p. 466). In the poster, there are two hands stretched toward each other, a black and a white one, each has a heart and below the hands is the message All Lives Matter.

First and foremost, the heart metonymically presents all human races residing in America. Second, racism evokes emotions such as fear, resentment, sadness, and aggression, which are feelings emanating from the heart under *the heart is a container of emotions*. Third, closely related to this, any injustices will weigh one down both physically and emotionally hence the need to remember that the *heart is a valuable object*. And fourth, the All Lives Matter ideology is enshrined in universal human rights principles and moral values pertaining to the sanctity of all lives worldwide, which is captured in the *heart is the seat of moral values*. The numerous heart conceptual metaphors are consistent with Mofarrej and Rabab'ah's (2020) observation that in Ancient Chinese, the human heart was conceptualized as a reasoning organ with the ability to unite the heart, will, desire, emotion, reason, and thought. Thus, both the intellectual and emotive functions of the heart are further conceptualized under *the heart is the ruler of the body* conceptual metaphor because the heart is the citadel of emotions and thought. With regard to the *Black and White faces facing the All Lives Matter campaign slogan is confronting racism* metaphor, whereby on the left of the poster, there are silhouettes of a black and a white face and the two faces are looking on the right where the words "All Lives Matter" are inscribed. This stems from the generic metaphor *face stands for the action it is involved in* where all races are engaged in confronting racism in America. Finally, *noting down major racial issues in America is advocating for equality in a racist society* pictorial metaphor was designed in a poster having the following capitalized messages: ALL LIVES MATTER, BLACK LIVES MATTER, WE CAN'T BREATHE, STOP RACISM, and YOU MATTER, all of which voice antiracism sentiments.

CONCLUSION AND RECOMMENDATION

Afreh (2015) and Mofarrej and Rabab'ah (2020) body organs are centers of emotions and thoughts. The analysis of color symbolism, conceptual metaphors, and metonymies of the hand and face within the Black Lives Matter campaign is consistent with the thesis advanced by cognitive linguists that human cognition is metaphoric and is embedded on our experience with phenomenon. Undeniably, racism is a societal truism and its mental and social representation within minority groups are pictorially represented in the Black Lives Matter posters in terms of clenched fists, clasped hands, raised hands, limp hands, joined hands, teary eyes, downcast faces, dialoging faces, gagged mouths, barbed wires, stocks, broken chains, and skulls. In the All Lives Matter posters that advocate for appreciating racial diversity, there is use of mental imagery of dyed colored eggs symbolism, joined hands, and the heart as a container of emotions. Indeed, such mental imageries resonate with racism issues recently echoed by President Joe Biden during his inauguration speech:

> A cry for racial justice, some 400 years in the making moves us. The dream of justice for all will be deferred no longer . . . . The rise of political extremists, White supremacy, domestic terrorism, that we must confront, and we will defeat. To overcome these challenges, to restore the soul and secure the future of America, requires more than words. It requires the most elusive of all things in democracy-unity. Unity . . . today, on this January day. My whole soul is in this. Bringing America, uniting our people, uniting our nation. And I ask every American to join me in this cause. (National News, 2021, p. 1)

From the foregoing, it cannot be overemphasized that for peaceful coexistence among the various races in America, there is a need for an inter-racial dialogue on matters touching on inequality, psychological trauma, social-class struggles and racism, which metaphorically and metonymically presented in both Black Lives Matter and All Lives Matter posters. This recommendation for inter-racial dialogue will serve everyone in the United States and will have a great chance of being replicated in other parts of the world where racism is rampant.

REFERENCES

Afreh, E. (2015). The metonymic and metaphorical conceptualizations of the heart in Akan and English. *Legon Journal of the Humanities* 26:38–57.

Al-Amoudi, K. (2018). The conceptual structure of 'hand' idioms in Arabic. *Internet Journal of Language Culture and Society* 37:30–41.

Alimentarium. (2021). Eggs as a symbol of life. Retrieved on January 11, 2021 from http://www.alimentation.org/en/knowledge/egg-symbol-life

Bertuccelli, P. M. (2013). Idiomatic and figurative uses of 'hand' in English and mano in Italian: Embodiment and cultural filters. *Rassegna di Linguistica Applicata* 1:17–38.

Black, M. (1962). *Models and Metaphors*. Ithaca, NY: Cornell University Press.

British Broadcasting Corporation. (2020). George Floyd: What happened in the final moments of his life. Retrieved on June 20, 2021 from https://www.bbc.com/news/world-us-canada-52861726

Croft, W. and Cruse, A. (2004). *Cognitive Linguistics*. Cambridge, UK: Cambridge University Press.

De Bortoli, M. and Maroto, J. (2001). Translating colors in website localization. *Proceeding of the European Language and Implementation of Communication and Information Technologies Conference*. University of Paisley.

Dur, B, I. U. (2015). Hand Image as metaphor and is usage in poster design. *Global Journal of Arts .Humanities and Social Sciences* 3:19–28.

Evans, V. and Green, M. (2006). *Cognitive Linguistics. An Introduction*. Edinburg, UK: Edinburg University.

Fan, H. (2017). A study of "Hand" metaphor in English and Chinese: Cognitive and cultural perspective. *Advanced Literary Studies* 5(4): 84–93. Retrieved on October 28, 2020 from https://m.scirp.org/papers/79776

Fang-fang, W. (2009). Metaphorical and metonymical expressions including face and eye in everyday language. Retrieved on December 12, 2021 from http://hkr.diva-portal.org/smasg/get/diva2:292843/FULLTEXT01.pdf

Forceville, C. (1996). *Pictorial Metaphor in Advertising*. London, UK; New York, NY: Routledge.

Ghafel, B. and Mirzaie, A. (2014). Colors in everyday metaphoric language of Persian speakers. *Procedia-Social and Behavioral Sciences* 136:133–143.

Hill, J. (2008). *Everyday Language of White Racism*. Oxford, UK: Blackwell Publishing.

Kövesces, Z. (2006). *Language, Mind and Culture: A Practical Introduction*. Oxford, UK: Oxford University Press.

Lakoff, G. and Johnson, M. (1980). Conceptual metaphor in everyday language. *The Journal of Philosophy* 77(8):453–486.

Lakoff, G. (1987). *Women, Fire and Dangerous Things: What Categories Reveal about the Human Mind*. Chicago, IL: The University of Chicago Press.

Lakoff, G. and Johnson, M. (2003). *Metaphors We Live By*. Chicago, IL: The University of Chicago Press.

Li, T. (2020). The metaphorical expressions of basic color words in English and Chinese. *English Language Teaching* 3(13):84–91.

Loadenthal, M. (2013). Jah people: The culture hybridity of White Rastafarians. Glocalism. *Journal of Culture, Politics and Innovation*. Retrieved on January 3, 2021 from https://glocalismjournal.org/wp-content/uploads/2020/03/loadenthal_gjcpi_2013_1.pdf

Magonya, A. L. (2017). Cross cultural variations of HIV/AIDS IS DEATH PICTORIAL metaphor. *Linguistics and Literature Studies* 5(5):375–389.

Mårup, E. (2016). Eye to Eye a contrastive view of metaphorical use of Eye in English and Japanese. Center for Language and Literature-Japanese Studies. Lund University, Sweden.

Mofarrej, O. B. and Rabab'ah, G. (2020). Conceptualization of the heart in Jordanian Arabic: A cognitive perspective. *International Journal of Linguistics* 12(4):65–80.

Negro, I. (2019). Metaphor and metonymy in food idioms. *Languages* 4(3):2–8.

Nguyen-Phuong-Mai, M. (2017). *Intercultural Communication: An Interdisciplinary Approach. When Neurons, Genes and Evolution Joined the Discourse.* Amsterdam, The Netherlands: Amsterdam University Press.

Niemeier, S. (2003). Straight from the heart: Metonymic and metaphorical explorations. In Barcelona, A. (Ed.). *Metaphor and Metonymy at Crossroads: A Cognitive Perspective.* Berlin, Germany: Mouton de Gruyter.

Pereira, L. M. (2014) Intercultural exodus: From Jamaica to the world. Centro de Estudos Interculturais. Retrieved on December 3, 2020 from https://core.ac.uk/download/pdf/47142906.pdf

Qiang, H. (2011). The study of the metaphor "Red" in the Chinese Culture. *American International Journal of Contemporary Research* 1(3):99–102.

Rasekh, E. and Ghafel, B. (2011). Basic colors and their metaphoric expressions in English and Persian. In the proceedings of the first *International Conference on Foreign Language Teaching and Applied Linguistics.* 211–224.

Rattansi, A. (2007). *Racism. A Very short Introduction.* Oxford, UK: Oxford University Press.

Richardson, S. (2020). What is Easter: Understanding the history and symbols. Retrieved on January 11, 2021 from http://www.crosswalk.com/faith/spiritual-life/understanding-the-history-and-symbol-of-easter-1256039.html

Sãnchez, T. M. (2012). Grasping metaphor and metonymic processes in Terminology. *Journal of Specialised Translation* 18:1–19.

škara, D. (2004). Reading the body in contemporary culture. *Coll Arthropol* 28(1):183–189.

Steinvall, A. (2007). 'Colors and Emotions.' In MacLaury, R., Paramei, G., and Dedrick, D. (Eds.). *Anthropology of Color: Interdisciplinary Multilevel Modeling.* Amsterdam, The Netherlands: John Benjamins Publishers.

Swan, T. (2009). Metaphors of body and mind in the history of English. *English Studies* 90(4): 460–475.

The National News. (2021). Transcript: President Joe Biden's inauguration speech in full. Retrieved on January 24, 2021 from www.thenationalnews.com/world/the-americas/transcript-president-joe-biden-s-inauguration-speech-in-full

van Dijk, T. (1987). *Communicating Racism. Ethnic Prejudice in Thought and Talk.* London, UK: Sage publications.

van Dijk, T. (1993a). *Elite Discourse and Racism.* Center of Discourse Studies, Madrid, Spain: Sage Publications.

van Dijk, T. (1993b). Political discourse and racism. Describing others in Western parliament. In S. H. Riggins (Ed.). *The Language and Politics of Exclusion: Others in Discourse.* Thousand Oaks, CA: Sage Publishers.

van Dijk, T. (Ed.) (1997). *Discourse Studies: A Multidisciplinary Introduction.* London, UK: Sage Publishers.

van Dijk, T. (2001). Critical discourse analysis. In Schiffin, D., Tannen, D., and Heidi, E. (Eds.). *The Handbook of Discourse.* Boston, MA: Blackwell Publishers.

van Dijk, T. (2005). *Racism and Discourse in Spain and Latin America.* Amsterdam, The Netherlands: John Benjamin Publishers.

Wang, C. (2015). Symbolism of colors and color meanings around the world. Retrieved on July 2, 2020 from https://colourofcity.files.wordpress.com/2018/03/symbolism-of-colors-and-color-meanings-around-the-world.pdf

Wodak, R. and Reisigil, M. (2001). Discourse and racism. In Schiffrin, D., Tannen, D., and Hamillton, H. (Eds.). *Handbook of Discourse Analysis.* Boston, MA: Blackwell Publishers.

Yu, Hui-Chich. (2014). A cross-cultural analysis of symbolic meanings of color. *Chang Gang Journal of Humanities and Social Sciences* 7(1):49–74.

Chapter 7
Sociological Perspective
Benson Waiganjo Kanyingi

This chapter offers a sociological perspective on social movement; Black Lives Matter (BLM) and All Lives Matter (ALM), which have been understudied by sociologists. As noted by Lubin (2016), sociologists have had a complicated relationship with activism. Therefore, they are still considering what can be done to address police brutality on people of color. Steven (1988) argues that sociology has an acute problem of attributing and assigning blame. Using a sociological perspective, this chapter argues that the effects of race and racism are felt differently by individuals having different identities, hence the existence of two social movements with different emphasis on social justice. BLM's awareness and call for action on racial discrimination is perceived as threatening the white supremacy, and therefore a counter group is plausible (Holt & Sweitzer, 2020). Given the little knowledge regarding the BLM and ALM, the chapter relies on analysis of new stories in different websites for broader understanding and the literature from different disciplines regarding how these two social movements have been represented. The following pertinent questions are asked to fill this information gaps: (1) How do institutions propagate racism? In this case, the schools, criminal justice system, and police who propel mass surveillance.

Indeed, the police officers exhibit individual racism, but they are part of institutions that continue and maintain racism in reality. Racism operates on different levels, from individual to structural. Reforming the police or disciplining the individual officer will not bring social justice. There is a need to interrogate the institutions that the police work for or relate with. (2) To what extent are different actors affected by multiple forms of oppression? Intersectionality at term originated in the work of Kimberlé Crenshaw (1995) will be employed to understand how people's identity at the intersection of race, class, gender, and sexual orientation face racist ideologies and racial oppression structures.

Combining these shapes how people experience racism as members of a racial group, gender, and class differently. By analyzing impacts of racism at different levels, diverse knowledge will be realized rather than focusing on the endless litany of dead black and police brutalities hence missing the bigger picture of racism in the American society. A person may benefit from white privileges while experiencing discrimination for being female or poor or gay. Therefore, multiple dimensions of social disadvantages and privileges can be experienced in different times and places regardless of race category. Andersen and Collins (2004) indicated that individuals such as blacks with intersecting identities of disadvantage are subjected to multiple systems of inequality. Hence, more emphasis on the lives of black people is justifiable as the suffering they endure is unique compared to other people of color.

The intersection of lived experiences of minorities for the construction of narratives and counter-narratives will inform this chapter because engaging in critical reviews of lived experiences of African Americans provides everyday experiences of racism. The lived experiences of African Americans portray a complex of discrimination that cannot be captured by most sociological theories associated with white scholars who set how people understand social life and make sense of it.

Racism is socially disruptive, and therefore a change in society can only occur when scholars engage in social justice efforts through objective research that appreciates different viewpoints. This chapter appreciates that there are African American problems similar to the white's problems that call for equal attention. Hence, there is a need for deep engagement. Sociology as a discipline is challenged to accept diverse ways of knowing rather than relying on the positivist theory, which operates within the loci of elites and, in this case, the whites. Sociology ought to challenge dominant color-blind ideologies in the United States and move toward an antiracist ideology for inclusivity and equity. This can be done through collaborative action, which involves public engagement to explain broader societal upheavals (Korgen et al., 2013).

SOCIOLOGY: CONCEPTUAL DISCUSSION

Sociology is a diverse and pluralistic discipline with many concepts. The selection of concepts depends on particular standpoint and assurance that those concepts will offer a comprehensive picture of the study's subject. In this chapter, concepts like civil society, community, deviance, elites, ethnicity, race, structural racism, institutions, race, and ethnicity will be used to offer guidance and explain certain complex human behaviors in the BLM and ALM social movements.

Civil society includes individuals coming together to associate on the basis of some shared interests. The association aims to influence public policy. Community denotes common experience and shared interests, for example, the black and white community, and this helps in exploring the relationship with one another. Deviance refers to behaviors, which break the rules and expectations of a society. Elite denotes superior groups. In this chapter, whites possess some power and occupy the top position on the hierarchy order. Elites are not always unified. Ethnicity is a claimed identity shared based on language, religion, and values of a group. In this case, ethnicity is explored in terms of ethnic relations examining why particular groups are disadvantaged. Race is a concept that describes and classifies human variation. In this case, the race is socially constructed where the human race is divided based on physical and cultural traits.

Sociologists have tried to understand racial dynamics by asking the important question of how race works and how people understand their racial subjectivity (Lewis et al., 2019). Sociologists also appreciate that race shape life experiences and opportunities. Besides, they conceptualize race differently depending on how it defines society. Research on race concept by sociologists has led to a claim that race is a social construct that changes as economic, historical, and political context changes. The lines that divide different races were created by humans and relate to power and resources. Structural racism is a system in which institutions of society have the power to reinforce burdens and give fewer benefits to the members of one race. And, institutions are deeply embedded in social life; different types of institutions perform specific functions. Institutions are a set of interrelated norms that are generalized across social groups.

This chapter uses a sociological perspective to make sense of institutions, laws, and policies that create more burden and give fewer benefits to black Americans because the BLM is synonymous with protesting police brutalities. How about institutions that work with the police to propagate racial prejudice? How do they interact with one another and reinforce inequities? Inequities intersect with other axes of oppression in "postracial era" beyond racial binarism. Therefore, it is hypothesized that the whites use the institutions below to reduce minority population (African American) progress, resulting in higher cases of prejudice and discrimination.

ZERO TOLERANCE POLICIES IN EDUCATION SYSTEMS

The American society holds the ideology of justice and pursuit of happiness. Nonetheless, such a claim is not matched by the reality as witnessed by match for justice by different social movement in the COVID-19 era. Justice's call shows a continued form of oppression of "others" produced and maintained by the elites who enforce white supremacy. The agitation for BLM actually occurred in the middle of the pandemic when United States was terribly devastated by COVID-19. The protesters preferred to ignore the ravages of the pandemic but fight against racism after George Floyd incidence. A clear illustration of how in post-racial times, practices of racism are hidden, and in some cases, they look natural. Racialized social systems create racial categories that experience covert racial practices propagated by institutions, laws, and policies differently.

One such policy is zero-tolerance policy (ZTP) in the United States, which started as a response to increasing crimes in and within schools. Schools that play a critical role in socialization are used to create power relationship rather than cognitive development of the learners. The get-tough initiative aimed at freeing schools from guns, drugs, and related violence, creating a safe and conducive environment for learners. For effective implementation and compliance with the act, the federal government allocated funds where each state was to meet conditions set for preventive discipline. To control deviant behavior, the local educational agencies could expel any student who carried a gun in a school or school-related function and modify terms of expulsion or act according to the state's perceived needs (Gjelten, 2019). Since the schools had the mandate to modify the action to perceived needs, they adjusted and enacted stringent policies, which were tough on students.

Interestingly in some states, the ZTP replicates the federal law and symbolic acts like carrying toy swords, fighting, and possession of over-the-counter drugs as disruptive rather than engaging in behavior support. Since the policy target terrible behaviors, it is not applied in all schools. Regrettably, it is commonly found within schools with large minority students, especially African American male students who are more severely disciplined than white students (The Civil Rights Project, Advancement Project, 2000). Kim et al. (2010) equates ZTP as a straightforward approach of "pushout" creating a school to prison pipeline. Decades of research reveal how the policy is highly discriminating. African American children are two to three times higher in expulsion, corporal punishment as compared to white students (Skiba, 2014; The Civil Rights Project, Advancement Project, 2001). The disciplinary laws permit school officials to determine the students' future on who to suspend or expel rather than coming up with innovative strategies to deal with student misbehaviors. Moore and Bellamy (2020) argue the approach has increased school discipline disparities in United States where the proliferation of ZTP has pushed the black children out of school to prison pipeline, especially marginalized students. Therefore, it calls the President Biden to reassess the policy and introduce non-discriminatory school's disciplinary action.

Thornhill (2019) argues that black students in historically and predominantly white institutions (HPWIs) face racism within the learning environment and public spaces adjacent to the learning institutions. The perpetrators of this heinous act include students, academic advisers, campus police, and staff members who marginalize black students. Black student's incapacitation makes it hard to earn a degree and secure a decent job after years of study (Johnson-Ahorlu, 2012). Dickey (2016) pointed out that the nationwide protests of 2015–2016 academic year made these schools acknowledge some of the student grievances and promised to diversify students and faculty members.

ZTP effects have primarily focused on black males who are most affected by this policy, neglecting the lived experiences of black girls (U.S. Department of Education Office for Civil Rights, 2014). The racialized gender approach conceals the lived experiences of black girls, which existing quantitative and qualitative data suggest they receive harsher discipline than white female students (Hines et al., 2020: Crenshaw et al., 2015). Hines et al. (2020) argue that the analysis of race, gender, and class reveal how African American girls are made invisible. Black female students are further marginalized as they fight for their identity while labeled loud and attitudinal. The educators perceive the girls as improper and deviant (perceived nonconforming), and discipline is inclined toward white femininity, which are perceived as fair and innocent. The black girls are always in surveillance and policing, because of the perceived criminal aspect. Black female students are pushed out of schools for asking questions, falling asleep in class, and wearing revealing clothes.

Morris (2016) noted that the pushout is a form of disempowering black girls go through and justified by the ZTP-tolerance policy. Therefore, the ZTP is racialized and directed by gendered interpretations of black identities that aim at killing black girls' creativity, confidence, and authentic selves. The racial bias and gender inferiority interact to affect the lives of black females. This helps interrogate race through the lens of gender and shows that similar to boys who are lauded for discrimination and pushout; black females are not special. Using intersectionality, multiple forms of inequality interrelate, such as how race interrelates with gender, class, sexual orientation, and so on. Indeed, African Americans, be it male or female, experience racism differently, and therefore there is a need to dig deep, go beyond conventional analysis to understand injuries inflicted on different class, gender, and so on.

The important question should be asked how does race intersect with lives of a black student with disability, how race intersects with lives of black male students as compared to girls because black child is always on the spotlight of the police and gangs notwithstanding surveillance (Gillborn et al., 2012). Gillborn et al. (2012) notes that heightened disciplinary scrutiny and criticism for black children of different backgrounds illuminate how race interrelates with class and gender inequality. If search questions are asked, they are possibility of unearthing many forms of oppression that shape laws, policies that govern these structures where racist inequities are created, sustained, and legitimized. It can also help to understand how white supremacy is maintained in the schools and subordination of black students is created and maintained, and the way to change it (Gillborn, 2015). Crenshaw et al. (2015, p. 14) states the school discipline policies are meant to, "funnel Black girls onto pathways to nowhere and make their academic and professional vulnerabilities invisible."

Supporting Views

ALM holds the color-blind racial attitudes that ignore the significance of race as they appeal to a humanistic appeal (Bonilla-Silva, 2003; Tawa et al., 2016). They blame the victim and hide the fact of domination. Therefore, despite overwhelming evidence as protests across the campuses, as noted by Dickey (2016), the school administrators cited race climate on campuses as excellent. Thornhil (2019) cites 84 percent of college presidents indicate race relations excellent and that race relations are improving. It clearly illustrates how being color-blind makes administrators delusional. They trivialize the call for justice by blacks as isolated cases that do not require intervention.

When issues related to racism are openly discussed, it is met with defensiveness and other forms of pushback. ALM dismisses BLM claims and legitimize specific policies and fight any approach that exposes the advantages of the white position. As noted by Apfelbaum et al. (2008), those who hold color-blind racial attitudes are people who are more concerned not to be perceived as prejudiced. Like how blacks and Latinos are controlled by the police more frequently, the black students receive harsher treatment in schools while white students' criminal behavior is attributable to external factors like bullied in school. At the same time, black crimes are attributed to something internal (Diangelo, 2018). One example is that minorities are poorly brought-up. They lack motivation and proper values to succeed in life as Bill Cosby acknowledged. The lower economic people are not holding up their end of the deal. These people are not parenting (Hymowitz, 2005). Cosby, just like the affiliates of ALM, believes African Americans are the most affected by ZTP because of poor parenting who rarely sit down with their children but blame racial injustices. Parents as socializing agents have failed in cultural socialization, which is vital in promoting culture and traditions, academic achievement, and higher self-esteem for adaptive functions (Burt et al., 2012). Rather than focusing on power and violence structures, ALM noted racism is associated with bad parenting (De Kosnik & Feldman, 2019).

Advocates for ZTP argue that schools must maintain a safe learning environment where discipline is a priority and policies put in place for serious offenses. Its implementation is fast to deal with dangerous students who pose a threat to other students. ALM accuses BLM to be hypersensitive, and use race at the expense of students' security. The rationale is that ZTP will refrain good children from breaking the rules, and therefore no measure is too great to protect a child. In reality, research has shown that ZTPs target black students as compared to their white counterparts. Because the disruptive student is associated with black bodies, black students are the most victims. In contrast, good or positive feedback is associated with the white student who benefit significantly from the pushout that disproportionately affects black students.

Opposing Views

BLM affiliates hold that institutional racism has been widespread in the American education system from the admission process, resource allocation, and stereotypical images in the curriculum. Institutional racism has led to blacks' exclusion through race-neutral policies, for example, employment through connections for remunerative positions. BLM calls for restorative justice; justice that promotes healing. Most have experienced ZTP as a disciplinary measure that needs mediation. They are afraid that if ZTP is not revisited, blacks will continue to be the majority in prisons. Pertinent questions are asked whether criminalizing every mistake against the law creates a better law-abiding citizen and whether this policy is an inclusive and effective mechanism for school discipline.

By criticizing ZTP, through mediation, there is the possibility of creating policies that value the contribution of black students in the schools. By listening to the voices of those who experience racism, a conclusion on racism can be drawn and understood through the lenses of marginalized communities. Discrimination still exists in the education system, although in subtle and hidden forms creating a disproportionate path for the African American student to reach actualization. BLM at schools acknowledges that racism had become more prevalent, overt, and therefore calls for honest conversation where people engage in racial justice. The argument is that black students have experienced oppression through the policies developed. Black students are automatically punished for various infractions in schools that have had a tremendous impact on their education. Black students have experienced higher expulsion and other criminal charges.

A report by the Civil Rights Project at Harvard University noted that the efforts to address school situation have span out of control as this act excludes children from educational opportunities and puts them into criminal prosecutions. As noted by Noam et al. (2001), the proponents of the approach did little research on its effects on children. Hagopean (2020) acknowledged that the schools began viewing children as criminals rather than young people with potential who faced different hurdles of live. He also noted that this approach targeted black students as most of them were suspended compared to white students. Therefore, the BLM comes in handy as they call for restorative justice that replaces ZTP approaches that propel racism in post racial America. These policies have made black students view themselves as deviant, a mindset that pushes them to further destructions. Bell (2015) argues that while ZTPs were intended to solve violence crimes and narcotic trafficking and possession of weapons, it has not achieved this. Still, it appears crafted for mass incarceration, expulsion for people of color. Even in post-racial America, the number of students arrested increases as of age ten to seventeen of black youth accounts for 25 percent arrests (Bonilla-Silva, 2014).

The policies have not been inclusive as black boys' suspension has been high and adversely impacted African American females and black children with disabilities. According to Bell (2015), the number of black girls suspended was high compared to other races. Yet, there is no data supporting the high incidence rate of weapons within the black family of people with disabilities. BLM understand that life outcomes are related to education, and therefore if racial-educational differences are not tackled, blacks are doomed to remain subordinate and systematically disadvantaged because educational achievements are measured in the form of opportunities for the next generation, social respect, as well as incomes. If racial equality has been achieved in the United States, there is no need for ALM to obscure any protests that seeks equality (Luttrell, 2019). But they cannot understand black American predicament because they lack in-depth knowledge of black people (Luttrell, 2019).

Those who oppose the ZTPs argue that studies have been done for a vast majority of states. Most states are moving from it because the policy criminalizes students, and has extreme consequences, hence a likelihood of repeat offenders or drop out of school completely. Research has shown that students who spent time in detention facilities are more likely to end in an adult prison (Kim et al., 2010). The majority of states are suspending ZTP because it has been found not the best measure to reduce negative behavior as it merely addresses the root cause of the problem (DeJong, Trupe & Zwingel, n.d.). They call for an avenue that creates a conducive environment that addresses the underlying issues rather than punishing the newer generation who have inadequacies in expressing themselves through words. This generation is characterized by Fakhoury (2017) as being vulnerable and resort to misbehaving rather than articulating issues. Hagopian (2020) argues the best approach in schools, as advocated by BLM at school, is restorative justice to build a healthy relationship. Restorative justice is viewed as a step in the right direction. It makes the student feel they matter.

THE CRIMINAL JUSTICE SYSTEM

Studies show incarceration in the United States is associated with family instability, recidivism, racism, poverty, unemployment, and restriction on social and political rights (Brown, 2015). From schools to the criminal justice system, it has become a series of a pipeline to black youths who are pushed out of schools. In the end, they become vulnerable to the criminal justice system, be it juvenile or adult prisons. Harlow (2003) noted that more than half of those entering prison lack high school diplomas, and also most of them underwent suspension nearly three times.

According to Shantel et al. (2020), the murder of black people is often state-sanctioned. The police and white neighbors kill suspicious or nervous black people. In some cases, black people are murdered by the police at their homes, and the officers get acquittal in the justice system. Surprisingly, the violence on black bodies does not end. It even continues in academic space. As noted by Ezorsky (1991), highly educated blacks face barriers to live in the same neighborhood whites. In a color-blind American society, the criminal justice system label black Americans as criminals to justify old forms of discrimination or overt racism that take places in racial structures that propel white supremacy. These structures are used to reinforce white supremacist racial order as a social reality, and any social movement that raises voices of black solidarity toward racial injustices makes them nervous and sense threatened, therefore BLM is associated with violence, and police brutalities is inevitable. Diangelo (2018) pointed out that the consequence of white fragility includes seeing others as a threat. This biased assessment has led many African Americans to land in trouble as criminal charges are instigated. In other words, Diangelo argues that the perception of criminal activity is influenced by race.

Black people's presence poses a threat to the white people. That being the case, he further notes that it has been documented that the police stop blacks and Latinos more times compared to whites. They also receive different treatment for the same crimes. Tabak (1986, p. 826) indicated in a survey carried out in thirty-two states, "The killer of a White is nearly three times more likely to be sentenced to death than a killer of a Black." Ingraham (2017) reported that blacks still receive long federal prison sentences nearly 20 percent longer than white people. He further notes that judges are less likely to revise sentences for the black offenders downward, and when they do, they reduce in small numbers compared to white offenders. Racial biases seep in the process as judges believe black Americans are more criminals who cannot be afforded any compassion. The dominant ideology is that black people are criminals, and also black neighborhoods are inherently dangerous and criminal. In prisons, black women face the oppressive system uniquely reinforced by stereotypes that they are deviant and dangerous. Ocen (2012) notes that due to negative historical constructs that have been normalized, black women are shackled even during childbirth, a clear sign of state-inflicted violence. After giving birth, the black women are labeled "bad mothers" who put their children at risk to escape from custody (Ocen, 2012).

Most literature and media attention focus on violent crimes or extrajudicial killings perpetrated toward black men without careful consideration of the invisible voices. For example, Trayvon Martin killing on February 26, 2012, by George Zimmerman received media attention and individuals taking to the streets and channeling anger on social media (CNN Editorial Research, October 19, 2020). The murder of George Floyd on May 25, 2020, by a Minneapolis police officer received considerable media coverage as well as public protests spearheaded by BLM, who called on the need for reforming the criminal justice system, as noted by Hill et al. (2020). But in reality, racism is deeply entrenched in the American system, especially to the invisible groups such as women of color and those of color who identify as LGBTQ (Berk et al., 2020). The hidden group faces multiple forms of oppression propagated by multiple hierarchical structures, including racial, gender, and sexuality hierarchies. Also, African American women who are incarcerated undergo similar treatment as men. Still, they do not receive equal attention as men, and when they react, they are labeled as insensitive.

White and black heterosexuals express rage on sexism. The black lesbians, gays, bisexuals, transgender, and queer face multiple systems of oppression such as race, gender, and sexuality, which intersect creating new forms of oppression. For example, despite racism, their sexual orientations attract verbal and physical attacks. It is worth noting three cofounders of the BLM movement, Alicia Garza, Patrisse Cullors, and Opal Tometi, are queer black women, a clear illustration of identity's marginalization. Therefore, black bodies in the United States with many marginalized identities experience more discrimination and fewer privileges. According to Human Right Campaign Foundation (2020), 2020 has been the worst year for gender nonconforming people in the United States. At least thirty-seven were killed and the number has been increasing because of systemic discrimination. The majority of victims have been black transgender women who face daily injustices of racism, transphobia, and sexism; a multiple marginalized identity. Even the stories portrayed in media and law enforcement deny or ignore the victim's gender identities, they engage in deadnaming (using the name assigned at birth rather than using the name they use currently), a clear illustration of lack of respect and dignity to transgender and gender nonconforming people.

Out of thirty-seven victims, at least thirty victims were transgender, and twenty-two were black. In 2020, twenty-one of the thirty-seven victims were initially misgendered by the media and the police, which impedes investigation and data collection (Human Right Campaign Foundation, 2020). The FBI annual statistics only reflected two anti-transgender murders a clear illustration of the level of negligence of the marginalized in society (Human Right Campaign Foundation, 2020). Intentional misgendering of many murders goes unreported, unlike other black victims. They disregard how a person self-identifies, as witnessed by Lamr Edwards's shooting in 2015 (Kellaway & Brydum, 2016).

Within the criminal justice system, those whose gender does not fit within binary expectations are overrepresented. Surprisingly, in the correctional facilities, trans-individuals are placed in prisons on gender identified on their birth certificate regardless of their identified gender. Within the correctional facilities, multiple aspects of their identity intersect to bring unique discrimination by the correction officers, courthouses who handle them as normal or less human. Also, black transgender women reported violence expressed by black cisgender men who, like whites, do not appreciate anyone who questions or threatens their masculinity (Hoston, 2020). Interestingly, the violence on LGBTQ has been on the rise, including castration, suffering, and sexual assault. The legal system in the United States has institutionalized racism, sexism, and homophobia. Since the system is color-blind, the authorities perpetuate violence on nonconforming people. Gender and race intersect with sexuality to increase the rates of victimization of people of color at the police's hand. Alexander (2010) and Mogul et al. (2011) noted that the police are more likely to stop people of color, especially LGBTQ people of color, who are vital targets. As compared to white gay men and transgender women, black counterparts are aggressively policed by law enforcement officers. In some cases, officers target areas where black gay men gather. Blacks have been sexualized as hyper-heterosexual, and therefore, homosexuality is linked to white privileges. Thus, racialized LGBTQ violence is a white reaction to reclaim their freedom. Also, heterosexual blacks detest it as incompatible with black identities. BLM is an intersection as it is concerned with black men and homophobic and transphobic violence to make them visible in the mainstream media (Weissinger et al., 2017).

Supporting Views

The call to reform the criminal justice system and the police at the local, state, and federal levels is meant with resistance by those who intend to obscure the experiences of those who are politically marginalized. Luttrell (2019) noted that those who have power deny self-reflection and, in this case, non-progressive white people and blacks who refuse to understand the black experiences.

To them, black mourning, an expression of anger and lamentation, is a threat. They feel white's supremacy is at threat. Thus, they work hard to dismiss any protest by BLM, which they deem irrelevant. They argue that despite black mourning, racial disparities in the criminal justice system and the police have reduced significantly. Anderson (2016) argues that black advancement is a trigger to white rage. The call for justice in the American system shows that the blacks are ambitious for equal citizenship, which undermines white supremacy. ALM opposes BLM mourning because they understand that mourning has ramifications for political establishments. It scares them because it calls for recognition and expands calling for solidarity and uncovers the injustices, which have remained invisible for a long time. Whenever BLM unites, ALM blames them for violence, making it hard for them to build their case. Also, it threatens whiteness, a racial category that is invisible, and the freedom and opportunities accorded to that race (Kamaloni, 2019).

ALM cites that the blacks want an excuse to do whatever they want to do. Their protests are riots. ALM uses tone-policing to admonish blacks for showing emotions. They agree that the criminal justice systems and the police may unfairly target people of color, but BLM protests are riots or equated with a terrorist group (Thompson, 2020). The Ferguson protests that involved riots in Missouri were perceived as a threat to the police as well to the white people. After George Floyd murder, critique on BLM and a call for equal attention, the acts of arson and looting were amplified. It makes BLM's call for policy intervention lack respect and its message perceived as illegitimate. Chapel (2020) argues that change should be accelerated, but BLM cannot change when they employ destruction and looting.

The issue of race has been brought into perspective; ALM argues that the individual's race is not vital in police shootings. They cite that blacks are not the target, but racial disparities are driven by police biased in areas where blacks are many. They argue that black and white civilians have equal exposure to situations in fatal officer-involved shootings (FOIS). They argue police shooting depends on the proportion of violent crime committed by a certain race. Johnson et al. (2019) noted as follows: As the proportion of violent crime committed by black civilians increased, a person fatally shot was more likely to be black. Conversely, as white crime rates increased, a person fatally shot was less likely to be black. Therefore, the concern that white officers disproportionately attack racial minorities is a way of illegitimatizing the police.

Opposing views

African Americans have similar stories on police behaviors and judges based on their lived experiences. The assertion is that the criminal justice system is racially biased. They argue that the criminal justice system and policing as an institution produces disparate outcomes. Vast numbers of blacks are incarcerated, on the streets, they are harassed, stopped more by the police, and frisked (Balko, June 10, 2020; Council of Criminal Justice, 2019). They feel they are punished because of the perception whites have of them. Blacks, irrespective of gender orientation, are more likely to be shot by the police than white people. U.S. Sentencing Commission in 2017 found, when black and white men commit a similar crime, the black men receive a longer sentence as compared to white men. Also, the justice system takes more serious crimes involving white's victimization from non-whites hence intense investigation. As Bjornstorm et al. (2010) put it, there is devalued interpretation of victims where the people of color are devalued while Whites are privileged.

All races sell drugs, but blacks are consistently charged (Balko, June 10, 2020). The stereotypical representation shape how judges perceive blacks, which also influences their judgment. Surprisingly, Uhlmann (1978) found out that black judges are harsher to black and white defendants than white judge. Based on this, both black and white judge sentenced black more harshly and therefore having more black judges cannot increase equality. BLM calls for accountability in the criminal justice system because held racial biases affect blacks. As of 2020, the nationwide acceptance of all races' BLM protests demonstrates an acknowledgment of racial justice (Gale, 2020). The call is for the inclusion of all in racial justice, including transgender people of color and gender nonconforming people who have been targeted by the all races. As witnessed on Hollywood Boulevard. The attacks have been normalized and accepted, where the onlookers recorded and celebrated the assaults. Most of the violent incidents are never taken seriously and, in most cases, the victims are misgendered by the courts and the police add more pain to the victims.

Synthesis of the Competing Views

Both BLM and ALM calls for greater accountability on the police brutality and peaceful protests directed on institutions where wrongs have been done. Justice is not really won until there is justice for all. Everybody is entitled to equal rights on anything, and therefore, BLM and ALM expresses concern about excluding others.

GOVERNMENT MASS SURVEILLANCE

While the deaths of black lives have attracted the attention of many, I argue that this is a narrow manifestation of racism. Massive surveillance of black's everyday life remains disguised and subtle, and difficult to challenge. It originates in the establishment of the governments and received less public condemnation, yet it fosters exclusion, subordination, and exploitation in different social contexts. I agree with Bonilla-Silva et al. (2011) who contend that white life is viewed positive while black life is negative based on how black life is contained through massive surveillance.

One of the existential threats to democracy in the United States is mass surveillance. As noted by Edward Snowden, the National Security Agency whistle-blower on his Twitter handle asked a pertinent question who suffers from unjustified surveillance and responds indeed the vulnerable suffer from mass surveillance (The Guardian June 9, 2013). The people of color have been the disproportionate victims of unjust surveillance justified under national security. Davis (1992) argues surveillance did not start yesterday. Federal Bureau of Investigation (FBI) designed the counter-intelligence program COINTELPRO to spy and harass citizens who deemed subversive in the 1960s. Under the surveillance radar are the people of color, a clear illustration that a narrative of risk is established on black Americans. Sue (2008) argues a narrative of risk creates unintended negative consequences, which include profiling, racism, and normalization. The ubiquitous surveillance on African Americans put them on a state of "abnormals" subjected to exclusion and mistreatment. A clear illustration is the algorithms for predicting recidivism, which is racially biased. Dressel and Farid (2018) analysis on correctional offender management profiling for alternative sanctions (COMPAS) overall accuracy noted that black defendants who did not recidivate were incorrectly predicted to reoffend twice as their white counterparts. The COMPAS scores favored white defendants over the blacks—a clear indication that whiteness is a normalized identity or the normative group.

Surveillance in the twenty-first century is unique where those in authority control data of the less powerful. On the study of pregnant mothers applying for medical aid, Professor Khiara Bridge found how women of color who relied on government assistance to give birth were drilled through forceful coercion about their livelihood. Those who do not comply are locked out of government assistance. Hence, infant mortality and other diseases affect women of color at higher rates; a clear indication that racism is a crucial contributor to health disparities. Also, poor African American women with children who apply for welfare received scrutiny about their personal lives as it is a requirement to verify professed needs. Apart from surveillance, they are stereotyped as welfare queens, promiscuous women who bear children to increase benefit receipts (Cohen, 2004; Gilman, 2013). With enhanced technology, the unannounced home visits, collecting mother's information and household composition and criminal background, can be easily accessible (Hughes, 2018). Bridge (December 4, 2015) argues that the courts authorized states to ask the questions beyond basic questions. For example, state officials enter the women of color houses to justify their eligibility, which illustrates informally disenfranchised poor mothers of privacy rights. The information gathered is then funneled to government institutions that used data on how they see fit.

As noted by German (2020), the FBI infiltrates groups that call for social change. They infiltrate those groups and disseminate false information to discredit those groups and plant a seed of hatred. As noted by intersectional theories, class, gender, race, and even religion shape individuals' experiences. Mass surveillance and intrusion of agencies are more experienced by those of lower class, predominantly poor. It shows how race intersects with the class to create multiple oppression. According to Lerman and Weaver (2014), the poor face the brunt of surveillance as neighborhood with poor communities' experiences police stops at a rate of 500 per 1000 residents. For Black bodies that are associated with movements for social change, the government uses technology to amplify their inequality. For example, if a black American is a Muslim, police may disproportionately observe him or her as a potential terrorist. As noted by Alice Goffman (2009, 2014), surveillance shapes and restructures the lives of those under surveillance. It creates tactics to avoid surveillance because they fear the repercussion of the criminal justice system. Avoidance technique adopted by people of color includes avoiding visiting hospitals, searching for formal employment, using bank, and renting apartments. In contrast, others use false documents to avoid surveillance (Remster & Kramer, 2018). Institutional avoidance reduces the competition and benefit the white race. The collective surveillance violates people's privacy, and this leads to overcrowding of prisons with one race.

Opposing views

Racial inequality is better explained by those who experience it. The impact of surveillance is only known to African Americans. When a group of white men stop in the street and have a chat, it is seen as normal compared to black men who stop in the street who are seen as beyond normal. In a public space shaped for and by the whiteness, black bodies in public space are seen as abnormal. The captured data is profiled and circulated between law enforcement agencies and further categorized by gender, religion, and economic status. BLM opposes mass surveillance as it infringes on citizen civil liberties and fosters a culture of fear among the activists hence silencing them. Ketels (2020) argues that widespread surveillance violates American democracy and hinders citizen freedom of expression and association. Those who face systematic racism tend to understand the events that are taking place in the United States. The Black body carries hypervisibility for surveillance and scrutiny; the ones who watch are White, while the object being watched is the person of color. Also, black police officers just like black judges' act in ways that reaffirm white supremacist agendas in their position.

The BLM has been on surveillance radar, the Department of Homeland Security has been monitoring the movements since the eruption of protests in Ferguson. The surveillance did not end there. Continuous media surveillance on activities of the BLM on Twitter, and key figures in the groups. A clear illustration was Mckesson tweeted Snowden: "I, & many other protestors, have been targets of state surveillance." Some protestors are even tracked and arrested in their homes. Such increased surveillance discourages activism and call for justice as noted by Funk (2020). As mentioned on Twitter, "Protests are happening all over the world for one cause." Social media allows youth of color across the globe to engage in transnational discussions about oppressive systems and state-sanctioned violence. Efforts to control this were put in place through surveillance on BLM, disrupt peaceful protests, and enhance the history of suppression of black movements that call for social justice (Linda & Silvio, 2017).

Supporting Views

Since the Seeing Eye is white and or the face recognizing technology is biased against the black, they argue that surveillance operates for the generalized public goods: protection. ALM participants, black and white hold the post racial frame mind. They believe racism is over, so no one should interfere with the state agencies to intervene BLM movement unruly and uncouth social action that is opposed to respecting the dignity of social activities (Swartz, 2019). ALM believes mass surveillance is a rhetoric of BLM, and surveillance is not only for blacks but for criminals.

Through surveillance, prevention and management of risk through anticipatory means is possible. It also enhances how things are ordered racially and defines what is in or out of control. Embracing technology is a sign of forward thinking and being modern. Through surveillance, the encroachment of activist's civil liberties is for the national security interests. It is easier for law enforcement agencies to diffuse information for control. As such, ALM tends to trivialize BLM claims by asserting all the people are the same without considering the BLM call for social Justice. Mass surveillance is ingrained in the American landscape and looks ordinary and natural to white people because its effects are not felt. To the BLM, their business will not be as usual as mass surveillance of black activism in their everyday lives is as a source of danger that needs control and management. The surveillance reveals a pattern for the black people getting stopped and frisked. The process makes them unsafe, fearful, and vulnerable; this is a clear illustration discrimination takes before an offence is done.

Synthesis of the Competing Views

The two groups believe that everybody has the right to give opinions, and therefore mass surveillance hinders the demand for justice (although call for justice for ALM is not synonymous with BLM). Surveillance on social media has hampered discussion on race and racial justice. Although it is their right to demand justice, and accountability, the two groups held back their ideas and opinions. The affiliates of the two groups engaged in self-surveillance, fearing personal consequences in workplace, relationships, and livelihood. It clearly illustrates how the government institutions censor those who lead justice movements for political control by the dominant groups. The American government has a history of threatening activists (Nell Edgar & Johnson, 2018). Judging from previous intimidation of movement leaders' perceived threats leads to self-censorship for hence killing conversation of racial Justice.

CONCLUSION AND RECOMMENDATIONS

First, racism is a global phenomenon, but as put forth by BLM in the call for justice, racism in United States is unique and a concern that promotes exclusion and oppression of minorities. Both ALM and BLM are committed to addressing social injustices, and police brutality, but they differ in the approach. Social justice is missing as expounded at macro-level systems; institutions and laws, policies and practices. These systems enhance structural violence that makes BLM members create the idea "I matter" is what matters because they have experienced racism differently compared to others in different institutions; schools, criminal justice systems, and under government mass surveillance. As discussed in preceding sections, racist inequities experienced in schools under ZTPs continue to affect the recipients and determine African American students' path. Suspensions affect academic performance and sometimes retention in the same grades leading to frustrations hence dropping out. Education is viewed as the only way out of poverty. Intersectionality helps us to capture the experiences of black female students within "blacks" and "women" who suffer similarly to male African counterparts. Black female students attempt to fight for their identity as they try to navigate the racialized education system. They are termed as loud and attitudinal, a clear example of considerable pressure and how race and gender tug on each other.

Second, in the criminal justice system, where the power favors one race (white), the relationship of race and crime were interrogated. It is evident that social inequalities due to structural racism influence behavior leading to the mass incarceration of black bodies in the United States. The black American community has been on the receiving end hence a unique social experience.

Men have been cited as most deviant, disregarding invisible groups like gender nonconforming people and transgender who suffer multiple forms of oppression before judges, the police, and correctional facilities, media as well white and black heterosexuals.

Third, government mass surveillance infringes people's rights to privacy, and the process does not subject everybody to equal treatment. The power of surveillance is heavy on disadvantaged groups. Stop and frisk, compulsory questions before given government assistance, recidivism, unannounced home visits, and infiltration are apparent in the black peoples' lives.

From the preceding discussion, it is clear color-blind post-racialism supported by the ALM dominates the government approach to policy making. It explains why policies created do not impact the marginalized as it is not permissible to use race as a point of discrimination. The study suggests that the marginalized groups within the blacks do not have a place in the public policy realm. Their rights are not considered in policy-making. Therefore, policy-makers should identify the issues they face as unique and deal with them differently for the sake of a common good because African Americans have been grievously harmed by slavery, and its aftermaths, for example, racism. Therefore, affirmative action should be implemented to show acknowledgment of such injustices. Second, BLM should ignore ALM's disruptions, and their mandate should go beyond police brutalities and focus more on subordinated groups within blacks who face double oppression to influence policy reforms. They should push for affirmative actions that emphasize programs intended to benefit the minorities within the black community.

REFERENCES

Alexander, M. (2010). *The New Jim Crow: Mass Incarceration in the Age of Color-Blindness*. New York, NY: The New Press.

Andersen, M., & Collins, P. (2004). *Race, Class, and Gender* (5th ed.). Belmont, CA: Wadsworth.

Anderson, C. (2016). *White Rage: The Unspoken Truth of Our Racial Divide*. New York: Bloomsbury Press.

Apfelbaum, E., Sommer, S., & Norton, M. (2008). Seeing race and seeming racist? Evaluating strategic color-blindness in social interaction. *Journal of Personality and Social Psychology* 95(4):918–932.

Balko, R. (June 10, 2020). There's overwhelming evidence that the criminal justice system is racist. Here's the proof. Retrieved on January 14, 2021 from https://www.washingtonpost.com/graphics/2020/opinions/systemic-racism-police-evidence-criminal-justice-system/

Bell, C. (2015). The hidden side of zero tolerance policies: The African American perspective. *Sociology Compass* 9(1):14–22.
Berk, C., Ezgi, T., Pamir, K., Deniz, C., & Fatih, I. (2020). Black Lives Matter movement - A comprehensive study on institutionalized racism, sexism and its approach towards intersectionality. Conference Paper.
Bjornstrom, E., Kaufman, R., Peterson, D., & Slater, M. (2010). Race and ethnic representations of lawbreakers and victims in crime news: A National study of television coverage. *Social Problems* 57(2):269–293.
Bridge, K. (December 4, 2015). What's the harm? Prof. Khiara M. Bridges on the poverty of privacy rights. Retrieved on January 16, 2021 from https://lawprofessors.typepad.com/reproductive_rights/2015/12/whats-the-harm-prof-khiara-m-bridges-on-the-poverty-of-privacy-rights.html
Bonilla-Silva, E. (2003). *Racism without Racists*. Lanham, MD: Rowman & Littlefield Publishers, Inc.
Bonilla-Silva, E. (2014). *Racism without Racists: Color-blind Racism and the Persistence of Racial Inequality in the United States*. Lanham, MD: Rowman & Littlefield.
Bonilla-Silva, E., Moon-Kie, J., and Vargas, J. (2011). *State of White Supremacy: Racism, Governance, and the United States*. Stanford: Stanford University Press.
Brown, W. (2015). An intersectional approach to criminological theory: Incorporating the intersectionality of race and gender into Agnew's General Strain Theory. *Ralph Bunche Journal of Public Affairs* 4(1), Article 6:229–243.
Burt, C., Simons, R., & Gibbons, F. (2012). Racial discrimination, ethnic-racial socialization, and crime: A micro-sociological model of risk and resilience. *American Sociological Review* 77(4):648–677.
Chapel, R. (October 7, 2020). Opposed to Black Lives Matter. Retrieved on January 12, 2021 from https://www.telegram.com/story/lifestyle/2020/10/07/opinionfirst-person-opposed-to-Black-lives-matter/114235446/
CNN Editorial Research (October 19, 2020). Trayvon Martin shooting fast facts. Retrieved on January 12, 2021 from https://edition.cnn.com/2013/06/05/us/trayvon-martin-shooting-fast-facts/index.html
Cohen, J. (2004). Deviance as resistance: A new research agenda for the study of Black politics. *Du Bois Review* 1(1):27–45.
Crenshaw, K. (1995). Mapping the margins: Intersectionality, identity politics, and violence against women of color. In Crenshaw, K., Gotanda, N., Peller, G., & Thomas, K (Eds.). *Critical Race Theory: The Key Writings that Formed the Movement*, pp. 357–383. New York, NY: New Press.
Crenshaw, K., Ocen, P., & Nanda, J. (2015). *Black Girls Matter: Pushed Out, Overpoliced, and Underprotected*. New York, NY: African American Policy Forum, Centre for Intersectionality and Social Policy Studies.
DeJong, P., Trupe, E., & Zwingel, E. (n.d.) Motivating students positively through restorative justice discipline. *Empowering Research for Educators* 4(1):Article 2.
De Kosnik, A., & Feldman, K. (2019). *#Identity: Hashtagging Race, Gender, Sexuality, and Nation*. Ann Arbor, MN: University of Michigan Press.

DiAngelo, R. (2018). *White Fragility: Why It's So Hard for White People to Talk about Racism.* Boston, MA: Beacon press.

Dickey, J. (May 31, 2016). The revolution on America's campuses. Retrieved on February 18, 2021 from https://time.com/4347099/college-campus-protests/

Dressel, J., & Farid, H. (2018). The accuracy, fairness, and limits of predicting recidivism. *Science Advances* 4(1). doi:10.1126/sciadv.aao5580.

Ezorsky, G. (1991). *Racism and Justice: The Case for Affirmative Action.* Ithaca, NY: Cornell University Press.

Fakhoury, L. (2017, November). Restorative justice [Video file]. Retrieved on January 11, 2021 from https://www.youtube.com/watch?v=MSy-qOiYjrA

Funk, A. (June 22, 2020). How domestic spying tools undermine racial justice protests. Retrieved on January 18, 2021 from https://freedomhouse.org/article/how-domestic-spying-tools-undermine-racial-justice-protests

Gale (2020). Black Lives Matter topic overview: Black Lives Matter. *Gale Opposing Viewpoints Online Collection.* Retrieved on January 14, 2021 from https://www.gale.com/open-access/Black-lives-matter

German, M. (June 26, 2020). The FBI targets a new generation of Black activists. Retrieved on February 24, 2021 from https://www.brennancenter.org/our-work/analysis-opinion/fbi-targets-new-generation-of-Black-activists

Gilman, M. (2013). The return of the welfare aueen. *Journal of Gender, Social Policy & the Law* 22:247–279.

Gillborn, D. (2015). Intersectionality, critical race theory, and the primacy of racism, class, gender, and disability in education. *Qualitative Inquiry* 21(3):277–287.

Gillborn, D., Rollock, N., Vincent, C., & Ball, S. J. (2012). You got a pass, so what more do you want? Race, class and gender intersections in the educational experiences of the Black middle class. *Race Ethnicity and Education* 15:121–139.

Gjelten, E. (February 5, 2019). What are zero tolerance policies in schools? Retrieved on January 4, 2021 from https://www.lawyers.com/legal-info/research/education-law/whats-a-zero-tolerance-policy.html

Goffman, A. (2009). On the run: Wanted men in a Philadelphia ghetto. *American Sociological Review* 74(3):339–357.

Goffman, A. (2014). *On the Run: Fugitive Life in an American City.* Chicago, IL: The University of Chicago Press.

Hagopian, J. (December 1, 2020). Making Black Lives Matter: The national movement has four key demands to eliminate racism in education. Retrieved from February 15, 2021 from https://progressive.org/magazine/making-Black-lives-matter-hagopian/

Harlow, C. (2003). *Education and Correctional Populations.* Bureau of Justice Statistics Special Report. Retrieved on January 20, 2021 from https://files.eric.ed.gov/fulltext/ED543577.pdf

Hines, D., Carter, A., & Dorinda. J. (2020). The effects of zero tolerance policies on Black girls: using critical race feminism and figured worlds to examine school discipline. *Urban Education* 55(10):1419–1440.

Hill, E., Tiefenthäler, A., Triebert, C., Jordan, D., Willis, H., & Stein, R. (May 31, 2020). How George Floyd was killed in police custody. Retrieved on January 12, 2021 from https://www.nytimes.com/2020/05/31/us/george-floyd-investigation.html

Holt, L., & Sweitzer, M. (2020). More than a black and white issue: Ethnic identity, social dominance orientation, and support for the black lives matter movement. *Self and Identity* 19(1):16–31.

Hoston, W. (June 24, 2020). Revealing a cultural truth: Not all Black Lives Matter. Retrieved on January 12, 2021 from https://www.pvamu.edu/blog/opinion-revealing-a-cultural-truth-not-all-Black-lives-matter/

Human Right Campaign Foundation. (2020). An epidemic of violence: Fatal violence against transgender and gender nonconforming people in the United States in 2020. Retrieved on January 25, 2021 from https://www.hrc.org/resources/an-epidemic-of-violence-fatal-violence-against-transgender-and-gender-non-conforming-people-in-the-u-s-in-2020

Hughes, C. (2018). From the long Arm of the state to eyes on the street: How poor African American mothers navigate surveillance in the social safety net. *Journal of Contemporary Ethnography* 48(3):339–376.

Hymowitz, K. (spring, 2005). What's holding Black kids back? Bill Cosby is right: The problem is the parents. Retrieved on January 23, 2021 from https://www.cityjournal.org/html/what%E2%80%99s-holding-Black-kids-back-12863.html

Ingraham, C. (November 16, 2017). Black men sentenced to more time for committing the exact same crime as a White person, study finds. Retrieved on February 11, 2021 from https://www.washingtonpost.com/news/wonk/wp/2017/11/16/Black-men-sentenced-to-more-time-for-committing-the-exact-same-crime-as-a-White-person-study-finds/

Johnson-Ahorlu, R. (2012). The academic opportunity gap: How racism and stereotypes disrupt the education of African American undergraduates. *Race Ethnicity and Education* 15(5):633–652.

Johnson, D., Tress, T., Burkel, N., Taylor, C., & Cesario, J. (2019). Officer characteristics and racial disparities in fatal officer-involved shootings *PNAS* 116(32):15877–15882.

Kamaloni, S. (2019). *Understanding Racism in a Post-racial World: Visible Invisibilities*. New York, NY: Palgrave Macmillan.

Kellaway, M., & Brydum, S. (January 12, 2016). The 21 trans women killed in 2015. *The Advocate*. Retrieved on January 11, 2020 from http://www.advocate.com/transgender/2015/07/27/

Ketels, C. (July 6, 2020). Black Lives Matter protests under aerial surveillance. Retrieved on January 19, 2021 from https://natoassociation.ca/Black-lives-matter-protests-under-aerial-surveillance/

Kim, C., Losen, D., & Hewitt, D. (2010). *The School-to-Prison Pipeline: Structuring Legal Reform*. New York, NY: New York University Press.

Korgen, K., White, J., &White, S. (2013). *Sociologists in Action: Sociology, Social Change, and Social Justice* (2nd ed.). Los Angeles, CA: Sage Publications.

Lerman, A., & Vesla, W. (2014). Staying out of sight? Concentrated policing and local political action. *Annals of the American Academy of Political and Social Science* 651(1):202–219.

Lewis, A., Hagerman, M., & Forman, T. (2019). The sociology of race & racism: Key concepts, contributions & debates. *Equity & Excellence in Education* 52(1):29–46.

Linda, S., & Silvio, W. (2017). *News of Baltimore: Race, Rage and the City*. New York, NY: Routledge Taylor & Francis.

Lubin, J. (2016). How sociology can support Black Lives Matter. Retrieved on January 19. 2021 from https://www.asanet.org/news-events/footnotes/dec-2016/features/how-sociology-can-support-Black-lives-matter

Luttrell, C. (2019). *White People and Black Lives Matter: Ignorance, Empathy, and Justice*. New York, NY: Palgrave Macmillan.

Mogul, J., Ritchie, A., & Whitlock, K. (2011). *Queer Injustice: The Criminalization of LGBT People in the United States*. Boston, MA: Beacon Press.

Moore, R., & Bellamy, J. (December 7, 2020). The Biden Administration must prioritize reversing Trump's damage to racial justice policy. Retrieved on January 4, 2021 from https://www.aclu.org/news/racial-justice/the-biden-administration-must-prioritize-reversing-trumps-damage-to-racial-justice-policy

Morris, M. (2016). *Pushout: The Criminalization of Black Girls in Schools*. New York, NY: The New Press.

Nell Edgar, A., & Johnson, A. (2019). *The Struggle over Black Lives Matter and All Lives Matter*. Lanham, MD: Lexington Books.

Noam, G., Warner, L., & Dyken, L. (2001). Beyond the rhetoric of zero tolerance: Long-term solutions for at-risk youth. *New Directions for Youth Development* 92:155–182.

Ocen, P. (2012). Punishing pregnancy: Race, incarceration, and the shackling of pregnant prisoners. *California Law Review* 100(5):1239–1311.

Remster, B., & Kramer, R. (2018). Race, space, and surveillance: Understanding the relationship between criminal justice contact and institutional involvement. *Sociological Research for a Dynamic World* 4:1–16.

Shantel, B., Cassi, C., San, G., Onoso, I., Verna, K., & Hadi, K., Catherine, L., Sarah, M., Victor, R., & Wendy, R. (2020). Systemic anti-Black racism must be dismantled: Statement by the American Sociological Association section on racial and ethnic minorities. *Sociology of Race and Ethnicity* 6(3):289–291.

Skiba, R. (2014). The failure of zero tolerance. *Reclaiming Children and Youth* 22(4): 27–33.

Steven, F. (1988). Explaining and blaming: Racism and Sociology. *Patterns of Prejudice* 22(1):21–30.

Swartz, O. (2019).The struggle over Black Lives Matter and All Lives Matter. *Rhetoric Review* 38(4):489–492.

Tabak, R. (1986). The death of fairness: The arbitrary and capricious imposition of the death penalty in the 1980s. *Review of Law & Social Change* 14(4):797–848.

Tawa, J., Ma, R., & Katsumoto, S. (2016). "All Lives Matter": The cost of color-blind racial attitudes in diverse social networks. *Race and Social Problems* 8(2):196–208.

The Civil Rights Project, Advancement Project (June 01, 2000). Opportunities suspended: The devastating consequences of zero tolerance and school discipline policies. Retrieved on January 4, 2021 from https://www.civilrightsproject.ucla.edu/research/k-12-education/school-discipline/opportunities-suspended-the-devastating-consequences-of-zero-tolerance-and-school-discipline-policies

The Guardian (June 9, 2013). Edward Snowden: the whistle-blower behind the NSA surveillance revelations. Retrieved on January 16, 2021 from https://www.theguardian.com/world/2013/jun/09/edward-snowden-nsa-whistleblower-surveillance

Thompson, C. (June 17, 2020). Abolish the (Tone) Police. Retrieved on January 12, 2020 from https://540westmain.org/2020/06/17/abolish-the-tone-police-by-chris-thompson/

Thornhill, T. (2019). We want Black students, just not you: How White admissions counselors screen Black prospective students. *Sociology of Race and Ethnicity* 5(4):456–470.

U.S. Department of Education Office for Civil Rights. (2014). Civil rights data collection data snapshot: School discipline. Issue Brief #. Retrieved on January 15, 2021 from https://eric.ed.gov/?q=source%3A%22Office+for+Civil+Rights%2C+US+Department+of+Education%22&id=ED577231

Uhlmann, T. (1978). Black elite decision making: The case of trial judges. *American Journal of Political Science* 22:884–895.

Weissinger, S., Mack, D., & Watson, E. (2017). *Violence against Black Bodies: An Intersectional Analysis of How Black Lives Continue to Matter.* New York, NY: Routledge Taylor and Francis Group.

Chapter 8

Gender and Sexuality Perspective

Cecy Edijala Balogun

This chapter places emphasis on the importance of women's lives in the narrative of the Black Lives versus All Lives Matter debate. The chapter considers gender-based violence (GBV) in Africa and argues that social issues like violence against women are a global menace that defies racial, cultural, religious, and socioeconomic boundaries because women everywhere experience diverse forms of violence that threaten their dignity and existence, from the home to the society in which they interact daily. The chapter aims to situate the importance of women's lives in the global sphere where a definition of whose life should be protected or ignored is fast becoming a debate among social movements globally.

The killing of a seventeen-year-old African American, Trayvon Martin by a neighborhood watch volunteer, George Zimmerman in Florida, and the discriminatory approach to justice generated protests on February 26, 2012, led by Patrisse Cullors, Alicia Garza, and Opal Tometi, which metamorphosed into the Black Lives Matter movement (Hoffman et al., 2016). On May 20, 2020, another African American, George Floyd was killed by a white police officer in the United States, leading to a fresh wave of protests that quickly spread to other countries with the social media hashtag #BlackLivesMatter. In a counter-protest, the All Lives Matter movement came out to the streets and also infiltrated social spaces with the #AllLivesMatter hashtag.

These protest movements, which attracted various groups from several countries, call to question, which life matters; black lives, blue lives, all lives, no life, and so on? Going by the narratives of the protests about black lives or all lives matter, what cannot be ignored is the undertone of racial discrimination as a driver of individual or group participation in these movements.

While the narratives of protest movements against racial discrimination against blacks are taking a global dimension, with people in the global south lending their voices to the brutality against blacks, especially in the United States, it is pertinent to draw the attention of such proponents and other apologists that other dimensions of social deprivations and discriminations exist; discrimination against women, either from the home, workplace, or society. These discriminations have reached alarming levels, especially violence against women, yet hardly mentioned, resisted, criminalized, nor condemned by the formal systems in different parts of the world.

The Black Lives Matter movement, which raises issues about people whose voices were silenced as a result of their identities, clearly explains the experiences of millions of women, who suffer marginalization and various forms of discrimination that infringe on their rights due to their gender. What however one cannot deny as the question of whose life matters is what perspective one focuses on in queries that have to do with abuse of human rights or denial to life as pursued by the social movements, like the Black or All Lives Matter movements or other social movements that permeate the global society.

In Africa, daily reportage of different forms of violence against women abound, and although pockets of cries from different social movements, both in off and on-line spaces are resulting in gradual changes in the approaches of African governments toward GBV, who provided laws to protect women. However, the poor implementation of such laws has continued to encourage perpetrators of such violence, and has made the crime prevalent in the continent.

The United Nations defined GBV as an act that results in or is likely to result in physical, sexual, mental harm, or suffering to women, including threats of such acts, coercion or arbitrary deprivation of liberty, whether occurring in public or private life (United Nations, 1993 cited in Muluneh et al., 2020).

The chapter attempts to address GBV in Africa by providing answers to three critical questions: (1) In what ways is GBV enabled and what forms of GBV are perpetrated against women in Africa? (2) what are the contributions of social movements in changing the narratives of GBV in Africa? (3) What have been the efforts of African governments toward curbing the menace of GBV on the continent?

This chapter argues that although diverse forms of discrimination abound that have threatened various groups and limit their aspirations to a better life and access to opportunities, violence against women has reached a red level, calling for critical attention; given its spread and prevalence in recent, particularly in Africa. Therefore, it should be seen as a collective social menace that should gain the attention of all social movements, irrespective of race, culture, social classes, or religions since it affects all women globally. The chapter further argues that GBV has persisted over the years because of the structural failures of the society, and with the opportunities offered by new media sources like the internet-enabled social media platforms, which are fast contributing to social change in this century, positive results can be achieved in the social transforming of women's experiences and aspirations for a better life.

This chapter uses secondary data sources from the internet, journal articles, publications, and personal observations on the trends of GBV in the Nigerian society and other African countries, vis-à-vis global reportage of issues of GBV to anchor the discourse on GBV in Africa.

The significance of this chapter hinges upon how the narratives of GBV in the African continent and the frightening huge number of victims that cut across generations are explicated. The need for governments at the global and country levels, social change proponents and movements, and policymakers to pay attention to this social crime against women in Africa becomes imperative. The chapter will provide evidential instances that will draw the attention of policymakers in Africa and at the global level, to move away from attempts at enacting laws against GBV to implementation of such laws, which is most needed if the growing trends of violence against women will be checked in the continent. The chapter will also help movements of social change to begin to pay more attention to issues like GBV that have a global implication on women's well-being than a discriminative approach with racial undertones that are harmful to the coexistence that globalization promotes.

The rest of the chapter will focus on the theoretical grounding of the chapter, using the African Feminist Theory, GBV in Africa with emphasis on its enablers, forms of GBV and the impact on women in the continent, social movements as avenues of changing the narratives of GBV in Africa, drawing attention to how the use of social media platforms and hashtags to protest against GBV in the continent is contributing to raising the voices of women in spheres where their cries were formally unheard, the responses of African governments to GBV, and recommendations for policymakers.

GENDER AND SEXUALITY: A CONCEPTUAL DISCUSSION

The concepts of gender and sexuality are conceptualized in the context of this chapter. They are presented separately for lucidity.

Gender

Gender is a social construct that describes the social attributes and opportunities that define men and women. It is not biologically ascribed but learned through socialization. Gender defines the roles and responsibilities of men and women that are created in the family, culture, or society in which people live (United Nations Educational, Scientific and Cultural Organization, UNESCO, 2003). It is the system of relations between men and women that describes their characteristics, behaviors, attitudes, roles, and status, which are ascribed by the society in a given social, economic, political, or cultural context to govern the relationships among the sexes and such roles are dynamic, modified by the systems that operate in a given society (Annan-Yao, 2004; UNESCO, 2003). Gender determines what is expected, allowed, and valued in women or men in a given context, and operate within the broader sociocultural context (United Nations (UN) Women, 2002).

UN Women (2002) noted that in many societies, inequalities between women and men abound in the responsibilities that are assigned, activities they partake in, access to and control over resources, and in opportunities to male decision. For example, Annan-Yao (2004) noted that gender relations in patrilineal communities are different from what is obtainable in matrilineal communities where women have liberty to express themselves and have a level of influence in decision-making processes, and access to inheritance. In patrilineal societies, which is the practice in Africa, women are expected to be submissive to men, are scarcely allowed to express themselves, and lack decision-making power.

Arguably in Africa, men's domination over women is not dependent only on whether the society is patriarchal; by the design of the African society, domination of men over women also prevails irrespective of social status of the women and the position they occupy in the society. Such male dominance over women in the African society encourages gender inequalities and gender stereotypes. Male dominance over women is expressed, among others, in GBV, which occurs from the home to the society. The social systems in Africa is designed in such a way that women are generally expected to be subject to men and are not allowed to express their views, even when they are subjected to oppressive behaviors. This makes it easy for men to take advantage of women and abuse them.

Additionally, the dynamic nature of the society is also providing a new narrative that is challenging the gender stereotypes in Africa, just as is obtainable in other parts of the world. Women are becoming more educated and economically empowered, they are beginning to rise to levels in the society once dominated by men and as a way of attempting to resist their enviable placement in the society, they are threatened and resisted by men through marginalization and various acts of discrimination, including GBV.

In order to bridge the gap that is created in the society due to the ascription of dominance of men over women, either as a result of culture, socioeconomic status, political, or religious systems that are inherent in a given society, which is creating grounds for marginalization against women in the society and exposing them to GBV, the call for gender equality and gender equity from various quarters of the society is apparent. Gender equality and equity are necessary for the full expression of women's rights and responsibilities in the society.

Gender equality implies equal conditions for men and women in realizing their full human rights and for contributing to and benefiting from economic, social, cultural, and political development (UNESCO, 2003). It implies equal rights, responsibilities, and opportunities that are available to men and women, boys and girls (UN Women, 2002). It means giving men and women equal rights and valuing the roles they play in the society equally, either in the home, work place, or society. Gender equity on the other hand addresses fairness to both women and men, that is, giving both an equal playing ground in the society. Gender equity is the means of achieving gender equality (UNESCO, 2003). That is when women are properly valued; their place in the society is given as much relevance as how men are valued, and at liberty to make decisions and express themselves, it will make it easy for gender equality to be achieved in the society.

The opportunities that social interaction offer in a global space that has reduced the world to a community through the internet and social media networks is fast changing the way gender is understood even in Africa. Women are becoming expressive, airing their voices in public spaces and changing decisions that affect them. They are beginning to raise their voices against violation of their rights in the society, especially GBV. Hence, an understanding of the roles and responsibilities of men and women, and a redefinition of equality of men and women in the African context, will help to change the way women are perceived in the society; as voiceless members of the society who should not speak out, even when they are badly treated, either by their intimate partners or abusers in the society, who want to take advantage of them because they are women.

Sexuality

Sex implies the biological characteristics that defines humans as females or males. It is the condition of being male or female, which is differentiated based on the reproductive roles of individuals. While sex is generally used to refer to sexual activity, technically, in the context of sexuality, sex is defined as the biological characteristics that define humans as female or male World Health Organization (WHO) (2021). It is the central aspect of being human, including sex, gender identities and roles, sexual orientation, erotism, pleasure, intimacy, and reproduction (WHO, 2006; cited in WHO, 2021).

Sexuality was traditionally understood as the concept that explains human relationships expressed through sex, either as a man or women. sexuality is the basis for the procreation of human beings, through sexual union of the opposite sex (Okechi, 2018). The concept of sexuality is differently implied in different parts of the world and across cultural groups. While it is understood in some societies as a sacred issue that is protected by the societal norms and value systems, in other cultures, sexuality is understood as an individual expression that is not premised on societal beliefs. While the latter is the understanding in most of the western societies, in Africa, notion of sexuality and how it is expressed is entrenched in the cultural beliefs and norms of the society. Sexuality is particularly held in high esteem in the African societies as it helps to define how men and women relate, within the communal norms and belief patterns.

The dynamism of the social and cultural definition of how men and women are perceived and understood in the society makes it easy for people's rights to be ignored. The wrong impression about human sexuality is being exploited globally for abusing women and in Africa, the eroded in the traditional African societies, the concept of sexuality was recognized as an individual right that is guided by the norms and values of the society where the individual lives. However, due to the influence of the western cultures on Africa, the notion of sexuality has taken new definitions, away from the traditional meanings that attach so much relevance on the sacredness of sexuality and sexual union. The western influence in Africa draws a new direction to how sexuality is understood and expressed; which is away from the group, communal, or societal checks and balances based on cultures, to a more liberal understanding as an individual perception on relating with the opposite sex.

Sexual rights are entrenched on the international conventions that protect human rights, in this regards, WHO (2006) cited in WHO (2021) defined sexual rights to include rights that are critical to the realization of sexual health; rights to equality and non-discrimination; the right to be free from torture or to cruel, inhumane or degrading treatment or punishment; the right to privacy; the rights to the highest attainable standard of health (including sexual health) and social security; the right to marry and be found a family and enter marriage with the free and full consent of the intending spouses and to equality in and at the dissolution of the marriage; and the right to an effective remedy for the violations of fundamental rights.

The rights of individuals and the social groups within which the individual interacts are defining considerations in sexual relationships in Africa and while the individual has the right to know and explore it, the social group has the right to maintain their collective conscience in what portrays the society as good or bad (Okechi, 2018). The unwritten rules that guided the behavior of members of the society help to maintain the sanctity of sexual union in the African society Okechi (2018).

Hence, while individuals have the rights to express their sexuality, the rights of others also have to be protected. The African perspective that dignifies sexuality has to be upheld to reduce the prevalence of GBV against women in the continent.

THEORETICAL FRAMEWORK

This section discusses the theoretical grounding of GBV in the African context. The African Feminist Theory forms the theoretical anchor for the discourses on GBV for the chapter.

Feminism describes movements that are established to challenge the social, political, and ideological issues that center around social equality between women and men in society. Feminist Theory analyzes how women and men are ascribed roles and responsibilities in society, condemn the subordination of women, which is engendered by gender inequalities that amplify patriarchy above womanhood. The theory focuses on such themes as discrimination against women, gender stereotypes, oppression, and patriarchy and is developed to challenge gender stereotypes, arguing that educational, professional, and interpersonal opportunities and outcomes for women should be equal to those that men enjoy. Proponents of Feminist Theory argue that society places priorities on the male's perspectives of issues, while women are largely ignored and treated unjustly in society.

The uniqueness of African women led to the development of African Feminist Theory, which addresses women's issues from the African perspective. African feminism was established by African women to address the challenges that African women who reside in the continent are confronted with. It explains the collective experiences of African women within the African context; their geographic location and ideology (Nkealah, 2006; Herr, 2017). The theory establishes a new, liberal, productive, and self-reliant African woman within the heterogeneous cultures of Africa in a bid to transform the cultural practices of the continent to address women's concerns in society (Nkealah, 2006). Terborg-Penn (1995) highlighted two dominant values in the African Feminist Theory to include advocating for self-reliance through the female networks and developing survival strategies, which have become entrenched in many African communities.

Most African feminists agree that African feminism stemmed from the global feminist movement, nevertheless, they argue that African feminism is grounded in their strength, challenges, and historical achievements as Africans (Nnaemeka, 2004 cited in Herr, 2017). They focus on the collectivistic nature of their societies, the importance of ethnic groupings, kinship, and extended families (Ouzgane & Morell, 2005 cited in Herr, 2017), thus differentiating themselves from the individualistic nature of western feminism, which runs contrary to the intricacies of the sociocultural environment of the African feminists (Herr, 2017).

Proponents of the African Feminist Theory contend that African women's bodies cannot be separated from their cultural environment, which is seen as a failure from the perspective of western feminists (Thiam, 1995; cited in Herr, 2017). They also argue that a self-definition of feminism from the African perspective highlights their needs, realities, oppression, and empowerment in the context of their particular environment (Kolawole, 2002).

Critiques of the African Feminist Theory have argued that Africa is not a monolith since the continent comprised differences in ethnicity and political and religious orientations (Kolawole, 2002). They contended that bringing these varied culturally different women under one umbrella affects their perception of the world. Mikell (1997) cited in Herr (2017) highlighted a weakness of African Feminist Theory as the absence of a clearly defined and established framework.

Given the threats that GBV poses to women's dignity and survival globally and in African in particular, African Feminist Theory provides a basis for situating the chapter. Firstly, the structural ascription of roles and responsibilities to men and women in the African context was designed in such a way that women are generally believed to be subordinates to men and are not expected to be heard, and in some cultures and religions, not even to be seen. This situation has been exploited by men to oppress women and perpetuates all forms of unimaginable violence against women, and out of fear for cultural norms and religious beliefs, women hardly cry out and not report such acts of abuse against them. Secondly, the weaknesses in the implementation of enacted laws that condemn GBV make the offense thrive since perpetrators are hardly brought to book. Hence, the African Feminist Theory fits appropriately for the discourse on GBV, which attempts to change the narrative of how GBV is seen and addressed in Africa, given the prevalence of the act, which occurs in all spaces of the women's endeavors.

GENDER-BASED VIOLENCE AGAINST WOMEN IN AFRICA

Women are pivotal to the development of the global community. They contribute to every facet of human development, working and adapting to very difficult terrains and situations. However, they are confronted by a host of social challenges in all places of their daily activities, from the home to the wider society. While society is quick to react to social issues that have a racial dimension, a common social menace that affects the white and the black, which has risen to a pandemic level, yet highly ignored, is discrimination against women, in all spheres of life. Discrimination against women is either racial or gender-based. Although racial discrimination tends to be limited to women who have migrant status, gender-related discrimination affects all women, irrespective of their racial positioning, cultural, religious orientation, and economic status. The United Nations Office of the High Commissioner for Human Rights (UNOHCHR, 2001) noted that the double exposure of women to discrimination as a result of their gender and race puts them at a greater risk of violence.

Over the years, there has been a growing level of marginalization and violence against women; their voices are inaudible and their social challenges given minimal attention in the actual sense of the word, particularly in Africa. Several factors account for the relative silence or negligence of governments toward the growing levels of GBV in the African continent. For example, the UNOHCHR (2001) observed that most societies have normalized GBV due to the racial, national, cultural, or religious beliefs that are practiced or the reluctance of the government to address situations that could further expose women to violence. The problem has persisted in the continent because when women attempt to speak against it, they are tagged disrespectful, anti-cultural, or corrupted by western cultures. Hence, some of the enablers of GBV are highlighted in the following subsections.

Migrant Status

Migrants are exposed to GBV as they attempt to escape from conflict zones or abuses by intimate partners either in transit or at their destinations (Anja, 2017). Like migrants, women who became refugees due to conflict or natural disasters are also highly vulnerable to gender-based abuses. Anja (2017) reported that 23 percent of female Burundian refugees admitted to experiences of GBV.

The inability of migrants to obtain means of livelihood in their countries of abode also exposes them to GBV as men often require sex from them as an alternative for providing opportunities for employment for them. As a result of such shameful exposures, several women have taken to prostitution as an aftermath of abuse for survival. In the view of the UNOHCHR (2001), migrant women are faced with triple discrimination of being women, foreigners, and prostitutes. As a result of their migrant status, such women hardly cry out; they bear their pain and exposures silently, with only pockets of their experiences made known to institutional forces that are saddled with the responsibility to address their plight.

Poverty and Lack of Employment among Women

In the African continent, women play prime roles in the family. Apart from child and home care, they contribute to the family's income by engaging in income-generating activities, either as low-income earners in low-paying jobs or as executives in high-profile positions in public and private spaces. Poverty contributes to GBV in several African countries, especially when the family's means of livelihood is low and can hardly cater to their socioeconomic needs. Most domestic violence against women especially intimate partner violence is driven by arguments over resources to meet family needs. For instance, Denney and Ibrahim (2012) noted that the occurrences of economic violence in homes trigger domestic violence, as the inability to contribute their quota to the upkeep of the family often results in instances where women are abused in the homes by their partners.

The limited employment opportunities for women also drive GBV against them in society. Even where employment opportunities are available, women are often discriminated against and sexually exploited by men in such work environments. UNOHCHR (2001) noted that women also constitute greater portions of employees in the services and entertainment sectors that have a high potential for abuse and discrimination.

Conflict

The Special Rapporteur on violence against women described conflict-related violence against women and girls as one of history's greatest silences (Ward, 2013). According to UNOHCHR (2001), in times of armed conflict, ethnic or conflict resulting from racial differences, systematic rapes, forced pregnancy or abortion, sexual abuse, sexual slavery, and other human rights violations against women are prevalent, and that women are the targets at such times not only because of their race and sex but because they are perceived to represent the honor of the opposing ethnic group, using it as a strategy to undermine the morale of a community. A countless number of women of all ages are exposed to GBV due to conflict situations in Africa, where conflict is persistently on the increase, ranging from civil wars, ethnic rivalries, religious upheavals, terror attacks, and so on, which have resulted in situations where entire communities have been sacked, and several million in displacement camps, thereby exposing women to all forms of GBV. Although more men are killed during wars, women are more disproportionately affected by the sexual and other forms of gender-related violence that are characteristics of conflict.

A 2010 study in the Eastern DRC on the prevalence of GBV at different stages of conflict revealed that almost 40 percent of women were survivors of sexual violence (Ward, 2013). The story is similar in Sierra Leone where an estimated 50,000 to 64,000 women who were internally displaced during the conflict in the country reported they had experienced conflict-related assaults (Ward, 2013). The 1994 genocide in Rwanda saw between 250,000 and 500,000 women raped and in a similar report, following the Sierra Leonean civil war, 94 percent of households reported that at least one member was sexually assaulted during the war (Anja, 2017). While several war crimes are placed within the purview of the international criminal court, a question that should be a focus in this century, if GBV in conflict situations would be addressed, is what efforts should be made to divorce women's abuse from the issues that should be the focus of wars. This is only achievable when attention is paid to the plight of women who are victims of wars they hardly know anything about, yet being used as bait, booty, and price for conquest.

Social and Cultural Norms

GBV has been identified by the European Council (2011) cited in Le Masson et al. (2018) as one of the social mechanisms through which women are held in subordination to men. In Africa, as is the practice in other parts of the world, women have always been dominated by men, suffering social and cultural discrimination. The cultural practices in Africa put women at a disadvantage compared to men. Although GBV is perpetrated not only against women and girls but also men as are they too are victims in some cases (Hook, 2010), however, the cultural dominance of women by men especially in patriarchal societies makes room for discriminative inequality between women and men. For example, the Gender Equality Index Report, which measures reproductive health, employment, and empowerment, reveals that twenty-seven of the thirty countries that display gender inequalities are in Africa (UN, 2015 in Muluneh et al., 2020). In the most recent report, Nigeria, Chad, and the Democratic Republic of the Congo, rank 128, 147, and 149 respectively, out of 153 countries assessed in the 2020 Global Gender Gap Index (World Economic Forum, 2020).

African cultures encourage patriarchy and since women are at the receiving end of practices that are inimical to their social wellbeing, culture is often exploited for abusing them. The society's design that provides a ground for power inequality creates an imbalance, which makes it even difficult for women who have suffered abuse to report their experiences or seek justice. Le Masson et al. (2018) noted that power inequality is an everyday experience for women and that violence against women is not restricted to conflict situations but represents a daily occurrence of patriarchal domination. The cultural beliefs that provide a thriving ground for women to be abused are so grounded in some societies that domestic violence by intimate partners is hardly frowned upon; it is seen as part of a cultural expression of love by the husband to the wife (Denney & Ibrahim, 2012). Where such beliefs are held, abused women have no voice to cry out as they are silenced by culture thereby empowering their abusers who would come to believe that their partners are only objects of abuse, rather than see them as partners to be treasured and protected.

Poor Access to Redress Mechanisms

Given the social imbalance in the society that holds women in subordination to men and the cultural and religious beliefs in Africa, which forbids women to speak out in public, expressing the pain, which women feel who have experienced GBV, is a serious challenge. As earlier observed, GBV has been described as a silent pandemic that is fast eating deep into the fabrics of the society and Africa in particular, with the frequent spate of its occurrences without any serious action by governments to curb it. From Nigeria to South Africa, Namibia to Burundi, the story is the same. It is not different in other countries around the world, where the news media are awash of reportage of women's abuse daily, with little or no stories of perpetrators of such crimes being punished.

A major limitation to redress for victims of GBV is the poor access to redress mechanisms in Africa. The lack of legal standing, limited access to public places, bias against women in the judicial system, cultural insensitivity, and illiteracy constitute barriers to women's access to redress mechanisms (UNOHCHR, 2001). Even though there are existing laws against GBV in several African countries, what is lacking is the implementation of such laws. Most of them have weak implementation frameworks as a result of which perpetrators are hardly punished, hence making the crime thrive in the continent. The UN Women (2020) report indicated that less than 40 percent of women who experience violence report it or seek support. Women hardly report cases of GBV due to fear of inaction or hostility by law enforcement agents who have also been indicted as perpetrators of such violence against them. The poor reportage of cases of rape in Nigeria is due to the lack of trust of the law enforcement agents, who themselves have also been accused of similar abuse of unsuspecting women. For instance, Amnesty International (2017) reported that many women who were detained for criminal offenses and lack the financial capacity to pay bribes are often victims of rape by security personnel in Nigeria. Independent Advisory Group on Country Information (IAGCI), (2015) also noted that allegations of rapes were hardly investigated and sentences for persons sentenced for rape and other sex-related offenses were often few and inconsistent in Nigeria, which may also serve as a discouragement to women in seeking redress.

Hence, one can safely say that changing the narrative of GBV will require the provision of a safe and credible environment for women to freely express themselves, not only by the enactment of laws that protect the rights of women but also the follow-through to ensure that such laws are carried to the letter as well as purging the law enforcement system that is also abetting the crime against women in distress.

FORMS OF VIOLENCE AGAINST WOMEN

Violence against women occurs in any form or place and is perpetrated by people that intimate or not intimate with them. Violence against women knows no cultural or racial barrier; women of all colors, socioeconomic status, or cultural background are exposed to one form of GBV or another. GBV is defined based on the relationship between the perpetrator and the victim into intimate partner violence or non-intimate partner violence and can be in the form of sexual, physical, or emotional violence (USAID, 2010 in Muluneh et al., 2020).

Intimate Partner Violence

UN Women (2020) noted that even before the outbreak of COVID-2019, an estimated 243 million women and girls were abused by an intimate partner in 2019. Intimate partner violence is the most known and researched form of violence against women and girls and is highly prevalent in Africa, especially Sub-Saharan Africa where it is as high as 65.64 percent (World Health Organization, WHO, 2013). The trend of intimate partner violence against women is similar across the continent. In West Africa, intimate partners have also been reported to be the main perpetrators of domestic violence against women. In a study on intimate partner violence in 1998, Ward (2013) noted that 66.7 percent of participants reported that they had been physically molested by intimate partners. In a similar report, the Guardian (2019) reported that about 137 sexual offenses are committed daily against women in South Africa, with about thirty women killed by their spouses each month. In Namibia, Oduah (2020) noted that between 2016 and 2019, over 3,000 cases of rape and 209 cases of domestic violence were reported, just as Melber (2020) decried the high incidences of intimate partner violence, rape, incest, and other forms of sexual abuses being on the rise in Namibia.

The prevalence of intimate partner violence in Africa is engendered by weak laws that fail to protect women from such violence. For example, The U.S. Department of State (2014) cited in IAGCI (2015) reported that in Nigeria, some federal laws permit the husbands to chastise their wives using physical means as long as such means do not result in injuries like loss of sight, hearing, speech, or life-threatening injuries. The high reportage of intimate partner violence notwithstanding, it has continued to be prevalent across the continent unchecked, further confirming the negligence by the governments in stemming the trend in the continent.

Sexual Violence

In Africa, diverse forms of sexual violence are perpetrated against women to frightening dimensions, ranging from raping of Septuagint women to minors as young as five years old, and gang-raping, which is becoming rampant. The Nigerian minister of women affairs and social development stated that about two million Nigerians, mainly women, and girls, are raped yearly (WHO, 2020). Ipas (2020) also noted that at least one in three girls are expected to experience sexual abuse before they attain the age of twenty-five. Similar stories are also reported in different countries in the continent of cases of rape. Gang rape is also becoming a common dimension of violence against women in Nigeria, especially minors. For example, there was a reported case of eleven men raping a twelve-year-old girl, as well as a trending case of a gang-raping of a twenty-two-year-old undergraduate student at the point of her studies in a church (Ipas, 2020).

High rates of sexual violence also permeate the educational institutions of several African countries, where female students are continually threatened and exposed to sexual abuse by male lecturers. For instance, between 2017 and 2018, about 3500 cases of pregnancy were reported among students in the northern region in Namibia, resulting in the dropping out of school of about 2,000 students (Melber, 2020). Also citing the UNESCO representative in Namibia, Melber (2020) noted that an estimated one-fifth of teenagers in Namibia was reported of having unintended pregnancies, with about 40 percent of such cases resulting from non-consensual sex, that is, rape-related cases. In recent, sex for grades has become common terminology in the university system in several African countries; a practice where female students are coerced by male lecturers to engage in sexual affairs with them in exchange for high academic scores. British Broadcasting Corporation (BBC) Africa (2019) reported several cases of academia who were caught on camera harassing female students for marks in Nigeria and Ghana, where the practice has been reported rampant. They were suspended by their institutions when such video recordings were made viral on social media.

Early Marriage

The prevalence of child marriage is also a global challenge, cutting across countries, cultures, and religions. However, the practice is highly prevalent in Africa, which is reported to having the highest record of child marriage in the world, accounting for six out of the ten countries with the highest child marriage prevalence in the world and over 50 percent of the global prevalence level (United Nations Children's Fund, (UNICEF), 2018). The report also indicated that child marriage in West and Central Africa is as high as 41 percent, which implies that four out of ten girls and young women, representing sixty million were married before the attainment of age eighteen (UNICEF, 2018). Niger Republic is credited for having the highest level of child marriage globally, accounting for 76 percent, Central African Republic 68 percent, and Chad 67 percent. In Chad, for example, a study showed that 30 percent of women aged twenty-five to forty-nine got married before the age of fifteen, and more than 70 percent got married before they were 18 (Le Masson et al., 2018). The narrative is the same in Nigeria, with an estimated twenty-two million child brides, representing 40 percent of all child brides in the African region (UNICEF, 2018). These figures portray another dimension of GBV that puts the future of millions of women at risk, since early marriage denies them access to a good life, not counting the health and other implications.

Structural Violence

The various forms of GBV described earlier, which have continued to threaten the survival of women in societies where their plights are hardly addressed, are engendered by the structures of the social, political, economic, cultural, and religious systems of the society. The structural problems also constitute forms of violence against women. Structural violence is entrenched in the gender inequality occasioned by the failures of the laws, institutions, and social norms that created the tolerant environment for GBV to thrive in Africa.

The notion of male dominance over women that is culturally promoted in the continent and expressed by the societal ascription of roles and responsibilities puts women in subordination to men and is exploited by men to perpetrate all forms of violence against women. Women are seen as powerless members of society (UNOHCHR, 2001) and are easy prey based on societal design. Women in rural areas (UN, 2015 cited in Muluneh et al., 2020), uneducated women, especially due to poverty and the preference of educating the males over the females, women who lack access to legal structures, either due to fear of being taken advantage of stigmatization or the absence of such legal structures in their localities, women who have low socioeconomic status, women who lack easy access to employment opportunities, and so on are all victims of the structural violence engendered by their societies

(UNOHCHR, 2001; Denny and Ibrahim, 2012; UN, 2015, cited in Muluneh et al., 2020; Le Masson et al., 2018).

IMPACT OF GENDER-BASED VIOLENCE ON WOMEN IN AFRICA

Violence against women is a broad-based problem that affects women in all walks of life, perpetrated by men, other women, family members, community, and even the state, and is experienced at various times in their lifecycle; from birth to old age (Solotaro & Pande, 2014). GBV has short and long implications on women's physical, sexual, reproductive, and mental health and their personal and social wellbeing (WHO, 2020).

GBV exposes women to injuries, unwanted pregnancies, sexually transmitted diseases, such as HIV, pelvic pain, urinary tract infections, fistula, genital injuries, pregnancy complications, and chronic conditions (WHO, 2020). Ward (2013) noted that thousands of women and girls in Congo suffer from tears in the vagina, bladder, and rectum due to rape experiences during the conflict in which guns and branches were used to violate them, in the same report, about 91 percent of rape survivors in the South Kivu region of the country were reported to suffer from severe rape-related illnesses. The exposure of young girls whose reproductive systems are not fully developed to early marriage destroys their reproductive systems, with many of them having complications like fistula. The WHO (2020) reported that GBV affects the mental health of women, as it leads to cases of posttraumatic stress disorders (PTSD), depression, anxiety, substance misuse, self-harm and suicidal behavior, sleep disturbances, and so forth.

Socially, pregnancies resulting from sexual abuse increase the likelihood of young girls dropping out of school, and they are forced into marriages for which they are hardly prepared, denying them a future of hope and accomplishment. The stigmatization that accompanies rape also exposes women to suicidal behaviors and in worse scenarios where the family or community fails to acknowledge their situation as cases of rape, but rather condemns them for an act that was beyond their control, many young women are denied family and communal support. Further, UNOHCHR (2001) noted that violence against women during times of war also exposes them to pregnancy and stigmatization, and they are also socially ostracized.

Given these narratives, the value that is placed on women is greatly eroded, and when several African countries were responding to the protests against blacks following the killing of George Floyd, one wonders what effort is being put in place to address the series of GBV that have led to the emotional and mental deaths of thousands of women in the continent. While the chapter does not condemn the Black Lives Matter movement, the issue of what constitutes what society perceives as socially acceptable in most cases is based on popular trends. Women are continually being abused in Africa, yet a persistent cry is necessary if the issue must gain the attention of those whose responsibility it is to address it, not only in the African continent but also globally, since GBV cuts across all races and cultures.

PROTEST MOVEMENTS: AVENUES OF SOCIAL CHANGE FOR THE MARGINALIZED IN THE TWENTY-FIRST CENTURY

Hoffman et al. (2016) stated that without disruption, there will be no change. If the rising problem of violence against women in all spaces of their endeavors is to be addressed, the orderly processes and systems that provide a breeding ground for such violence to thrive have to be disrupted. Hoffman et al. (2016) argued that sometimes disruptions of the formal system is necessary for the existence of a fair democratic process as failure to disrupt the system that hardly addresses the social concern of the marginalized implies that the channels of change, which ordinarily are not accessible to the marginalized, will continue to elude them. In systems where the social concerns of women are not visible to those in authority, protests can be used to challenge unsocial behaviors, tendencies, and policies that discriminate against the rights and privileges of women in society.

Analyzing the Black Lives Matter movement in America, the protests following the killings of black African Americans that led to the establishment of the movement challenged the political institutions in the country, when it appeared justice was miscarried, in favor of the whites, trivializing the lives of the blacks through a discriminating legal system. Both the protests against the killing of Trayvon Martin in 2012 and George Floyd in 2020 amplify the relevance of social movements in changing the silence and injustice against the marginalized in the society, which in these cases relate to racial discrimination.

Protest movements have also been used to challenge unacceptable social treatments in Africa, since colonial times. Following the amalgamation of Nigeria in 1914, women protested against the British colonial and indigenous leaders when they were denied opportunities in decision-making processes (Salami, 2018). Another popular protest that was staged by women in Nigeria as early as 1929 was the Aba women's riot, which was on the instance of the plans by the colonial rulers to include women in tax payment. The protest attracted over 10,000 women who challenged the government of the day and succeeded in changing the policy, which was detrimental to their socioeconomic well-being. Similarly, in Sierra Leone, about 10,000 women challenged British rule in 1951 by staging a protest against a proposed increase in market dues and the inflation in food prices by the Lebanese, who were sole distributors of food (Chioma, 2005 cited in Medie, 2013).

A major achievement of the social movements in the late twenty-first century, especially in these contemporary times, is the visibility and freedom of expression they enjoy due to the technological advancement through social media networks. Drawing from the pieces of evidence of the Black Lives Matter in the United States and the End SARS protest against police brutality in Nigeria in 2020, the place of protest movements in challenging unfriendly government policies, abuse of public office, and marginalization against women cannot be overemphasized. Hoffman et al. (2016) pointed out that people who lack the privilege and power to address their social challenges will seek alternative ways to draw the attention of the government, and protest movements in social spaces are fast adopting this approach.

Drawing from the historic and recent shreds of evidence of women who succeeded in making their grievances known through protests in Africa, the problem of GBV, which has assumed an alarming rate, stands a chance of being curbed when women in African countries rise up to the challenge to put forth their protests against such social menace.

SOCIAL MEDIA AND PROTEST MOVEMENTS IN AFRICA

The internet and social media platforms increase the speed, reach, and effectiveness of social movements, making a positive impact on the result of social mobilizations for challenging societal ills. For example, Buettner and Buettner (2016) noted that the Egyptian revolution of 2011, which was mobilized to overthrow the president, Hosni Mubarak was made effective through the internet as a tool for mass mobilization.

While Africans have previously cried to the international community for support in addressing social challenges in the continent, the story is taking a new dimension. This new perspective to social movements that challenge societal ills is driven by a self-help approach anchored on the possibility and ease of mobilization for support, either financial, human, or emotional, using social media platforms, with the creation of hashtags that quickly go viral, thereby attracting the attention of the global community.

Social media are enhancing the voices of protesters of social movements in Africa and are currently widely used to challenge issues of GBV in the continent. Through the social media platforms like Facebook, YouTube, Twitter, blogs, Instagram, and so on, stakeholders of women's well-being are creating awareness and transforming the social relations in the continent. Aside from the postings of audios and videos of abuse against women, the use of hashtags in social media platforms have also become very popular, as such hashtags specify the social issue for public support, making it easy to raise voices against societal ills around the world.

For instance, the uniqueness of the Black Lives Matter movement played out in its use of social media platforms and digital technologies, which enhanced the reach and popularity of the movement as it gained mass support globally. The #BlackLivesMatter Hashtag draws attention to the population of people demanding social changes from societal mishaps that discriminate against their individual or collective rights in society. The hashtag was first coined by Patrice Cullors and Alicia Garza on Facebook in 2013 in the agitation for the acquittal of George Zimmerman in the shooting of Trayvon Martin (Guynn, 2015 cited in Arif et al., 2018). The hashtag spread to other social media platforms and further metamorphosed into online and offline social movements that brought racial discourses to the limelight, especially the shooting of African Americans by police officers (Guynn, 2015 cited in Arif et al., 2018). The #AllLivesMatter hashtag was also widely distributed calling for the need to place value on all lives without segregation.

In Africa, the use of hashtags is similarly driving social change, arm-twisting governments on issues that would have ordinarily gone unnoticed. Oduah (2020) noted that in 2020 alone, hashtags were used for various campaigns in Namibia, Zimbabwe, Cameroun, DRC, Nigeria, and a host of other countries in the continent and globally. Through social media hashtags, governments' attention is being drawn to several structural problems that enable violence against women, and the need for strict legislation that protects women from all forms of violence.

The #BringBackOurGirls is a popular hashtag that was trendy after the abduction of 276 schoolgirls from Chibok in Nigeria by the Boko Haram in April 2014. Although most of the girls have since regained freedom, but not at the cost of their dignity, as several of them were impregnated and returned as nursing mothers. Social media and hashtags were also highly used during the END SARS protest against police brutality in Nigeria in 2020. Social media were used to share videos of extra-judicial activities of police officers and military men, making the event become viral and attracting international attention. Obia (2021) reported that the #ENDSARS hashtag attracted over two million tweets on Twitter, including protesters from the United States and the United Kingdom. The raping of an undergraduate student while studying in a church also sparked off social media outcry in Nigeria, with the hashtag #WeAreTired (BBC, 2020).

The #MeToo hashtag is a prominent hashtag that was used to challenge gender violence against women, especially sexual violence, though started in America, also became popular in Africa, where it was used to challenge sexual abuse of women in the continent. The #MeToo hashtag was also used in Nigeria, against sexual abuse. For instance, in the northern part of the country where women are particularly meant to be heard and not seen due to cultural and religious beliefs, the Twitter message by a twenty-four-year-old northern lady who has been persistently abused her boyfriend led to the social discourse around the #MeToo hashtag as young women who had been abused sexually shared their experiences on social media.

In South Africa, following the killing of women due to sexual violence, protests pervaded the social media platforms as women expressed their anger, using hashtags like #NotInMyName, #AmINext, #SAShutDown (Bambalele, 2019).

In another vein, the #ShutItAllDownNamibia hashtag started as an outcry due to the discovery of a young woman who was buried in dunes in Walvis Bay, a port town in Namibia. Through the social media protest, protesters called on the government to declare a state of emergency against femicide and rape in the country and for the creation of sex offenders register to prosecute perpetrators of the crimes (Oduah, 2020). The #CongoIsBleeding protest was similarly mobilized due to the prevalence of sexual violence against women and child labor in the Congo (Oduah, 2020).

All the aforementioned scenarios amplify the seriousness that women have come to attach to their experiences as victims of GBV in the continent, which portrays what is obtainable in all parts of the world, where women are continually being abused and yet silenced in their pain due to structural systems that were designed to hold them insubordination, without voice justice to their plights.

OUTCOMES OF PROTEST MOVEMENTS AGAINST GENDER-BASED VIOLENCE IN AFRICA

Social media have provided veritable media for victims of social crimes to express their anger and dissatisfaction against the failures of the structures that put women on the receiving end of all forms of GBV. The power of hashtags in advancing or transforming social narratives, attracting wide coverage of sympathy to a cause of action by protesters, makes the global space a unifying ground to changing societal anomalies. For example, Bambalele (2019) noted that barely three weeks after the #BringBackOurGirls hashtag was used, it attracted over a million users of the hashtag globally, an indication that social media are prime as an avenue for driving social change in contemporary global spaces, especially on issues that border on GBV, which affect women of all races and cultures.

Pieces of evidence of the impact of social media on the social transformation of African society abound. The legal environment in the continent, which hitherto had been described as highly ineffective in addressing GBV, is being arm-twisted through the use of social media protest movements to drive social transformation in Africa. In Namibia, for example, following the arrest of protesters against the killing of women, social media became the public instrument for the outcry against the injustice, leading to the release of the protesters (Oduah, 2020).

The END SARS protest against police brutality in Nigeria led to the institution of judicial panels in at least twenty-eight out of the thirty-six states in the country for an investigative inquiry into the various forms of violence by the police officers against the citizens, including women (Oduah, 2020). Additionally, during the END SARS protest in Nigeria, networking through social media networks with other protesters in the country enabled the release of arrested protesters who were illegally detained by law enforcement agents. Further, the sharing of footage of attacks on protesters of END SARS in Nigeria on YouTube, Instagram, Twitter, Facebook, and so on served as evidence against the activities of law enforcement officers, which would have gone unnoticed, without the social media outlets.

The place of social media in the social transformation of society was acknowledged by Gladwell (2010) who noted that social medial platforms are greatly reinventing social movements. However, several scholars have mentioned some problems of using social media driving social change in society. The use of the internet for social activism encourages the existing inequalities among citizens who are not technology savvy, thereby excluding them from a cause even when they may be interested in supporting the need for social change. For instance, Christensen (2011) faulted the role of the internet in enhancing social change, arguing that it is the well-educated and politically interested that utilize the benefits of technology. In a similar vein, Shulman (2004) contended that the impact of the internet in changing social interaction may not be felt since it hardly impacts political outcomes in real-time.

Taken as a whole, the gains that social media offer to women are enormous. Before now, their causes are hardly addressed and GBV has been described as a silent pandemic that knows no economic, social, cultural, or racial boundary. While uproar against social malaise in the society occurs from time to time following a social crime, GBV is a daily occurrence in all societies of the world and Africa in particular. The debate about black, white, or blue lives has at its center women as victims in all spaces where these social injustices occur, yet there have hardly been a global or in the case of Africa, a regional cry against the perpetrators of the crime either as intimate partners, family members, neighbors, law enforcement agents, or superiors in workspaces. The new dimensions that social media offer as a channel for making their experiences known and raising their voices in society provide a forum that will not only attract the attention of their immediate governments but also, the attention of the global community.

GOVERNMENT RESPONSES AGAINST GENDER-BASED VIOLENCE IN AFRICA

There are international conventions that protect the rights of women against GBV, to which African countries are signatories like the UN Convention on the Elimination of All Forms of Discrimination against Women (CEDAW), the African Charter on the Rights of Women in Africa, and other subregional laws. Individual countries also have laws that criminalize GBV, most of which were on the instances of pressures from women's movements (Denney and Ibrahim, 2012; Tripp et al., 2009, cited in Medie, 2013), although several countries in the continent still lack protective laws against GBV. For instance, García-Moreno and Avni (2016) cited in Muluneh et al. (2020) noted that only twenty-two out of the fifty-four countries in Africa have adopted laws that prohibit GBV.

Nigeria ratified the CEDAW in 1985, and the Nigerian 1999 constitution also prohibits discrimination against sexual offenses (IAGCI), 2015). To address the gap in access to legal redress against GBV in Nigeria and also with the promptings of various interest groups, the Violence against Persons Prohibition Act was passed into law in 2015, which prohibits, among others, violence against women and girls (IAGCI, 2015; Ipas, 2020). The Namibian constitution also contains a clause that addresses GBV, which was reinforced in other legislations like the Combating of Domestic Violence Act 4 of 2003 and the Combating of Rape Act 8 of 2000 (National Plan of Action on Gender-Based Violence, 2012–2016). The country also ratified the SADC Protocol on Gender and Development, which is committed to promoting the principles of gender equality in the country.

There have been drawbacks in the implementation of these laws in the continent, which have continued to encourage the prevalence of crime against women. Medie (2013) stated that the failure of most African governments to implement the laws that prohibit GBV prevents the victims from being served justice. Ipas (2020) reported that in Nigeria, even though there is a federal law, the Violence against Persons Prohibition Act, which was enacted in 2015, the adoption of the act is only in sixteen of the thirty-six states in the country. Amnesty International (2017) noted that even though the law was passed, it is only applicable in the Federal Capital Territory. Lending its voice to the poor state of protective laws against GBV in Nigeria, Amnesty International (2017) noted that many laws against violence against women in

Nigeria have limited scope and fail to guarantee the rights of women and in the views of Ipas (2020) the adoption and implementation of the act against violence at the state levels will help to check the spate of violence against women in Nigeria.

The opposing laws in Nigerian society make it difficult for the implementation of the law prohibiting violence against women. IAGCI (2015) noted that customary and religious laws that are at variance with the federal laws prevent the implementation of gender laws, hence, making it difficult to curb the discriminatory issues against women in the country. Furthermore, the legal framework in Nigeria, which places more credibility on the testimony of men compared to that of women in many criminal courts in Nigeria (IAGCI, 2015), also puts women at a disadvantage in reporting and getting redress against GBV in the country. For example, the customary laws in some states offer different penalties for sexual assaults; penalties of men exceed the penalties for the same offense committed against women (United States State Department, cited in IAGCI, 2015). Additionally, IAGCI (2015) noted that discriminatory laws and practices, violence against women, and gender stereotypes constitute hindrances toward the attainment of gender equality. The poor reportage of GBV in Nigeria was also attributed to the attitude of law enforcement agents, who are nonchalant in investigating such allegations (IAGCI, 2015).

Similarly, although Liberia ratified the UN Convention on the Elimination of All Forms of Discrimination against Women (CEDAW), the Advocates for Human Rights (2015) reported the implementation of the convention and other national laws is weak such that sexual violence thrives due to the poor state of legal infrastructures. The report noted that corruption of law enforcement personnel who demand bribes from victims of GBV limits their demand for a formal process of redress. The committee on the elimination of Discrimination against women in Liberia reported that the measures that are put in place to address GBV are not enforced in practice and that they lack coordination and are concentrated in urban areas (Advocates for Human Rights, 2015).

War-torn countries like Liberia, for example, with weak implementing agencies further limit the implementation of such laws (Amnesty International, 2010, cited in Medie, 2013). The weakness of such conflict-affected countries in implementing laws that protect women's rights, in the view of Ward (2013), is due to the absence of reliable data since the systems to collect data at such times may not be in place. Medie (2013) noted that even though GBV is prevalent in postwar Liberia, most of the reported cases hardly get to the courts. This puts to question the importance that is attached to women's rights when formal policy processes fail to address social malaise like GBV, which is a crime against the dignity of the woman.

Given the discourse, the prevalence of GBV in Africa will primarily be anchored on the weakness of the systems that are designed to protect the rights of women. Places where women go for formal processes of redress are characterized by high risk to their safety, which reflects a lawless society with nowhere to go to seek justice. The key alternative which has proven effective from the recent experiences in several African countries is taking their cases to social media spaces to attract the attention of stakeholders, either for support to make their plights known or to bring attract the attention of their governments through popular demand for justice, which has been proven effective in the Black Lives Matter, Bring Back Our Girls movements and other social media enabled protests that have been enhanced using various forms of hashtags.

CONCLUSION AND RECOMMENDATIONS

Several questions that come to mind, in conclusion, is whose lives matter in the global community and Africa in particular? What criteria are used to measure the level of injustice committed when there is the killing of a white or black man in America, Nigeria, Afghanistan, France, or India? Who is more or less important where justice is needed? What social crime is perceived as important by the government, public law enforcement agents, or even protesters who cry out against acts of injustice in society? The position one takes in giving an honest thought to these questions might be influenced by the biases of the environment where one is operating from. However, a dispassionate stance is required where social problems are concerned. A society that will succeed in driving a socially safe environment especially one where women will be able to carry out their daily activities and also accomplish their life's aspirations will have to be blind to the social identification women carry and address their risks in a socially acceptable way. Given the foregoing, the following recommendations are suggested.

(1) Governments in Africa need to move away from law enactment to putting structures in place that protect the rights of women in the continent.
(2) The formal legal processes in the continent should be reassessed and repositioned to encourage victims of GBV to seek redress using the formal legal processes.
(3) African governments need to make concerted efforts to ensure that perpetrators of GBV are punished to build public confidence and increase the reportage of cases of GBV by victims.
(4) Social movements and Africa and the world at large need to pay close attention to fighting GBV, which is not limited to Africa, but cuts across all cultures; rather than engendering racial divide.

(5) Social media campaigns should be capitalized upon by social movement groups that are involved in challenging GBV in Africa, given its potential for making the voices of women who have experienced GBV known and to seek justice on their behalf.

Expectantly, addressing the issues recommended from this discourse will help to curb the prevalence of GBV in Africa, and also encourage women who are victims of the crime to approach the formal judicial processes to seek justice, instead of dying in silence.

REFERENCES

Advocates for Human Rights. (2015). Liberia's compliance with the convention on the elimination of all forms of discrimination against women. Report for the Pre-Sessional Working Group of the Committee on the Elimination of Discrimination against Women. Retrieved on February 28, 2021, from https://tbInternet.ohchr.org/LBR/int_cedaw_lbr_19364_e.pdf

Amnesty International, Nigeria. (June 7, 2017). Submission to the United Nations Committee on the elimination of discrimination against women 67th session, July 3–21, 2017. Retrieved on February 25 2021, from https://primarysources.brillonline.com/browse/human-rights-documents-online/submission-to-the-united-nations-committee-on-the-elimination-of-discrimination-against-women;hrdhrd92112016111

Anja, P. (September 7, 2017). Gender-based violence against women: Both cause for migration and risk along the journey. Retrieved on February 25, 2021, from https://www.migrationpolicy.org/article/gender-based-violence-against-women-both-cause-migration-and-risk-along-journey

Annan-Yao, E. (2004). Analysis of gender relations in the family, formal education and health. *Gender Economies and Entitlements in Africa. CODESRIA*: 1–17. Retrieved on March 2, 2021 from https://www.codesria.org/IMG/pdf/GE-Chapter-1-annan.pdf

Arif, A., Stewart, G. L., & Starbird K. (2018). Acting the part: Examining information operations within #BlackLivesMatter discourse. In Proceedings of the ACM on Human-Computer Interaction, 2 (CSCW): 1–27. Retrieved on February 15, 2021 from https://faculty.washington.edu/kstarbi/BLM-IRA-Camera-Ready.pdf

Bambabele, P. (December 19, 2019). Hashtag activism finds a home in social media sites. Retrieved on February 22, 2021, from https://www.sowetanlive.co.za/news/south-africa/2019-12-19-hashtag-activism-finds-a-home-in-social-media-sites/

British Broadcasting Corporation (BBC) Africa. (December 16, 2019). Nigerian university lecturer sacked over sexual harassment. Retrieved on February 19, 2021, from https://www.bbc.com/news/world-africa-50817098?intlink_from_url=https://www.bbc.com/news/world&link_location=live-reporting-story

British Broadcasting Corporation (BBC) Africa. (June 5, 2020). #WeAreTired: Nigerian women speak out over wave of violence. *BBC News*. Retrieved on January 12, 2021 from https://www.bbc.com/news/world-africa-52889965

Buettner, R., & Buettner, K. (2016). A systematic literature review of twitter research from a socio-political revolution perspective. In *2016 49th Hawaii International*

Conference on System Sciences (HICSS) (pp. 2206–2215). IEEE. Retrieved on February 20, 2021, from https://www.researchgate.net/publication/282150020_A_Systematic_Literature_Review_of_Twitter_Research_from_a_Socio-Political_Revolution_Perspective

Christensen, H. S. (2011). Political activities on the internet: Slacktivism or political participation by other means? *Peer-Reviewed Journal on the Internet.* Retrieved on February 25, 2021, from https://firstmonday.org/article/view/3336/2767

Denney, L., & Ibrahim, A. F. (2012). Violence against women in Sierra Leone. How women seek redress. *Overseas Development Institute.* Retrieved on January 12, 2020, from https://www.refworld.org/pdfid/523ac7a94.pdf

Gladwell, M. (2010). Small change. *The New Yorker* 4:42–49. Retrieved on February 22, 2021 from https://www.newyorker.com/magazine/2010/10/04/small-change-malcolm-gladwell

Herr, K. (2017). A Black African Feminist theory to examine Female Genital Mutilation (FGM) within African immigrant families, in the United States, Mame Kani Diop, Doctoral Candidate Pearl Stewart, PhD Retrieved on January 22, 2021 from https://www.ncfr.org/sites/default/files/2017-08/TCRM%204%20-%20A%20Black%20African%20Feminist%20Theory.pdf

Hoffman, L., Granger Jr, N., Vallejos, L., & Moats, M. (2016). An existential–humanistic perspective on Black Lives Matter and contemporary protest movements. *Journal of humanistic Psychology* 56(6):595–611. Retrieved on January 21 2021, from https://doi.org/10.1177/0022167816652273

hooks, b. (2010). *Feminism Is for Everybody: Passionate Politics.* Cambridge, MA: South End Press. Retrieved on February 12, 2021, from https://excoradfeminisms.files.wordpress.com/2010/03/bell_hooks-feminism_is_for_everybody.pdf

Independent Advisory Group on Country Information (IAGCI). (2015). Country information and guidance Nigeria: Gender-based discrimination/harm/violence against women. Retrieved on February 28, 2021 from https://www.refworld.org/pdfid/55dda9204.pdf

Ipas. (August 6, 2020). As sexual violence continues to rise in Nigeria, Ipas and partners advocate for state-level protections. Retrieved on February 24, 2021, from https://www.ipas.org/news/as-sexual-violence-continues-to-rise-in-nigeria-ipas-and-partners-advocate-for-state-level-protections/

Kolawole, M. M. (2002). Transcending incongruities: Rethinking feminism and the dynamics of identity in Africa. *Agenda* 17(54):92–98. Retrieved on February 12, 2021, from https://researchgate.net

Kwasi, G. A. (August 14, 2019). Internet clicktivism. Retrieved on February 24, 2021, from https://www.dandc.eu/en/article/ghanaian-feminists-are-using-social-media-change-public-discourse

Le Masson, V., Benoudji, C., Reyes, S. S., & Bernard, G. (2018). Violence against women and girls and resilience links, impacts and perspectives from the Chadian context. Working and Discussion Papers. Retrieved on January 12, 2021, from https://www.odi.org/publications/11026-violence-against-women-and-girls-and-resilience

Medie, P. A. (2013). Fighting gender-based violence: The women's movement and the enforcement of rape law in Liberia. *African Affairs* 112(448):377–397. Retrieved on February 24, 2021, from https://doi.org/10.1093/afraf/adt040

Melber, H. (October 29, 2020). #ShutItAllDown in Namibia – the fight against gender-based violence. Retrieved on February 24, 2021, from https://theconversation.com/shutitalldown-in-namibia-the-fight-against-gender-based-violence-148809

Muluneh, D. M., Stulz, V., Francis, L., & Agho, K. (2020). Gender-based violence against women in Sub-Saharan Africa: A systematic review and meta-analysis of cross-sectional studies. *International Journal of Environment and Public Health*. Retrieved on January 12, 2021, from https://www.mdpi.com/1660-4601/17/3/903

Nkealah, N. (2006). Conceptualizing feminism(s) in Africa: The challenges facing African women writers and critics. *English Academy* Review:133–141. Retrieved on February 16, 2021, from https://www.researchgate.net/publication/232977377_Conceptualizing_feminisms_in_Africa_The_challenges_facing_African_women_writers_and_critics

Obia, V. A. (November 11, 2020). ENDSARS, a unique Twittersphere and social media regulation in Nigeria. Retrieved on February 26, 2021, from https://blogs.lse.ac.uk/medialse/2020/11/11/endsars-a-unique-twittersphere-and-social-media-regulation-in-nigeria/

Oduah, C. (December 9, 2020). Rest of the world. The revolution will be hashtagged. Retrieved on February 25, 2021, from https://restofworld.org/2020/the-revolution-will-be-hashtagged/

Okechi, O. S. (2018). The indigenous concept of sexuality in African tradition and globalization. *Global Journal of Reproductive Medicine* 6(1):1–5. Retrieved on March 2, 2021 from https://www.researchgate.net/publication/328192431_Globalization_and_the_Indigenous_Concept_of_Sexuality_in_African_Tradition_Charting_a_New_Course_for_Sexual_Right_and_Safe_Society

Olaoluwa, A. (December 1, 2020). EndSars protests: The Nigerian women leading the fight for change. *BBC News 2020*. Retrieved on February 20, 2021 from https://www.bbc.com/news/world-africa-55104025

Republic of Namibia Ministry of Gender Equality and Child Welfare. (2012–2016). *National Plan of Action on Gender-based Violence*. Retrieved on February 28, 2021 from www.undp.org.dam.docs

Salami, M. (September 2018). Feminism in Nigeria – By and for who? Retrieved on February 15, 2021 from https://www.zeitschrift-luxemburg.de/feminism-in-nigeria-by-and-for-who/

Shulman, S. W. (2004). The Internet still might (but probably won't) change everything. *Journal of Law and Policy* 1(1). Retrieved on February 24, 2021 from https://core.ac.uk/download/pdf/159565779.pdf

Solotaro, L. J., & Pande, P. R. (2014). Violence against women and girls: Lessons from south Asia. World Bank, Washington DC, ISBN 978-1-4648-0171-6. Retrieved on January 12, 2021, from https://openknowledge.worldbank.org/handle/10986/20153

Terborg, P. R. (1995). Through an African feminist theoretical lens: Viewing Caribbean women's history cross-culturally. In Sheperd, V., Brereton, B. & Bailey, B. (eds.). *Engendering History: Caribbean Women in Historical Perspective*. Retrieved on February 22, 2021 from https://link.springer.com/chapter/10.1007/978-1-137-07302-0_1

The Guardian. (September 5, 2019). Thousands protest in South Africa over rising violence against women. Retrieved on February 24, 2021 from https://www.theguardian.com/world/2019/sep/05/thousands-protest-in-south-africa-over-rising-violence-against-women

United Nations Educational, Scientific and Cultural Organization (UNESCO). (2003). *UNESCO's Gender Mainstreaming Implementation Framework Baseline Definitions of Key Concepts and Terms.* Retrieved on March 2, 2021, from http://www.unesco.org/new/fileadmin/MULTIMEDIA/HQ/BSP/GENDER/PDF/1.%20Baseline%20Definitions%20of%20key%20gender-related%20concepts.pdf

United Nations International Children Emergency Fund (UNICEF). (2018). Child marriage in west and central Africa at a glance. Retrieved on February 22, 2021, from https://www.unicef.org/wca/media/2596/file#:~:text=The%20prevalence%20of%20child%20mrriage

United Nations Office of the High Commissioner for Human Rights (UNOHCHR). (2001). Gender dimensions of racial discrimination. Retrieved on January 12, 2021, from https://digitallibrary.un.org

United Nations (UN) Women. (2002). *Gender Mainstreaming: An Overview.* New York: United Nations. Retrieved on March 2, 2021 from https://www.un.org/womenwatch/osagi/conceptsanddefinitions.htm

United Nations (UN) Women (December 2020). In focus: 16 days of activism against gender-based violence. Retrieved on February 12, 2021 from https://www.unwomen.org/en/news/in-focus/end-violence-against-women

Ward, J. (2013). Violence against women in conflict, post-conflict and emergency settings. *UN Women.* Retrieved on February 22, 2021 from https://www.endvawnow.org/uploads/modules/pdf/1405612658.pdf

World Economic Forum (WEF). (2020). Global gender gap report 2020. Retrieved on February 12, 2021 from http://www3.weforum.org/docs/WEF_GGGR_2020.pdf

World Health Organization (WHO). (2013). Global and regional estimates of violence against women: Prevalence and health effects of intimate partner violence and non-partner sexual violence. Retrieved on February 12, 2021 from https://apps.who.int/iris/bitstream/handle/10665/85239/9789241564625_eng.pdf;jsessionid=26C5EE024F9574130FAC506880560355?sequence=1

World Health Organization (WHO). (2021). Sexual health. Retrieved on March 3, 2021, from https://www.who.int/health-topics/sexual-health#tab=tab_2

Chapter 9

Economic Perspective

Abdul Amin Kamara

This chapter examines the ideologies and actions the Black Lives Matters and All Lives Matters movements from the perspectives of economics, which is the systematic study of production, consumption, and transfer of wealth, and also the condition of a region or group as regards material prosperity. Although the two movements are new phenomena, they are currently making headlines in the United States and other parts of the world.

Since this chapter interrogates the economic perspective of this book, it should be noted that economics itself forms an integral part of the social human construct and it is almost impossible for human beings to live without any form of exchange going on; even in primitive societies, there were means of exchange and, hence, humans in their pluralistic form cannot exist without exchange.

Also, as Black Lives Matter activists are demanding holistic social reforms based on the principles of equality, the economic aspects of their followers in terms of "upliftment" and livelihood must be taken into consideration, as there is nothing like the "State of Black Economy." It neither exists in Africa, nor does it exist in any other part of the world. It is an illusion to think there is a situation called the State of Black Economy. Blacks have been dubbed by some observers as "economic slaves" (e.g., see: Onyeani, 2012, p. 43).

In addition, organizers of the Black Lives Matters movement should take into consideration the fact that mass rallies and violent demonstrations will not lead to economic emancipation. Rather, they should seek collaboration from the majority of people right across the globe. This will not lead to economic emancipation, but it will help them to build their success on what others are doing for them (Onyeani, 2012, p. 60).

This chapter therefore further explores the "powernomics" concept to demonstrate that the more wealthy people that are in a particular race or place will determine the respect they will command among their peers. Both movements investigated are seeking attention on what has been done to them either because of the color of their skin or because they are a minority.

Furthermore, the chapter investigates major economic concepts like fundamental economics, macroeconomics, microeconomics, international economics, and personal finance economics and how they are related to the two movements. Moreover economic questions like what goods and services and how much of each to produce, how to produce, for whom to produce, and who owns the factors of production are probed.

Before getting into the analysis, the chapter offers a backdrop by exploring racism in the past and present and extrapolates how it will look like in the future by reviewing related literature that will illustrate facts to show that there is a close link between racial discrimination and socioeconomic status; more specifically, whether civilians or men in uniform will deal with an individual not based on the color of his or her skin but socioeconomic condition. Imagine how harshly a police officer will stop a person in a Toyota; it will not be the same as how he or she will stop another person in a Rolls Royce. This applies to neighborhood raids, schools, hospitals, shopping malls, and so on. Furthermore, people will be ready to listen to you when you show them how to make money, or invest in people or places. This verity is captured by Lee Kuan Yew when he recounts the following:

> On my first official visit to America in October 1967, I recounted to 50 business people at a luncheon in Chicago how Singapore had grown from a village of 120 fishermen in 1819 to become a metropolis of 2 million. This was because its philosophy was to provide goods and services "cheaper and better than anyone else, or perish." They responded well because I was not putting my hand out for aid, which they had come to expect of leaders from newly independent countries. I noted their favourable reaction to my "no begging bowl" approach. (Yew, 2000, p. 56)

As stated earlier, the Black Lives Matter and All Lives Matter movements are new phenomena that are making waves. Thus, it is very important to examine how they operate and what some of their gains would be losses in the near future, whether the two groups are politically motivated movements or just groups that are yearning for attention, or whether they were established for personal gains or for selflessness based on equality for all.

ECONOMICS: A CONCEPTUAL DISCUSSION

To start with, for a subject whose history began in Ancient Kemet/Egypt in c. 6000–c. 3150 BCE (Mark, 2017), but is now ubiquitous across the globe, it is only inevitable that there is no one universally accepted definition of economics today. Nonetheless, there are similarities among the many definitions. Paul A. Samuelson and William Nordhaus, for example, define economics as "The Queen of the Social Sciences," which studies "how men and society end up *choosing*, with or without the use of money, to employ *scarce* productive resources which could have alternative uses, to produce various commodities and distribute them for consumption, now or in the future, among various people and groups in society" (2010, p. 4). S. Charles Maurice, Owen R. Phillips, and C. E. Ferguson denote economics as "a study of the method of allocating scarce physical and human resources among unlimited wants or competing ends" (1986, p. 2). And, Lloyd G. Reynolds elucidates economics as the study of "*economizing*, which is something we do every day. We are forced to economize because of *scarcity*" (1985, p. 3). Given these definitions, I therefore proffer the following general definition for economics: that is, an area of knowledge that is engaged in the scientific study of the production, consumption, and transmission of wealth.

Next, from the preceding definitions, we can notice that study of economics entails at least following five aspects:: (1) *choice*—an act of selecting or making a decision when faced with two or more alternatives; (2) *scarcity*—when a resource is insufficient for the demand; (3) *production*—the action of making or manufacturing from components or raw materials, or the process of being so manufactured; (4) *consumption*—the using up of a resource; and (5) *transmission*—the action or process of passing on something from one place or person to another. Thus, as one can glean from Samuelson and Nordhaus, the study of economics includes the following phenomena:

> Those activities which, with or without money, involve exchange transactions among people ... how men choose to use scarce or limited productive resources (land, labor, capital goods such as machinery, technical knowledge) to produce various commodities (such as wheat, beef, overcoats, concerts, roads, bombers, yachts) and distribute them to various members of society for their consumption ... how men in their ordinary business of life, earning and enjoying a living ... how mankind goes about the business of organizing its consumption and production activities ... and wealth. (2010, p. 4)

Also, according to Samuelson and Nordhaus, economics is employed "to *describe, analyze, explain* and *correlate* the behavior of production, unemployment, prices, and similar phenomena" (2010, p. 4). Nonetheless, these scholars do not provide the denotations of the very important italicized terms, which are often used interchangeably by some writers, so I do so here: (a) *describe* involves giving an account in words of (someone or something), including all the relevant characteristics, qualities, or events; (b) *analyze* is to examine methodically and in detail the constitution or structure of (something, especially information), typically for purposes of explanation and interpretation; (c) *explain* entails making (an idea, situation, or problem) clear to someone by describing it in more detail or revealing relevant facts or ideas; and (d) *correlate* involves showing a mutual relationship or connection, in which one thing affects or depends on another.

In addition, just as many other economists have pointed out, Maurice et al. (1986) and Reynolds (1985) talk about the two major branches of the study of economics, that is, *macroeconomics* and *microeconomics*. *Macroeconomics* is concerned with large-scale or general economic factors, such as interest rates and national productivity. Whereas, *microeconomics* is concerned with single factors and the effects of individual decisions.

Contrastingly, on the one hand, *macroeconomics* focuses on aggregate over the economy in its entirety; for instance, the overall level of employment in a country will be a focal point of this branch of economics. On the other hand, *microeconomics* focuses on the organization of individual behavior or the behavior of a small group of individuals; for example, the forces that determine the price and the amount of rice consumed by a customer or a small group of customers will quality as a pivot for this branch of economics (Maurice et al., 1986, pp. 8–9). Concomitantly, in Reynolds's *Macroeconomics* book (1985), the following topics are broached: how a market economy organizes production; supply and demand; measuring national output and income; income differentiation: simplest case; income differentiation: steps toward reality; inflation; prices, public spending, and fiscal policy; banking and the money supply; the federal reserve system; monetary policy and aggregate demand; fluctuations in national income; short-term stability: targets and instruments; long-term growth: explanation and appraisal; external balance and the world monetary system; the basis of international trade; and trade flows and trade policy. And, in his *Microeconomics* book (1985), Reynolds interrogates these topics: how a market organizes production; economic decisions under central planning; supply and demand; consumer choice; producer choice; profit as a business objective; competition among the many; competition among the few; market power: antitrust and regulation; market failure: public goods; quasi-public goods: education and healthcare; externalities, common resources, and the environment; factor prices: wages, interest, profit; labor markets: discrimination, unionism, and minimum wages; income distribution: before and after taxes; and inequality, poverty, and public policy.

THE DAWN OF RACISM AND ITS EMERGENCE IN THE UNITED STATES

We learn from the Holy Torah, the Holy Bible, and the Holy Qur'an that when God created our ancestors (that is Adam and Eve), He did not state their race. Instead, what we are told in the books is "Let Us make man (Adam) in our image, according to our likeness. So God created man (Adam) in His own image; He created them male and female." In regard to the so-called Curse of Ham, many Christian philosophers in the past and even today and may be in the future are abusing or will abuse it, distort, twist, or misinterpret the verses in the Book of Genesis 9:18–27 (Holy Bible, King James Version, 2002 edition). Thus, it is important to clarify what this passage actually says and does not say. We learn from the passage that after the flood is over and his family has settled down, Noah got drunk and passed out, lying naked in his tent. His son Ham, specifically as the father of Canaan (9:22), saw him and told his two brothers, Shem and Japheth, who then carefully covered up their father. When Noah woke up and found out what had happened, he pronounced a curse on Canaan, the son of Ham, stating: "Cursed be Canaan! the lowest of slaves will he be to his brothers." Noah then blessed Shem and Japheth, declaring: "Blessed be the LORD of Shem! May Canaan be the slave of Shem. May God extend the territory of Japheth . . . and may Canaan be his slave" (9:26-27).

In the nineteenth century, both before and after the Civil War in the United States (April 12, 1861—April 9, 1865), the "Curse of Ham" text was frequently cited by whites pastors and writers to argue that the slavery or subjugation of the black race was, in fact, a fulfillment of the prophecy in this text. These pastors and writers argued that the (a) the word "Ham" really means "black" or "burnt" and, thus, refers to the black race; and (2) God commanded that the descendants of Ham (black people) become slaves to Japheth, who, they argued, represents the white race. It is, indeed, quite speculative to assume that the name "Ham" actually means "black" and, thus, refers to the people in Black Africa when to the Ancient Kemetians or Egyptians the word $ḥm$ ("ham") refers to "servant" or "majesty."

The act of racism can be traced back to the name Kemet, which means "the black land," a reference to the land of Egypt and to the dark fertile soil associated with it. Yet, to assume that the Hebrew name Ham is even connected to this Egyptian word is questionable. Then even if it is, to say that "the black land," a reference to fertile soil, is actually a reference to the black race in Africa is likewise quite a leap in logic. Thus, the etymological argument that "Ham" refers to the black people of Africa is not defensible. Likewise, as aforementioned, the actual curse is on Canaan, who is clearly identified as the son of Ham. Thus, the curse is placed on the Canaanites and not on the supposedly (and unlikely) descendants of Ham in Black Africa (Moore & Walker, 2016).

MEANS, METHODS OF MOBILIZATION, AND EXECUTION OF ACTIVITIES

The means, methods of mobilization, and execution of activities by both the Black Lives Matter and All Lives Matter organizations are almost the same. The difference between the two is in terms of size; Black Lives Matter has more followers as compared to All Lives Matter. Black Lives Matter started as a hashtag # movement in 2013 and metamorphosed itself into a global movement. Proof of this can be found on the internet, especially using search engines like Google. And, according to Caroline Forsey, "Google is the most popular search engine with more than 70% of the search market share" (2020, p. 1).

Using Google to compare popularity of both movements you will notice that Black Lives Matter is more popular as compared to All Lives Matter. The majority of the results—59,818,181 generated in .60 seconds—were about the Black Lives Matter movement. The All Lives Matter movement had 3,100,000 results generated in .60 seconds. Based on the results generated by Google, it is clear that Black Lives Matter gets more attention as compared its counterpart movement on the internet. The internet is one of the fastest ways of transmitting information especially in the twenty-first century when more than half of the world's population is trying to gain access to it. By 2020, more than half of the world's population—that is, 4.5 billion people—was determined to have access to the medium (Kahn, 2020).

Also, Kahn points out that the internet is accessible to anyone who connects to any of its integral networks because the medium makes available very powerful and universal capabilities that can be employed for any purpose that is contingent on information. Thus, people can work cooperatively at many different places as the medium can facilitate human communication through audio and video transmissions: that is, "chat rooms," ee-mail, newsgroups or listservs, and social media. In addition, the medium provides ingress to digital information via many applications such as the World Wide Web (WWW). As a result, e-businesses and their traditional subsidiaries have found the internet to be a very efficient medium to conduct most of their sales and services (Kahn, 2020).

The movements also make use of newspapers, television, lobbying, and popular among them all is mass demonstrations worldwide, especially by the Black Lives Matter movement because it has a global membership that ranges between 24,000,000 and 26,000,000 million people worldwide. In recent times, especially after the brutal death of George Floyd in the hands of the police, Black Lives Matter demonstrations were sometimes not 100 percent peaceful and slogans like "defund the police" were very popular especially in the United States. The Black Lives Matter movement has to be understood in the context of the historical legacy of the ill-treatment of blacks by the police, the criminal justice system, and the American political and social institutions more generally. That legacy is a fact, according to Cynthos Lum and Daniel Nagin (2017).

As is often the case when new movements capture our attention, the Black Lived Matter movement is now a hot topic of debate in both the public sphere and academia. The debate in both quarters is focused on the tactics and organizational structures that BLM activists employ to promote social change. Some critics of the movement have argued that its focus on disruptive protest tactics, decentralized organizational structures, and unwillingness to negotiate with political elites in the gradualist realm of public policy formation will ultimately limit the success of the movement. On August 24, 2015, for example, Barbara Reynolds, who described herself as a "septuagenarian grandmother" and "activist in the Civil Rights Movement of the 1960s," penned a powerful opinion editorial in *The Washington Post* that urged Black Lives Matter activists to embrace the "proven methods" of the Civil Rights Movement of the 1960s. "The loving, non-violent approach is what wins allies and mollifies enemies," Reynolds argued in her piece, "[but] what we have seen come out of Black Lives Matter is rage and anger—justifiable emotions, but questionable strategy" (Reynolds, 2015, p. 1).

Former President Barack Obama, who got his start in politics as a community organizer in Chicago, Illinois, made a similar critique of the movement on a trip to England in 2016. While speaking at a town hall event in London on April 23, 2016, President Obama summed up the Black Lives Matter movement as follows:

[The Black Lives Matter movement is] really effective in bringing attention to problems.... Once you've highlighted an issue and brought it to people's attention and shined a spotlight, and elected officials or people who are in a position to start bringing about change are ready to sit down with you, then you can't just keep on yelling at them. And you can't refuse to meet because that might compromise the purity of your position. The value of social movements and activism is to get you at the table, get you in the room, and then to start trying to figure out how is this problem going to be solved. (Shear & Stack, 2016, p. 1).

It is very clear from the preceding exploration that both movements employ the mass media as in integral means of mobilization and execution of their activities.

SPONSORSHIP OF THE MOVEMENTS

Like many nonprofit organizations, both the Black Lives Matter and All Lives Matter movements rely on grants, contributions, and donations from their members and other charitable organizations. For example, as Kailee Scales, the founding director of the Black Lives Matter Global Network Foundation, revealed:

> On Wednesday, the Black Lives Matter Global Network Foundation was setting aside $6 million from money it received in donations to support black-led grassroots organizing groups. Last week, the foundation unveiled a separate $6.5 million fund for its network of affiliate chapters. Beginning July 1, affiliated chapters can apply for unrestricted funding of up to $500,000 in multi-year grants, the foundation announced. Grants from both funds will be administered through a fiscal sponsor. (Scales, 2019, p. 1)

Scales added the following:

> In this watershed moment for black power building...it is critical that we democratize giving to ensure all of us have access to the resources we need to reverse centuries of disinvestment in black communities, and invest in a future where we can all be connected, represented and free. (Scales, 2019, p. 1)

As stated earlier, the All Lives Matter movement does not have as large a following compared to that of the Black Lives Matter movement; thus, it will not be able to mobilize as much funds as the Black Lives Matter movement. It is therefore clear that mega multinational companies will find it very difficult to fund small organizations that will not influence their financial gains in the near future. Even though these companies are donating, those donations are also investments because they will want to gain access to communities or markets that are not easily accessible to them but through donations it will be very easy for them to gain access.

THE ECONOMIC GAP BETWEEN BLACKS AND WHITES IN THE UNITED STATES

As we learn from Mehrsa Baradaran, "When the Emancipation Proclamation was signed in 1863, the Black community owned less than one percent of the United States' total wealth. More than 150 years later, that number has barely budged" (2017, p. 1). There are two banking systems in the United States.

One is the regulated and heavily subsidized mainstream banking industry; the other is the unregulated, costly, and often predatory fringe industry. The black community has historically been under the latter system, having been left out of the former. This has come at great expense to the black community (Baradaran, 2017).

As noted by Baradaran (2017), Richard Thaler and Cass Sunstein found that blacks pay on average of $425 more for loans than white customers. Most black neighborhoods are "banking deserts," neighborhoods abandoned by mainstream banks. Federal Deposit Insurance Corporation (FDIC) surveys on the "unbanked and underbanked" reveal that 60 percent of blacks are either unbanked or underbanked. In striking contrast, only 3 percent of whites do not have a bank account and 15 percent are underbanked. Those without bank accounts pay up to 10 percent of their incomes, or around $2,400 per year, just to use their money. That is a meaningful amount of money for low-income Americans, and it is being sucked up by alternative financial services. This problem has been exacerbated since the crisis of 2008, when 93 percent of all bank closings occurred in low-income neighborhoods (Baradaran, 2017).

From the preceding observation, it is evident that black communities find it very difficult to have access to adequate finance within their communities due to the step up of the banking institutions within the United States. Consequently, when a bank withdraws or withholds its activities from a particular community, it leaves a void that affects both its customers and noncustomers: that is, people who benefit directly or indirectly from the banking industry within the community. Job loss is the first direct impact on employees within the community, and the value for other banking-related activities (services) like real estate development, microfinance institutions downsize their activities drastically and sometimes even disappear totally. Also, the gap between the rich and poor widens greatly; and since it is very difficult for humans to transact without the use of money as a medium of exchange, creditors will now step in to fill the void of the financial institutions that wrapped up their activities in the community and, hence, a bank desert or a bank drought is created.

Therefore, movements such as Black Lives Matter and All Lives Matter should pay keen attention to the economic gap that exists between blacks and whites in addition to going out to match. Also, organizers or leaders of these movements should know the difference between demonstration and mobilization. Demonstration is short-term, while mobilization is long-term; but both organizations, especially Black Lives Matter, are well known for their mass demonstrations worldwide and such activities will never uplift the Black race from their current situation.

Although the African American population continues to increase, its average income does not reflect the increasing demographics. In 2018, the annual median income of African Americans reached $41,361, which is below the national average of $61,937, and far below the white median income valued at $70,642. The disparities continue when comparing African Americans with Asian American households that earn an average of $87,194, and with Hispanics who earn a median income of $51,450. In 2018, the median income for Native Americans was estimated to be $41,882 compared to the median income of African Americans, thereby making the two groups the lowest earning races (Collins et al., 2019).

Also, according to the U.S. Census Bureau, approximately 21 percent of African Americans live below the poverty line, compared to an overall poverty rate of 11.8 percent. Poverty rate disparities are exacerbated when compared across racial lines. Only about 10 percent of white Americans and Asian Americans live below the poverty line, a poverty rate half that of African Americans. A total of 17.6 percent of Hispanics live below poverty, while Native Americans have the highest poverty rate, with 25.4 percent living below the poverty line (United States Census Bureau, 2010, 2017).

With all these been said or written by different authors and activists, it will be very important for Black Lives Matter leaders to change the narrative of mass demonstration that sometimes lead to violence or clashing with the police and embark on massive mobilization of both human and material resources for the next generation not to be swimming in the cycle of police brutality and other forms of injustices that are taking place in various black communities.

Nonetheless, the Civil Rights Movement that was established by different prominent black leaders was not done by accident. It was purposefully established to counter the racial injustices that were meted on the black race. The same is true for the Black Lives Matter movement as the organization itself was formed during the regime of Barack Obama, considered by many to be "the first Black President," albeit other contrary evidence exists about the claim. This is to show how blacks were oppressed even under the leadership of Obama. In an interview conducted in 2012 when Obama was asked to respond to criticism that his administration had not done enough to support black businesses, the premise being that helping black businesses was akin to addressing black poverty, he responded: "I'm not the president of Black America. I'm the president of the United States of America" (quoted by Baradaran, 2017, p. 1). So, with such a statement coming from a president that was voted for by a majority of black voters, what will be the future of black businesses in the United States?

UNFULFILLED PROMISES BY DIFFERENT ADMINISTRATIONS TOWARD BLACK AND OTHER MINORITY BUSINESS ENTERPRISES

The Obama administration attempted to make inroads into poverty alleviation, specifically with the Affordable Care Act aimed at lowering healthcare costs, which are a major source of financial distress for low-income earners. Obama, like his predecessors, did not specifically target the racial wealth gap, nor did he advocate a race-based economic agenda. The administration's efforts were a continuation of theories underlying black capitalism and an updated community capitalism of the Clinton administration. In several speeches, Obama heralded the importance of small businesses and minority businesses, including renewing Minority Business Enterprise Week and praising the importance of minority businesses in several small fora. On the campaign trail, he had promised "to help bring businesses back to our inner-cities." He envisioned creating institutions akin to the World Bank to "spur economic development." He lamented, "less than one percent of the $250 billion in venture capital that is invested each year goes to minority businesses that are trying to breathe life into our cities. This has to change." He promised that he would make sure every community had "financial institutions that can help get them started" on the road to building wealth. These promises were not pursued, either because of the game-changing financial crisis, the antagonistic legislative environment, or perhaps due to Obama's lack of conviction on black capitalism. As mentioned earlier, when Obama was asked in 2012 to respond to criticism that his administration had not done enough to support black business—the premise being that helping black business was akin to addressing black poverty—he responded: "I'm not the president of Black America; I'm the president of the United States of America" (Baradaran, 2017, p. 1).

The Treasury under Obama did announce in 2015 that it would name its newly created wing after the Freedmen's Bank. This would be the first time, of course, that the Treasury would actually be linked to the bank. (The last time, the link was purely speculative and the depositors paid the price.) The Treasury also decided to put Harriet Tubman on the $20 bill. And, banking agencies are still carrying out the 1989 Financial Institutions Reform, Recovery, and Enforcement Act (FIRREA) legislative mandate to support minority banks (Baradaran, 2017).

As shown in the preceding paragraphs, little or no action has been made by different administrations to alleviate poverty in minority communities, and black communities are no exception to the unfulfilled promises. Until the political class makes it a point of duty to pass and enforce legislations that encourage and protect minority businesses that will lead to growth, it will be very difficult for the businesses to get off from embryonic their stage.

BLACK ENTERTAINMENT AND POVERTY REDUCTION IN BLACK COMMUNITIES

The entertainment industry (particularly sports) has been an escape route for most people to become rich within the shortest possible time. From the late 1980s to the present, the proportion of blacks that are celebrated in the entertainment industry from music, athletics, and so on, is very high and a majority of these entertainers have moved to either the middle class or the upper class in their diverse communities.

Nevertheless, income and employment only display partial components of economic well-being. Wealth levels account for total debt, financial assets such as investment funds and nonfinancial assets such as residential property ownership. Thus, net worth is a broader depiction of wealth, and starkly highlights the racial wealth division. While white households have a median family net worth of $147,000, black households have a median family net worth of a mere $3,600. In other words, the median white family has forty-one times more wealth than the median black family. Much of this can be attributed to disparities in homeownership, as housing is known to make up two-thirds of a typical household's wealth. Access to quality jobs and residing in asset rich neighborhoods are also key to boosting the financial security of African American households (Collins et al., 2019).

However, even though the number of blacks who are wealthy or rich is far below the number of those who are not, it is imperative to know that a majority of these sports men do not engage in poverty reduction ventures within their various communities. Economic activities like building factories or the setting up of industries that will produce tangible goods and services that will reduce the high rate of unemployment amongst black people are not visible in most black communities. Instead, a majority of them are engaged in lavish life styles that most of the time ushers them into bankruptcy or even poverty. There are over 47.8 million African Americans residing in the United States, which makes blacks 13 percent of the total U.S. population; but there are less wealthy blacks in black circles as compared to other races. A majority of these wealthy blacks got their wealth through entertainment. Blacks like Robert F. Smith, Oprah Winfrey, Michael Jordan, Jay-Z, Kanye West, and Tyler Perry gained their wealth through entertainment, save David Steward who became rich as an information communication technology (ICT) expert.

The total net worth of these black entertainers is more than enough to reduce poverty and unemployment among blacks in America, if they decide to invest their monies in black communities with the sole aim to reduce or alleviate poverty from their various neighborhoods.

BLACK CAPITALISM/ECONOMY AND GLOBAL WHITE CAPITALISM/ECONOMY

The concept of black capitalism or black economy is a new phenomenon as compared to white capitalism or white economy, which has been in existence for the past 400 years. The looting of Africa's natural resources by colonial masters and the disrespect and disdain that these colonial masters accorded Africans would be harbingers of inhuman history.

As argued earlier, there is nothing like the "State of Black Economy." It does not exist in Africa or in any other part of the world. It is an illusion to think there is such a situation called the "State of Black Economy." Blacks are economic slaves. There is no group of people in this world who have abandoned any ambition of being economically independent from the grip of others as the black race. Whether Africans in the continent or Africans in the Diaspora, blacks are more economic slaves now than when the Caucasians conquered and sold them into slavery (Onyeani, 2012).

Even though economists have demonstrated that, in theory, black capitalism should have little direct impact on the well-being of black non-capitalists, indirect and noneconomic effects have not been investigated. Empirical tests of this relationship have been inadequate. And, although not denying that black economic well-being may affect black businesses, it is argued that the effect is at least reciprocal, and probably stronger in the other direction. It has been found that for cities, the extent of black entrepreneurial activity has a strong statistical effect on the well-being of the black population, even when controls are introduced for the many other factors that affect aggregate black welfare. Therefore, it is argue that the apparent effect is a sociological one, operant through variables such as group status and group power. The introduction of intervening measures of black "clout" into the model produces results that support this hypothesis (Villemez & Beggs, 1984).

Indeed, oil has become one of the most important products in the world. It is what created fortunes for people like Rockefellers; it is what created companies like Standard Oil, which was broken up to become the juggernauts like Exxon, Mobil, Texaco, and so on. A lot of the African countries possess oil in abundance. It has become the economic life blood of most African countries. But Africans do not have an iota of knowledge of the process of finding oil and bringing it to use. To discover the oil, a Caucasian has to bring in his equipment to survey African lands or shores. If there is oil, he estimates the amount of oil located in the area. Africans award him the contract of drilling for oil. He brings his own men. Unlike in his own country, whatever environmental damage the drilling does is none of his concerns. Africans also award him the contract to take the oil from them. He pays less than $12 per barrel for the crude oil. He refines the crude into several products, which are then sent back to Africans at more than $65 per barrel. In 1998 alone, Exxon generated revenues of $100 billion, Mobil $47 billion, Texaco $32 billion, and Chevron $27 billion. The revenues of these four companies almost outstripped the revenues of all the fifty black African countries south of the Sahara combined (Onyeani, 2012).

For blacks in the United States, as mentioned earlier, they on average have a lower net worth than whites. This is especially pertinent in the creation of new businesses. One of the most common forms of collateral for loans to open businesses is home equity. With the historical and current differences in lending patterns toward blacks and whites, the option of using home equity to borrow against in order to open a business has diminished.

CONCLUSION AND RECOMMENDATIONS

From the analyses in the preceding sections, it is quite clear that racism has always been present in human society, and it is most times linked to the socioeconomic condition of a particular racial group. Indeed, racism in the mid-twentieth century and racism in the first quarter of the twenty-first century are almost similar, but racism after the end of slavery is totally different from what we see today. At least, immense progress has been made, but it is vital for all blacks to know that nobody will set them free from the world's socioeconomic condition, which is a cornerstone of the current racial prejudices that is meted on black folks. I therefore conclude that racism is economics: one is treated based on his or her economic condition, and his or her economic capacity determines his or her class in society.

As aforementioned, it is very difficult to separate the racism and economics because the inequality that exists among human beings is actually based on economic stratification. Concomitantly, I will recommend the following:

(a) Both Black Lives Matter and All Lives Matter should try their level best to create ways and means that will uplift blacks and other minority groups by educating their followers and non-followers about the essence of professional education that will create jobs and will earn them a decent living standard.

(b) Entrepreneurship education and economic freedom for blacks must be prioritized; it must be systematic in its approach for building an economy purely for blacks (black capitalism) that will go hand-in-hand with the white economy. Although this will be difficult, it will be achieved in less than a generation because all the blueprints are there.
(c) Diaspora Africans, especially the successful ones, should be ready and be given incentives to return to Africa and invest what they have amassed aboard in other to help inject new ideas and better ways to compete in all spheres of life as compared the present unhealthy competition that is taking place in the continent.
(d) Mass demonstration is a short-term solution for the problems that are affecting the black race. There must be a systematic and lasting solution to the problems that are affecting blacks and other minority groups. The slogan Black Lives Matter in itself has already segregated blacks from other minority groups, also marching will never solve the current situation of the black race because the problem itself is a systemic problem rather than conventional one.

Indeed, it is not farfetched to say that the agendas of the purveyors of the Black Lives Matter and All Lived Matter movements will not be successful if economics does not occupy a central role in their thoughts and activities.

REFERENCES

Agozino, B. (2018). Black Lives Matter otherwise all lives do not matter. *African Journal of Criminology and Justice Studies* 11(1):1–11. Retrieved on October 28, 2020 from https://www.umes.edu/uploadedFiles/_WEBSITES/AJCJS/Content/AJCJS%20VOL11.%20Agozino.pdf

Al-Heeti, A. (July 7, 2020). Black Lives Matter: Netflix movies, TV shows and books that touch on systemic racism. *CNET*. Retrieved on October 28, 2020 from https://www.cnet.com/news/black-lives-matter-movies-tv-shows-and-books-on-systemic-racism/

Baker, P. K. (June 23, 2020). Why saying 'All Lives Matter' misses the big picture. *CNN*. Retrieved on November 4, 2020 from https://www.cnn.com/2020/06/23/opinions/all-lives-matter-misses-the-big-picture-baker/index.html

Black Lives Matter. (2018). Black Lives Matter 13 guiding principles (a project of teaching for change by the DC area educator for social justice). Retrieved on October 31, 2020 from https://www.dcareaeducators4socialjustice.org/black-lives-matter/13-guiding-principles

Black Lives Matter. (2020). BLM's #WHATMATERS2020 resources. Retrieved on October 27, 2020 from https://blacklivesmatter.com/

Bouie, J. (September 30, 2015). Elizabeth Warren just gave the best response to Black Lives Matter. *Slate*. Retrieved on November 1, 2020 from https://slate.com/news-and-politics/2015/09/elizabeth-warrens-black-lives-matter-speech-was-the-best-one-yet-its-still-not-enough.html

Buchanan, L., Bui, Q., & Patel, J. K. (July 3, 2020). Black Lives Matter may be the largest movement in U.S. history. *The New York Times*. Retrieved on October 28, 2020 from https://www.nytimes.com/interactive/2020/07/03/us/george-floyd-protests-crowd-size.html

Cohn, N., & Quealy, K. (June 10, 2020). How public opinion has moved on Black Lives Matter. *The New York Times*. Retrieved on October 28, 2020 from https://www.nytimes.com/interactive/2020/06/10/upshot/black-lives-matter-attitudes.html

Collins, C., Hamilton, D., Asante-Muhammed, D., & Hoxie, J. (April 2019). Ten solutions to bridge the racial wealth divide. *Institute for Policy Studies*. Retrieved on October 28, 2020 from https://ips-dc.org/report-racial-wealth-divide-solutions/

Communications Workers of America—CWA. (2020). Black Lives Matter, All Lives Matter: Resolution 75A-15-9. Retrieved on August 30, 2020 from https://cwa-union.org/pages/black_lives_matter_all_lives_mattercwa-union.org/pages/black_lives_matter_all_lives_matter

Holy Bible (King James Version). (2002 edition). Grand Rapids, MI: Zondervan.

Lum, C., & Nagin, D. (2017). Reinventing American criminal justice. *Crime and Justice* 46. Retrieved on October 28, 2020 from https://www.journals.uchicago.edu/doi/10.1086/688462

Mark, J. J. (June 15, 2017). Trade in Ancient Egypt. *Ancient History Encyclopedia*. Retrieved on January 18, 2021 from https://www.ancient.eu/article/1079/trade-in-ancient-egypt/

Maurice, S. C., Phillips, O. R., & Ferguson, C. E. (1986). *Economic Analysis: Theory and Application*. Homewood, IL: Richard D. Irwin, Inc.

Onyeani, C. (2012). *Capitalist Nigger: The Road to Success, A Spider Web Doctrine*. London, UK: Timbuktu Publishers.

Reynolds, L. G. (1985). *Macroeconomics: Analysis and Policy*. Homewood, IL: Richard D. Irwin, Inc.

Samuelson, P. A., & Nordhaus, W. (2010). *Economics* (19th ed.). New York, NY: McGraw-Hill Book Company.

Villemez, W. J., & Beggs, J. J. (1984). Black capitalism and Black inequality: Some sociological considerations. *Social Forces* 63(1):117–144.

Yew, L. K. (2000). *From Third World to First World: Singapore Story (1965–2000)*. New York, NY: Harper Publishing.

Chapter 10

Psychological Perspective

Lilian Anyango Olick

The continued murders of blacks are the result of the failure of the United States to fight the effects of the past five decades of continued systemic racism, with the death of George Floyd being one of the most recent. For blacks, these events are repetitive and traumatic and, as such, represent a severe ongoing threat to everyone's mental health. This chapter examines the impact of racial discrimination against blacks in the United States. It features the need for improving mental health support for this group from a psychological perspective: that is, the systematic analysis of the human mind and its roles, most specifically those affecting behavior in a given context. Thus, the chapter delineates a sociocultural model to the psychology of racism that integrates diverse programs of theory and the concept of racism as a psychological defense mechanism within the debate between advocates of the Black Lives Matter (BLM) and All Lives Matter (ALM) ideologies.

According to the World Health Organization (WHO) (2004), as cited in Galderisi et al. (2015), mental health is a disposition of well-being in which a person recognizes their capabilities, can cope with the ordinary stresses of life, can operate productively, and can contribute to the community. The WHO accentuates that mental health is more profound than just the lack of mental disorders or limitations (WHO, 2004 as cited in Galderisi et al., 2015). Peak mental health is about not only avoiding operational fitness but also looking after ongoing happiness and wellness. Multiple biological, cultural, psychological, and social factors determine an individual's mental health under any circumstance. Some of the most recognized risks to mental health include persistent socioeconomic pressures and violence. The most unmistakable evidence is associated with sexual violence and racism (Thompson et al., 2012; Bryant-Davis et al., 2010). With the advent of the science of positive psychology and happiness, there is a notable shift in mental health research and practice. Positive psychology has initiated a new way of looking into challenges. It recognizes happiness and well-being as constituting a fundamental human skill (Ralph & Corrigan, 2005). Generally, positive psychology goes hand-in-hand with conventional mental health intercessions.

Various scholars describe racism from an individual, cultural, social, biological, or humanistic perspective. Salter et al. (2018) defined *racism* as an individual prejudice and systemic, enduring in the benefits and limitations designated in ideological discourse, cultural elements, and institutional and social actualities that operate collectively with personal biases and inclinations. Racism is now recognized as a system of superiority based on race, fueled by everyone, whether they mean to or not, and whether they identify as racist or not (Salter et al., 2018). Generally, the concept of racism is frequently employed equivalently with discrimination (differential treatment or the absence of equal treatment), stereotyping (prejudiced opinions and ideas, flawed generalizations), prejudice (bias or profiling), and bigotry (intolerance or hatred).

This system inevitably imagines prejudice as a collection of primary social-psychological means accommodating the psychologies of people (i.e., discrimination, bias, stereotyping, and ideological discourse) employed in the race setting (Salter et al., 2018). Although most studies do not treat the context of race as unique in social and psychological studies; instead, scholars typically extrapolate precursors for prejudice or racism and psychological outcomes from low status (versus high status), subordinate (versus dominant), minority (versus majority), out-group (versus in-group), and low status (versus high status) research paradigms (Salter et al., 2018). This proposition can simulate the objective function that race rooted in cultural and social circumstances has participated in deciding which identities and individuals consistently constitute dominant and marginalized assemblages.

Thus, the role of psychological science in cultivating racial discrimination in the community and the widespread racial inequality that persists in critical and crucial life realms (e.g., education, health, housing, and wealth) remains unknown. More specifically, has racism been utilized as a psychological defense mechanism within the debate between advocates of the BLM and ALM ideologies? Furthermore, can the science of psychology pervade revived efforts to combat racism and its effects, primarily on mental health, particularly from a social-cultural perspective? Generally, the chapter focuses on the discussion regarding racism from a sociocultural perspective, how it impacts personal cognition and mental health, and, critically, how to deal with it. Correspondingly, significant prepositions are the following:

(a) Psychological science has played a significant role in advancing societal racial prejudice and the widespread racial differences that persist in many essential life realms.

(b) All ideologies utilize racism as a psychological defense mechanism.
(c) Psychological science viewed from a social-cultural phenomenon can eradicate racism and its effect, especially on mental health.

Finally, a constructivist paradigm assumes that reality is subjective, multiple, and socially constructed, informing the study. The study will adopt a qualitative case study approach to identify the "patterns of meaning" given within texts (Merriam, 1998, p. 31) about the case-psychological sociocultural model to the psychology of racism that integrates diverse programs of theory and the concept of racism as a psychological defense mechanism within the context of the debate between advocates of the BLM and ALM ideologies. Data will be collected through a document review of selected texts to explore and uncover meaning and understanding (Merriam, 1998). Purposive sampling, specifically, criterion and maximum strategies, will be used to identify information-rich documents and sites (Miles & Huberman, 2014). The researcher verifies all articles for relevance, credibility, accuracy, and representativeness (Scott as cited in Bryman, 2016).

PSYCHOLOGY: A CONCEPTUAL DISCUSSION

For starters, it is not farfetched to state that no academic discipline has dealt with the idea of conceptualization, which the American Psychological Association (APA) defines as "the process of forming concepts, particularly those of an abstract nature, out of experience or learned material" (2020, p. 1) more than the field of psychology. In fact, the *Journal of Theoretical and Philosophical Psychology* dedicated an entire volume to "conceptualizing psychological concepts" in 2011 (APA, 2011).

Next, in addition to the general definition of psychology presented earlier, the field has also been characterized as the scientific investigation of behavior, experience, and mental processes in all living creatures (Fernald, 2008). In short, it is the science of mind and behavior. The two parts of the word "psychology" expressed in terse order mean (1) "the study of" (2) "the mind." But the discipline of psychology today extends far beyond the mind in both directions: inward and outward toward the environment. Its topics of inquiry range from neural messages to cultural influences. Few fields offer such breadth and so many practical applications (Fernald, 2008). Economists concentrate on financial behavior, theologians on religious behavior, sociologists on group behavior, and so forth, but psychologists include the study of the behavior of all living creatures anywhere—a broad mandate, indeed. Sometimes, psychologists simply use the term *behavior* to refer to the extensive array of reactions produced by diverse creatures. It should be made clear, however, that modern psychology reaches far beyond health and illness, mental, and physical. In such instances, it may include thoughts, feelings, and psychological responses as well. In fact, the discipline of psychology entered the twenty-first century with a mandate from the APA to engage in more intensive study of happiness, fulfillment, and the sense of well-being. Modern psychology seeks to discover and foster the ways in which people and societies can flourish (Seligman & Csikszentmihalyi, 2000).

Also, the psychology discipline has been conceptualized in terms of its general approaches and major theories. Commencing with the general approaches, there are four major ones. First, the *Physiological-Biological Approach* focuses on how the normal functions of living organisms and their parts impact behavior. Operating from the premise that everything an organism does must be controlled by some physical process in its body, the approach proffers that discovering the nexus between the physiology and the behavior will assist a researcher to comprehend why the organism behaves the manner that it does. In addition to delineating physical mechanisms, a researcher can also examine how intrinsic characteristics also contribute to the behavior (Freedman, 1982).

Second, the *Behavioral Approach* concentrates on the activities of an animal that can be observed directly, instead of concentrating on internal activities. The approach is often times referred to as *Stimulus-Response* or *S-R* psychology since it highlights an organism's response to a stimulus while ignoring what happens inside the organism. It is also dubbed *black box* psychology because the behavioral psychologist perceives an animal as a "black box" that is closed and unknowable. According to this approach, "internal changes are important only in so far as they produce changes in behavior, and any internal change should produce some change in behavior. Therefore, the behaviorist need not study the internal processes, because they will show up in the behavior" (Freedman, 1982, p. 9).

Third, the *Cognitive Approach* pays attention to how thought shapes behavior. The postulate of the approach is that beliefs, expectations, linkages among events, memories, and other mental processes that control behavior comprise cognition. Thus, psychologists operating from a cognitive perspective focus on the mental processes that control the behavior of the subject under investigation (Freedman, 1982).

Fourth and finally, the *Humanistic Approach*, while it does not reject the preceding approaches, nonetheless, foregrounds the individual as a unique person as opposed to being simply a representative of the human species. Humanists delineate the following two characteristics that separate people from other animals: (1) people are free to act and, thus, must take responsibility for their actions; and (2) people have a goal, which is to achieve self-actualization—that is, "the full and complete expression of their own potential" (Freedman, 1982, pp. 10–11). Consequently, humanistic psychologists focus on subjective experience: that is, the experience that is interpreted mentally or felt emotionally. Therefore, unlike behavioral psychologists who deal with internal events, cognitive psychologists treat internal events (Freedman, 1982).

In addition, vis-à-vis the major theories, there are six. First, *Cognitive Developmental Theory* accentuates the "person as knower." Thus, a person is portrayed as a being that is capable of (a) interpreting meaning, (b) solving problems creatively, (c) synthesizing information, and (d) critically analyzing a statement. These capabilities, according to the theory, allow a person to shape his or her experience, select certain elements of the environment to which to attend, and plan actions to accomplish goals (Newman & Newman, 2017).

Second, *Learning Theory* focuses on elements that explain the relatively enduring changes that take place due to experience. The four strands of this theory are the following: (1) *classical condition*, which suggests that when two phenomena occur very close together in time, they come to acquire similar denotations and to yield similar responses; (2) *operant conditioning*, which postulates that repetition and the consequences of behavior are they major factors in learning; (3) *social learning*, which purports that much learning occurs as a result of observing and imitating the behaviors of other people, not an outcome of the intentional manipulation of rewards and punishments; and (4) *cognitive behaviorism*, which proposes that a complex set of expectations, goals, and values comprise behavior and impact performance (Newman & Newman, 2017).

Third, *Social Role Theory* deals with how a person's participation in increasingly diverse and complex social roles shapes the process of socialization and development. Role, then, is commonly defined as any combination of "behaviors that has some socially agreed-upon function and for which there exists an accepted code of norms" (Newman & Newman, 2017, p. 18). Four dimensions that are profitable for examining the effects of social roles on development are as follows: (1) the number of roles in which a person is involved, (2) the intensity of involvement that the roles require or a person brings to them, (3) the pattern of participation in the roles over time, and (4) the degree of structure specified for the roles (Newman & Newman, 2017).

Fourth, *Psychoanalytic Theory*, with an emphasis on the development of a person's emotional and social life, offers the perspective that all behaviors, except one that emerges from tiredness, are motivated. This perceptive postulate is accompanied by a tacit need for a psychology of behavior—a behavior that has meaning and does not occur randomly without purpose. Rooted in the supposition that motives precipitate behavior, the theory offers the following two hypotheses: H_1: there are two fundamental psychological motives—(1) aggression and (2) sexuality—upon which all psychological events are based; H_2: the area of the psyche named the "unconscious" is the residence of strong, primitive emotions (Newman & Newman, 2017).

Fifth, *Fulfilment Theory* tenders the notion that in order to comprehend experience, it is vital to examine it from the point of view of the person. Thus, according to this theory, "self-concept" is a major variable for understanding behavior, as it is the key to knowing how a person classifies experiences and the manner he or she denotes his or her goals and needs. As such, the theory puts forward the view that people strive toward a more fully functioning state (Newman & Newman, 2017).

Sixth, *Psychosocial Theory* focuses on the ability of a person to subscribe to his or her own development. According to this theory, development takes place throughout a person's lifespan, from childhood to adulthood. The five organizing concepts that undergird the theory are the following: (1) *stages of development*—prenatal, infancy, toddlerhood, early school age, middle school age, early adolescence, later adolescence, early adulthood, middle adulthood, and later adulthood; (2) *developmental tasks*—a set of skills and competences a person acquires as s/he gains mastery over the environment; (3) *psychological crisis*—a person's psychological efforts to adjust to the demands of the social environment at each stage of development; (4) *the central process for resolving the psychological crisis*—the presiding milieu in which the conflict is resolved; and (5) *coping behavior*—the active efforts to resolve stress and to establish novel solutions to the challenges of each developmental stage (Newman & Newman, 2017).

PREPOSITION ONE: PSYCHOLOGICAL SCIENCE AND SOCIETAL RACIAL DISCRIMINATION

Most studies define racism from an individual psychological perspective by using prejudice, stereotyping, or discrimination. However, as identified in the previous sections, racism is ingrained in the individual mind and established at past and cultural levels. Concentrating on personal bias can disguise the position that institutional and cultural means work in sustaining race-based bureaucracies. In the article *Current Directions in Psychological Science*, Salter et al. (2018) suggested a cultural-psychological strategy to prejudice. The authors recommended that everyday settings sustain support and control racist processes and reproduce racism. People form and sustain these racist means through their choices and behaviors. For instance, individuals might select some descriptions of the past, fashioning history and intervening in collective thought in a way that serves racialism. This reciprocation connecting people and culture makes it more challenging to demolish racism. According to Salter et al. (2018), prejudice cannot be undone by singularly changing people's biases because features of our ordinary systems support those preferences. Thus, the goal of this section is to investigate the function psychological science has performed in sustaining societal racial prejudice and the widespread racial disparities that continue to exist in any number of essential life domains from a sociocultural model of psychology and within the context of the debate between advocates of the BLM and ALM ideologies.

The campaign, BLM, was conceived in July of 2013 after the state absolved Zimmerman George in the death of Martin Trayvon, a seventeen-year-old African American, and with the passing of Floyd George on 20th 2020 being one of the most current events that sparked the campaign's response and actions and this study. The campaign's initiators designated it as "a rejoinder or countered to structural anti-Black racialism permeating the US, and *a confirmation of Black communities'* contributions to the humankind, community, and resilience in light of lethal abuse and oppression" (Garza, 2014, p. 1). BLM became the rallying call of a present social action that defeated the premise of a *post-racial* United States and reoriented state psychological discourse on anti-black prejudice (Petersen-Smith, 2015). Over the earlier few ages, BLM demonstrations have taken place in every primary U.S. city.

Even though the campaign has been black-led, supporters of varied races have marched within cities and communities, interrupted presidential election campaign events, and invaded city halls, malls, and divisional police units. Public knowledge and appreciation of BLM are widespread, influential, and nearly twice as many U.S. citizens back BLM (43 percent) as opposed to it (22 percent) (Horowitz & Livingston, 2016). In support of this reformist campaign, there have been attempts from counter-movements such as ALM. These counter-campaigns, nevertheless, have been primarily overpowered in the streets and outnumbered in social media and online engagement by BLM (Anderson & Hitlin, 2016). Based on the conceptions of these two campaigns, this portion examines the relationship between psychological science and societal racial prejudice by investigating relevant literature.

First, psychological science, particularly from a socio and cultural perspective, can significantly influence the interpretation and meaning of the two movements by supporters from either side. For instance, when the BLM motto appeared, oppositionists conjectured the expression as divisive and confrontational, taking it to eliminate other races (Sherfinski, 2015). The expression *ALM* emerged to argue that all lives are equal because all are human beings. Nevertheless, BLM advocates asserted that the campaign does not suggest that other lives do not matter; instead, in a world that discriminates against, marginalizes, and stigmatizes black individuals, societies recognized BLM, too (Tucker & Hegg, 2015). The diverse arguments from both parties, with each side noting its isolation and non-existence in the opposition campaign, evidence the impact of psychological science on deciphering meanings, primarily from a cognitive, behavioral, humanistic, and sociocultural cognitive position.

For instance, Gallagher et al. (2018) examined how rallies and counterprotests diverge by a multilevel examination of over 860,000 tweets quantifying aspects their discourse. The study discovered that #AllLivesMatter promotes opposition within #BlackLivesMatter and hashtags like #PoliceLivesMatter and #BlueLivesMatter in such a manner that historically reverberates the tension between black reformers and law enforcement. Besides, the investigation confirmed that a notable portion of #AllLivesMatter utilization originates from hijacking by #BlackLivesMatter advocates. Beyond solely introducing #AllLivesMatter with #BlackLivesMatter content, these hijackers employ the hashtag to face the counter-protest notion of ALM undeviatingly. The review's conclusions suggest that the BLM campaign could develop, display various discussions, and dodge derailment on social media by examining counter-protest views, a primary subject of #AllLivesMatter, instead of the campaign itself.

Sawyer and Gampa (2018) estimated the extent to which antiracist social campaigns influenced blacks' and whites' explicit and implicit racial views versus each other. Precisely, the investigation explored whether explicit and implicit racial biases evolved throughout the evolution and growth of BLM and high periods of the BLM exertion. The research established that antiracist social campaigns contribute a latent societal-level dilemma for decreasing racial segregation. The investigation also considered racial views before and throughout BLM, including its high effort utilizing 1,369,204 members from 2009 to 2016. Overall inherent attitudes were less pro-white throughout BLM than before BLM becoming successively less pro-white after and beyond BLM, and were less pro-white during most points of high BLM activists after controlling for abnormalities in participant attributes and characteristics. Whites became less intrinsically pro-white as BLM, whereas blacks conferred slight variation considering variations in implied biases by participant race. Whites became less pro-white concerning definite biases, and blacks became less pro-black through BLM, each approaching an equal "no inclination" status. The study explicitly defined racial views in BLM settings, with no center on ALM, even though its goal was not to discover the link and connection between psychological science and societal racial prejudice.

Watson-Singleton et al. (2021) considered perseverative perception and BLM activism as modifiers in evaluating racism's impact on depressive symptoms. The investigation further examined the connection between psychological science and racial prejudice, specifically depressive manifestations over time, and the resilience and risk modifiers that influence this connection. One understudied concept that may exasperate this connection and link is perseverative cognition-chronic activation of stress-related cognitive descriptions, an aspect that the inquiry established. Nevertheless, race-specific organizations, such as BLM activism, attenuate this relationship. Thus, across two-time periods and over half a year, the research reviewed autoregressive and cross-lagged connections between racial prejudice and depressive signs. It also experimented if BLM actions and perseverative cognition modified the cross-lagged relationships between depressive traits and racial prejudice. Verdicts established a notable cross-lagged effect of Time 1 racial segregation on Time 2 depressive traits using data from 232 African Americans. The cross-lagged influence modifies both perseverative cognition and aid for BLM actions identifying that Time 1 racial discrimination joins with Time 2 depressive traits at lower points of perseverative cognition and lower points of BLM aid.

Hoffman et al. (2016) researched the existential-humanistic viewpoint on BLM. Current rally campaigns differentiated from past campaigns through decentralized management and employing technology and social media were fundamental in dealing with social justice matters. The investigation confirmed that BLM represents one of the most prominent and contentious modern rally campaigns. Most of the contention is related to the misconstruction, distorted depictions, and strives to undermine the campaign. An analysis of the evolution of BLM and examination of concepts like polarization and privilege conceded that the BLM movement produced a potent sociocultural evaluation and inventive utilization of anger, suffering, and pain from advancing human pride and positive cultural transformation.

Moreover, the postulates of existential-humanistic psychology heighten the recognition of BLM and other protest campaigns while further extending essential direction on evading various latent risks to the campaign's achievement. Critical psychology (Prilleltensky & Fox, 1997 as cited in Hoffman et al., 2016) found out that psychology has often augmented the status quo. Unquestionably, existing-humanistic psychology aligns with this exposition and critique suggested by Prilleltensky and Fox (1997) that "reassuring the poor, people of color, the working class, and women to explain their predicaments as individuals guarantees that they strive to transform themselves instead of the community" (1997, p. 12). If existing-humanistic psychologists only fight these inequalities as they provide therapy services inside the counseling rooms, they will fail to realize the real potential of existing-humanistic postulates in the world.

Leach and Allen (2017) reviewed a recent social science investigation on BLM by applying a model of dynamic dual-pathway of a rally to the campaign to conjecture the social psychology of the movement. The study ascertained that the reality and dynamics of global campaigns such as BLM might improve psychology methodologically, practically, and conceptually.

The suggested framework interlocks with macro-social model campaigns such as BLM since it centers on the social and cultural division of facts and reality as an effective method over a period explaining that individuals get to describe their encounters in peaceful manners. This social validation produces more potent identity, assessment, sensation, and motivation providing psychological evidence of corporate and joint operations such as demonstration. Compatible with the framework, a review of BLM insinuates that potency and anger are founded, in part, on perceived social assistance from people who share values either online or in person (De Choudhury et al., 2016; Freelon et al., 2016a, b). As suggested in Leach and Allen's (2017), anger about police prejudice and the perceived potency of demonstration are fundamental interpretations of black people's behavior and motivation underpinning BLM (Freelon et al., 2016a, b).

PREPOSITION TWO: RACISM AS A PSYCHOLOGICAL DEFENSE MECHANISM

Another different view from research is that racism (and discrimination against people of all races) has no evolutionary or biological origin but is fundamentally a psychological factor—principally a defense mechanism constituting feelings of anxiety and insecurity. There is further evidence of this view from the psychological concept of terrorism management (Greenberg et al., 1986 as quoted in Hoffman et al., 2016). Studies have shown that people feel anxious and insecure when reminded of their death and react by being more inclined to obstinate goals, materialism, greed, prejudice, and anger (Greenberg & Kosloff, 2008). They are more prone to adapt to socially asserted views and identify themselves with their tribal or racial groups. The purpose of this section is to investigate the concept of racism as a means of psychological self-defense within the context of the conflict between BLM advocates and the views of ALM by analyzing existing literature.

According to Terror Management Theory, the motive for using prejudice as a means of psychological protection is to increase one's self-esteem in the face of death or to feel secure or to be at risk of death (Greenberg et al., 1986, as stated in Hoffman et al., 2016; Greenberg & Kosloff, 2008). According to some studies, racism is the same as feeling inferior, uncomfortable, or unworthy (Greenberg & Kosloff, 2008). Studies identify psychological protection from five different aspects of prejudice. This aspect is seen in the various categories, which lead to extreme forms of discrimination. First, if individuals feel vulnerable or notice a lack of identity, they are inclined to join a group to reinforce their sense of self-worth and gain a feeling of belonging. Joining a group or becoming a part of something better than them and collectively participating with other team affiliates makes one feel whole and essential (Greenberg & Kosloff, 2008). Nonetheless, this group status could lead to a second stage: hostility to other assemblages.

Second, to further reinforce their sense of connections, team participants can grow feelings of animosity toward other groups. A group can be further defined and merged into something else and compete with other parties. A third factor is when team participants withdraw compassion from other group participants, reducing their anxiety and empathy for others (Greenberg & Kosloff, 2008). They can do good to their team members but be cruel and insensitive to anyone outside it. This feature is closely related to the fourth factor: the homogenization of people from other teams. Therefore, the research identifies people not by their personality or behavior; instead, general prejudice and group thinking (Greenberg & Kosloff, 2008). Fifth and lastly, in the most severe and toxic form of racism, personages may expose their psychological imperfections and their failure to one party to avoid responsibility and blame. Some groups become goats. Therefore, they should be punished, attacked, or killed, in retaliation for the charges against them (Greenberg & Kosloff, 2008). Individuals with distorted temperaments and traits are more inclined to this approach since they cannot accept any of their blunders and are more likely to praise others.

Similarly, a study by Juby (2005) on racial, ethnic, and defensive practices of white counselors has found that apart from reinforcing the notion that white counselors use self-defense strategies for color client counseling, there is no dynamic study on what constitutes self-defense counseling. Moreover, while most of the recent literature on modern forms of apartheid focused on white rights and the psychological effects of apartheid, this study established a small study investigating how white people supported racism. This article has suggested two perspectives that explain the implications of racial defense measures (Juby, 2005).

The first is the Modern Theory of Racism, which holds that today's misunderstandings reflect race conditions. The acceptance of good and bad conditions by people of color leads to white Americans who see themselves as righteous and just. The Racial Identity Theory proposes that information processing techniques, such as self-defense strategies, help whites process and address racial issues. The primary purpose of this study was to examine the perceptions that racial discord and racial profiling contribute to anti-apartheid measures. Documents affirming white people's self-defense against apartheid often do not take into account individual differences. Research considers that whites use racist-related defenses without considering the possible differences between group members in number or the types of protections used (Juby, 2005).

Therefore, an additional objective of the study was to investigate individual differences in racial protection. Participants were 236 white counselors and psychologists. The results showed that racial disagreements and particular racial identities were related to the full-fledged defense in situations of interracial counseling. Ambivalence was associated with intellectual self-defense and the fight against aggression and racial identity issues associated with racist ideologies. The results also suggested that racial protection is becoming more complex. The study converts racial identity scores into profiles for further experimental analysis. Profile analysis showed that certain types of profiles were associated with low levels of ambiguity and self-defense. The study's findings highlight the importance of using multidisciplinary methods to assess the complex relationship between race and other race-related factors (Juby, 2005).

Similarly, Utsey and Gernat (2002) conducted a study examining the relationship between racial status and self-defense strategies by white counselors during racial counseling and surveillance dyads. The sample consisted of 145 white trainers enrolled in royalty and doctoral programs at two small private northeastern universities in the United States. The results showed that white counselor trainees with low levels of nationalistic maturity relied on the initial protection of the ego to manage the anxiety experienced during provocative counseling and guarding dyads.

PREPOSITION THREE: PSYCHOLOGICAL SCIENCE AS A TOOL TO ERADICATE RACISM AND ITS EFFECT ESPECIALLY ON MENTAL HEALTH

Experiences of racism, both direct and indirect in the form of minimal harassment or racial expression through the media, can have severe outcomes for the mental well-being of African Americans. These effects referred to as "racial trauma" can lead to fatigue, depression, energy conservation, chronic stress, and symptoms such as posttraumatic stress disorder. Police cruelty and widespread unfairness of past and present origins of violence in African American communities are significant. Both BLM movements and counseling suggest addressing this reality at many levels. The BLM attempts to promote and foster awareness of systemic prejudice and advance resilience among African Americans. Consequently, counseling services should focus on promoting and fostering multicultural values, social equity, and advocacy.

For example, French et al. (2019) proposed a different psychological framework for the dynamic healing of black people in the United States. The research is founded on existing models focused on social justice activism and education and suggested a mode of transformation and healing that includes liberal psychology, Intersectionality Theory, and black psychology. The study has reviewed these concepts as an antecedent to acquainting a dynamic healing approach and its five-pronged elements: (1) integration, (2) critical awareness, (3) strong hope, (4) strength and resilience, and (5) cultural trustworthiness and self-awareness. It culminates with a discourse on applying more extraordinary healing in clinical work, training, research, and social justice support (French et al., 2019).

Specifically, the study found that psychological healing requires a transition to traditional psychological therapies that focus on helping the person deal with discrimination and eliminating players that advance race-based trauma. Consequently, efficacious healing recognizes the pain of cruelty while promoting the hope of justice and freedom. Sensitive knowledge, hope, resilience, resistance, and integrity transform the process of dynamic healing. Studies have suggested that counselors should go beyond looking at social justice and multiculturalism as criteria for placing social justice in the middle of our research, training, clinical practice, and advocacy (French et al., 2019).

Thomas and Zuckerman (2018) discussed the link between BLM and community psychology, highlighting similarities with the new frameworks provided by the organization. The study provided an overview of BLM, discussed development, and highlighted ideas and approaches to each review article. Research has shown that knowledge of human history plays an essential role in promoting mental health, and the West African Sankofa concept reflects this fact. Research has also shown that Black Liberation Psychology supports the Black History Framework (Chapman-Hilliard & Adams-Bass, 2016), especially when the history of encounters is more important than the individual's passing. According to the study, members of the black diaspora face risks ranging from migrant segregation, institutional pressure, vandalism, and financial ruin. Finally, the study found that Black History Knowledge (BHK) and Black Liberation have created awareness of racial discrimination and discrimination, the contributions and achievements of black people, their financial status (social, political, economic), and cultural power. The authors, therefore, have suggested completing these activities by finding the effects of mental health awareness (Thomas & Zuckerman, 2018).

CONCLUSION AND RECOMMENDATIONS

A review of evidence in the context of BLM and ALM ideologies reveals that psychological science has played a significant role in

(a) sustaining societal racial prejudice and the widespread racial inequalities that remain existence in any number of fundamental life realms;

(b) all ideologies that have utilized racism as a psychological defense mechanism; and
(c) psychological science that viewed from a social-cultural phenomenon can eradicate racism and its effect, especially on mental health.

Generally, data relating to BLM and ALM ideologies reveal, from a psychological perspective, that findings on the three preceding prepositions were limited. Even though racism as a psychological defense mechanism existed, none focuses on BLM and ALM's context. Consequently, the literature suggests more studies to fill this knowledge gap.

In sum, the deaths of Floyd George and many other blacks, and the subsequent BLM protests that followed across the globe, have exerted their damage on the mental health of African Americans. Historically and in today's world, the critical role of race and ethnic order should continue to affect people psychologically. Black clients in the consulting room feel strongly about the impact of discrimination, and powerlessness, anger, fatigue, and anxiety characterize the system. Experiences of racism, both direct and indirect in the form of minimal harassment or racial expression through the media, can have severe consequences for the mental health of black people. These effects, designated as "phylogenetic trauma," can lead to energy loss, chronic stress, fatigue, depression, and symptoms such as posttraumatic stress disorder. Police cruelty and widespread prejudice of past and present origins of violence among African Americans are common effects. Both the BLM campaign and the psychology behavior suggest addressing these realities on many levels, with BLM seeking to raise awareness of systemic racial injustices and promote stability for black people. In contrast, psychology enunciates multicultural values, social justice, and the promotion of improving the mental health of blacks and all.

REFERENCES

American Psychological Association (APA). (2011). Conceptualizing psychological concepts. *Journal of Theoretical and Philosophical Psychology* 31(2):73–125.

American Psychological Association (APA). (2020). *APA Dictionary of Psychology*. Washington, DC: APA Publications.

Anderson, M., & Hitlin, P. (2016). The hashtag #BlackLivesMatter emerges: Social activism on Twitter. Pew Research Report. Retrieved from http://www.pewinternet.org/2016/08/15/thehashtag-blacklivesmatter-emerges-social-activism-on-twitter/

Bryant-Davis, T., Ullman, S. E., Tsong, Y., Tillman, S., & Smith, K. (2010). Struggling to survive: Sexual assault, poverty, and mental health outcomes of

African American women. *The American Journal of Orthopsychiatry* 80(1), 61–70. https://doi.org/10.1111/j.1939-0025.2010.01007

Chapman-Hilliard, C., & Adams-Bass, V. (2016). A conceptual framework for utilizing Black history knowledge as a path to psychological liberation for Black youth. *Journal of Black Psychology* 42(6), 479–507. https://doi.org/10.1177/0095798415597840

De Choudhury, M., Jhaver, S., Sugar, B., & Weber, I. (May 2016). Social media participation in an activist movement for racial equality. Paper presented at the 10th International AAAI Conference on Web and Social Media, Cologne, Germany. Retrieved from http://www.munmund.net/pubs/BLM_ICWSM16.pdf

Freedman, J. L. (1982). *Introductory Psychology*. Boston, MA: Addison-Wesley Publishing Company, Inc.

Freelon, D., McIlwain, C. D., & Clark, M. D. (2016a). Beyond the hashtags: #Ferguson, #BlackLivesMatter, and the online struggle for offline justice. Washington, DC: American University, Center for Media and Social Impact. Retrieved from http://cmsimpact.org/wp-content/uploads/2016/03/beyond_the_hashtags_2016.pdf

Freelon, D., McIlwain, C. D., & Clark, M. D. (2016b). Quantifying the power and consequences of social media protest. *New Media & Society*. Advance online publication. https://doi.org/10.1177/1461444816676646

French, B. H., Lewis, J. A., Mosley, D. V., Adames, H. Y., Chavez-Dueñas, N. Y., Chen, G. A., & Neville, H. A. (2020). Toward a psychological framework of radical healing in communities of color. *The Counseling Psychologist* 48(1), 14–46. https://doi.org/10.1177/0011000019843506

Galderisi, S., Heinz, A., Kastrup, M., Beezhold, J., & Sartorius, N. (2015). Toward a new definition of mental health. *World Psychiatry: Official Journal of the World Psychiatric Association (WPA)* 14(2), 231–233. https://doi.org/10.1002/wps.20231

Gallagher, R. J., Reagan, A. J., Danforth, C. M., & Dodds, P. S. (2018). Divergent discourse between protests and counter-protests: #BlackLivesMatter and #AllLivesMatter. *PloS one* 13(4), e0195644. https://doi.org/10.1371/journal.pone.0195644

Garza, A. (2014). A history of the #BlackLivesMatter movement. Retrieved from http://blacklivesmatter.com/herstory/

Greenberg, J., & Kosloff, S. (2008). Terror management theory: Implications for understanding prejudice, stereotyping, intergroup conflict, and political attitudes. *Social and Personality Psychology Compass* 2(5), 1881–1894. https://doi.org/10.1111/j.1751-9004.2008.00144.x

Greenberg, J., Pyszczynski, T., & Solomon, S. (1986). The causes and consequences of a need for self-esteem: A terror management theory. In R. F. Baumeister (Ed.), *Public Self and Private Self*. New York, NY: Springer-Verlag.

Hoffman, L., Granger, N., Vallejos, L., & Moats, M. (2016). An existential-humanistic perspective on Black Lives Matter and contemporary protest movements. *Journal of Humanistic Psychology* 56(6), 595–611. https://doi.org/10.1177/0022167816652273

Horowitz, J. M., & Livingston, G. (2016). How Americans view the Black Lives Matter movement. Pew Research Report. Retrieved from http://www.pewresearch. org/fact-tank/2016/07/08/howamericans-view-the-black-lives-matter-movement/

Juby, H. L. (2005). Racial ambivalence, racial identity and defense mechanisms in white counselor trainees. *Dissertation Abstracts International: Section B: The Sciences and Engineering* 66(5-B), 2855.

Leach, C. W., & Allen, A. M. (2017). The social psychology of the Black Lives Matter meme and movement. *Current Directions in Psychological Science* 26(6), 543–547. https://doi.org/10.1177/0963721417719319

Newman, B. M., & Newman, P. R. (2017). *Development through Life: A Psychological Approach* (13th ed.). Homewood, IL: The Dorsey Press.

Petersen-Smith, K. (2015). Black Lives Matter. *International Socialist Review* 96. Retrieved from https://isreview.org/ issue/96/black-lives-matter

Prilleltensky, I., & Fox, D. (1997). Introducing critical psychology: Values, assumptions, and the status quo. In D. Fox & I. Prilleltensky (Eds.), *Critical Psychology: An Introduction*. Thousand Oaks, CA: Sage.

Ralph, R. O., & Corrigan, P. W. (2005). *Recovery in Mental Illness: Broadening Our Understanding of Wellness*. Washington, DC: American Psychological Association.

Salter, P. S., Adams, G., & Perez, M. J. (2018). Racism in the structure of everyday worlds: A cultural-psychological perspective. *Current Directions in Psychological Science* 27(3):150–155. https://doi.org/10.1177/0963721417724239

Sawyer, J., & Gampa, A. (2018). Implicit and explicit racial attitudes changed during Black Lives Matter. *Personality & Social Psychology Bulletin* 44(7), 1039–1059. https://doi.org/10.1177/0146167218757454

Sherfinski, D. (October 15, 2015). Ben Carson: Of course all lives matter-and all lives include Black lives. *The Washington Times*. Retrieved on November 2, 2020 from https://www.washingtontimes.com/news/2015/oct/15/ben-carson-course-all-lives-matter-and-all-lives include Black lives

Thomas, D., & Zuckerman, A. (2018). Black Lives Matter in community psychology. *Community Psychology in Global Perspective* 4(2), 1–8. 10.1285/i24212113v4i2p1

Thompson, N. J., McGee, R. E., & Mays, D. (2012). Race, ethnicity, substance use, and unwanted sexual intercourse among adolescent females in the United States. *The Western Journal of Emergency Medicine* 13(3):283–288. https://doi.org/10.5 811/westjem.2012.3.11774

Tucker, B., & Hegg, S. (October 22, 2015). Tactics of Black Lives Matter. IN Close. Episode 216. KCTS-TV. Archived from the original on November 2, 2015. Retrieved on October 30, 2020 from https://web.archive.org/web/20151102024356/http://kcts9.org/programs/in-close/tactics-black-lives-matter

Utsey, S., & Gernat, A. (2002). White racial identity attitudes and the ego defense mechanisms used by White counselor trainees in racially provocative counseling situations. *Journal of Counseling & Development* 80(4). https://doi.org/10.1002/j.1556-6678. 2002.tb00214.x

Watson-Singleton, N. N., Mekawi, Y., Wilkins, K. V., & Jatta, I. F. (2021). Racism's effect on depressive symptoms: Examining perseverative cognition and Black Lives Matter activism as moderators. *Journal of Counseling Psychology* 68(1), 27–37.

World Health Organization (WHO). (2004). *Promoting Mental Health: Concepts, Emerging Evidence, Practice (Summary Report)*. Geneva, Switzerland: WHO.

Chapter 11

Business Perspective

Olumuyiwa Adekunle Kehinde

This chapter focuses on how race interrelates with business, which can be generally denoted as the study of a person's regular occupation, profession, or trade, and also as the practice of making one's living by engaging in commerce. In a broader sense, the chapter accounts for how race and business can influence each other and how both are speaking to Black Lives Matter and All Lives Matter calls around the world over the death of George Floyd, a black man killed by a group of police officers in Minneapolis, United States. It also shows how race reminds the world about other killings of blacks such as Philando Castile, Freddie Gray, Eric Garner, and Michael Brown.

Human beings cannot set apart their "work selves" from their "community selves." The United States like many other nations has been preaching diversity and equality, but systemic racism, white supremacy, and privilege in corporations around the globe persist. Now, the Black Lives Matter and All Lives Matter movements have magnified their voices to ensure reduction or eradication of historic white privilege. This chapter therefore investigates how these movements are motivating the need for distinct actions among business owners and corporations to rethink and support true equality in workplaces and communities. Concomitantly, perceptions of individuals, corporations, and chief executive officers (CEOs) concerning why every life matters within and outside workplaces are examined.

The concept of *race* and its associated issues remain what humankinds have to live and grapple with for years unknown and, thus, further reinforced W. E. B. Du Bois's 1903 declaration that remains prophetic till now. In a society such as the United States, race issues are fundamental to understanding the functionality of relationships existing among people and formal and informal organizations. As has been observed by many scholars, race permeates all nooks and crannies of society, and Thomas and Alderfer (1989) opined that every aspect of people's lives are incorporated into race. These aspects may include systems such as education, economy, business, employment, justice, health, politics, and religion, among others; however, racialization when allowed in any degree can distort any system.

Business as a concept is a worldwide phenomenon that may be ranked among what and who shaped or rules the world because of its economic hegemony that asserts unprecedented influence on almost everyone in a society. As a culture, most businesses are attributed to active engagement of entrepreneurs (of whatever backgrounds, color, and culture) toward producing goods and services for people. Noticeably, as no single race has a monopoly of all products and services that its people needed, so do businesses rely heavily on multicultural and multiracial markets. However, the major questions that guide this chapter are the following: How does race and business or entrepreneurship or market interrelate? What is the nature of business ownership in the United States and what group constitutes the most underrepresented and why? What is the implication of this uneven representation? What are big business owners doing currently to bridge these gaps after the recent uproars against structural racialization and inequality in the United States? Furthermore, based on these questions, the following propositions are tendered: (a) there is a relationship between race and business or market/entrepreneurship; (b) business ownership in the United States is dominated by whites while other races are underrepresented; (c) there are numerous impacts of racialization and inequality persisting within the business or entrepreneurship sector in the United States where people with different racial backgrounds operate; (d) in response to recent protests against large racial/ethnic gaps existing within the United States, businesses, big company owners or entrepreneurs are capable to bridge the existing gaps in their corporations. Before addressing these aspects, the conceptual discussion of Business and the methodology upon which the analysis is grounded are first presented in the next two sections.

BUSINESS: A CONCEPTUAL DISCUSSION

As can be gleaned from the definition of the discipline of business provided earlier, it is obvious that the phenomenon does not strictly follow a particular formula as many experts have different approach of discussing business as part of socioeconomic and financial endeavors of humankinds. Notably, business entails any entity such as any enterprise or organization that involves in either commercial, industrial, and or professional endeavors. Business entities may be established toward making profits or as nonprofit organizations, which focus on rendering charitable services to individuals or group(s) or fighting for a particular social issue (Hayes, 2020). Similarly, business can also be described as a chain of activities that entails conceiving ideas on what to be produced or service to be rendered, for whom, how, when, and with anticipated cost, anticipated profit, or to be cost-free. The *Britannica Online Encyclopedia* (2020) added that business may be based and be operating under the existing laws such as those governing right of owing property, contract and exchange, and incorporation.

Explicitly, business type varies, and experts have identified sole (individual) proprietorships, partnerships or joint ventures, and limited liability companies (corporation) (Hayes, 2020; Britannica Online Encyclopedia, 2020). Furthermore, Hayes (2020) asserted that understanding business administration requires some theoretical underpinnings such as strategic management, organizational behavior, as well as Organization Theory. Business can be conceptually framed as re(occurring) human activities that have been existing from time immemorial, and it entails providing goods or services for specific customers free of charge or to make profit. Business can also be described as a chain of economic activities that involve sourcing for raw materials and employees, production or trading goods or services, identifying relevant or potential customers, selling or exchanging goods and services to those customers, and sustaining the business, whether profit is made or not.

Over time, the concept of business and entrepreneurship, or in another words small business versus big business, has been debated (QuickMBA, 2010; Leiber, 2009; Mills Communication Group, 2009). From such arguments and other extant literature, this chapter establishes that in the United States, both forms of businesses exist with the majority being classified as small businesses. Contrary to the notion that big entrepreneurs (or businesses mostly found at Wall Street) are contributing immensely to American economic growth, the Chief Counsel of the Small Business Administration's (SBA), Thomas M. Sullivan (2006), reiterated that small business is pivotal to the U.S. economy as these businesses have been found innovating and creating new jobs rapidly than their competitive larger sizes. Furthermore, Sullivan (2006) stated that across all communities in the United States, small businesses are nimble and creative and playing a significant role. Hait (2021) also mentioned that as a crucial segment of the economy (both national and local), small business remains a main driver of financial growth in the United States.

Importantly, some yardsticks to gain insights into the nature of small and big businesses in the United States include the number of the employees; the size of where the business is located; the company's size; legal structure; sales, shipment, or revenue. While the nature or definition of small businesses is debatable; what is essential in this chapter is to understand that most businesses are created as small startups and eventually drive economic growth in their own capacity (see Hait, 2021).

Similarly, the U.S. Census Bureau's 2021 report titled *Business Formation Statistics by State* revealed that 423,095 business applications were obtained in February of 2021 alone; and, this figure indicated a sharp decline compared to 488,519 business applications received in January of 2021. Despite the fact that no mention is made of the actual percentage of applications submitted in favor of small business or big business, it is crucial to note that many minority groups have been forced to directly or indirectly practice small business culture (even if these groups have bigger business ideas) due to certain constraints like the inability to secure loans and practicing in the mainstream economy due to their race or color. The concept of business in this context implies that any form of standard business (sole proprietorship, partnership, or limited-liability) will require ideas, raw materials, employees, funding, and markets from diverse ethnic groups or cultures before long-term sustainability can be assured. Essentially, doing business in the United States has been misaligned with the supremacy of white people at the detriment of other minority groups, and this is manifesting in different forms, such as challenges in securing funding, transiting to a bigger business, and operating in mainstream markets. Some of these challenges have become visible components of business or entrepreneurship in the United States, and they need to be understood by everyone, especially the existing or intending investors, business owners, and entrepreneurial support organizations.

METHODOLOGY

The methodology adopted for this chapter is a content analysis of both extant literature and new voices that emerged after the recent protests against the brutal killing of George Floyd in June of 2020. The chapter therefore examines the process and forms of racism, and the nature of existing entrepreneurships in the United States. Importantly, themes were formed around how owners of big corporations have responded to the agitation of the masses on equality and deracialized America. This is worth investigating as race and business or market are part of the political economy where enactment of social forces as well as power relations can be linked back to existing interplays of social institutions, history, culture, and markets.

All these issues can be controlled and distorted by various forms of racism, which have all the means of producing "race-based economic inequities" (Hinson et al., 2012, p. 11). Furthermore, this chapter makes some substantial correlates of what previous literature has highlighted concerning means of closing racial and inequality gaps, and why the majority of big and successful business owners just shifted their attention to in support of Black Lives Matter and All Lives Matter movements. The rest of this chapter discusses some concepts that include processes and forms of racism, why to examine race and business, the nature of minority and majority business enterprise in the United States, and how gaps and inequalities have been created, thereby making the lives of certain races matter. Some case studies are also highlighted, with discussion and conclusion on how business owners have responded toward closing such inequalities with the aims of making all lives matter.

PROCESSES AND FORMS OF RACISM

Racialization or racism is a huge social menace, and most developed countries are not immune to it. Historically, racism in the United States has generated a humungous amount of varied concerns from different people depending on the aspect one experiences it. However, its dynamism is noticeable each day and, according to Hinson et al. (2012), five eras—(1) Colonial to Mexican-American War, (2) Civil War to Jim Crow, (3) New Deal to Civil Rights, (4) Civil Rights Era, and (5) Post-Civil Rights Era—are associated with mechanisms for dominating and controlling others, especially through certain social and economic practices.

Despite organized resistance to such control and domination, the eras have shown enough racialized activities and race-based inequalities that have accumulated from the social structure in the United States. As the trend is ongoing and ever changing, the reality is that structural racialization is "America's major piece of unfinished business" (Foreman, 2000, p. 30), which is now part and parcel of corporate ventures and business enterprises. In addition, when racial prejudice is injected into businesses, its effects will remain unpalatable to a particular race or individual while the actors may not be focused and thereby circumventing real actions against them, or in another words "diverting our attention from the structural changes that are required in order to achieve racial justice" (Hinson et al., 2012, p. 4).

To better understand race within the precinct of this chapter, four forms have been identified and they can be linked back to the colonial era, according to Hinson et al. (2012):

(1) Interpersonal racism involves one group making presumptuous statements or acting with prejudice and discrimination about other groups' personalities, intentions, and abilities based on their race, which altogether may lead to intended or unintended cruel actions against other groups.

(2) Internalized racism arises from intentional or unintentional self-aggrandizement of dominant groups with their constant show of their political, social, and economic hegemony; experiences; and work done to remind other stigmatized groups of their own abilities and intrinsic worth. Such situations are internalization of those negative messages that may rob the less privileged groups of ascertaining their own worth and reaching their potential fully. Solemnly, racism is this form reinforces racial oppression but at the same time beclouds their true structural and systemic nature.
(3) Institutional racism may happen across various intuitions such as schools, businesses, justice department, and police, among others. Such racism may be perpetrated (in)directly and or (un)intentionally with the aim to limit some people's rights or to make them suffer unnecessarily based on their race.
(4) Structural racism occurs based on the accumulated results and influence of a racialized society over the centuries. An example is the creation of the white middle class, which has offered opportunities for some to be wealthy and owing sumptuous properties until today. One example is this: "in the 17th Century, Africans from diverse nations were categorized under the label 'Negro,' which was a racialized category; in the space of one century, different forms of labor were racialized so that 'worker' was white and 'slave' was Negro; and, over time, different groups of immigrants have been assigned to the broad categories of white (European immigrants) or 'of color' (Latin American, African, Asian-Pacific Islander and more recently, Middle Eastern immigrants), and also for today's struggles over immigration policy" (Hinson et al., 2012, p. 5).

Racialization in America is truly an "unfinished business" (Foreman, 2000, p. 30; Norton, 2009). According to Edelman, a public-relations firm's poll (published in published on June 9, 2020) showed that about two-thirds of Americans (plus 57 percent of white people) attested that systemic racism exists in the United States (The Economist, 2020). If not well-redefined, as the U.S. population grows, racism may be a potential reason for more wild and wide violence, and thereby having unpalatable impacts on social cohesion, national development and cultural diversity as individuals, groups, and institutions, including the police, which is the main antagonist in the recent protests that rocked the United States following the death of George Floyd, may be on collision cause. This has also called for looking inwardly to an aspect of institutionalized racial issues with a focus on how business ventures visualize why the lives of both blacks and whites should matter.

WHY A NEED TO EXAMINE RACE AND BUSINESS

It is doubtful if any country can survive economic wise and attain sustainable development without business ventures from different groups and races. Even China, the most populated country in the world, understands this economic necessity. This is in line with Silverman's (2000) argument that color cannot be hidden by the invisible hand of the market, and that when the colonial paradigm is internally employed as a model for analyzing the business development of the minority group in minority markets, some institutional constraints entangling doing business can be spotted in such minority markets.

Understanding the preceding verity within the periscope of race in the United States is another fundamental mechanism to unravel the institutionalized nature of businesses and people involved in their daily operations as well as those exerting power in those businesses. Whatever their interactions are will produce a set of intersections of race, respect for minorities or the rights of the less-privileged, and their quality of life. Reasons for examining race and businesses are profound; and, from the understanding culled from U.S. opinion polls, religion is subliminal to police rank, and businesses are far less ranked to the policing system that the law enforcement agency knows, and which directly or indirectly empowers them to act and overact in both private and public places (see Braithwaite, 2020). Corroborating this assertion on Twitter, Slack CEO Stewart Butterfield (who is one of the most recent voices against police brutality and high-handedness in American society) stated that the need to overhaul police powers and that any police that commits atrocities in the line of duty should be prosecuted, and any abuse of the solemn/sacred power (especially one attached to the office) to maim people without necessity should be counted as federal offense and be viewed as a hate crime and others.

Additionally, firms and businesses have for ages reinforced some section of race and group (especially the minority ones) to suffer in their organizations or in the general public by failing to address, support, and activate mutual and classless relationships among people of varied perspectives, backgrounds, colors, and cultures (Blake-Beard et al., 2006). Importantly, most entrepreneurs, business owners, organizations, and companies have not taken equality of race and culture into a cognizance or right perspective (see Caproni, 2005).

The demographic nature of the United States has some projection toward the dynamics of majority versus minority population in the near future. Referring to the new statistics from the U.S. Census Bureau, Frey (2018) noted that the future growth of the country is tied with the population of youth from the minority races, and that by 2045, the population of the whites in the United States will become a minority as it contracts to 49.7

percent. PolicyLink (2019) also affirmed that the new demographic will engulf the American market by year 2040 when the majority of the people are projected to be colored, and this claim has been backed up with an evidence from the demographic of young people in the United States who are now a colored majority. If this becomes true, it implies that people referred to as color will become a majority and this may change the face of American business and market in terms of their revenue and market share increment, enlarging and retaining customers and continual market expansion (see PolicyLink, 2019).

In Alba's (2018) analysis of the latest version of the projections, the group that is significant in this purported demographic change will be from mixed minority-white family backgrounds, and without such classification, the projection of majority-minority society by 2060 may never come true or be as people have imagined it. In addition, Mohan (2020) believed that if even the country witnessed such a change or not, the American society is far from being a nation without racial discrimination, which, according to Alba (2018), is at a high level especially against blacks. Mohan (2020) further reported that the immediate reactions of many toward the projections got them freaked out, and it accelerated many things including the greater bias against minorities shown by many white Americans who were privy to the information despite noticeable challenges minorities, especially blacks, faced in securing financial aids, enjoying good health, education, and career, as well as receiving deserved criminal justice.

It is also believed that whether the projections become a reality or not, the American society will never remain the same in the future as workplace and business will need really diversity unlike the previous lip service many CEOs had given. Quoting Porter Braswell, one of the founders and the CEO of diversity hiring startups, Jopwel, Mohan (2020) reported that by 2040, having a diverse workforce in a company and doing business will be well-understood by people because they will need to consider and have a personnel (workforce) that understands the new demographic before they can easily sell their products to them. However, if racial discrimination increases or persists against minorities, it implies that racial inequality may negatively influence the majority of the consumers of goods and services, suppliers, and employees, and this may lead to strained businesses because of fewer suppliers, unproductive workforce, as well as missed market segments.

The preceding scenarios all make every life to matter as advancing racial equity will definitely add values to all forms of systems in the country, including businesses and companies. Notably, the minority or the underrepresented people are found mostly in poor communities with amenities, and their economic standards are worse due to fewer or no investment by institutions from mainstream markets, and in another situation whereby these markets are distinct from minority markets as the latter were formed to tackle mainstream society filled with racialization (Silverman, 2000).

Meanwhile, market decisions made from such communities and markets may not thrive because they lack support of those *big guys and gals* in the mainstream markets, thereby making it glaring how market systems and institutions support racial discrimination that makes all lives not to matter, even though there are opposing views concerning some racial issues, including what makes black or minority business owners or entrepreneurs to be lagging behind their white counterparts.

Silverman (2000) asserted that scholars have divergent opinions on racism in the United States as they fail to approach it from colonialism viewpoints, which literarily have formed a heritage from which dominant groups economically and politically subjugate the minority groups. Furthermore, the history of colonialism and racial discrimination in the United States cannot be erased or altered; therefore, according to Silverman (2000), social relations are formed and stabilized by racial and ethnic stratifications in all societies. But, unlike America with a history of internal colonialism (with influence of European colonialism that gave shape to American social relations), the modern racial and ethnic stratification system can be linked to its colonial heritage. Therefore, any opposing argument on the issue can be critically analyzed using internal colonialism to foreground the social experiences of blacks, Latinos/as, native Americans, and other groups (Silverman, 2000).

In agreement with Silverman, some business-related cases mentioned in this chapter show similar social experiences that culminated from both the economic and political dominance of whites over the blacks and other minority groups since the colonial period in U.S. history.

A CASE OF POLITICAL ECONOMY AND CONTROL OF COMMUNITY ASSETS AND BUSINESS

Owing and doing business constitute a part of community assets under broader economic auspices, which in one way or the other is influenced by politics. Hinson, Healey and Bester (2012) mentioned that the conservatives understand and press for an economy whose markets are not pressured externally or by government—to create for the agitators—an unregulated economy devoid of workers' protection, demands for community investments, and the possibility of a racism-free society.

One of the best ways to understand the significance of business perspectives to racial issues in the United States is through political economy and its nexus with markets, unfixed government roles, history and culture, and social institutions, and doing so will reveal more about the influence of racialization on economic structures which transcend markets. Importantly, because of a wider scope of structural racism, political economy and racialization interplay widely to the point of decisions and control of wealth (factors of production), whereby people get education, live, and secure healthcare (Hinson et al., 2012), including who hires who, for what, and how, as well as who owns a business, at what place, and what type. These are ultimately cases that the minority or marginalized people have faced and are still facing in the United States as people who control wealth and resources (that is the conservative politicians, and big corporations) are potential controllers of the economy.

How these corporations responded to the Black Lives Matter movement is discussed later in this chapter. For synthesis, the usual opposing views are centered on times when economic resources were given to communities of color and, historically, the periods are truly useful to analyze today's reality. The first period was during the Reconstruction Racial Order of 1865–1877 when African Americans were allowed to start small businesses, formed cooperatives, build farms, and form political associations and societies. However, after Southern whites massively resisted, the period was short-lived and replaced by Jim Crow that restored white supremacy and control over land and capital.

The second time was in 1965 when Community Action Programs were launched, and in their first year, it made Office of Economic Opportunity to disburse millions of dollars to low-income communities. The money was utilized to establish community institutions, businesses, and training program for job creation by those with or without little capital. After the first year, the programs were hijacked by the governors and mayors after sensing that people were becoming economically buoyant and they long to taste political power. The third period was known for Community Reinvestment Act in 1977 when government regulated banks and thereby offered communities of African Americans and Latinos/as the means of receiving loan opportunities in which billions of dollars were secured as small business and mortgages loans. The Act made it imperative for banks to prioritize loans to small businesses and homeowners within the bank communities, but only for those who have deposits with the banks.

Meanwhile till today, it is hard if not impossible for anyone to empirically say the markets and the economy in the United States are favorable to blacks and other minority or underrepresented races because the markets and that economy are still under the control of those who strictly or slightly believe in colonial and slavery heritage, and promoting contemporary and internal colonialism. A case of black farmers' struggles as earlier experienced during post-Reconstruction and post-Jim Crow periods continue to meet high level of resistance as found on the floor of the House of Representatives when

Steve King vehemently stood against reparation to farmers with authentic cases of discrimination against them (Hinson et al., 2012).

Furthermore, the markets and the economy are notably under rebranded power relations and racialization heritage, which when placed side-by-side with features and nature of racial inequality in the United States, one will arrive at historical, contemporary, and possible future realities of what can be obtained from the economy, markets, and businesses in the next decades. Norton (2009) underscored the complexity of racial inequality in America from historical points of view to the contemporary time, and in another case study relevant to business perspectives on which this chapter focuses.

Silverman (2000) explored crucial experiences of black and Korean business owners in minority markets, and explicates that both black and Korean entrepreneurs were made to react to how agency of the institutional environment of these business owners made them respond to their business environments. After studying Chicago's ethnic beauty aid industry, the author reported that Korean entrepreneurs acted as middlemen, while the blacks were not, thereby showing that various actions of blacks and Korean entrepreneurs in Chicago minority markets are predicated on stratification of race and ethnicity in the mainstream society, as well as in the mainstream markets. Similarly, two distinct existing niches (the professional niche and the retail niche) were studied within Chicago's beauty aid industry; and separate suppliers and creators of demand were identified along racial line as follows:

> In the professional niche, black manufacturers often sold products to black distributors, who in turn sold to black merchants and salons. In the retail niche, white manufacturers often sold products to Jewish and Korean distributors, who in turn sold to chain stores and Korean merchants. There are exceptions to these general patterns of business networking; they reflect the dominant modes of business interactions in the ethnic beauty aids industry. (Silverman, 2000, p. 195)

Moreover, Silverman (2000) stressed the institutional arrangements in contemporary America and society that decide and help people to comprehend the economic functions of minority groups and the severity of blacks' subordination, which, in turn, reduces the extent to which minority entrepreneurship can reach in America. The author stated numerous economic roles that have distinctively emerged with some yardsticks under stratification of race and ethnicity in America. From the case study the author presented, other characteristics of this industry represent what many minority entrepreneurs and minority markets experience in contemporary America from the mechanism that produces racial and ethnic inequality.

In such racial stratification and financial constraints, the black entrepreneurs' business survival has been by looking inwardly to their own race through mobilization of their own people and resources within their community, thereby making control of the professional niche possible as black manufacturers and black entrepreneurs are able to achieve a close relationship (Silverman, 2000). Another reported strategy of how black business owners have been able to survive declining opportunities and tight markets as reported by the author was based on mobilization of ethnic resources beyond America. The reason was that even when their niche is less capital-intensive, there was no money to expand it, and the whites with financial buoyance leveraged on such financial constraints and then placed them on stiff competitions which the black business owners found daunting. Therefore, opening businesses and exporting abroad to countries like Iran, Iraq, Nigeria, South Africa, Uganda, Ghana, and other black nations with huge black populations are part of the business strategies they employed to maximize mobilization of their ethnic resources in order to stay in business in America (Silverman, 2000). As much as the U.S. mainstream markets are concerned, the internal colonialism heritage mentioned earlier till now reinforces numerous impacts of racialization and inequality persisting within the business or entrepreneurship sector in the United States where people with different racial backgrounds operate. The next section shows the case of the state of business startups in the United States and the opportunities they could have had being missed due to racialization processes to which they were subjected and are still experiencing.

THE CASE OF THE STATE OF BUSINESS STARTUPS IN THE UNITED STATES

The United States for many decades has been experiencing rapid startups; however, white entrepreneurs really outnumber the colored entrepreneurs who without dissimulation remain underrepresented. This further portrays the United States as a country on a fast lane of becoming racially diverse, and in which the repercussions of such action may be tantamount to disparity between white and black owners of businesses and missed opportunities (Kauffman, 2016). Notably, race can be used to categorize business owners in the United States, and this categorization means African American ("Black"), Asian, Hispanic, and white people as owners of various businesses.

Nonetheless, the Small Business Administration as of 2013 stipulated that of all U.S. businesses, only 7 percent of the firms were owned by blacks; 4.3 percent were owned by Asians, and 10.6 percent were owned by people of

Hispanic origin. Based on what has been reported and noticed by Kauffman (2016), the racial gap and ethnic coloration among entrepreneurs of diverse backgrounds persist in the United States. Accordingly, influences on owning and running business in the United States have been linked to some factors, which have been systematically enshrined into business ownership and widen the already-existing gaps. Kauffman (2016) explicated that how firms owned by the minority perform is predicated on the following factors, which are also instrumental to their thriving or failure.

(a) Management: This means who owns what firm and how much training or education including skills he or she possesses. In this context, the racial/ethnic gap exists as black and Hispanic families hardly own family businesses that can be transferred from one lineage to another. Also, black entrepreneurs have lower education and managerial acumen compared to white and Asian entrepreneurs. These existing gaps may witness reduction as more black and Hispanic entrepreneurs acquire more education.
(b) Money: Owning money or access to credit facilities has shown that racial/ethnic differences persist among business owners in the United States. White families are richer than black and Hispanic families, thereby leading to inequality among businesses owned by these different races. Also, both black and Hispanic businesses have a low level of successful loan application compared to businesses owned by white and Asian entrepreneurs. The resultant effect of this phenomenon is low capitalization, exposure to failure, hardship in running the business, and lower survival rate.
(c) Markets: Location of minority-owned businesses or firms are hardly found in urban centers, thereby are mostly serving or being patronized by ethnic minorities or retailers, which, in turn, adversely affects their businesses or firms unlike those entrepreneurs who concentrate or have access to sell to retailers from diverse ethnic groups. Kauffman (2016) stated furthermore that some studies have reported increment in sales of some minority-owned businesses through government procurement programs, but the future effect and sustainability of such a program remain debatable.

Essentially, in Kauffman's index showing start-up activity according to race, the Latinos/as have the highest rate of new entrepreneurs, while African Americans have the lowest over the years. This serves as one of the evidences of racial/ethnic attachment to owing, running, and succeeding as entrepreneurs in the United States.

THE CASE OF BIASED AND DISCRIMINATORY FINANCIAL PRACTICES IN THE UNITED STATES

This section is devoted to a case study on financial constraints people of color have been facing in doing and sustaining their businesses in the United States, and it digs deeper into biased and discriminatory financial practices that have been affecting people of color and impeding their initiatives of doing business in the United States for a long time. Applewhite (2018), a member of the Forbes Council, explained the extent to which power and structural racism have limited, slowed, and ruined businesses owned by people of color.

According to the Applewhite (2018), there was a decrease of one-third in venture capital financing in 2016 as the capital fell from $77.3 billion to $52.4 billion, and made those seeking early-stage financing to seriously suffer. Since 2012 also, it was reported that below the accounted deals, angel and seed investments have fallen by half, which implies that when a business owner has less or no early-stage capital, he or she will be forced to borrow capital from friends and family members, a case that has been found as a great challenge to most entrepreneurs of color (Applewhite, 2018).

Relatedly, discrimination and bias have been found to be influencing financing disbursement to companies mainly owned or operated by white males according to a 2016 report by the Center for Global Policy Solutions (Applewhite, 2018). Based on such financial practices, minority-owned businesses (over 1.1 million of them) have been found dysfunctional and unable to cope with the startup ecosystem, thereby stalling 9 million potential jobs with their possibility of pumping $300 billion into the national treasury (Applewhite, 2018).

Furthermore, the model of business, which the United States is running, has showed that blacks hardly occupy decision-making positions within Venture Capital (VC) and also that blacks who are capital-backed founders in American venture are less than 1 percent; and, based on pattern recognition, the risk has been reduced by VC. However, the potential to earn high profit has been inhibited by inherent funding bias (Applewhite, 2018). These scenarios also suggest that doing business in the United States right from the early stage is faced with the absence of capital and the absence of representation within the business ecosystem that allows for investing due to racially enshrined financial discrimination against communities of color.

In the United States, raising fund personally by an entrepreneur from friends and family members has been linked to bias in financial practices and the poor financial state of most African Americans as their average net worth does not surpass $11,000 compared to white American's $144,000 average net worth. Importantly, many African Americans have problems in investing or starting a business due to lacking access to early capital as well as generational wealth (Applewhite, 2018). While the minority population is growing, its businesses or investments die easily at the early stage due to the impact of the critical financial situation on their startup in the United States. For instance, biased financial practice has been noted in the early stage and seed round investments as it has decreased over 40 percent since 2014; however, only companies like Uber, Space X, and Airbnb largely owned or managed by whites have enjoyed more than $55 billion in late-stage investments (Applewhite, 2018).

The opposing voices on biased and discriminatory financial practices have not been commonly heard publicly may be due to the widespread empirical evidences concerning the said practices against people of color in general. Another possible reason for the lack of notable counterarguments concerning biased financial practices against certain businesses owned by blacks and Latinos/as may be that many CEOs and corporations have publicly admitted that racial discrimination and social injustice have impeded the ease of securing finance to start or grow businesses mostly owned by people of color in the United States. Notably, all of these practices portend adverse risk and demotivation for existing and upcoming business owners or entrepreneurs within the startup ecosystem as well as for those trying to sustain their businesses or vying to move their business to the mainstream markets.

Applewhite (2018) added that at VC companies, only 2 percent of African Americans were found in senior positions, thereby showing the degree of underrepresentation being exercised in such a growing industry. Therefore, investors who fail to align with the reality of a present-day business concept and consumer interests may eventually flutter or collapse as only businesses or entrepreneurs that align and allow diversity of perspectives and workers may be sure of succeeding in their ventures based on the projection of having a majority-minority population in the United States by 2044. Thus, Applewhite advised that addressing funding bias requires exposure, education, training done intentionally, and representation.

Similarly, organizations that focus on developing, investing, and accelerating entrepreneurial talent need to take inequalities existing within their own establishments serious, and getting experts' help as well as organizing staff training on bias are paramount steps to intentionally curb biased financial practices and other racial issues. The aforementioned funding phenomena with their historical evidences within the business ecosystem in the United States might have further spurred many CEOs and firms to keep pledging for social equity in words and in practice beginning from their workplaces or firms. While the preceding case seems wider and encompassing, the following is a brief description of another case that illustrates disparity among black and white owners of businesses or firms.

THE CASE OF THE ETHNIC BEAUTY AIDS INDUSTRY IN CHICAGO

In this section, the case of Chicago's ethnic beauty aids industry is examined. Some scholars of entrepreneurship might have claimed that African Americans have no worthwhile business tradition, but one of the counterarguments has been attributed to Butler (1991; see Feagin and Iman, 1994 for details). In closeness to what Kauffman (2016) reported, Butler also mentioned that in the 1700s, many black businesses were serving both black and white customers and for a period up to two centuries; their businesses were succeeding and expanding to cities and towns until discrimination by whites commenced and violent attacks on their business (like what was experienced in Tusla before World War II) brought a decline to their business activity.

One of the case studies that can confirm what attacks on and discrimination against black businesses has led to is the ethnic beauty aids industry in Chicago where the manufacturers were black. A thorough exploration of black and Korean entrepreneurs in Chicago's ethnic beauty aids industry was reported by Silverman (2000) and the findings are relevant in this context. Silverman (2000) explained that from the inception to this modern time, the industry has faced racism and racial discrimination that emanated from mainstream society according to the experiences of three generations of Black manufacturers who were operating in Chicago.

As Silverman (2000) asserted, the racial/ethnic peculiarity and implications on minority businesses or firms can be better understood by alluding to three historic periods. The first was the period of Great Migration and the Great Depression. This period saw the emergence of the ethnic beauty aids industry as solely an institution of blacks.

The second period was between the Great Depression and the Civil Rights Movement. The period witnessed how this industry withstood economic and social woes instigated by racial tensions between blacks and whites. The implications of this period include disappearance of some black-owned institutions as many failed to survive the Great Depression period, and got unfavorable public discussion during the Civil Rights movement (Silverman, 2000).

The third period ranged from the time of Civil Rights Movement to 1990. This period marked a noticeable and wide loss of firms owned by black manufacturers, and acquired by white conglomerations in the United States. Silverman (2000) further elaborated that the significance of this period is that it has confirmed the idea of reproduction of racism and racial discrimination even in modern time as participation of these black manufacturers of ethnic beauty aids witnessed stiff barriers to enter and operate in the wider and popular economy.

Furthermore, Silverman (2000) maintained that these barriers have remained difficult to be removed as white-owned conglomerates keep expanding, and the unfavorable effects of the global economy on businesses or firms also keep affecting black businesses. Notably, what Silverman reported also included the Jewish and Korean merchants operating in the South Side of Chicago. While racial discrimination faced by black manufacturers of ethnic beauty aids received much attention, the overarching effect of racism and racial discrimination on other minority groups (Jews and Korean) and their industries have limited the success rate of businesses and firms owned by black entrepreneurs in the United States. Several personal narratives of many entrepreneurs or manufacturers who have experienced racism and racial discrimination in relation to black beauty aids manufacturers in the city of Chicago were presented by Silverman (2000).

In the response of S. B. Fuller (a Black manufacturer in the city of Chicago who joined the ethnic beauty aids industry after the Great Depression), it was noted that he confronted several race-related challenges even though the period seemed promising to young entrepreneurs. Examples of obstacles witnessed by Fuller then included the inability to obtain loans from mainstream banks, which then hampered the growth and development of his company. This experience and others might have shaped the belief, ideology, and experiences of many blacks, including Fuller, on race relations in mainstream American society in general. This problem faced by black and Hispanic minorities in the United States has also been explicated by Kauffman (2016). In acknowledging the extent of interest whites have in probing black businesses, Fuller said in an interview with *U.S. News & World Report* the following:

> Here, in our organization the white people are very sensitive about being treated as inferior in our organization. They are more concerned about discrimination than the Negroes are. One thing I find in my organization is this: If I don't watch very closely, the Negro bosses here will discriminate, and hire all Negroes and no Whites. I'm constantly watching them to see that they hire people on their merit and not on the color of their skin. (U.S. & World Reports, 1963; quoted by Silverman, 2000, p. 63)

The preceding statement came after Fuller's business had been boycotted by a supremacist group (White Citizens' Council) in Chicago as retaliation for a boycott staged in the South by blacks. Fuller mentioned specifically that racial problems had made him lose substantial amount of income; and, after his products like Jean Nadal and H. A. Hair Arranger were removed from shelves in many stores in the South, he reiterated the need for selling products made by blacks to whites and vice versa (Silverman, 2000).

While the majority of the people whose ideology misaligns with Fuller's and other black owners of companies in the United States may be untenable, the recent calls (after and during the Black Lives Matters protests) for equity in business ventures and related racial relations have reinforced Fuller's ideology and weakened the opposing views such as blacks' inability to establish and thrive in business ventures even today.

RESPONSES TO BLACK LIVES MATTER AS A CASE OF RACIAL DISCRIMINATION IN BUSINESSES

The case presented in this section focuses on numerous voices that have condemned the systemic racism and white supremacy or privilege in corporations as a result of protests in the United States and other nations against the brutal killing of George Floyd. The case presented in this section shows that both black and white business owners (either in the mainstream economy or local sphere) are aware of the reality of racial discrimination in modern businesses and companies.

The essence of this section is its potential to portray how modern business owners most of who are even white are quickly acknowledging the significance of making all lives matter economically and in doing business across the United States, in particular. As captured by some thriving entrepreneurs, there are intriguing cases of race and racial discrimination in both small and big companies. In their reaction to the protests, the owners and CEOs of big corporations who are mostly white identified motifs like injustice, racial discrimination, inequality, racism, and violence against minority ethnic groups in the United States and how markets and big corporations should stand against the practices.

The technology industry, for instance, saw the need to eradicate or reduce racial discrimination in United States markets among black and white entrepreneurs and among their employees. For realistic purposes, some notable positions about the issue of race, racism, and racial discrimination were made and captured in FoxNew as reported by Genovese (2020). Apple's CEO, Tim Cook, said: "As difficult as it may be to admit, that desire is itself a sign of privilege. George Floyd's death is shocking and tragic proof that we must aim far higher than a 'normal' future, and build one that lives up to the highest ideals of equality and justice" (Genovese, 2020, p. 1). Also Amazon showed that the company took a firm stance against ethnic and racial tensions, especially between blacks and whites by commenting that "Amazon stands in solidarity with the Black community—we remain steadfast in our support for our employees, customers, partners, and the communities where they live and work. And we stand in support of organizations that are making a difference" (Genovese, 2020, p. 1). Twitter also reechoed the historical racism and persecution of blacks and other minority group by saying this: "Amid the already growing fear and uncertainty around the pandemic, this week has again brought attention to something perhaps more pervasive: the long-standing racism and injustices faced by Black and Brown people on a daily basis" (Genovese, 2020, p. 1).

Additionally, Microsoft identified the race problem and its plan to make a change in its company and communities. Accordingly, the Microsoft CEO Satya Nadella explained: "There is no place for hate and racism in our society. Empathy and shared understanding are a start, but we must do more. I stand with the black and African American community and we are committed to building on this work in our company and in our communities" (Genovese, 2020, p. 1). Essentially, such messages have reechoed the voices of this company's workers many of who are black and showing a pathway to having equity at the workplace and in the company in general.

The preceding cases tilt toward ensuring the reduction or eradication of social injustice; but, in a deeper sense, the calls may also help in making blacks and other minority ethnic groups own and manage businesses in the mainstream economy of the United States with little or no hindrance from the sociopolitical sphere of the country. This will replicate and reinforce the past calls (see Silverman, 2000). The opposing views to calls of these major CEOs about making Black Lives Matter have not been widely heard may be as a result of the tension in the country. Conversely, as the protests reached climax, a banner bearing Black Lives Matter atop Amazon's homepage linking to a blog where the company voiced out and supported the subject of the protests made one of the Amazon's customers to negate the slogan Black Lives Matter and maintain that All Lives Matter (McCulloch, 2020).

Some observers have also challenged many CEOs who claimed that they are in support of the Black Lives Matter movement to check inwardly and commence racial equity at their companies. For example, Nike's advertisement against racism was criticized for the absence of racial diversity, especially within the company's executive leadership team. In response, the company quickly published a few blacks who were their executive team members (Graham, 2020). Similarly, Braithwaite (2020) reported that in 2018 when Nike launched an advertisement that featured former National Football League quarterback Colin Kaepernick about police violence, some people opposed the company and made #NikeBoycott trend on Twitter as they threatened to burn their shoes. These actions led to a 3 percent fall in the company's sportswear shares; however, Nike's sales jumped up in the aftermath of the campaign and stood at 30 percent during the All Lives Matter protests in the United States.

MORE CALLS FOR RACIAL JUSTICE, EQUITY, AND DIVERSITY: A CASE OF NATIONAL AND LOCAL U.S. BUSINESSES AND MARKETS

Individuals and organizations that focus on developing, investing, and accelerating entrepreneurial talent need to take inequalities existing within their own establishments seriously, and getting experts' help as well as organizing staff training on bias, since they are paramount steps to intentionally curb biased financial practices and other racial issues. Even before the protests, Applewhite (2018) reported that some organizations had pledged to address funding bias and close the gap in the representation of youths and young professionals. The initiative includes Village Capital that devised the peer selection process to combat investor bias; New York City-based startup Jopwell that has recently increased job placement and advancement of career of professionals from black, Latino/a, and Native American populations; and other establishments such as Black Girls Code, Code2040, HBCUvc. Applewhite also emphasized the collaboration among business owners, entrepreneurial support organizations, and investors to remove funding bias and to achieve profitable as well as equitable ecosystem.

Furthermore, many pledges against social injustice by some owners of big businesses, investors, and entrepreneurs (including whites) during and after of All Lives Matter protests indicated that contrary to opinions about racial injustice in America, including its business ecosystem, carry no weight any longer. Friedman (2020) stated that Adidas has pledged to increase its black and Latino/a workers at Adidas and Reebok by 30 percent; while Andreessen Horowitz (an investment firm) has pledged $2.2 million for training and as seed capital through its Talent x Opportunity fund for upcoming entrepreneurs at less-served communities. Friedman also mentioned that Apple (a technology company) has promised to establish a camp for black software developers and multiply the number of blacks who are suppliers of the company's materials used for production.

Friedman (2020) added that Estée Lauder Companies (a cosmetic brand) also said that in the next five years, black workers in the company will reflect the true population of this race in the United States, and also that the next two years will witness recruitment of graduates from historically black colleges and universities (HBCUs). Estée Lauder Companies like Apple also promised to double the patronage of black-owned businesses by purchasing ingredients and other materials from them. Based on what Friedman (2020) reported, table 11.1 was formulated for clarity and summary purposes. The table shows how CEOs or businesses have responded and pledged to tackle racism and reduce or eliminate its associated practices in the United States,

Table 11.1 Responses by CEOs or Businesses to Tackle Racism

Name of Company	Brand/Product or Service(s)	Pledge, Promise, or Plan of Action	Year in Focus
Facebook	Social Media/ Tech	1. Target 2023 to double its black and Latino/a Employees.	3
		2. The company pledged 30 percent increment in leadership posts for black people	5
		3. To expend $100 million (at minimum per year) on black-owned suppliers, marketing firms to construction companies.	NS
FitBit	Mobile Fitness/ Tech	The promise was made to support research on black people's health, including COVID-19, and getting and featuring of social media influencers who are blacks.	NS
PayPal	Finance and Tech	1. The company promised to create a $500 million fund mainly for supporting businesses owned by blacks and other minority groups through creation and strengthening of relationship with community banks.	NS
		2. Servicing credit unions to the underrepresented communities and making direct investment at startups owned by black and other minority groups was also promised by this company.	NS
		3. For the black-owned businesses affected by COVID-19, a separate $10 million grants was also pledged.	NS
		4. Another $5 million was also pledged toward funding grants and employee program that aimed at matching gifts for nonprofits and those black business owners working with them.	NS
		5. Ensuring and creating long-lasting internal diversity and inclusion program with a separate $15 million.	NS

(Continued)

Table 11.1 (Continued)

Name of Company	Brand/Product or Service(s)	Pledge, Promise, or Plan of Action	Year in Focus
PepsiCo	Beverage	1. A pledge of 30 percent increment in black managers was made. This will be executed by adding 250 black employees to the managerial positions, with at least 100 black employees to be among various executive positions.	2025
		2. Doubling of purchases from black-owned suppliers as well as creating more marketing agency jobs for black people.	NS
Pinterest	Search Engine/ Lifelong Learning	Designing and publishing content regarding racial justice, and ensuring that users learn about Black Lives Matter on its platform.	NS
Sephora and Rent the Runway	Beauty Chain	This establishment promised to ensure that products from businesses owned by blacks are given 15 percent space on their shelves.	NS
SoftBank	Tech, Energy, and Finance	This conglomerate promised to commence a $100 million fund that is will mainly target investing in minority-owned or led companies in the U.S.	NS
Trek	Bicycle Manufacturing	1. This manufacturer pledged to create 1,000 jobs for black people in its cycling industry through $2.5 million investment that will include bicycle training scholarship program as well as in retail management.	over 10 years
		2. Invest of another $5 million to new bike shops in communities known for been underserved was also pledged with a goal of building another 50 stores was made.	over 3 years (10 years to achieve the goa.
		3. Trek further pledged to work on ethnic diversity by establishing a scholarship that will fund and equip 25 teams that have children from diverse ethnics through National Interscholastic Cycling Association program.	10 years

Walmart	Retailer of Different Products	1. A promise to stop storing cosmetic products from multicultural manufacturers in locked cases was made as the same promise was announced by CVS and Walgreens.	NS
		2. Walmart also pledged to invest $100 million to create a Center on Racial Equity that will work against systemic racism in the U.S. and ensure reform in criminal justice as well as offering job training in partnership with philanthropic initiatives.	5
WarnerMedia	Mass Media, Advertising, and Entertainment	1. This company affirmed its readiness to support Color of Change (which is a nonprofit civil rights advocacy organization) as well as the NAACP Legal Defense and Educational Fund Inc. with on-air advertising.	NS
		2. The company also plans to fund its content innovating program with $500,000 from which 1/5 of it will be used to promote shows on development issues in underrepresented communities.	NS
YouTube	Video/ Film and Tech	A pledge to invest a $100 million fund was made by this Google-owned to support black artists and creators. The company further promised to protect black artists and users of YouTube from content that indicates white supremacy and bullying.	NS

Note: NS = Not specified.
Source: Self-generated by the author.

thereby implying their admittance of racial, biased, and discriminatory practices in corporate America and in the United States as a whole.

The preceding pledges and plans of action(s) by business leaders align with the message about myths that UK's CEOs must understand as proffered by values, equality, respect, culture, inclusion, diversity, and accessibility (VERCIDA). Cole (2020) reported that three myths are untrue as the corporate world seemed to accept the mantras of Black Lives Matter and All Lives Matter. The first myth is that the protests against the unjust killings of black people are also an issue that white people in power should condemn. The second is that the issue concerns both politics and business as the world is interconnected. This implies that what people experience outside their workplace has influence on their feelings and input at work. The third myth is that the issue of racial injustice is purely a United States' matter and not a UK's matter. Dan Robertson, a D&I professional and consulting director with VERCIDA, believed that leaders of companies may not provide answers to all matters, but they need to show kindness, voice out when it matters, listen and act, use their networks to make other leaders in them act as necessary (Cole, 2020).

In this context, racial injustice in business is a global issue; and, while Cole (2020) mentioned that the event (racial injustice and protests by the Black Lives Matter movement) occurred in the United States, the pains black people in the United Kingdom suffer are as much as those of blacks in the United States. It was noticed during the protests that some people, including the non-business owners in Africa, Asia, and Europe, felt the same sentiment against racial injustice in general. Cole also reported statements credited to Etsy's CEO Josh Silverman who promised to ensure the welfare of black-led institutions as well as organizations working for criminal justice through the donation of $500,000 each to Equal Justice Initiative and Borealis Philanthropy (see other pledges in table 11.1). Essentially, accepting the truthfulness of the aforementioned myths has established more understanding about diversity and inclusion at the corporate world.

The aforementioned assertion, as reported by *The Economist*, commensurate with the observation made by Jeffrey Sonnenfeld of Yale University's School of Management that CEOs have avoided talking about race and other controversial topics but now acting due to the widespread acknowledgment of racial injustice in the United States (The Economist, 2020). Currently, the concerns of several bosses of businesses in the United States concerning racial injustice seem to be serious, despite the absence of substantive changes within firms in the past (The Economist, 2020). Meanwhile, before the Black Lives Matter and All Lives Matter movements, few experts and entrepreneurs openly advocated the need for diversity in business as one of the ways to increase reasonable representation of different ethnic or racial groups in business and investment in the United States. For instance, in 2015, McKinsey reported that there is a likelihood of public companies that prioritize gender and ethnic diversity to outperform their peers (Applewhite, 2018).

BOSSES' PERSPECTIVES ABOUT TACKLING RACIAL INJUSTICE IN THE UNITED STATES: A CASE OF QUESTIONS AND ANSWERS

As a matter of fact, voices against racial injustice in the American corporate world may hardly be contested by opposing voices as many people especially owners of businesses have shown. *The Economist* (2020) explicated following four questions that need to be answered to understand and explain the nature of racial injustice in the American corporate world: (1) Are black people truly disadvantaged or not? (2) To what extent can a business be blamed rather than society? (3) What are the impacts of those disadvantages on business' performance? (i4) Is there anything businesses can do to correct problem? Although the federal government requests the publication of data on the specific numbers of peoples of various ethnic groups in individual American firms, due to fear of lawsuits against racial discrimination, no much data are available (The Economist, 2020). It was also revealed that only few technology companies (including Intel) have made available their payment and ethnicity data available for examination, and, based on what *The Economist* (2020) reported, responses to all the aforementioned questions are summarized and presented in table 11.2.

In sum, due to much awakening about the need for racial justice by corporate America, there seems to have emerged a greater hope to tackle racialization of their businesses, as the 2020 protests had the same echoes of what happened in 1918, 1935, and 1968, when America's economy and its underlying structures were shaken (The Economist, 2020). The fact remains that many CEOs have seen the need to take a stand as Facebook employees also expressed their anger against inaction of the company to emulate Twitter's action of flagging down former U.S. President Donald Trump's comments about shooting the looters (President Joe Biden during the 2020 election campaign said the same but was never reprimanded). It is not time to give huge applauds to companies like Adidas, Facebook, FitBit, NASCAR, PayPal, PepsiCo, Pinterest, Sephora and Rent the Runway, SoftBank, Target, Trek, Viacom CBS, Walmart, WarnerMedia (in addition to those mentioned earlier and others not mentioned here), and their owners who are mostly white for announcing their intentions to effect needed changes on race relations, starting from their companies or organizations and reflecting on how they

Table 11.2 Business Owners' Voices against Racial Injustice in the American Corporate World

Questions	Answers Based on Verified Past or Current Situation(s)
(i) Are Black people are truly disadvantaged or not?	1. Only four black people (no female) are part of Fortune 500 CEOs with only seventeen in the past twenty years. 2. Fewer than 3 percent African American are among those at senior corporate jobs, while less than 8 percent of them are in white-collar jobs. Among these people, only 3 percent are found as employees of Silicon Valley. 3. With their 13 percent in American population, unemployment of black people has for long remained twice the unemployment rate of White people 4. The disparity in black–white wage over the past two decades has spread from blue-collar jobs to those with advanced degrees.
(ii) To what extent can the business be blamed rather than the society?	1. The longstanding view of corporate world in America is that racial injustice is a society problem, and it must also solve it because inequality is linked to the laws and the legacy of slavery and Jim Crow. These laws are believed to be at the detriment of Black Americans. 2. It is also believed that only government can address issues like poverty, injustice, and racialized schools, among others, but discrimination is also found at many firms that are even mostly respected in America. 3. A lawsuit on racist corporate practices was instituted against Coca-Cola in 2000, and the firm was compelled to find remedy to such practices. Starbucks in 2018 closed all its coffee shops, offered training to all its workers after black patrons were removed in one of their outlets in Philadelphia. After being found guilty in a racial-discrimination suit, a whooping sum of $176m was paid by Texaco (the oil mogul that has been merged with Chevron now), and Angela Vallot who was the then Texaco's chief diversity officer attested to racism at work.

(iii) What are the impacts of those disadvantages on business' performance?	1. Lack of diversity in business for instance has huge negative impacts on business performance. From 2014 to 2020, Sundiatu Dixon-Fyle and colleagues at McKinsey investigated racial and gender diversity at many firms in fifteen countries. Their three separate reports confirmed that those firms that maintained good employee diversity were on top quartile of performance in their businesses having good profit margins unlike those firms with poor employee diversity that were at the bottom quartile on the same metrics. 2. Based on Nelson James of Bridgespan's research, it was reported that black people are not in the social circle of 3/4 of white people. It has also been found that black and white people attend separate churches, separate schools, live in different neighborhoods, and only meet at business but absence of true diversity may stall having conversations on issue such as race at their workplaces. 3. It is believed that failure of corporation to act against racism may have adverse effects on companies in diverse ways. For instance, a research paper published in the *American Economic Journal* investigated ethnic prejudice among some firms, and reported that in order for discriminators to avoid working among or with people of diverse ethnicity, they (the discriminators) were willing to forfeit earnings up to 8 percent. The scenario above implies that shareholders' interests in such firms are at risk. 4. In Edelman's survey, over 1/2 of whites expressed the need for brands to take a stand concerning racial inequality; and more than 2/3 of Republicans indicated that a company's response to race protests will influence its brand to either gain or lose acceptance or trust. Accordingly, an American law firm, Paul Weiss, was widely rebuked for having white people as all its new partners in 2019.

(Continued)

Table 11.2 (Continued)

Questions	Answers Based on Verified Past or Current Situation(s)
(iv) Are there anything businesses can do to correct or improve the matter?	Some of those actions that businesses can do to improve unpalatable situation surrounding racial inequality and lack of diversity are as follows. 1. Placing faith in raced-based quotas should not be done by business bosses. Quoting Michele Meyer-Shipp of KPMG, *The Economist* (2020) reported that many black people, including the professionals, like to avoid being among the executive teams due to lack of having voice when reaching such position. 2. Meritocracy should also be avoided by business bosses. Quoting Ms Hills, *The Economist* (2020) revealed that true meritocracy can only be found among few firms as only people who are similar to the managers are empowered, thus paving ways for systemic racism. 3. It was further reported that race should be focused on by firms that truly wanted to advance black people. Doing so also require having a means of diversity that targeted at black people, and enshrining and implementing fixed means of promoting and securing a commitment of those at the top to avoid bias that may emanate from middle managers. 4. Teaching the managers how to implement diversity among different people is essential to avoid personal bias that may subvert corporate efforts. Quoting Ms Meyer-Shipp, *The Economist* (2020) reported that black employees do not get frequent and candid response from their white managers, and these employees get sacked when they believe they are fully functional while most managers will back up their decision with untenable euphemisms like inability of the employees to portray volume of executive duties required of them.

Source: Self-generated by the author.

do business. While time is awaited to see these pledges and good intentions come true, their plans of actions have shown that both Black Lives Matter and All Lives Matter.

CONCLUSION AND RECOMMENDATIONS

The business perspective on Black Lives Matter versus All Lives Matter has been explored in the preceding sections of this chapter. First it was shown that there has been unfriendly race relation between blacks and whites and other minority groups in the United States, and that this race relation has spread across many aspect of human life, including owning and doing business in the United States.

Next, the sections briefly narrated how racism and racial discrimination have led to several violent attacks and boycotts of businesses owned by both blacks and whites. Historically, black business owners and entrepreneurs have suffered from both sociopolitical and economic policies like the inability to secure financial facility, and restriction from operating in the mainstream economy, among others.

Also, some cases of unhealthy race relations and their effects on business were elucidated. Drawing from views and reactions of many corporations and their owners to social injustice and racial discrimination that were reechoed during the violent protests tagged Black Lives Matter; the chapter highlighted the contemporary ideology and future solution proffered by these business owners to racism and racial discrimination in the United States.

It is recommended, therefore, that to ensure that Black Lives and All Lives Matter, businesses or organizations owned by either blacks or whites should embrace inclusiveness of diverse cultures and races, which, in turn, may lead to equal opportunities to be hired, to be suppliers of raw materials, being buyers of products made by any race, being beneficiaries of loans, and so on. Next, the need for contemporary autonomous economic institutions for black Americans and other minority ethnic groups should be revisited. This has been even advocated by observers such as Anthony Overton in the 1900s. Entrepreneurs from underserved communities should be helped to be able to compete without fear in the mainstream economy.

REFERENCES

Alba, R. (2018). What majority-minority society? A critical analysis of the Census Bureau's projections of America's demographic future. *Sociological Research for a Dynamic World* 4:1–10.

Applewhite, D. (2018). Founders and venture capital: Racism is costing us billions. *Forbes*. Retrieved on March 19, 2021 from https://www.forbes.com/sites/forbesnonprofitcouncil/2018/02/15/founders-and-venture-capital-racism-is-costing-us-billions/?sh=3b805f862e4a

Blake-Beard, S., Murrell, A., and Thomas, D. A. (2006). Unfinished business: The impact of race on understanding mentoring relationships. Working Paper No. 06-060.

Braithwaite, T. (June 2020). How companies decided that black lives matter. Retrieved on July 30, 2020 from https://www.ft.com/companies/the-top-line

Britannica Online Encyclopedia. (October, 2020). Business organization. Retrieved on March 17, 2021 from https://www.britannica.com/topic/business-organization

Butler, J. S. (1991). *Entrepreneurship and Self-help among Black Americans*. New York, NY: State University of New York Press.

Caproni, P. J. (2005). *Managing Cultural Diversity: Management Skills for Everyday Life: The Practical Coach* (2nd ed.). Upper Saddle River, NJ: Pearson Prentice Hall.

Cole, C. (June, 2020). Black Lives Matter—and that applies in the corporate world too! Retrieved on March 21 from https://diversityq.com/blacklivesmatterandthatappliesinthecorporateworldtoo

Feagin, J. E., and Imani N. (1994). *Racial Barriers to African American Entrepreneurship: An Exploratory Study*. Omaha, NE: Black Studies Faculty Publications.

Foreman, C. H. (2000). Facing up to racial disparity. *The Brookings Review* 8(2):29–30.

Frey, W. H. (2018). Diversity explosion: How new racial demographics are remaking America. Retrieved on March 5, 2021 from https://www.brookings.edu/blog/the-avenue/2018/03/14/the-us-will-become-minority-white-in-2045-census-projects/

Friedman, G. (August, 2020). Here's what companies are promising to do to fight racism. *The New York Times*. Retrieved on March 19, 2021 from https://www.nytimes.com/article/companies-racism-george-floyd-protests.html

Genovese, D. (June, 2020). How are big tech companies responding to George Floyd killing? From public sentiments to multi-million donations big tech is responding in big ways. *Fox News*. Retrieved on June 10, 2020 from https://www.foxbusiness.com/howarebigtechcompaniesrespondingtogeorgefloydilling

Graham, M. (2020). The right way for companies to weigh in on racism, according to experts. Retrieved on July 31, 2020 from https://www.cnbc.com/technology/

Hait, A. (January, 2021). What is a small business? Retrieved on March 18, 2021 from https://www.census.gov/library/stories/2021/01/what-is-a-small-business.html

Hayes, A. (July, 2020). Business. *Investopedia*. Retrieved on March 17, 2021 from https://www.investopedia.com/Business%20Definition.html

Hinson, S., Healey, R., and Bester, D. (2012). *Race, Power and Policy: Dismantling Structural Racism*. Berkeley, CA: National People's Action by the Grassroots Policy Project.

Kauffman, M. E. (2016). Kauffman compilation: Research on race and entrepreneurship. Retrieved on July 31, 2020 from www.kauffman.org

Leiber, N. (July, 2009). The anatomy of an entrepreneur. *Bloomberg Business Week*. Retrieved on March 18, 2021 from www.BusinessWeek.com/smallbiz/running_small_business/archives/2009/07/anatomy_of_an_e.html

McCulloch, A. (2020). Global businesses embrace Black Lives Matter movement. Retrieved on July 31, 2020 from https://www.personneltoday.com

Mills Communication Group. (July 2009). Entrepreneur vs. small business owner: What's the difference? Retrieved on March 19, 2021 from www.millscommgroup.com/blog/2009/06/entrepreneur-vs-small-business-owner-whats-the-difference

Mohan, P. (2020). How the end of the white majority could change office dynamics in 2040. Retrieved on March 5, 2021 from https://www.fastcompany.com/90450018/how-the-end-of-the-white-majority-could-change-office-dynamics-in-2040

Norton, W. (2009). Racial inequality in contemporary American society. Retrieved on July 31st, 2020 from https://www.ssc.wisc.edu/~wright/ContemporaryAmericanSociety/Chapter%2014%20--%20Racial%20inequality--Norton%20August.pdf

PolicyLink. (April 2019). How companies can advance racial equity and create business growth. Retrieved on July 31, 2020 from https://www.policylink.org/

QuickMBA. (2010). A definition of entrepreneurship. Retrieved on March 18, 2021 from http://www.quickmba.com/entre/definition/

Silverman, R. M. (2000). *Doing Business in Minority Markets: Black And Korean Entrepreneurs in Chicago's Ethnic Beauty Aids Industry*. New York, NY: Garland Publishing, Inc.

Sullivan, T. M. (2006). Small business by the numbers. *National Small Business Administration*. Retrieved on March 18, 2011 from www.nsba.biz/docs/bythenumbers.pdf

United States Census Bureau. (March 2021). Business formation statistics by state. Retrieved on March 18, 2021 from https://www.census.gov/library/visualizations/interactive/bfs-by-state.html

U.S. News & World Reports. (August 1963). A Negro businessman speaks his mind. *U.S. News & World Reports*, 58.

Chapter 12

Political Perspective

Omosefe Oyekanmi

Unlike many other sensational events, the death of George Floyd on May 25, 2020, in South Minneapolis, United States, created a momentum in history, bringing to reality the value and disvalue of the human life by humans. Following the circumstances of his death by white police officers on a harmless black American, screaming "I can't breathe," yet again the discourse on racial discrimination and man's inhumanity against humanity took a global twist. The situation was further heightened, as statistics on white police brutality on black citizens in America were reeled out. According to statistics compiled by *The Washington Post*, between 2015 and 2019, police shot and killed between 962 and 1,004 Americans each year, with black Americans (who represent approximately 13 percent of the population) proportionally nearly three times as likely as whites (who represent about 76 percent of the population) to be killed by the police, according to the database Mapping Police Violence (Altman, 2020), albeit more whites are killed by the police each year in terms of actual numbers (Agozino, 2018).

This debate resonated around the world, producing expressions of solidarity from virtually every continent. Blooming into a political force, the caption "Black Lives Matter" quickly awakened calls and demands on human right violations, political and economic exploitation by citizens, national governments, and international community alike against Africans. This accentuated the systemic injustice and rape by Western influence against Africa's development and quest for a peaceful continent. Consequently, the devastating effect of foreign intrusion into African affairs since the partition of Africa in 1885 for selfish interests and political domination, at the detriment of ethnic violence in Africa, comes to the fore. Although conflict in Africa is a function of national governance crises and the failure of governmental institutions in African countries to mediate internal conflicts and promote development, the genesis of protracted conflict in Africa cannot be disconnected from European and American invasion. As Achakeng (2013) posits, the root cause of most latent and manifest conflicts can be traced to colonialism and the decolonization process. This, according to Cohen (1995), suggests that the conflictual tendencies in most African states, informed by gross inequalities in power relations and uneven distribution of national wealth, were created by colonial powers out of ethnic and regional diversities.

From Sudan to Rwanda, Mali, Congo, Côte d'Ivoire, and Nigeria, to mention a few, the characterization of protracted conflicts in Africa reflects the influence of Western exploitation of black lives. Although these recurrent conflicts in recent past have taken new dimensions in the position of claims for separatist agitations and group dissents, it nonetheless tailors governance principles, national politics, the allocation and distribution of national resources and public appointments along ethnic lines. Basically, these ethnic lines crafted by colonial desperation for administrative convenience, political domination, and economic exploitation of Africa for the West have endured till date and are creating more divided and polarized societies in Africa.

More worrisome is the fact that sixty years after most African states got independence and 2020 being projected by the African Union as the year of "silencing the guns," armed conflicts still remain a quagmire in Africa's development. As it would appear, conflict on the continent is getting worse, not receding. According to the Armed Conflict Location & Event Data Project, by November 30, 2018, Africa accounted for 15,874 armed conflicts and in 2019 of the same period, 21,600 incidents of armed conflict were recorded in Africa, translating to about a 36 percent increase within 12 months (Allison, 2020). Be that as it may, the global outcry springing out of the gruesome murder of a young black man by white police officers in May of 2020 was not only a tipping point on the narratives emanating from racism and human discrimination against human, but further punctuates the universal value of man or woman and his or her rights from the perspective of Africa's encounter with slavery, colonialism, imperialism, and capitalism.

Hence, with an overall objective to unmask the complex causes of Africa's contemporary crises, this chapter examines Western political exploitation and subjugation in Africa and their counter-effects, including ethnic conflict and war. Hinged on the 1948 Human Rights Declaration, which values human life as sacrosanct, regardless of race, color, and sex, the position of this chapter is couched on the supremacy of all lives. Situating the debate from a political perspective, the chapter argues that all human lives matter and none should be sacrificed for another. Although literature on Western subjugation and domination is plethoric, the point of analysis in this chapter is anchored on the universality of human rights and the supremacy of all lives. To this end, major terms such as ethnic conflict, human rights, and politics are adequately clarified.

Politics, derived from the Greek word *polis*, literally means city-states, as the ancient Greek city was divided into a collection of independent city-states, each with its own system of government. The term *politics* understood differently by different thinkers from different traditions is by far very complex to define, given that it is intricately linked to cooperation and conflict as instruments guiding human activities. Hence, politics has a very broad in scope.

In general literature, politics is viewed from the realm of public affairs as an art of government, compromise, and consensus. Nonetheless, since a conflict resolution system, exercise of power, and the distribution of scarce resources as the making of collective decision are involved, the study of politics is also perceived as the science of government. As a discipline and the practice of deception and manipulations, politics is seen as a bargaining chip (Modebadze, 2010). Considering the relevance of politics in human interactions, Arendt (1958) defines politics as the most pivotal aspect of human action, because it affirms the uniqueness of each individual, involving interactions between free and equal citizens, thereby giving meaning to life. However, a classic and famous definition of politics by Harold Lasswell in 1936 as "the process of who gets what, when and how" captures the analysis in this chapter.

Ethnic conflict is an assemblage of two words, ethnic and conflict. Ethnic culled from ethnicity is a social construct shaped by European and African tendencies. The word ethnic is derived from the Greek word *ethnos*, which denotes race or nation. As Berman (1998) opines, ethnicity was constructed by Africans through the formations of communities that created protection and wealth in exchange. It is a distinct group of people bound by unifying charters like culture, language, values, history, and so on. Hence, on the one hand, ethnic refers to a group created on the basis of shared traditions and culture, bound by governed rules and traditions, which make them distinct. Conflict, on the other hand, refers to the friction between two or more opposing views induced by goal divergence, frustration, and limited resources (Pondy, 1967; Schmidt & Kochan, 1972). It is important to note that conflict is not exclusively violent in form. While it can be violent or uncontrollable, dominant or recessive, resolvable or insolvable (Aremu, 2010), it can also be really mild. Hence, as Coser (1998) puts it, conflict involves the struggle over values and claims to scarce influence, power, and resources, with an objective by conflicting parties to either injure or eliminate the opponent.

Ethnic conflict therefore refers to tensions between two distinct communities arising out of separate ethnic identities competing for scarce interests or divergent opposing interests. Within the point of analysis, ethnic conflict is therefore a situation in which the interest of one party is shaped along ethnic terms, whereby the major fault lines aggravating the confrontations is based on ethnic distinctions. In other words, ethnic conflict in Africa has taken the posture of collective violence emanating from toxic interactions between subgroups as well as the suppressive nature of the state competing for scarce resources and political influence.

Constituting a political doctrine independent of a philosophical one, human rights are grounded by the functions they have within political practice (Gusman, 2015). Intrinsic to all persons, human rights therefore refer to the basic rights and freedom of people all through their life time. Within the context of this chapter, human rights are not characterized as determined by states; instead, they are framed as inalienable rights regardless of nationality, sex, ethnic origin, color, religion, language, or any other status (Brown, 2016). Thus, as pointed out by Griffin (2010), human rights interest centers around autonomy, welfare and liberty.

Consequent on the conceptualization of basic terms, the general aim of this chapter is to analyze the debate on the value of the black life in view of Western economic, social, and political interference in Africa. However, the specific objectives are to (1) establish a nexus between universal human rights and European influence in Africa, (2) examine the influence of European political and economic domination in exacerbating ethnic conflict in Africa, (3) evaluate factors promoting protracted conflict in Africa, (4) determine the intended and unintended consequences of Western interference in Africa, and (5) assess the effects of ethnic conflict on Africa's development.

In view of the aforementioned objectives, the chapter proposes that ethnic conflict and contemporary crises in Africa will systematically increase until the root cause of the conflict is properly situated and addressed outside of Western solutions to Africa's problems. To this end, the relevance of this chapter cannot be overemphasized. By the nature of the devastating effects of ethnic conflict and war, vis-à-vis the unbalanced relations between the developed North and undeveloped South in the international scheme of events, a discourse on the supremacy of all lives is sacrosanct. Similarly, with national governments and international community alike now regarding ethnic conflict as a security problem of global proportion and ethnic conflict becoming a platform for evaluating a new morality of promoting peace, stability, and human rights globally (Wimmer, 2004), the chapter brings to reality the question of universal human rights. More so, the flagrant abuse of human rights and the audacity of crime and violence tearing Africa apart have been a function of ethnic, racial, and religious intolerance, which account for the growing challenges to peace and development in Africa. Again, given that ethnic conflicts in Africa in time past have been addressed from either the posture of national institutional failure, ethnic diversity, poor management of internal conflict by the state, and competition for natural resources, attempt to understand the root causes of ethnic conflict in Africa is poorly conceived. Thus, this chapter is appropriate for a number of reasons: (1) An analysis of the political perspective from the realm of Western influence brings a broader and balanced position to the discourse on Black Lives Matter versus All Lives Matter discourse; (2) it redirects the focus of human rights issues to the subject (individual) and not the government, race, religion, or organization, which better places the theory of universal human rights; (3) it gives a lucid explanation for the conflicts in Africa and a lasting solution to this quagmire truncating Africa's development; and (4) it provides a policy direction for national governments, nongovernmental organizations (NGOs), civil societies, academia, policy experts, and international organizations on the best plausible management of ethnic conflicts in Africa.

In terms of the methodological approach, the chapter adopts a descriptive case study, with a random selection of a multiethnic country that has experienced ethnic conflicts-cum-civil war in Africa. Based on a random selection, Rwanda's 1994 genocide forms the base for analysis. This is because the Rwandan crisis is one of the worst case scenarios of ethnic discord planted by colonialism (Cocodia, 2008). Relying on content analysis, through reports, observations, and historical accounts of ethnic conflicts in the selected country, and the debate on Black Lives Matter versus All Lives Matter, data sources were systematically analyzed within the scope of slavery, colonialism, imperialism, and capitalism in Africa. This chapter is therefore divided into three major analytical and a concluding section. The first section begins with an account of the European partition and domination in Africa, while the second section examines the influence of Europe in the Rwandan ethnic conflict. The third section explores the debate on Black Lives Matter versus All Lives Matter within the context of Western intrusion in Africa and the final section concludes the chapter with summary of the findings and a recommendation. Before doing all this, however, a conceptual discussion of political science, which is the academic discipline that undergirds this chapter, is first presented in the section that immediately ensues. This is followed by a discussion of the theoretical grounding that underlies the analytical sections.

POLITICAL SCIENCE: A CONCEPTUAL DISCUSSION

The perennial issue in the conceptualization of political science has been about whether the discipline is a science, as its name infers, or not. Indeed, the relations between humans and how they are organized have attracted debates for as long as humans coexisted. As such, where humans have created seemingly systems of coordination and effective relations, a system of politics has been established. From the early writings and ancient cultures of Confucius in China (551–479 BCE) and Ibn Khaldun in Africa, the influence of politics in humanity was demonstrated. However, the significant contributions of Plato, in his unprecedented publication, *The Republic*, and Aristotle's introduction of empirical observation earning him the title of "Father of Political Science," remain profound in the development of a political perspective of humanity. In essence, Fair cites Easton as stating that "from the days of Aristotle, political science has been known as the master science" (Farr, 1995, p. 207). Weisberg (1986) also states that even though the study of political issues as a distinct body of knowledge is about 100 years old, concerns with such questions is as old as human society.

Following the gradual emergence of the modern world, the fifteenth century witnessed European renaissance in art, economics, culture, politics, religion, and science with new ways of understanding the world. Several studies show that the pathway of ideas in political science has transited from traditional approaches (Lindblom, 1977; Brown & Ainley, 2005). In effect, new thinkers and political philosophers hinged on Aristotle's contribution of empirical methods to the study of politics opened up the discipline to several debates and analytics. Among such thinkers are Machiavelli, Hobbes, Locke, and others, who attempted to understand the world through several dimensions of politics.

Central to the debate on politics was the scientific nature of the discipline. With the eighteenth-century Industrial Revolution and twentieth-century World Wars, politics developed, first, along the ideas of traditional philosophers and the ideas of behavioralists to the behavioral revolution debate. The traditional or normative approach sought to understand political systems from the prism of institutions such as legislatures, executives, judiciaries, and so on, whereby a science of politics was out rightly discredited based on it being a qualitative and normative study with less credence for rigor and scientific methods typical of the natural sciences.

However, by the 1930s, following the discontent with traditional approaches to politics, which focused on legal norms rather than examining the political behavior of political actors, a new method of understanding politics and defining its science was developed (Wogu, 2013). Basically, after World War I, several political scientists, especially those of American stalk, were motivated to empirically analyze political behaviors in a manner that could foretell political issues and events. This charge was informed by the behavioralist movement of political science, which focused on advancing political analysis through scientific methods. The behavioralist approach was a movement geared toward analyzing the political behavior of political actors in relation to political activities. As Berkenpas (2016) states, the behavioral revolution was a significant point in history, marking the transition of the political science discipline from traditional methods to an identity of modern social science. Following this development, the science of politics gained fame after the two World Wars.

The behavioralist approach to the study of political phenomena became prominent among American political thinkers and philosophers through the published works of Graham Wallas (*Human Nature in Politics*), Arthur Bentley (*The Process of Government*), and Charles Merriam (*New Aspects of Politics*). This approach of politics engaged scientific methods and empirical research to study human political behavior, challenging previous approaches not based on facts but institutional laws. To this end, different divisions of the movement arose, stemming from those preferred to be called theoretical behavioralists and others preferred to be named behavioralists (Nitisha, n.d). Nevertheless, the development of this modern approach did not develop fully until after World War II through the influence of thinkers like Truman, Dahl, Easton, and others. This approach created controversies and academic confusion given that it was accused of its inability to predict the World Wars and other global events using its mathematical and systematic modeling approach. In effect, this new revolution or political science, which was expected to understand the dynamics of man as a political and social being, created more hullaballoo to the discipline, thereby attracting more critics. David Easton, however, developed the following eight intellectual foundation stones of the behavioralist movement, which further entrenched the science of politics:

(1) Regularities—generalization can be made and regularities in political behavior can be predicted.
(2) Verification—emphasis on empirical and scientific results.
(3) Techniques—an experimental attitude toward techniques.
(4) Quantification—express results as numbers where possible or meaningful.
(5) Values—emphasis on empirical values over ethical values.
(6) Systemization—research must be "theory oriented and theory directed."
(7) Pure Science—deferring to pure science as solving social problems.
(8) Integration—political and social issues cannot be studied in isolation; they must be Integrated to other social sciences and value.

By adopting Easton's eight intellectual foundation stones, political science embraced a higher possibility of generality and reliability. However, the scope of most political investigations was at the micro level, with few attempts of macro-level generalizations (Wogu, 2013).

Although the behavioral approach was not without flaws, as more emphasis was placed on quantification and systematization, its contribution to the development of politics and its scientific attribute is noteworthy, given the enormous political studies and investigations, it has afforded the discipline. Such approaches, enabled by the behavioralist perspective to political science, are case study, content analysis, observation, and so on. Importantly, the research design adopted in this chapter, case study, which is an offshoot of the behavioralist strand of politics, afforded an unchallenging data analysis and presentation in this chapter. Hence, the traditional, behavioralist and several other approaches of political science have improved the discipline as an analytical tool for understanding political processes, whether at the state, national government, international, or individual level of political inquiry.

The Science of Politics

Like economics, sociology, and other social science disciplines, political science is a scientific approach studying social phenomena (Chanthamith et al., 2019). By defining the two major concepts—that is, politics and science—many introductory books on political science inform us that, as mentioned earlier, politics is derived from *polis*, the Greek word for state or nation. Politics generally refers to the forces "that constitute and shape the government of the state and its policies and actions" (Pennock & Smith, 1964, p. 6). Again, contemporary dictionaries indicate that the word science is derived from the Latin verb *scio* and the noun *scientia*—"knowledge." Therefore, science has to do with the way questions are formulated and answered. For this reason, one can define science as a method of systematic inquiry. Thus, the methods or tactics involved in managing a government or state can be examined systematically by employing theory and research methods. About systematic inquiry, the first major aspect is theory, which can be defined as a logical, generalized statement that shows the relationship between two or more hypotheses. Theories are the core of any scientific process, whether it is the natural sciences, "hard sciences," or the social sciences. There are two types of theory (1) inductive and (2) deductive. Inductive theory moves from specific observations to the general, whereby phenomena of interest are objectively observed and recorded, and the pattern or regularity observed in the data is then explained with a theory (Johnson & Joslyn, 1991). Deductive theory moves from the general to the specifics. Therefore, "on the basis of theory certain phenomena are predicted, then events are observed and measured to see if they occur as predicted" (Johnson & Joslyn, 1991, p. 22). In sum, scientific research can utilize both inductive and deductive theories.

Political science is therefore a science because of its research methods. Research methods can be defined as a body of tools or techniques that allow an investigator to conduct a systematic study of a problem. According to Chava Frankfort-Nachmias and David Nachmias, "the research process [or methods] consists of seven main stages: problem, hypothesis, research design, measurement, data collection, data analysis, and generalization" (1996, p. 20). They forgot to state the eighth stage, theory, even though they present it in their diagram.

Although the elements of reliability, verifiability, precision, and accuracy found in natural sciences are absent in political science, it, however, does not limit its sense of systematic study, observation, or experience. Again, the science of politics may not conform to the rules of cause and effect as the other natural sciences do; it, however, is sufficient to explain and draw conclusions on individuals and their relations with the state and government.

Consequently, political science is that branch of the social sciences which studies the principles of the state and government by delving into the foundations of the past and how it interacts with the future (Maddocks, 2020). From the perspective of the Black Lives Matter versus All Lives Matter debate, the science of politics is reflected in the ability of the discourse in this chapter to explore the interactions from slavery, colonialism, capitalism, and neocolonialism in Africa. Politics, therefore, deals with power in terms of who has it? Who doesn't and why? As such, political science is the study of political institution, policies, values, and processes that focuses on governance structures that guide societies through their public priorities and policies on how government touches the individual (Saxena, 2011). In an attempt to apply the science of politics in an ideal research process, this chapter on the political perspective of the Black Lives Matter versus All Lives Matter debate seeks to unbundle and analyze the political phenomenon of Western and European exploitation in Africa since the era of slavery till date.

THEORETICAL GROUNDING

Considering the dynamics of politics and the complexities of Western variance in African systems, a theoretical underpinning is critical in any analysis of this sort. The chapter therefore explores two theories essential for understanding fissures of ethnic-conflict and underdevelopment in Africa. Thus, the Social Dominance Theory (SDT) and Conflict Theory (CT) are employed to root the exploration in this chapter.

Social Dominance Theory

Propounded in 1992 by Pratto et al. (2006), the SDT infers that human societies are organized along group-based social hierarchies where at least one group fares better than other groups in social status and power. For Islam (2014), the theory has been useful in explaining persistent inequalities of group based on marginalized social categories like religion and ethnicity.

Hence, through the use of disproportionate forces like the Bretton woods institutions, World Trade Organization (WTO), members of dominant social groups tend to enjoy desirable material and symbolic benefits such as international policies, economic power, political influence, wealth, and military power. According to the theory, three primary ways of maintaining group-based inequalities are (1) aggregated individual discrimination, (2) behavioral asymmetry, and (3) institutional discrimination. Captured along institutional discrimination, the theory argues that the least oppressive kind of peace that societies can realize can be harnessed from reducing the social inequality in a society and advancing social inclusion to promote the empowerment of all groups toward collective needs. Evidently, the unbalanced institutional order in the international system enables the continuous wealth of the globalized North and the prevalence of poverty and conflict in the globalized South.

Roberts (2011) assuages that the campaigns against genetically modified organisms (GMO) by green NGOs and European agricultural interest groups, for instance, are misleading because they are geared toward protecting a few wealthy United States and European agribusinesses at the detriment of throwing more millions into a higher risk of starvation. Also, Roberts claims that decades ago for environmental and public health reasons, the use of dichlorodiphenyltrichloroethane (DDT) was banned worldwide, without consideration for its propensity to prevent millions of malaria-induced deaths in Africa and most malaria-infested states. Today, ample evidence shows that the ban on DDT spraying has been a tragic mistake. These protectionist western policies continue to increase the suffering of the poor around the world and stiffen competition for public goods and resources, which then exacerbates violent conflicts.

The SDT is anchored on the premise that the intentional creation of unequal structures by the West results in the domination of the West, leaving the underdeveloped nations of Africa, Latin America, and Asia perpetually struggling for scarce resources. This is evident in the economic sabotage of underdeveloped nations by the West, with little or no regard for the counter-effects in those countries. In other words, the global South in most cases is only served unfavorable economic and political opportunities that not only make fair competition in a global economy impossible but also incite intra-ethnic violence and pit religious groups against one another, saddled with influencing group interests over state-based interests. Accordingly, African and most of the other underdeveloped nations of the world are socially dominated and conditioned in international politics to breed diseases, poverty, low standards of living, and conflict, with the West grandstanding as its liberator. In this sense, the proposition by Pratto et al. (1999) that "legitimizing myths," which connotes the institutionalization of these abnormalities, infers that over time people and society are convinced that the existing structures are desirable and just, despite their unequal outcomes with respect to low-status countries in Africa.

Conflict Theory

CT is a theoretical perspective of the social sciences, which states that stratification is inimical to any society. Thus, the theory is a macro-level approach influenced by the writings of German philosopher and sociologist Karl Marx (1818–1883). For him, societies are fragmented into groups that compete for social and economic resources caused by slavery and, ultimately, colonization. The result of this social order was the creation of artificial states and societies. These Western artificial processes and configuration, evident in slavery, colonization, and capitalism, underscore the genesis of the full blows and unending conflicts in the African continent.

The theory suggests that although conflict is inevitable, societies are perpetually in a state of conflict due to competition for scarce resources resulting in the powerful dominating the powerless. This competition is, however, sustained by the construction of inherent inequalities in the international social structure, which reinforces the unequal balance in economic and political power between the West and Africa and within African states and their communities. For instance, the inequalities across the educational, political, and economic structures in a multiethnic society like Nigeria have exacerbated intra-ethnic conflicts in that country. According to Marx, there are two classes of societies: (1) the bourgeoisie class that maintains social order through domination and (2) the proletariat, which is perpetually oppressed by the bourgeoisies. As such, there is a basic conflict of interests between the two classes. Inferring from Lumumba-Kasongo (2017), the core propositions of Marxism is that social conflict is situated in the ownership of the means of production and the social relations of production. As he avers, most African conflicts are in the structure of the capitalist economy and its power base. Speaking of capitalist disorders, as sponsored by the West in most developing countries of Africa and Latin America, conflict is situated as follows: (a) a social-class phenomenon (social consciousness), (b) materially defined, (c) the outcome of unequal wealth distribution (social inequality), and (d) not natural or organic.

Consequently, the four basic features of CT—that is, (1) competition, (2) revolution, (3) structural inequality, and (4) war—are central to understanding the incessant intra-state violence and civil wars in Africa. The structures of political opportunity and political economy in most African communities are trapped by the imbalance of power distribution along ethnic lines. Although the weak state structures and politics of the ruling class hold sway as major influencers of African conflicts, it is, however, pertinent to note that the present state structure and power elite dynamics in most African states are pitfalls of European colonial structures and capitalist expansion of the West. Acemoglu et al. (2005) submit that the principal narratives on the root cause of contemporary African development are envisaged on European influence since the era of colonialism. As Routley succinctly puts it:

> It's remarkable to note that a full third of the world's borders are less than 100 years old. This is especially apparent in Africa, where many existing borders still resemble those haphazardly set up by colonial powers around the turn of the 20th century. The average border on the continent is only 111 years old. In 1964, independent African states chose to maintain colonial borders, primarily to prevent widespread conflict over territory. Though colonial divisions were maintained in theory, only about one-third of Africa's 51,000 miles (83,000 km) of land borders are demarcated—an issue that continues to cause headaches today. (2018, p. 10)

Furthermore, the colonization processes created multilayered conflicts that affected the African life as a whole, where borders were crafted and new lands imposed thereby restructuring ownership. Hence, the key factors propelling intra-ethnic conflict and violence in Africa stem from struggles over access to landed properties and control of natural resources. The condition of Africa's development and violence profile is enmeshed in the inequality division in the international system, which is unfavorable to Africa's economy, thereby creating artificial scarcity, weak state institutions, poverty, corrupt elites, stiff competition and violent intra-ethnic conflicts. Routley (2018) further asserts that African institutions were designed by colonial officials to enable swift movement and transfer of Africa's resources for the benefit of Europe, which became vital even after independence, subject to the inheritance of African political elites who maintained the legacy of perverted institutions as instruments of oppression against the citizens. By extension, the postcolonial African state is a continuum of Western colonial exploitation, faring as an agent of corruption, bad leadership (Iheukwumere & Iheukwumere, 2003; Anazodo et al., 2015) and extreme violence.

Based on the two theories engaged in this analysis, several positions like that of Michalopoulos and Papaioannou (2013) suggest that the political centralization of the precolonial era at the group level is a significant determinant of contemporary states' relations and global development both across and within countries. Inferring from this, inequality across and within ethnic lines presents a lucid basis for civil wars (Huber & Mayoral, 2014; Esteban & Ray, 2011). However, for Fearon and Laitin (2003), the present order reflected in ethnic fragmentation and civil war does not show a strong correlation sufficient to explain Africa's contemporary development.

EUROPEAN PARTITION AND DOMINATION OF AFRICA

Western exploitation lucidly described as "European robber statesman" by Walter Rodney (1972, p. 161) began in the year 1500 with the massive transportation of Africans into Europe and America for forced labor. As early as the fifteenth Century, the Trans-Atlantic Slave Trade commercialized the movement of people in the black race, thereby contributing to the wealth and development of Europe and to the depopulation and strangulation of human and economic freedom in Africa. This period was a devastating era in African history, as over twenty-five million Africans over a span of 400 years were sold into slavery, with harsh and inhumane conditions meted out to them. More so, the Trans-Atlantic Slave Trade created the conditions that enabled European colonial quest and the unequal power relations between Africa and the West that exists till date. Hence, the 1884–1885 scramble for Africa was a slanting point in Africa's civilization story.

The Otto von Bismarck organized conference, as popularly referred, although discussed only the boundaries of Central Africa (the Congo Free State), it however symbolized ethnic partitioning, laying the foundation that would be used among Europeans to divide the continent, which saw the signing of hundreds of treaties that divided the largely unexplored continent into protectorates, free-trade areas, and colonies by the Europeans (Michalopoulos & Papaioannou, 2016) alone. Significantly, the far-reaching effects of the European partition of Africa cut across the political, economic, and cultural consequences for African men and women, with an enduring impact on African peoples and societies. Bailey puts it plainly, when he states: "The political map of Africa is a western colonial creation, drawn by western powers with little regard to the boundaries of historic ethnic homelands or the ethnic compositions of the subject population, and today these artificial or multi-ethnic nations lack the internal political cohesion necessary for survival as nations" (1994, p. 4).

Leading to an exponential expansion of European territorial control over Africa, the Berlin Conference signified the ethnic partitioning of Africa basically to prevent conflict among European countries over the struggle for African territories and resources. Dolorously, border lines were crafted without due consideration for inherent boundaries, enduring traditions and customs that have existed for centuries (Michalopoulos & Papaioannou, 2016). Thus, Lord Salisbury, the British prime minister, stated: "We have been engaged in drawing lines upon maps where no white man's feet have ever trod; we have been giving away mountains and rivers and lakes to each other, only hindered by the small impediment that we never knew exactly where the mountains and rivers and lakes were" (quoted by Chelwa, 2013, p. 1).

Consequently, with only Liberia and Ethiopia earning the status of an independent nation by 1914, about 90 percent of African states had been divided between seven European states (Faal, 2009). In essence, in a bid to avert possible war between a group of European countries over territorial allocations, the artificial mapping of African territories has translated into an overwhelming consequence of intra-ethnic conflict and incessant violence. Following the flagrant contempt for precolonial boundaries, most contemporary African conflicts are sprouts of this international disorder (Faal, 2009). Similarly, as assuaged by several contributors to Africa's underdevelopment discourse, the Industrial Revolution in Europe was made possible due to the colonization of Africa. Hence, the sudden transformation of European technological innovation evident in steam engine production, electric power, and the availability of raw materials placed the continent as a major producer of goods for the international market. Africa, therefore, served as three major economic points of benefits to Europe. First, Africa served as a ready market for European surplus goods; second, as a cheap, available, and abundant source of raw materials to feed European manufacturing industries; and second, as a territory to advance European expansionist quest (given the availability of economic surplus and financial progress generated from the gains of European's extortion in Africa) by investing in capital projects like mining, cotton industries, banks, and plantations. According to Hiribarren, apart from Ethiopia and Liberia:

> In 2018 most African borders were defined in Europe in a very short period of time between the end of the nineteenth century and the end of the First World War. Nearly 44% of them were defined after astronomical lines (meridians and parallels), 30% after mathematical lines (arcs and lines) and 26% after geographic landmarks (mainly rivers and mountains). France is behind the creation of 32% of African borders, the United Kingdom 26.8%, Germany 8.7%, Belgium 7.6%, Portugal 6.9%, the Ottoman Empire 4%, Italy 1.7% and Spain 1.5%. (2018, p. 1)

Thus, in order to justify European encroachment on African soil, the European legal invention, terra nullius (Borch, 2001), was adopted, giving credence to the absurd notion that African land belonged to no one. This human right violation crystalized the domination of Africa and the nature of its conflicts. In effect, the domination of the African continent was further enforced by a perspective of European renaissance geared toward the freedom to plunder the world through intellectual freedom, whereby Africa became the guinea pig (Mekoa, 2019). As Boahen (1985) posits, the period between 1890 and 1910, which saw the conquest and occupation of virtually the whole continent of Africa by the imperial powers and the establishment of the colonial system, signified a tumultuous period for the black continent. The Europeans stealthily walked into Africa's air, transforming its social and religious structures, gaining economic influence, political control, and global dominance.

Originally, Africans did not fold their arms to this fragrant violation of their human rights. Severe resistance from most quarters, especially as regards the African economy, was posed against European domination, as European lords systematically impeded the political sovereignty of Africans. In essence, most African leaders and traditional rulers were determined to maintain their status quo by retaining their sovereignty and independence (Boahen, 1985), However, given the sophistication of European weaponry and political grandeur imbued by the principle of divide and rule, Africa was defeated. The conditions of structural imbalance ultimately made the defeat of Africa inevitable. According to Ocheni and Nwankwo (2012), the direct take over and control of the African economy, through imposed taxation system, forced labor, introduction of a currency value over the traditional barter system, higher price value of European commodity over African commodities, forceful acceptance of the international division of labor system, monetization of the economy and payment of low wages were the scores for European successful domination of Africa, which forlornly still constructs African relations in the international system till today.

Nonetheless, following the exploitative tendencies of colonialism, the 1930s were distinct as an adverse point of transformation for Africa. From the 1930s, when the Great Depression, the World War II, creation of international organizations like the United Nations, the Universal Declaration of Human Rights, and the Cold War took place, colonialism and its influence began to wane out, as it provoked radical movements on the universality of human rights, freedom, and equality for all. These developments were instrumental in reawakening nationalist calls throughout the continent, evident in international conferences, national rallies, and riots. The new African states as created by colonial machinery were confronted with the higher mandate of obtaining independence from their colonial administrators; hence, they absorbed the ethnic and boundary creation of Europeans, without taking cognizance of its counter-effects.

Furthermore, the new African states had a common and more compelling motive of ousting colonial powers from African soil. This common front served as a unifying charter among ethnic divisions, religious fronts and social groups in the quest for political independence among African states. African nationalist leaders and freedom fighters therefore trivialized salient factors bred by the West and this invariably led to several military coups and civil wars at the wake of independence in most states like Nigerian and Sudan. Moreover, the Cold War between the United States and the Union of Soviet Socialist Republics (USSR), which streamed into the period African states got independence, saw these two power blocs dumping tons of weaponry on Africa at a time when the erstwhile European colonial masters continued to extort their ex-colonies economically.

Mekoa (2019) affirms that the colonial legacy bequeathed to new African states was disproportionately aligned, with some regions more developed than others, due to the capital exploitation of the colonial economy linked to the metropolitan trade and capital circuits. As such, the colonial legacy sowed the seeds of inequality and uneven development, which still hunt Africa till this day. Colonialism in Africa defied the principle of the "accelerator and multiplier effect" (Ocheni & Nwankwo, 2012), since raw materials produced by Africans were transported to the West only, without engaging it in local industries, and the surplus gains from the economy were not ploughed back into African economies, where the raw materials were sourced, but rather concentrated in the West. Considering the inequality division colonialism birthed, colonial Africa was stratified into class structures, thereby intensifying class struggle and ethnic divisions within the African colonies. Although the poor demarcation of African territories by Europeans contributed marginally to the various border disputes among African states, which sometimes degenerated into wars, the stratifications within African colonies and ethnic groupings evident in unequal development have led to several inter-ethnic wars in many African countries over the years.

EUROPEAN ROLES IN AFRICAN CONFLICTS: THE RWANDAN GENOCIDE AS AN EXAMPLE

A recurring decimal in Africa's development discourse is the many protracted conflicts. As Fawole (2004) points out, a distinct characterization of the African continent is its regularity with conflict. Hence, since postcolonial Africa, one of the most serious problems exacerbated by underdevelopment resonates from the series of violent conflicts and civil wars in the continent. The characterization of these conflicts tainted by ethnicity sometimes metamorphose into civil wars like in Sudan (1995–1990); Chad (1965–1985); Angola since 1974; Liberia (1980–2003); Nigeria (1967–1970); Somalia (1999–1993); Burundi, Rwanda, and Sierra Leone (1991–2001), and so on. However, the Rwandan genocide with its grave devastating effect on black lives and humanity as a whole underscores the devaluation of human lives by European hegemony.

Rwanda: A Brief Background

Rwanda, a land-locked country located in the eastern part of Africa, has a population of about 13,172,530 (worldometer, 2021), with three major multi ethnic groups (Hutu 85 percent, Tutsi 14 percent, and Twa 1 percent). It has a total land area of 24,670 Km^2 (9,525 sq. miles), with an urban population of 17.6 percent. Prior to 1916, the relationship between Hutu and Tutsi was tolerable, despite Tutsi's dominance. Assuming a bureaucratic composition, the powers of the chiefs were dependent on the blessings of the Mwami (king) in such manner that they did not claim their position by right or inheritance or by virtue of any prior connection with the area to which they were appointed (Isabirye & Mahmoudi, 2000). According to Isabirye and Mahmoudi (2000), the unequal relationship in Rwanda was sustained through an ideology of ethnic superiority, signifying different roles where Tutsis are herders and Hutus are farmers, except for the Tutsis who grow crops and the Hutus who keep cattle. This socioeconomic distinction and social customs are defined by economic activities and have created different social classes within pre-colonial society (Beauchamp, 2014), suggesting that ethnic groups were designated based on social classes and not traditional clan networks.

Initially colonized in 1899 by the German Empire, Rwanda became a Belgian colony in 1962 following the defeat of the German Empire in World War I. Subsequently, mandated by the League of Nations to be absorbed under the Belgian empire, the Belgian colonial occupation had more lasting effect than that of Germany in Rwanda. Intrinsically, both European empires ruled Rwanda through the kings and promoted a pro-Tutsi policy. This enduring effect was envisioned in the Belgian subtle act of racializing the differences between Hutu, Tutsi, and Twa. As Dumarz (2019) avers, under the Belgian colonial empire, precolonial socioeconomic structures were crafted along ethnic lines. Hence, Rwanda had a bitter, violent experience among ethnic groups, considering the Belgian administrative order that placed the Tutsis in a much higher position over the Hutus. As a follow up, the Belgian colonial construction was the offshoot of animosity and resentment against ethnic groups in Rwanda. Bearing in mind that the differentiation between the Hutus and Tutsis was not couched on ethnicity or religion, wherein the primary identity of all Rwandans in the precolonial era was originally associated with eighteen different clans including Hutu and Tutsi. Unarguably, most contemporary heterogeneous societies in Africa like Rwanda experienced the creation of the colonial masters (Dumarz, 2019).

Preeminent influence and educational opportunities were significantly assigned to the Tutsis over the Hutus by the colonial powers. As the Tutsis dominated the political and economic circles, the Hutus were motivated by Western values like democracy and equality, which ultimately polarized the ethnic groups into separate political entities. Despite the policy reversal of Belgian colonial authorities in 1959, which toned down support for minority Tutsis and empowering Hutus, disruptive affinities had been entrenched in the polity sufficient to draw a continuous pattern of ethnic violence

(Dumarz, 2019). Colonialism, therefore, birthed two extreme identities with clearly defined and opposing ends. The Tutsis assumed themselves better with leadership competence, while the Hutus were considered the oppressed.

Three years before gaining independence in 1962, the Hutus overthrew the ruling Tutsi king and this culminated into thousands of Tutsis being killed and some 150,000 driven into exile in neighboring countries by the Hutus (nationsonline, n.d). Although Rwanda gained independence from Belgium in 1962, this did not help to ease ethnic tension but rather institutionalized it and fanning the postcolonial period with ethnically motivated violence. Subsequently, in 1963, following an incursion by Tutsi rebels based in Burundi, about 20,000 Tutsis in Rwanda were killed (BBC News, 2018). Again in exile, rebel groups under the Rwandan Patriotic Front (RPF) were formed by the children of exiles, which ushered in the famous Rwandan civil war in 1994 that saw the genocide of about 800,000 citizens with more victims from the Tutsi stalk. On April 6, 1994, the plane of Rwandan President Juvénal Habyarimana was shot down by a missile of unknown origin. His death set the motion for a carnage that lasted for the next 100 days. Consequently, President Paul Kagame of Rwanda charged Rwanda's colonial masters and France in 2014 for their "direct role" in the factors that exacerbated the Rwandan genocide (Cowell, 2014) and its multiplier effects on Africa's underdevelopment. For instance, the identity cards introduced in 1932 under the Belgian administration, which mandated Rwandans to identify themselves according to the ethnic groups they belonged, was a death trap for most Tutsis at checkpoints during the genocide in 1994. Commemorating the 1994 genocide in 2014, President Kagame assuages that although the genocide act and all gross human atrocities were committed by Rwanda nationals, the historical antecedents and root cause of the ethnic cleansing were engraved in the international composition (Cowell, 2014).

The Role of France in the Rwandan Conflict

The influence of the West was not limited to the interference of Germany and Belgium alone, as France played a pivotal role in post-colonial Rwanda. The interaction of France in Rwanda was solidified by the close friendship between Presidents Francois Mitterrand of France and Habyarimana of Rwanda (Wallis, 2006), which defined the political and economic structure of Rwanda thereafter. Similarly, the elite structure was designed along Francophone and Anglophone identities. In essence, French-speaking political elites, educated in Catholic Francophone culture, saw in Paris a source of sociopolitical identity and perceived Anglophone Tutsis as a potential threat against who they should be protected. The Hutus became an offspring and a vital partner to France's network, while the Tutsis, by aligning with the British, migrated to Uganda, an Anglophone culture. Thus, Rwanda's political class was torn between a Francophone and Anglophone cultures of identities. This intrinsically shaped the interactions that culminated into the genocide. As Dumarz (2019) asserts, Paul Kagame, who fled to Uganda at the age of two, trained in the U.S. military, an ally of Ugandan leader Yoweri Museveni, and the leader of the Tutsi-led Rwandan Patriotic Front (RPF), was automatically by design, an unfavorable choice to France. These manifestations were convenient elements for France's subtle institutionalization of discriminations against Tutsis in Rwanda upon which the genocide festered. Without lessening Africa's many complex issues of corruption, poverty, underdevelopment, and so on, as motivating intra-ethnic conflicts, the Rwandan genocide is instructive. This is because it suggests that the gruesome event was not the tale of two supposedly savage ethnic groups in an African country, but a case of European colonialism planting the seeds of future tragedy.

More so, beyond the political trajectories of manipulation and domination in Rwanda by the West, the body language and international inaction of the United Nations and major powers were a slant not only on black lives but on humanity as a whole. According to Canadian General Romeo Dallaire, prior information on the genocide was available to relevant authorities of the United Nations as early as January of 1994, but decisive actions were not taken in a timely manner (Shiffman, n.d). Thus, the greatest regret of the Bill Clinton Administration remains the failure to intervene in the Rwanda genocide (Beauchamp, 2014). Significantly, the complex phenomenon, stemming from colonial disvalue for humanity and a combination of inherent structural failures in Rwanda and Africa in its entirety, still hampers Africa's political and economic development. In other words, the profound impact of this historical error embodied in colonial cartography has continually posed as Africa's nightmare in its developmental quest in all global relations.

WESTERN INFLUENCE IN AFRICA WITHIN THE CONTEXT OF BLACK LIVES MATTER VERSUS ALL LIVES MATTER

The Black Lives Matter movement is an international human rights phenomenon that has existed since 2013 but has spread across the world after the murder of George Floyd. Although the murder of unarmed black men and women in the United States launched the movement, the crusade has sunk into all forms of human rights abuses and discrimination. Accordingly, from the United States to the Caribbean, Europe, the Middle-East, and most parts of Africa, black people face common issues of discrimination, miseducation, sub-optimal development, health disparities to bottom-of the-barrel status in almost all indicators of development and wellbeing (Fairchild & Fairchild, 2017). As Fairchild and Fairchild (2017) posit, these problems cannot be isolated from the common origin of exploitation against Africans, evident in colonialism, imperialism, capital flight, and resource exploitation spanning for more than 500 years till this day.

In essence, the debate on which lives matter is grounded in the prism of human rights, whether, black, white, blue eyes, Negro, and so forth. Thus, two basic questions seeking answers are the following: (1) Whose life is less important than the other? (2) What accounts for such basic importance to a life? No doubt, the nature to which the debate and subsequently political movement on Black Lives Matter versus All Lives Matter was decentralized across race, continent, regions, religion, ethnic, and the international community reaffirms that human rights are not only basic but individualistic. In effect, the global movement infers that human rights issues are exclusively about the right to life. Even though the general assumptions infer that human rights are Western-oriented and not universal as they claim because of the theory that supports the stance that the practice of human rights regime is unequal, Eurocentric and power-centered, human rights are universal in their entirety. They are intrinsically universal because they rest on the equal rights of all humans. As such, systemic, unjust, institutional violation and exploitation of Africa through international organizations and unequal terms of relations in a supposedly global terrain operating under the theory of universal human rights is an aberration. Therefore, all lives, including Black lives, matter.

The 1948 Universal Declaration of Human Rights (UDHR), which is the ground norm of the modern theory on human rights, identifies with the inherent dignity, equal and inalienable rights of all humans as the foundation of freedom, justice, and peace in the world. In light of this verity, the development of Western multinational corporations, Europe and America was as a result of the more than 400 years of slave trade in Africa (Hardy, 2020). The theft of mineral resources, natural resources, and human capital has further impoverished the black race and subjected citizens to fight one another over Western remnants in their soil. More worrisome is that with more international awareness on human rights and an informed impact of Western exploitation and discrimination in Africa, the West is still engulfed in the disvalue of African life.

Aliyu Modibo Umar, a former Nigerian commerce minister, queried the sincerity of European Union (EU) African trade agreements, stating that thirty years of nonreciprocal free market access into the EU did not improve the economic situation of Africa, the Caribbean, and the Pacific (ACP) (Ighobor, 2014). As Seery and Caistor (2014) contend, the root of inequality in Africa stems from the exploitative practices and institutions forced on much of the continent by the colonial powers into the hands of a few. Situating that rapid market liberalization under structural adjustment programs, deregulation, public spending cuts, privatization, and tax cuts for the rich and corporations, a "race to the bottom" on labor rights entrenched inequality further and increased poverty and hunger. Hence, the debt crises of the 1980s and 1990s and the Western liberal policies engraved poverty, inequality, and conflict in Africa. To further entrench this inequality division in Africa, about 75 percent of the wealth of African multi-millionaires and billionaires is held offshore, with the continent losing $14bn annually in uncollected tax revenues as a result (New World, 2018).

Significantly, the influence of the international financial system that facilitates the theft of resources from Africa to developed nations has contributed maximally to the inequality gap in Africa and the spiral effect of intra-ethnic conflicts. Importantly, most international initiatives like the Economic Partnership Agreements (EPA), designed to solve the excesses of colonialism and the uneven terms of relations between European countries and African states, will remain a quest in futility, so long as tax subsidies are instituted for the West. In essence, the African poverty chain and agricultural stagnancy have deepened due to the tax subsidies offered to Western producers. This creates disproportionate effect on poverty and, by extension, crisis, since many citizens of the low-income countries in Africa live in rural areas. As local small holder goods are destroyed, the advancement of the Western market is expanding at the detriment of African development. For instance, the EU forecasts that its agricultural subsidies will total €365 billion ($423 billion) between 2021 and 2027, while Brussels' entire European-Africa policy is worth just €39 billion a year (DW, n.d., p. 14).

As a member of the left-wing Linke Party suggests, "Instead of more free trade to create more reasons for migrants to leave, we finally need to stop plundering Africa's raw materials," adding that "fair trade" was a more appropriate term (quoted in DW, n.d, p. 16). In other words, African collective rights to a just and prosperous life have been truncated by the continued influence of the West. Until the continent braces up to a protectionist system envisioned in total freedom, Africa may remain in this debacle of poverty, conflict, war, and death trap.

CONCLUSION AND RECOMMENDATION

The chapter discussed the debate of Black Lives Matter versus All Lives Matter from the prism of Western exploitation and discrimination in Africa. Adopting the SDT and Conflict Theory, the chapter assessed the inequality gap within the international system and the inequality division constructed by Westerners in Africa. The chapter also argues that this inequality gap has consistently resulted in violent conflicts. Using a descriptive content analysis methodology, the Rwandan genocide was the base line for interrogating European colonialism and capitalist expansion in Africa. The chapter submits that all lives matter, considering the baseline of the Universal Human Rights Declaration of 1948. Hence, Black lives matter too and should be assessed from the realm of international institutions and international trade.

Apropos the preceding verities, the chapter therefore recommends that Africa should embrace a protectionist policy of international trade and power relations. While the impact of colonialism and Western intrusion is evidently a root cause of Africa's problems, it cannot answer for ethnic tensions, corruption, poverty, and state failure after about sixty-four years of postcolonialism. Africa should look inward to find the causes of ethnic tension rather than blame colonialists.

REFERENCES

Acemoglu, D. & Robinson, J. A. (2010). Why is Africa poor? *Economic History of Developing Regions* 25(1):21–50.

Achankeng, F. (2013). Conflict and conflict resolution in Africa: Engaging the colonial factor. *African Journal on Conflict Resolution* 13(2):11–38.

Agozino, B. (2018). Black Lives Matter otherwise all lives do not matter. *African Journal of Criminology and Justice Studies* 11(1):1–11. Retrieved on October 28, 2020 from https://www.umes.edu/uploadedFiles/_WEBSITES/AJCJS/Content/AJCJS%20VOL11.%20Agozino.pdf

Allison, S. (January 6, 2020). Conflict is still African's biggest Challenge in 2020. *ReliefWeb*. Retrieved on January 9, 2021 from https://reliefweb.int/report/world/conflict-still-africa-s biggest-challenge-2020

Altman, A. (June 4, 2020). Why the killing of George Floyd sparked an American uprising *Time*. Retrieved on January 9, 2021 from https://time.com/5847967/george-floydproteststrump/

Anazodo, R. O., Igbokwe-Ibeto, C. J. & Nkah, B. C. (2015). Leadership, corruption and governance in Nigeria: Issues and categorical imperatives. *African Research Review* 9(2): 41–58.

Aremu, J. O. (2010). Conflicts in Africa: Meaning, causes, impact and solution. *African Research Review* 4(4):549–560.

Arendt, H. (1958). *The Human Condition*. Chicago, IL: The University of Chicago Press.

Bailey, G. A. (1994). Rebirth of the non-western world. *Anthropology News* 35(9):1–5.

Beauchamp, B. (April 10, 2014). Rwanda's genocide—what happened, why it happened, and how it still matters. *Vox*. Retrieved on February 27, 2021 from https://www.vox.com/2014/4/10/5590646/rwandan-genocide-anniversary

Berkenpas, J. R. (2016). The behavioral revolution in contemporary political science: Narrative, identity, practice (doctoral dissertation, Western Michigan University, Michigan, USA). Retrieved on March 7, 2021 from https://scholarworks.wmich.edu/cgi/viewcontent.cgi?article=2404&context=dissertations

Berman, B. J. (1998). Ethnicity, patronage and the African state: The politics of uncivil nationalism. *African Affairs* 97(388):305–341.

Borch, M. (2001). Rethinking the origins of terra nullius. *Australian Historical Studies* 32(117):222–239.

British Broadcasting Corporation (BBC) News. (September17, 2018). Rwanda country profile. *BBC News*. Retrieved on February 27, 2021 from https://www.bbc.com/news/world-africa-14093238

Brown, C. & Ainley, K. (2005). *Understanding International Relations* (3rd ed.). Basingoke, UK: Palgrave Macmillan.

Brown, G. (2016). *The Universal Declaration of Human Rights in the 21st Century*. Cambridge, UK: Open Book Publishers. Retrieved on February 26, 2021 from https://www.equalrightstrust.org/ertdocumentbank/Brown-Universal-Declaration-Human-Rights21C.pdf

Chanthamith, B., Wu, M., Yusufzada, S. & Rasel, M. (2019). Interdisciplinary relationship between sociology, politics and public administration: Perspective of theory and practice. *Sociology International Journal* 3(4):353–357.

Chelwa, G. (May 22, 2013). The scramble for Africa, fractionalization and open borders. Retrieved on March 9, 2021 from https://openborders.info/blog/the-scramble-for-africa-fractionalization-and-open-borders/

Cocodia, J. (2008). Exhuming trends in ethnic conflict and cooperation in Africa: Some selected states. *African Journal on Conflict Resolution* 8(3):9–26.

Cohen, H. J. (1995). What should we do when nations get angry? *Nexus Africa* 1(2):11–14.

Cowell. A. (April 10, 2014). Colonialism, bloodshed and blame for Rwanda. *The New York Times*. Retrieved on February 27, 2021 from https://www.nytimes.com/2014/04/11/world/europe/colonialism-bloodshed-and-blame-forrwanda.html

Durmaz, M. (April 5, 2019). It's time to accept the west failed Rwanda during genocide. *TRT World*. Retrieved on February 27, 2021 from https://www.trtworld.com/opinion/it-s-time-to-accept-the-west-failed-rwanda-during-genocide25593

DW (n.d). EU-Africa free trade will create more imbalances, say critics. Retrieved on February 28, 2021 from https://www.dw.com/en/eu-africa-free-trade-will-create-more-imbalances-saycritics/a-45018168

Esteban, J. & Ray. D (2011). A model of ethnic conflict. *Journal of the European Economic Association* 9(3):496–521.

Faal, C. (February 21, 2019). The partition of Africa. *Blackpast*. Retrieved on 23 February, 2021 from https://www.blackpast.org/global-african-history/partition-africa/#:~:text=This%20conference%20was%20called%20by,were%20invited%20to%20the%20conference

Fair, J. (1995). *Remembering the Revolution: Behaviorism in American Political Science: Political Science in History*. Cambridge, UK: Cambridge University Press.

Fairchild, H. H. & Fairchild, H. F. (2017). *Reflections on Black Lives Matter: Lifespan Perspectives.* Delhi, India: Indo American Books.

Fearon, J. D. &. Laitin. D. D. (2003). Ethnicity, insurgency, and civil war. *American Political Science Review* 97(1):75–90.

Frankfort-Nachmias, F. & Nachmias. D. (1996). *Research Methods in the Social Sciences.* New York, America: St. Martin's Press.

Gusman, J. (2015). The concept of human rights: Political and moral approaches. (Master's thesis, Radboud University, Nijmegen, The Netherlands). Retrieved on January 6, 2021 from https://theses.ubn.ru.nl/bitstream/handle/123456789/1160/Gusman%2C_Jesse_1.pdf?sequence=1

Hardy, W. (September 25, 2020). Riches & misery: The consequences of the Atlantic slave trade. *OpenLearn.* Retrieved on March 17, 2021 from https://www.open.edu/openlearn/history-the-arts/history/riches-misery-the-consequences-the-atlantic-slave-trade

Hiribarren. V. (2018). Scramble for and partition of West Africa. In N. Achebe, S. Adu-Gyamfi, J, Alie et al. (eds.), *History Textbook: West African Senior School Certificate Examination.* Retrieved on February 23, 2021 from https://wasscehistorytextbook.com/wpcontent/uploads/sites/334/2018/06/WASSCE_History_Textbook.pdf

Huber, J. D. & Mayoral, L. (2014). *Inequality Ethnicity and Civil Conflict.* New York, NY Columbia University.

Ighobor, K. (2014). Trade between two unequal partners. *Africa Renewal.* Retrieved on February 28, 2021 from https://www.un.org/africarenewal/magazine/august-2014/trade-between-two-unequal-partners

Iheukwumere, E. O. & Iheukwumere, C. A. (2003). Colonial rapacity and political corruption: roots of African underdevelopment and misery. *Chi.-Kent J. Int'l & Comp. L.,* 3, 1.

Isabirye, S. B. & Mahmoudi, K. M. (2000). Rwanda, Burundi, and their "ethnic" conflicts. *Ethnic Studies Review* 23(1):62–80.

Islam, G. (2014). Social dominance theory. *Encyclopedia of Critical Psychology* 28(1):1779–1781.

Johnson, J. B. & Joslyn. R. A. (1991). *Political Science Research Methods.* Washington, DC: America: Congressional Quarterly Press, Inc.

Lindblom, C. E. (1977). *Politics and Markets.* New York, NY: Basic Books.

Lumumba-Kasongo, T. (2017). Contemporary theories of conflict and their social and political implications. In T. Lumumba-Kasongo & J. Gahama (eds.), *Peace, Security and Post-Conflict Reconstruction in the Great lake Region of Africa.* Dakar. Senegal: CODESRIA.

Maddocks, K. G. (June 26, 2020). What is political science all about? South New Hampshire University. Retrieved on March 9, 2021 from https://www.snhu.edu/about-us/newsroom/2018/08/what-is-political-science

Mekoa, I. (2019). How Africa got into a mess: Colonial legacy, underdevelopment, corruption and human rights violations in Africa. *Journal of Reviews on Global Economics* 8:43–52.

Mende, J. (2019). Are human rights western—And why does it matter? A perspective from international political theory. *Journal of International Political Theory.*

Retrieved on January 25, 2021 from https://journals.sagepub.com/doi/10.1177/1755088219832992

Michalopoulos, S. & Papaioannou, E. (2013). Pre-colonial ethnic institutions and contemporary African development. *Econometrica* 81(1):113–52.

Michalopoulos, S. & Papaioannou, E. (2016). The long-run effects of the scramble for Africa. *American Economic Review* 106(7):1802–1848.

New World Wealth. (2018). *The AfrAsia Bank: Africa Wealth Report*. Retrieved on February 18, 2021 from https://enterprise.press/wp-content/uploads/2018/09/africa-wealth-report-2018.pdf

Nitisha. (n.d). Behaviouralism in politics: Definition, origin and credo. *Political Science*. Retrieved on March 8, 2021 from https://www.politicalsciencenotes.com/behaviouralism/behaviouralism-in-politics-definition-origin-and-credo/717

Ocheni, S. & Nwankwo, B. C. (2012). Analysis of colonialism and its impact in Africa. *Cross-Cultural Communication* 8(3):46–54.

Oneworldnationsonline. (n.d). Rwanda. Retrieved on February 27, 2021 from https://www.nationsonline.org/oneworld/rwanda.htm#:~:text=Population%3A%2011.5%20million%20(2016%3B,1.7%25%20claim%20no%20religious%20beliefs

Pennock, R. J. & Smith. D. G. (1964). *Political Science: An Introduction*. New York, NY: The Macmillan Company.

Pondy, L. R. (1967). Organizational conflict: Concepts and models. *Administrative Science Quarterly* 12:296–320.

Pratto, F., Sidanius, J. & Levin, S. (2006). Social dominance theory and the dynamics of intergroup relations: Taking stock and looking forward. *European Review of Social Psychology* 17(1):271–320.

Roberts, J. (January 24, 2011). How western environmental policies are stunting economic growth in developing countries. *The Heritage Foundation*. Retrieved on February 13 from https://www.heritage.org/global-politics/report/how-western-environmental-policies-are-stunting-economic-growth-developing

Routley, N. (January 12, 2018). Map: All of the world's borders by age. Retrieved on February 22, 2021 from https://www.visualcapitalist.com/map-worlds-borders-by-age/

Saxena, N. (2011). Political science: A conceptual analysis. *The Indian Journal of Political Science* lxxii(1):129–134.

Schmidt, S. M. & Kochan, T. A. (1972). Conflict: Toward conceptual clarity. *Administrative Science Quarterly* 17:359–71.

Seery, E. & Caistor A. A. (2014). Even It Up: time to end extreme inequality. Oxfam. Retrieved on February 28, 2021 from http://policy-practice.oxfam.org.uk/publications/even-it-up-time-to-end-extreme-inequality-333012

Shiffman, K. (n.d.). Scream bloody murder. (CNN). Retrieved on March 9, 2021 from https://edition.cnn.com/2008/WORLD/africa/11/13/sbm.dallaire.profile/

United Nations. (1948). *Universal Declaration of Human Rights*. Retrieved on January 7, 2021 from https://www.un.org/en/universal-declaration-human-rights/

Wallis, A. (2006). Rwanda rift in La Francafrique. *Open Democracy*. Retrieved on February 27, 2021 from https://www.opendemocracy.net/en/rwanda_france_4183jsp/

Weisberg, H. F. (1986). *Political Science: The Science of Politics.* New York, NY: Agathon Company.

Wimmer, A. (2004). Toward a new realism. In A. Wimmer & R. Goldstone (eds.), *Facing Ethnic Conflicts: Toward a New Realism.* Lanham, MD: Rowman and Littlefield.

Wogu, I. A. P. (2013). Behaviouralism as an approach to contemporary political analysis: An appraisal. *International Journal of Education and Research* 1(12):1–12.

Worldometer. (February 27, 2021). Rwanda population (LIVE). Retrieved on February 27, 2021 from https://www.worldometers.info/world-population/rwanda-population/

Chapter 13

Juvenile Justice Perspective

Gerald K. Fosten

This chapter utilizes the juvenile justice perspective (i.e., the history of youth services; current theories of adolescent development; the impact of community disadvantage; and child abuse and neglect on behavior) to examine the treatment of black bodies—in particular, black males—as they matriculate into adulthood. Treyvon Martin, Tamir Rice, Jordan Edwards, and other black youths' deaths at the hands of institutionalized policing reveal patterns of systemic institutionalized behavior that oftentimes manifests in the overuse of force and deaths of black youths. Parents of black youths having "the talk" with their black children are challenged to protect their children from societal norms that criminalize black youths in their earliest stages of development. The chapter therefore also investigates the challenges of black youths as they attempt to exist in a societal construct that places the full weight of the criminal justice system on their necks. In order for effective change to produce positive outcome, it is proposed here that proponents of Black Lives Matter (BLM) and All Lives Matter (ALM) must address juvenile justice policies with foci given to juvenile delinquency behavior, systemic racism, and structural racism. Juvenile justice reform policies must be centered around developing adolescents' mental capabilities, physical nature, cognitive awareness, emotional sensory, social constructs, and behavior practices.

The juvenile justice and Delinquency Prevention Act (JJDPA) was first authorized in 1974. It was established to ensure that states and territories of the United States meet certain common standards for how youths across the country are treated in the justice system. It did this by establishing two core protections: (1) a prohibition on the incarceration of youths charged with status offenses (conduct that is not criminal if engaged in by an adult, such as skipping school or breaking curfew), and (2) a requirement that youths have sight and sound separation from adult inmates. Two additional protections were added in a subsequent reauthorization: (1) a prohibition against housing young people in adult facilities while awaiting trial as juveniles, and (2) requiring that states address disproportionate minority contact. States receive federal formula grant funding for complying with these protections. The act was last reauthorized in 2002 and expired in 2007. On December 13, 2018, Congress passed H.R. 6964, the Juvenile Justice Reform Act of 2018, with broad bipartisan support (CFJJ, 2018). In FY 2019, the Office of Juvenile Justice and Delinquency Prevention (OJJDP) awarded more than $323 million to support state, local, and tribal efforts to deter delinquency and safeguard children (OJJDP, 2020). In FY 2020, the OJJDP awarded nearly $370 million in grants (OJJDP, 2020).

The Department of Justice (DOJ) defines "juvenile" as a person who has not attained her or his eighteenth birthday and "juvenile delinquency" as the violation of a law of the United States committed by a person prior to his eighteenth birthday, which would have been a crime if committed by an adult. A person over eighteen, but less than twenty-one years of age, is also accorded juvenile treatment if the act of juvenile delinquency occurred prior to his eighteenth birthday. See 18 U.S.C. § 5031 (USDOJ, 2020).

The OJJDP defines the term *community-based* facility, program, or service as a small, open-group home or other suitable place located near the juvenile's home or family and programs of community supervision and service, which maintain community and consumer participation in the planning operation, and evaluation of their programs, which may include, but are not limited to, medical, educational, vocational, social, and psychological guidance, training, special education, counseling, alcoholism treatment, drug treatment, and other rehabilitative services (OJJDP, 2019). OJJDP defines the term *federal juvenile delinquency program* as any juvenile delinquency program, which is conducted, directly, or indirectly, or is assisted by any federal department or agency, including any program funded under this chapter (OJJDP, 2019). It denotes a "juvenile delinquency program" as any program or activity related to juvenile delinquency prevention, control, diversion, treatment, rehabilitation, planning, education, training, and research, including drug and alcohol abuse programs; the improvement of the juvenile justice system; and any program or activity designed to reduce known risk factors for juvenile delinquent behavior, provides activities that build on protective factors for, and develop competencies in juveniles to prevent and reduce the rate of delinquent juvenile behavior (OJJDP, 2019).

BLM is a social movement seeking to address challenges of institutional and systemic racism by bringing awareness to challenges of African descendants of slaves and descendants of other Africans experience in the United States. BLM is largely characterized by liberal and progressive supporters challenging white supremacy and institutions that facilitate the existence of white supremacy. BLM does not promote black dominance. Instead, it promotes equality with all humankind and seeks to end racially biased practices in all its forms. #BlackLivesMatter is self-described as "a call to action and a response to the virulent anti-Black racism that permeates American society" (Vote Smart, 2016). The intention of the #BlackLivesMatter hashtag is to broaden the conversation around state violence to include all of the ways in which black people are intentionally left powerless at the hands of the state (Vote Smart, 2016). BLM and #BlackLivesMatter represent an umbrella term for a techno-ubiquitous digital assemblage movement coalition advocating ideas, objectives, and groups combined to confront, challenge, and change dominant societal structural norms, institutionalized systems, and patterns of behavior. Currently, there is no one "leader" or typical power structure to the BLM movement (Barron-Lopez, 2020). BLM considers itself "leaderful" with the ability to wage battle on multiple fronts using "multi-tactical" approaches encompassing everything from organizing and protesting to pushing new legislation at various levels of government (Barron-Lopez, 2020). According to the National Institute of Health (NIH), numerous organizations use BLM terminology in some form or manner to identify and advance the movement. The most prominent is the Black Lives Movement Global Movement (BLMGN), which has grown to become one of the most recognizable entities in the BLM movement. BLMGN is a chapter-based organization made up of more than forty chapters worldwide (NIH, 2020). BLMGN's stated goals are to "eradicate white supremacy and build local power to intervene in violence inflicted on Black communities by the state and vigilantes" (NIH, 2020). Initially started to address law enforcement killings and overuse of force against unarmed black men and women, its mission-focus has expanded beyond not only to address the criminal justice system but also to include equity advancement in other policy institutions such as education, housing, and other social frameworks. In furtherance of these goals, it organizes programs around black arts and culture, protests to achieve policy change, and provides toolkits and other resources for discussing and responding to systemic and institutionalized forms of racism (NIH, 2020).

BLM identifies itself as nonpartisan in its political affiliation (NIH, 2020). However, BLM's mission-activities result in advocacy activities that address and target political party organizations. It has supported and opposed policy positions held by both the Democratic Party and Republican Party. Historically, varying ideological perspectives in the United States have been influential in the current evolution of criminal justice policy. All too often, the juvenile justice perspective is not mentioned in the larger discussion of criminal justice perspectives. Such discussion rarely encompassed the juvenile justice perspective.

Thus, there are two major objectives in this chapter. The first is to determine whether using BLM terminology is inherently a political activity. And the second is to find out whether the Black Lives Matter Global Network (BLMGN)—the owner of www.blacklivesmatter.com and arguably the most prominent BLM-related organization—is a partisan political group. As to be further described later, using BLM terminology is not inherently a political activity and BLMGN is not currently a partisan political group (NIH, 2020).

ALM #AllLivesMatter is a broad federation term arguably designed as a counter-movement response to challenge, refute, and discredit ideals championed by the BLM movement. According to Pew Research Center data, ALM is largely supported by a conservative base (Horowitz, Juliana and Livingston, 2016). ALM is an alternative ideological movement to BLM. Both #BlackLivesMatter and #AllLivesMatter hashtags (trending topics on social media) have ignited a national conversation on the use of police brutality and the mistreatment of minorities in America. While they don't have to exist separately, the way they have been discussed in the political arena, especially during the 2016 election, has pitched them against each other (Vote Smart, 2016). ALM does not challenge white supremacy and domination. ALM does not advocate for equality and equity for all humankind in the sense that it seeks to address historical and contemporary inequality, oppression, and injustices experienced by descendants of slavery and Africa in the United States. South Carolina's first black senator since Reconstruction, Tim Scott, used the statement in an interview on CNN, asserting that this statement allows us to see what we have in common and bridges racial divisions. The ALM movement therefore places emphasis on inclusion as a motivator behind its use of the phrase (Vote Smart, 2016),

Significant focus of criminal justice policy is devoted to adult perspectives on criminal justice. The juvenile justice perspective relating behavior of youth and juvenile actors is often not included in the larger policy issue framework of criminal justice. Hence, while the deaths of Treyvon Martin, Tamir Rice, Jordan Edwards, and other black youths trend on social media platforms, lesser policy and practice is devoted on social media to addressing broader issues affecting juvenile justice and adolescents' outcomes and policy outcomes in comparison to the attention social media platforms address adult criminal justice reform.

This chapter seeks to highlight important perspectives stakeholders and policymakers must consider if monumental criminal justice reform is to become a reality in the United States. If goals are criminal justice reform, saving of taxpayers' dollars currently spent in the corrections system, and advancement of American ideals of democratic freedoms for traditionally underserved and oppressed subpopulations of U.S. citizens, both Republicans and Democrats will be more influential, and the nation will be better served if party ideological positions take a back seat to partisan politics. The two parties must establish, embrace, and adopt mutually common goals that realign their respectful ideologies into mutually held juvenile justice and criminal justice policy decisions equitably advancing underutilized subpopulations of minority men into more positive and productive outcomes offered in the United States' highly advanced economic society. This is preferable to the perpetual conditioning of subpopulations of largely underutilized and unproductive black males as participants ensnared in the criminal justice system. Once entangled and ensnared in the criminal justice system, oftentimes, insurmountable collateral damage and challenges from which many never recover academically are inflicted on black youths and juveniles impacting their abilities to live productive outcomes as they matriculate into adulthood (Radice, 2018). States play a pivotal role in orchestrating long-term and permanent collateral damage through statues that partially protect the confidentiality of juvenile records (Radice, 2018).

How do current policies and approaches promote prevention, deterrence, retribution, rehabilitation, restorative justice, and so forth? How has #BlackLivesMatter evolved from a social media platform advocating against criminal justice and law enforcement killings of black men to broader policy issues advocating against societal racism (structural racism) and institutional racism (systemic racism) facilitating white domination?

The major proposition here then is that #BlackLivesMatter social media digital technology platforms (internet, Facebook, Twitter, TikTok, etc.) represent a practical evolution of technology to address the black struggle for justice and equality. Television's role in the 1960s has been augmented in the twenty-first century by internet-based platforms to advance the black struggle for equality. The #BlackLivesMatter hashtag is an archetypal example of a hashtag tied to a political issue or cause. It has maintained a relatively high baseline level of usage on Twitter over a period of several years (Anderson et al., 2018).

This chapter refers to the juvenile justice system or criminal justice system as a general framework that is more or less representative of what happens in any given state. Each state has its own individualized juvenile justice structure with dramatic differences in maximum age of juvenile jurisdiction, appointment of counsel, treatment options, probation caseloads, and adjudication of docket in the same (or separate) courtroom as adults (Radice, 2018). The two movements should provide transparency regarding their political positions on juvenile justice and criminal justice perspectives in three key areas: (1) the history of youth services, (2) theories of adolescent development, and (3) the impact of community disadvantage.

Concomitantly, the research methodology that undergirds this chapter is qualitative, which means that emphasis is placed on words instead of numerical values. More specifically, a Descriptive Case Study approach that seeks to answer the question "What is?" is utilized. Thus, the analyses in the sections that follow give accounts in words of the phenomena broached, including all the relevant characteristics, qualities, or events (for more on this methodology, see Bangura et al., 2019).

Effective public policy cannot be based on instinct or anecdote; rather, it must be based on solid information that enables policymakers and practitioners to identify and quantify problems in the system, propose and implement solutions, and then evaluate whether the solutions are, in fact, effective (CFJJ, 2018).

In theory, the two movements represent nonpartisan political movements. In practice, a social and demographic trends survey finds the two movements differentiate along racial lines and largely represent ideologies of the Democratic Party and Republican Party establishments (Pew Research Center, 2016). Both movements comprised supporters favoring one political ideology or policy position in opposition to the political ideology and policy position advocated by the other movement (Horowitz, Parker and Anderson, 2020). Despite this, the public still remains confused and conflicted on the debates advanced by BLM and ALM (Vote Smart, 2016). A study conducted by Pew Research Center found that only 12 percent of whites and 33 percent of blacks say they understand the goals of BLM. In particular, for white adults, support for BLM is divided among party lines, with just 4 percent of white Republicans expressing support for the movement, in comparison to 29 percent of white Democrats (Vote Smart, 2016). In lieu of BLM, the ALM movement lacks substantial exposure revealing its policy positions on issues pertaining to juvenile justice and criminal justice. Pew Research Center survey studies have shown that support for BLM has decreased since June of 2020 but remains strong among black Americans (Horowitz and Thomas, 2020).

This issue is still hotly debated within the general public. Moreover, public debate is likely to continue about what #AllLivesMatter means as a response to the #BlackLivesMatter movement. If these two social movements continue to be exclusive from each other, then the stances individual policymakers and the ideological positions of their respectful political party will be evident based upon their pursuit and enactment of policy outcomes relating to juvenile justice. Before engaging in the broader conceptualization of the juvenile justice perspective, it is important to first ideologically conceptualize and discuss contexts of the major notions underlying this chapter.

The study of juvenile justice is a subcomponent of the larger criminal justice system and is divided into four perspectives: (1) deterrence, (2) retribution/punishment, (3) rehabilitation, and (4) restorative justice. Deterrence focuses on prevention. Retribution focuses on aspects of punishment.

Rehabilitation centers on readaptation. Restorative justice centers on responsibility and reconciliation.

THE HISTORY OF YOUTH SERVICES: A CONCEPTUAL DISCUSSION

A separate juvenile justice system was established in the United States about 100 years ago with the goal of diverting youth offenders from the destructive punishments of criminal courts and encouraging rehabilitation based on the individual juvenile's needs (McCord, Spatz-Widom and Crowell, 2001). This system was to differ from adult or criminal court in a number of ways. It was to focus on the child or adolescent as a person in need of assistance, not on the act that brought him or her before the court. The proceedings were informal, with much discretion left to the juvenile court judge. Since the judge was to act in the best interests of the child, procedural safeguards available to adults, such as the right to an attorney, the right to know the charges brought against one, the right to trial by jury, and the right to confront one's accuser, were thought unnecessary (McCord et al., 2001). Juvenile court proceedings were closed to the public and juvenile records were to remain confidential so as not to interfere with the child's or adolescent's ability to be rehabilitated and reintegrated into society. The very language used in juvenile court underscored these differences. Juveniles are not charged with crimes, but rather with delinquencies; they are not found guilty, but rather are adjudicated delinquent; they are not sent to prison, but to training school or reformatory (McCord et al., 2001).

In practice, there was always a tension between social welfare and social control—that is, focusing on the best interests of the individual child versus focusing on punishment, incapacitation, and protecting society from certain offenses (McCord et al., 2001). This tension has shifted over time and has varied significantly from jurisdiction to jurisdiction, and it remains today (McCord et al., 2001).

Each of the fifty states with the District of Columbia has its own laws that govern its juvenile justice system. How juvenile courts operate may vary from county to county and municipality to municipality within a state (McCord et al., 2001). The federal government has jurisdiction over a small number of juveniles, such as those who commit crimes on Indian reservations or in national parks, and it has its own laws to govern juveniles within its system. States that receive money under the federal JJDPA must meet certain requirements, such as not housing juveniles with adults in detention or incarceration facilities, but it is state law that governs the structure of juvenile courts and juvenile corrections facilities (McCord et al., 2001).

Tracking changes in practice is difficult, not only because of the differences in the structures of the juvenile justice systems among the states but also because the information collected about case processing and incarcerated juveniles differs from state to state and because there are few national data (McCord et al., 2001). Some states collect and publish a large amount of data on various aspects of the juvenile justice system, but for most states, the data are not readily available. Although data are collected nationally on juvenile court case processing, the courts are not required to submit data, so that national juvenile court statistics are derived from courts that cover only about two-thirds of the entire juvenile population (Stahl et al., 1999; McCord et al., 2001). Furthermore, national data on the number of juveniles convicted by offense, the number incarcerated by offense, sentence length, time served in confinement, or time served on parole are not available to the public. Such national information is available on adults incarcerated in prisons and jails (McCord et al., 2001).

Broader public policy must therefore be advocated and addressed concerning the juvenile justice perspective if the school-to-prison pipeline is to be dismantled. Social media can be utilized to influence the criminal justice system and to bring greater awareness to the root issues of juvenile delinquency. Also, more than one aspect of public policy must be addressed. This entails addressing multiple systems and services addressing young people of color transitioning to adulthood. The education system offers the greatest opportunities to impact change.

In response to the increase in violent crimes in the 1980s, state legal reforms in juvenile justice, particularly those that deal with serious offenses, have stressed punitiveness, accountability, and a concern for public safety, rejecting traditional concerns for diversion and rehabilitation in favor of a get-tough approach to juvenile crime and punishment (McCord et al., 2001). This change in emphasis from a focus on rehabilitating the individual to punishing the act is exemplified by the seventeen states that redefined the purpose clause of their juvenile courts to emphasize public safety, certainty of sanctions, and offender accountability (Torbet and Szymanski, 1998; McCord et al., 2001). Inherent in this change in focus is the belief that the juvenile justice system is too soft on delinquents, who are thought to be potentially as much a threat to public safety as their adult criminal counterparts (McCord et al., 2001).

Legal reforms and policy changes that have taken place under the get-tough rubric include more aggressive policing of juveniles, making it easier (or in some cases mandatory) to treat a juvenile who has committed certain offenses as an adult, moving decision making about where to try a juvenile from the judge to the prosecutor or the state legislature, changing sentencing options, and opening juvenile proceedings and records (McCord et al., 2001).

Changes in laws do not necessarily translate into changes in practice. In addition to the belief that at least some juvenile offenders are amenable to treatment and rehabilitation, other factors limit overreliance on get-tough measures. They are the following: (a) the expense of incarceration; (b) overcrowding that result from sentencing offenders more harshly; and (c) research evidence that finds few gains, in terms of reduced rates of recidivism, from simply incapacitating youths without any attention to treatment or rehabilitation (McCord et al., 2001). Practice may also move in ways not envisioned when laws are passed. For example, many jurisdictions have been experimenting with alternative models of juvenile justice such as the restorative justice model (McCord et al., 2001). The traditional juvenile justice model, however, focuses on offender rehabilitation and the current get-tough changes focus on offense punishment; the restorative justice model focuses on balancing the needs of victims, offenders, and communities (McCord et al., 2001).

CURRENT THEORIES OF ADOLESCENT DEVELOPMENT

Factors influencing adolescent social development are complex. Many variables are at play when examining adolescent behavior relating to behavior and mental health. Family influence, school and education, community and environment, and biological factors can influence behavior outcomes. A theory can try to explain crime for a large social unit or area (macro), or it can attempt to explain crime at the individual or smaller unit level (micro) (Akers and Sellers, 2012). Many disciplines factor into criminological theories, such as psychology, sociology, biology, political science, and criminal justice (Akers and Sellers, 2012).

Research has shown that age is one of the most significant predictors of criminality, with criminal or delinquent activity peaking in late adolescence and decreasing significantly with time.

According to the National Juvenile Justice Network, in a paper titled "Using Adolescent Brain Research to Inform Policy: A Guide for Juvenile Justice Advocates":

> Brain development takes place in stages and is not fully complete in adolescence. The frontal lobe, especially the prefrontal cortex, is one of the last parts of the brain to fully mature, and undergoes dramatic development during the teen years. It is this 'executive' part of the brain that regulates decision making, planning, judgment, expression of emotions, and impulse control. This region of the brain may not be fully mature until the mid-20s. (National Juvenile Justice Network, 2012, p. 1)

Since we are dealing with human behavior, the social sciences will never be like the hard sciences. In the hard sciences, the theory of relativity does not change. In the social sciences, however, we deal with probabilities. A number of theories provide explanations of adolescent development and implications to juvenile delinquency behavior (Akers and Sellers, 2012). The social scientist will say things such as, "A severely neglected child will probably commit, or tend to commit, delinquent acts" (Akers and Sellers, 2012, p. 1).

Studies of crime and labeling practices occur at the individual level (micro), the institution level, and the state or national rule making body (macro). Labeling Theory investigates the role of government agencies, state institutions, and social processes in the creation and realization of deviance and crime focusing more on external processes involving social and societal responses to the label, including increased surveillance as well as reduced social opportunities and interactions (Liberman et al., 2014). Devah Pager in *The Mark of a Criminal Record* defines Labeling Theory as: "The 'negative credential' associated with a criminal record represents a unique mechanism of stratification, in that it is the state that certifies particular individuals in ways that qualify them for discrimination or social exclusion" (Pager, 2003, p. 942).

Subculture Theory advanced by Albert Cohen consists of a culmination of multiple theories. It posits that juveniles that do not meet the social standards seek validation from a subculture. The subculture group is formed of other juvenile peers that do not meet the subculture standard and who may influence an individual to commit criminal acts in order to receive approval from the group. These groups act in manners that are not socially acceptable and rebel against the socially acceptable standards (Akers and Sellers, 2012).

Travis Hirschi's Social Bond Theory posits that an individual's ties to his or her community develop in early childhood to explain why people conform to social norms or participate in delinquent behavior. The theory encompasses four elements: (1) weak attachment to parents, education and peers; (2) belief in conventional values and low respect for the police, law and authority; (3) commitment (cost factor involved in engaging in deviant activities outweighing lack of aspiration toward measures of legitimate success); and (4) involvement in conventional activities driven by boredom (Krohn and Massey, 1980).

Psychological theories comprise general perspectives that look to the psychological functioning, development, and adjustment of an individual in explaining criminal or deviant acts. Under this set of approaches, the criminal act itself is important only in that it highlights an underlying mental issue (Akers and Sellers, 2012). Personality theorists believe that criminal behavior is the result of an improper or defective personality or personality traits. Instead of developing a conforming appropriate-social personality, the criminal develops a personality based on conflict, impulsiveness, and aggression. The criminal does not have the ability to feel empathy, remorse, or guilt for his or her actions, and does not develop a sense of right and wrong (Akers and Sellers, 2012).

Deterrence Theory states that if punishment is certain, severe, and swift, then people will refrain from committing criminal acts. The theory also proffers that crime can be controlled through the use of punishments that combine the proper degrees of certainty, strictness, and swiftness (Akers and Sellers, 2012). The theory is at the core of the criminal justice system and the basis for most strict punishments and long prisons sentences (Akers and Sellers, 2012). Retribution embraces the notion that the punishment fit the crime. The notion is also referred to as "an eye for an eye" (Akers and Sellers, 2012).

The term *rehabilitation* itself simply means the process of helping a person to readapt to society or to restore someone to a former position or rank. However, this concept has taken on various meanings over the years and wavered in acceptance as a principle of sentencing or justification for punishment. The means used to achieve reform in prisons have also varied over time, beginning with silence, isolation, labor, and punishment, then moving onto medically based interventions, including drugs and psychotherapy. More recently, educational, vocational, and psychologically based programs, as well as specialized services for specific problems, have been promoted as means to reform prisoners during their sentence. Between the 1950s and 1970s, the ideal model of correctional administration was founded on the belief that skilled experts could administer individualized assessment and treatment that would "diagnose" and "treat" the causes of criminality similar to the way that medical doctors cure other forms of illness. This medical model of inmate services was referred to as the "rehabilitative ideal," a correctional philosophy deeply rooted in the idea that prison inmates could be reformed and returned to the free world as law-abiding citizens, and was crucial to the development of correctional professionals and most corrections departments across the United States throughout the 1950s and 1960s. Many in the field believed that the rehabilitative ideal would be the paradigm for corrections indefinitely and that penal reformers would be able to craft increasingly technical and sophisticated prison environments and programs (Phelps, 2011).

Restorative justice refers to programs that are designed to make offenders take responsibility for their actions and restore them and their victims, as much as possible, back to things as they existed before the offense. The restorative justice model focuses on balancing the needs of victims, offenders, and communities (Wilson et al., 2017). Often, offenders will apologize to the victims and to the community and attempt to financially compensate the victims for their losses (Akers and Sellers, 2012).

Most adults agree about the kinds of things that are important for adults to do with young people—encourage success in school, set boundaries, teach shared values, teach respect for cultural differences, guide decision making, give financial guidance, and so on (American Psychological Association, 2002). Nonetheless, fewer actually act on these beliefs to give young people the kind of support they need (American Psychological Association, 2002). As writer Ryan Dedmon points out, "By exploring the environmental influences of family and school on adolescents, the nature and extent of juvenile delinquency can better be explained." Dedmon continues, "The family is a key social institution that provides first-line nurturing socialization and support systems of young children. The assumed relationship between delinquency and family life is critical today because the traditional American family is rapidly changing" (Dedmon, 2017). When the family support system becomes broken, severed, fractured, or dismantled, huge voids in youth development are negatively impacted. Families today can take many forms—single parent, shared custody, adoptive, blended, foster, and traditional dual parent (American Psychological Association, 2002). Ethnic diversity must be taken into consideration if individual development is to be truly understood in order to produce effective policy with the goal of positive outcomes. Becoming aware of racism and gaining an understanding of the manifestations of social injustice is an inevitable and important part of building a sense of ethnic identity. Professionals who work with ethnic minority youths can help them to make sense of the discrimination they may face and to build the confidence and skills necessary to overcome these obstacles (American Psychological Association, 2002).

The family unit is vulnerable to external influences upon its members. Family conditions and influences have significant impact on shaping the extent to which children are exposed to other major agents of socialization. Generally, a child's first socialization process begins in the home and learns values, beliefs, and behaviors from parents and other family members. Dysfunction and disjunction destabilize an orderly family structure and can have significant negative impacts on a child's outcome.

Despite good motives and efforts, it is more challenging for one parent to provide the same degree of control, discipline, and support as two. Therefore, the composition of a household can be a strong determinant of a child's delinquent behavior. Single-parent households increase the likelihood of youths being unmonitored and unsupervised to participate in high-risk behavior. This unmonitored and unsupervised time becomes an opportunity to experiment with sexual behavior, crime and delinquency, or substance abuse (American Psychological Association, 2002). Numerous studies have found that a positive relationship with at least one caring adult—a parent, teacher, coach, extended family member, mentor, and so on—with a strong positive, emotional attachment to the child is associated with resilience and positive outcomes (American Psychological Association, 2002).

Schools are a basic channel through which community and adult influences enter into the lives of adolescents. Education is a general path towards occupational prestige. When juveniles are deprived of this avenue of success through poor academic performance, there is a greater likelihood of deviant behavior. Correspondingly, delinquency could be another manifestation of whatever characteristics got the child into trouble with school authorities in the first place (National Research Council and Institute of Medicine, 2000). Some studies have shown reductions in delinquent behavior when a teenager drops out of school. Others have shown increasing rates of delinquency following school dropout. In addition, many other studies have shown that family and child characteristics predict both problems in school and an increased likelihood of delinquent behavior (National Research Council and Institute of Medicine, 2000).

Despite the ongoing discussion of the direction of causality, the evidence is clear that poor school performance, truancy, and leaving school at a young age are connected to juvenile delinquency (National Research Council and Institute of Medicine, 2000). Students who show signs of hyperactivity and aggression tend to deliberately disobey authority figures and, thus, are more likely to be labeled as "bad students," which can have a lasting impact on a student's entire educational career. According to the Labeling Theory, negative labeling has projection and impact upon the juvenile's self-concept and very well may influence future behavior, which manifests into the label. Stated another way, students who are labeled early in their educational career may participate in types of behavior, which are expected to accompany those labels.

As aforementioned, families today can take many forms—single parent, shared custody, adoptive, blended, foster, traditional dual parent, to name a few. Regardless of family form, a strong sense of bonding, closeness, and attachment to family have been found to be associated with better emotional development, better school performance, and engagement in fewer high-risk activities, such as drug use (American Psychological Association, 2002).

The restorative justice theoretical framework views crime as violations of people and relationships. These violations, in turn, create an obligation to make things right (Wilson et al., 2017). As stated earlier, restorative justice aims to reestablish the balance that has been offset as a result of a crime by involving the primary stakeholders (i.e., victim, offender, and the affected community) in the decision-making process of how best to restore this balance. The focus is on healing as opposed to punishment. Other important principles of restorative justice include offender accountability for wrongdoing, respect for all participants, and the centrality of the victim throughout the process (Wilson et al., 2017). Victims overwhelmingly prefer criminal justice approaches that prioritize rehabilitation over punishment and strongly prefer investments in crime prevention and treatment to more spending on prisons and jails. These views are not always accurately reflected in the media or in state capitols and should be considered in policy debates (Alliance for Safety and Justice, 2016).

The Micro-level Labeling Theory is an inadequate framework to understand the social impact of mass criminal justice intervention in inner-city communities. Whereas the individual social psychological impact of the official labeling process has weakened, the mass criminalization of inner-city African American youths has exacted collective costs in terms of social exclusion and diminished social expectations (Hirschfield, 2008).

Thus, opponents of the Micro-level Labeling Theory argue that while deterrence is a factor in preventing individuals from committing criminal acts, it most likely is not the deciding factor. Most people will not commit criminal acts because they believe it is wrong to do so, and because they have been socialized to follow the norms of society (Akers and Sellers, 2012). Programs that offer therapy and counseling in attempts to reduce delinquency have not been shown to be particularly effective (Akers and Sellers, 2012). While the role of psychology in criminal justice and criminology is indeed important, we have not yet reached a place where the key concepts of psychological and personality theories, along with their recommended treatments, have had a measured impact on criminal activity (Akers and Sellers, 2012). Starting in the early 1970s, rehabilitation was publicly discredited, making rehabilitation "a dirty word"; corrections departments turned to drastically different rhetorical strategies to justify their existence; and the sentencing structures that undergirded the rehabilitative ideal were dismantled (Phelps, 2011).

Research has indicated that some rehabilitative efforts do in fact have some positive outcomes on reoffending. Using recidivism as a means of assessing the effectiveness of rehabilitative programs may be somewhat misleading. Rates of reoffending reveal little about the effectiveness of rehabilitation programs, per se, as they could well ignore improvements that may have occurred in other areas, because much crime remains undetected, and because reoffending behavior may have little to do with areas targeted by initial programming efforts. Generally, no specific ethnicity rehabilitation programs are geared toward African American, Hispanic (or Latino/a), and Native American prisoners. However, formal and informal support groups based on ethnicity often develop, are largely composed of community organizations and volunteers, and serve to provide a strong means of support for prisoners who may feel culturally and spiritually isolated. Thus, it is not surprising that findings compiled by the Alliance for Safety and Justice in a 2016 report titled *Crime Survivors Speak* show that seven out of ten victims prefer that prosecutors focus on solving ongoing problems in communities, and also to emphasize rehabilitation over jails and prisons (Alliance for Safety and Justice, 2016).

THE IMPACT OF COMMUNITY DISADVANTAGE

Black boys lag behind in most social indexes measuring academic progress and advancement (NCES, 2019). Black boys are disciplined at a higher rate far disproportionate to their population (NCES, 2019; Riddle and Sinclair, 2019). Black boys come into contact with school resource officers (law enforcement) at a rate significantly higher than that of their peer groups (NCES, 2019). Black boys are placed in special education more than their peers (NCES, 2019). Black boys are more likely to lag behind in reading and literacy (NCES, 2019; Lynch, 2016).

Logically speaking, since so much of children's time is spent in school, there exists a relationship between delinquent behavior and what is happening, or not happening, in their classroom and learning environments. Numerous studies have confirmed that delinquency is related to academic achievement, and experts have concluded that many of the underlying problems of delinquency are intimately connected with the nature and quality of children's experiences at school (NCES, 2019).

Both the juvenile justice system and education system are pivotal actors in the school-to-prison pipeline. According to data from the National Center for Education Statistics (NCES) and the Individuals with Disabilities Act (IDEA), children of color with disabilities face disparate rates of suspension and expulsion. Suspension and expulsion are associated with poor academic and life outcomes (NCES, 2019). Students who are suspended and expelled are more likely to drop out or come into contact with the criminal justice system than their peers (NCES, 2019). There exist sizeable disparities in the identification of education disabilities. Black children in grade school are 40 percent more likely to be identified with a disability than their peers and twice as likely to be identified as being emotionally disturbed (NCES, 2019). Black children, in particular black boys, receive more punishment than their peers. Educators are more likely to recommend suspension for a black child than a white child for the exact same behavior (NCES, 2019).

Because of the school's significant role in the socialization of juveniles, the education system must assume more responsibility and take a more active role in preventing delinquency. There are serious problems associated with implicit bias, labeling, tracking, and programming failure and some students (NCES, 2019; Radice, 2018). Education officials need to institute more programs that will make schools more effective instruments of delinquency prevention. Schools must take a proactive approach to improving students' psychological assets and self-image, equipping them with the resources to positively handle and resist antisocial behavior. Schools should also focus on the continued cognitive development of students by increasing students' awareness about the dangers of violent behavior, substance abuse, and delinquency. Counseling services must be more available to help students who have already demonstrated behavioral problems.

Proactive policing practices target high-crime, disadvantaged neighborhoods, affecting individuals already facing severe socioeconomic disadvantage. Findings suggest that young men stopped by the police face a parallel but hidden disadvantage: compromised mental health. It has been found that young men reporting police contact, particularly more intrusive contact, also display higher levels of anxiety and trauma associated with their experiences (Geller et al., 2014). Despite these differences, the substantive associations between respondents' experiences with the police and their mental health are strong and largely robust across samples and models—particularly among respondents reporting stops carried out in an intrusive fashion. This raises concerns that the aggressive nature of proactive policing may have implications not only for police-community relations but also for local public health (Geller et al., 2014).

The National Center for Biotechnology Information's *Involvement in the Juvenile Justice System for African American Adolescents: Examining Associations with Behavioral Health Problems* study underscores that low-income African American youths are not a homogenous group and that those who come into contact with the juvenile justice system differ significantly from their counterparts with no such contact with regard to behavioral and health problems (National Center for Biotechnology Information, 2017). Findings also highlight that those with multiple juvenile justice system contacts report higher behavioral and health problems on some factors but not all and, thus, future research with larger samples and more in-depth methods are needed to better understand why. These findings, notwithstanding, suggest that juvenile justice–involved youths are a highly vulnerable population and that detention represents an opportunity to provide a wide range of comprehensive services addressing mental health, substance use, sexually transmitted infections (STIs) education, and violence prevention services (National Center for Biotechnology Information, 2017).

CHILD ABUSE AND NEGLECT ON BEHAVIOR

Decades of child welfare and juvenile justice research highlights racial disparities among black children. In child welfare, black children are more likely to experience racial disparities across key decision points, including child abuse reporting, investigation and removals, and they are least likely to be reunified with parents (Simmons-Horton, 2020). Little has changed since the juvenile and child welfare systems were established. Current policies embodying the targeting of black children are damaging to the black family (Simmons-Horton, 2020). In the juvenile justice system, an amendment made to the JJDPA of 1974 mandated juvenile justice jurisdictions to reduce disproportionate numbers of black youths in all processing stages or they face fiscal penalties. Improvements have been made in tracking racial disparities, yet race bias in arrests, adjudications, and sentencing continues (Simmons-Horton, 2020).

Many youths grow up in dysfunctional families headed by substance abusing parents, live in deteriorated neighborhoods, have access to dangerous weapons, are lured by criminal gangs, and are constantly exposed to extremes of poverty and violence. Some suffer from psychological and emotional problems. The United States faces many challenges in areas of child welfare and many social categories. This generation of adolescents faces many potential problems different from the challenges faced by preceding generations of youths. By age eighteen, many have spent more time in front of a cell phone and television than in a classroom; exposing themselves to murders, sexual topics, and violent assaults through various media platforms. Many juveniles text, upload, and post incriminating delinquencies on social media sites. Oftentimes, juveniles, friends, acquaintances, people with whom they know, or complete strangers post incriminating content to social media sites. It is nearly impossible to delete uploaded content from every site on the World Wide Web (internet) someone's stored files, or social media account(s).

Youths who are victims of emotional or physical trauma may suffer from a delay in brain maturation because of the disruption in brain development (NJJN, 2012). Youths and young adults incriminating between the ages of eighteen and twenty-four are particularly vulnerable following victimization and can suffer from the long-term impacts of unaddressed trauma, such as difficulty with school, work, relationships, and poor physical health. They are also the most at-risk for later becoming involved in criminal activity if their needs go unmet (Alliance for Safety and Justice, 2016).

Failing grades, truancy, and dropping out of school are only some of the response options available to struggling students who do not succeed in the education system. Students who cannot cope with the unsuccessful school experience feel that they essentially have two options: (1) drop out or (2) go to school and cause trouble. Consequently, school attendance laws limit those options to the latter. Oftentimes, feelings of frustration are vented and categorized as acts of aggressive behavior toward teachers and peers. Unfortunately, many youths will not receive proper resources to assist them along the most chaotic moments as their young physical bodies, brains, emotions, and hormones, which evolve from children into young adults. For myriads of reasons, many distressed youths experience this transition as difficult and overwhelming. Many are labeled as "disruptive," "unruly," and "troublemakers," and systematic process efforts to remove them from the classroom environment become the course of action path chosen by education officials (Aldrich, 2021).

Through the lens of slavery, child welfare, and juvenile justice systems, we see that there are policies and practices with unreasonable expectations pointed toward black families. The time is now for these systems to look internally at their "well-meaning" policies that are destructive to the black family (Simmons-Horton, 2020). One consequence of the decline in support for welfare policies and trust in experts or professionals was a shift in the balance of power among the public, criminal justice professionals, and legislators (Phelps, 2011). Instead of experts setting criminal justice policies and professionals implementing decisions for individual cases, this new mode of governance focused on populist and racially-coded "law and order" rhetoric (Phelps, 2011). This new rhetoric was matched with increased legislation around criminal justice policies (e.g., sentencing guidelines, mandatory minimum sentences, and repeat offender laws) that transferred decision-making power away from administrators, judges, and parole boards to legislators and voters (Phelps, 2011). With politicians in greater control of correctional policy and increasingly worried about appearing "soft on crime," it became harder to continue funding prison programs (Phelps, 2011).

Many researchers argue that while we have discovered much in recent years, there is much more that we do not yet know about brain development and juvenile delinquency, such as specific evidence of causation. And, thus, it is just too early to start using this research to inform policy (NJJN, 2012).

Unconscious racial bias has been found in many corners of the criminal justice system. A study in Washington state found that in narrative reports used for sentencing, juvenile probation officers attributed the problems of white youths to their social environments but those of black youths to their attitudes and personalities (Ghandnoosh, 2015).

Juvenile justice involves youths that are a highly vulnerable population and that detention represents an opportunity to provide a wide range of comprehensive services addressing mental health, substance use, STI education, and violence prevention services (Voisin et al., 2017).

CONCLUSION AND RECOMMENDATIONS

As previously mentioned, effective juvenile justice policy must be based on evidence-based data that enable policymakers and practitioners to identify and quantify problems in the system, propose and implement solutions, and then evaluate whether the solutions produce positive outcomes. Youths who are connected to their family, school, and community are more likely to have the resources needed to deal with the stresses and challenges they face. This requires cross-collaboration of data from juvenile justice, criminal justice, education, health, social welfare, housing, and other agencies.

The social development of adolescents is best considered in the contexts in which it occurs: that is, relating to peers, family, school, work, and community. It is important to keep in mind when interpreting the findings of research on the social development of adolescents that most of the research to date is based on samples of white, middle-class adolescents (American Psychological Association, 2002). Research done with more diverse groups of adolescents has revealed differences among youths of different ethnic backgrounds; so, generalizations to specific ethnic groups should be made with care when the research is based solely on samples of white adolescents (American Psychological Association, 2002).

Historical child welfare and juvenile justice research highlights racial disparities among black children. In the juvenile justice system, black youths are five times more likely to be detained or committed compared to white youths and four times more likely to be certified to adult courts (Simmons-Horton, 2020). The American juvenile justice system was established during the early 1900s for protection and rehabilitation of wayward disobedient and unsupervised children. The population of black youths, largely located in the South, remained enslaved (Simmons-Horton, 2020). Despite laws changing over time, black youths were denied access to reformatory institutions, and it would be a decade later before special sections were made available for black children. Still, "Black Codes" forced black adolescents into incarceration for behaviors, only deemed criminal, because of being black (Simmons-Horton, 2020).

Child welfare professionals oblivious to or unconcerned of possible systemic racial bias are unlikely to address disparities as they are occurring. Involvement of concerned community members of color in key staffing decisions creates opportunities for objective, in-depth decision-making. Zero-tolerance policies in schools are a primary source of juvenile intakes targeting black children (Simmons-Horton, 2020). Furthermore, juvenile courts must evaluate adjudication and adult certification decisions, disproportionately placing black youths in detention centers, residential treatment facilities, and adult prisons (Simmons-Horton, 2020).

Major findings indicated that adolescents who reported juvenile justice system involvement versus no involvement were 2.3 times as likely to report mental health problems, substance abuse, and delinquent or youth offending behaviors (Voisin et al., 2017). Additional findings documented that the higher the number of juvenile justice system contacts, the higher the rates of delinquent behaviors, alcohol and marijuana use, sex while high on drugs, and commercial sex. These findings suggest that identifying and targeting youths who have multiple juvenile justice system contacts, especially those in low-resourced communities for early intervention services, may be beneficial (Voisin et al., 2017).

Overrepresentation of African Americans occurs at every level of the U.S. juvenile justice system, from initial contact with law enforcement to sentencing and incarceration (Voisin et al., 2017). Not surprisingly, this overrepresentation continues into adulthood, with African American males representing the overwhelming majority of the incarcerated adult population in the United States (Voisin et al., 2017). Juvenile records do not just disappear when youths turn eighteen years of age. Those records can significantly affect a child's employment, housing, and educational opportunities, leaving many young people with tremendous hurdles as they attempt to become successful adults (National Reentry Resource Center, 2017). Therefore, a better understanding of correlates associated with juvenile justice system contacts can help to identify possible interventions to slow the pipeline from juvenile justice system involvement to adult penal institutions (Voisin et al., 2017). The major problem areas of most concern for high-risk adolescents living in lower socioeconomic environments are alcohol and drug abuse, pregnancy and sexually transmitted diseases, school failure and dropping out, crime, delinquency, and violence (American Psychological Association, 2002).

Disparate treatment of African Americans occurs at every stage of the juvenile legal system. Race and socioeconomic status explain some but not all of the factors contributing to delinquency. Applicable arrest data reveal that African Americans are disproportionately involved in delinquency, with larger differences for serious crimes (Voisin et al., 2017). Recent analysis has indicated that these racial differences have declined in recent years. Criticism of these studies note that crimes committed by African Americans may be more likely to come to attention of the police and that African Americans offenders are more likely to be arrested than their white counterparts (Voisin et al., 2017).

Adolescence is an opportunity to help youths become responsible adults and to lay a foundation for youths that will help them make informed decisions. Few studies to date have examined the relationship between frequency of juvenile justice system contacts and rates of delinquency among low-income African American youth and adolescents (Voisin et al., 2017). The developing adolescent brain means that the personalities and behaviors of youths are not fixed or stagnant; therefore, youths are highly amenable to treatment and rehabilitation (National Juvenile Justice Network, 2012). With this concept as the center of focus, policymakers need to adopt and implement effective evidenced-based policy solutions.

Due to its effectiveness, advocates will continue to use brain development research to inform and influence juvenile justice policy reform (National Juvenile Justice Network, 2012). Apropos the major questions become the following: What are the implications of using this research? How can we use this research while still being respectful of our young allies? And, how might this research be used for other policy agendas? (National Juvenile Justice Network, 2012).

Few studies exist that have examined the ability of BLM or ALM to influence policy legislation at national, state, local, and institution decision-making levels. BLM's efforts in bringing attention to racial disparities and disparate treatment in the criminal justice system have influenced political debate on criminal justice system reform, and to a lesser extent larger policy issues that contribute to root causations of delinquency such as poverty, violence, and education.

Explicit mentions of race and references to law enforcement are the most common topics in collection of tweets prior to fall 2017 (Anderson et al., 2018). Tweets that mention protests and fatal encounters with police are quite common at certain points in time but less common at others (Anderson et al., 2018). Mentions of national politicians and political parties were relatively rare prior to fall 2017 (Anderson et al., 2018).

It remains to be seen how influential social media platforms can be in influencing public policy in matters that do not have the emotional effect as seeing acts of questionable justifiable or excessive police violence. The challenge for social media-based movements is overcoming divided political rhetoric and ideology and addressing broader public policy areas that influence juvenile delinquency. Support for BLM has decreased since June of 2020 but remains strong among black Americans (Horowitz and Thomas, 2020). Both the BLM and ALM movements are deeply supported along partisan and racial lines (Rothchild, 2020). Support along party lines provides insight into policy positions held and advanced by the Democratic Party and Republican Party. If these two social movements continue to be exclusive from each other, then the stances candidates take on them may change future legislation to come (Vote Smart, 2016). Perhaps, in this regard, social media-based advocacy groups can influential in pressuring policymakers into a particular political position on a specific issue area or policy matter.

The ALM movement would have more validity if it formed its political ideology in an organic manner. Stated another way, ALM should offer its own public policy positions in spite to BLM. #BlackLivesMatter or #AllLivesMatter? Both hashtags (trending topics on social media) have ignited a national conversation on the use of police brutality, and the mistreatment of minorities in America. While they don't have to exist separately, the way they were discussed in the political arena of the 2016 election pitched them against each other (Vote Smart, 2016). The fact that the ALM movement was created as a response to BLM begs questions to be asked regarding ALM's authenticity, purpose, and objectives as championed by its supporters. A question that can be asked is this: Would there be an ALM without the BLM movement? If ALM is sincere, it should take the lead in advocacy of policy reforms, overcoming racial injustice and systemic racism and advancing conditions for historically oppressed and marginalized subpopulations.

Questions must be asked and genuinely discussed regarding the path juvenile justice and criminal justice reform should pursue. Solutions to the issues discussed must be collectively adopted, enacted, and implemented. What are the alternatives to the present paths pursued? Consequently, what are the projections if public policy remains unchanged? A better understanding of correlates associated with juvenile justice system contacts can help to identify possible interventions to slow the school-to-pipeline from juvenile justice system involvement to adult penal institutions (Voisin et al., 2017). This requires incorporating successful prevention and diversion models after identifying correlates associated with juvenile delinquency. These key recommendations are briefly summarized as follows:

(a) Adopt national uniform confidentiality, nondisclosure statutes, and extinguishing statutes (using sealing or expungement) for how states should protect juvenile records.
(b) Advocate for more reform in the education system, particularly on matters that disproportionately impact African American youths.
(c) Examine BLM's or ALM's ability to influence policy legislation at national, state, local, and institution decision-making levels.
(d) Study how social media platforms can be utilized to positively influence policy, civic issues, and agendas.
(e) Examine, explore, and implement ways to get juvenile justice reforms into mainstream criminal justice reform.
(f) Share successful reform measures occurring at state and local levels.

REFERENCES

Akers, R. L. and Sellers, C. S. (2012). *Criminological Theories: Introduction, Evaluation, and Application* (6th ed.). New York, NY: Oxford University Press.

Aldrich, M. W. (2021). Tennessee teachers could seek to remove unruly students under bill approved by legislature. *Chalkbeat Tennessee*. Retrieved on March 13, 2021 from https://tn.chalkbeat.org/2021/3/11/22326158/tennessee-teachers-could-seek-to-remove-unruly-students-under-bill-approved-by-legislature

Alliance for Safety and Justice. (2016). Crime survivors speak: The first-ever national survey of victims' views on safety and justice. Retrieved on December 8, 2020 from https://allianceforsafetyandjustice.org/crimesurvivorsspeak/

American Psychological Association. (2002). Developing adolescents: A reference for professionals. Retrieved December 7, 2020 from https://www.apa.org/pi/families/resources/develop.pdf

Anderson, M., Toor, S. R. and Smith, A. (July 11, 2018). 2. An analysis of #BlackLivesMatter and other Twitter hashtags related to political or social issues. Pew Research Center. Retrieved on December 8, 2020 from https://www.pewresearch.org/internet/2018/07/11/an-analysis-of-blacklivesmatter-and-other-twitter-hashtags-related-to-political-or-social-issues/

Bangura, A. K., Obando, J. A., Munene, I. I. and Shisanya, C. (2019). *Conducting Research and Mentoring Students in Africa: CODESRIA College of Mentors Handbook*. Dakar, Senegal: CODESRIA Publications.

Barron-Lopez, Laura. (2020). Why the Black Lives Matter movement doesn't want a singular leader. *Politico*. Retrieved on November 20, 2020 from https://www.politico.com/news/2020/07/22/black-lives-matter-movement-leader-377369

Coalition for Juvenile Justice. (2018). Summary of the Juvenile Justice Reform Act of 2018. Retrieved on December 9, 2020 from https://www.juvjustice.org/sites/default/files/resource-files/Summary%20of%20the%20Juvenile%20Justice%20Reform%20Act%20of%202018.pdf

Dedmon, Ryan. (2017). Roles of family and school in preventing juvenile delinquency. *Operation 10–8*. Retrieved on November 29, 2020 from http://operationt8.com/roles-of-family-and-school-in-preventing-juvenile-delinquency

Geller, A., Fagan, J., Tyler, T. and Link, B. G. (2014). Aggressive policing and the mental health of young urban men. *American Journal of Public Health*. Retrieved on December 08, 2020 from https://www.ncbi.nlm.nih.gov/pmc/articles/PMC4232139/

Ghandnoosh, N. (2015). Black Lives Matter: Eliminating racial inequity in the criminal justice system. *The Sentencing Project*. Retrieved on December 02, 2020 from https://sentencingproject.org/wp-content/uploads/2015/11/Black-Lives-Matter.pdf

Hirschfield, P. J. (2008). The declining significance of delinquent labels in disadvantaged urban communities. *Sociological Forum* 23(3):575–601.

Horowitz, J. M. and Livingston, G. (2016). How Americans view the Black Lives Matter movement. Pew Research Center. Retrieved on December 03, 2020 from https://www.pewsocialtrends.org/2020/06/12/amid-protests-majorities-across-racial-and-ethnic-groups-express-support-for-the-black-lives-matter-movement/

Horowitz, J. M. and Thomas, D. (2020). Support for Black Lives Matter has decreased since June but remains strong among Black Americans. Pew Research Center. Retrieved on December 03, 2020 from https://www.pewresearch.org/fact-tank/2020/09/16/support-for-black-lives-matter-has-decreased-since-june-but-remains-strong-among-black-americans/

Horowitz, J. M., Parker, K. and Anderson, M. (2020). Amid protests, majorities across racial and ethnic groups express support for the Black Lives Matter movement: deep partisan divides over factors underlying George Floyd demonstrations.

Pew Research Center. Retrieved on December 03, 2020 from https://www.pew socialtrends.org/2020/06/12/amid-protests-majorities-across-racial-and-ethnic-gr oups-express-support-for-the-black-lives-matter-movement/

Krohn, M. D. and Massey, J. L. (1980). Social control and delinquent behavior: An examination of the elements of the social bond. *Sociological Quarterly* 21(4):529–544. Retrieved on December 15, 2020 from https://www.ojp.gov/ncjrs/virtual-lib rary/abstracts/social-control-and-delinquent-behavior-examination-elements-social

Liberman, A. M., Kirk, D. S. and KiDuek, K. (2014). Labeling effects of first juvenile arrests: secondary deviance and secondary sanctioning. Urban Institute. Retrieved on December 12, 2020 from https://www.urban.org/sites/default/files/publication/ 33701/413274-Labeling-Effects-of-First-Juvenile-Arrests-Secondary-Deviance-a nd-Secondary-Sanctioning.PDF

McCord, S-W. and Crowell, N. A., eds. (2001). *Juvenile Crime, Juvenile Justice.* National Academies of Sciences. National Academies Press. Retrieved on December 03, 2020 from https://www.nap.edu/read/9747/chapter/7

National Center for Education Statistics. (2019). Condition of education: Students with disabilities. Institute of Education Sciences. Retrieved on December 13, 2020 from https://nces.ed.gov/programs/coe/indicator_cgg.asp?referer=raceindicators

National Center for Education Statistics. (2019). Status and trends in the education of racial and ethnic groups. Institute of Education Sciences. Retrieved on December 15, 2020 from https://nces.ed.gov/programs/raceindicators/indicator_RDA.asp

National Institute of Health. (2020). Black Lives Matter and the Hatch Act. U.S. Office of Special Counsel. Retrieved on November 20, 2020 from https://www.tra ining.nih.gov/assets/Black_Lives_Matter_Opinion.pdf

National Juvenile Justice Network. (2012). Using adolescent brain research to inform policy: A guide for juvenile justice advocates. Retrieved on December 19, 2020 from http://www.njjn.org/uploads/digital-library/Brain-Development-Policy-Paper_Updated_FINAL-9-27-12.pdf

National Reentry Resource Center. (2017). Collateral consequences of a juvenile adjudication: how juvenile records can affect youth even after the case is over. Retrieved on December 12, 2020 from https://nationalreentryresourcecenter.org/

National Research Council and Institute of Medicine. (2000). Education and delinquency: summary of a workshop. National Academy of Sciences. Retrieved on December 10, 2020 from https://www.nap.edu/read/9972/chapter/1

Pager, D. (2003). The mark of a criminal record. Harvard University. Retrieved on December 18, 2020 from https://scholar.harvard.edu/files/pager/files/pager_ajs.pdf

Pew Research Center. (2016). On views of race and inequality, Blacks and Whites are worlds apart: About four-in-ten Blacks are doubtful that the U.S. will ever achieve racial equality. Retrieved on December 12, 2020 from https://www.pewresearch.o rg/social-trends/2016/06/27/on-views-of-race-and-inequality-blacks-and-whites-ar e-worlds-apart/

Phelps, M. S. (2011). Rehabilitation in the Punitive Era: The Gap between Rhetoric and Reality in U.S. Prison Programs. National Institutes of Health. National Center for Biotechnology Information. U.S. National Library of Medicine. Retrieved on December 18, 2020 from https://www.ncbi.nlm.nih.gov/pmc/articles/PMC3762476/

Radice, J. (2018). The juvenile record myth. *The Georgetown Law Journal*. Retrieved on December 12, 2020 from https://www.law.georgetown.edu/georgetown-law-journal/wp-content/uploads/sites/26/2018/02/zt100218000365.pdf

Riddle, T. and Sinclair, S. (2019). Racial disparities in school-based disciplinary actions are associated with county-level rates of racial bias. Retrieved on December 15, 2020 from https://www.pnas.org/content/116/17/8255/tab-figures-data

Simmons-Horton, S. (2020). Ending anti-Black racism in child welfare and juvenile justice systems. University of Texas at San Antonio. Retrieved on December 03, 2020 from https://www.utsa.edu/today/2020/07/story/ending-anti-black-racism.html

United States Department of Justice. (2020). Criminal resource manual. U.S. Department of Justice Archives. Retrieved on November 08, 2020 from https://www.justice.gov/archives/jm/criminal-resource-manual

United States Department of Justice. (July 2020). Office of Juvenile Justice and Delinquency Prevention. 2019 Annual Report. Retrieved on January 18, 2021 from https://www.ojjdp.ojp.gov/sites/g/files/xyckuh176/files/media/document/253179.pdf

United States Department of Justice. (July 2020). Office of Juvenile Justice and Delinquency. OJJDP Fiscal Year 2020 Awards at a Glance. Retrieved on January 18, 2021 from https://ojjdp.ojp.gov/publications/fy-2020-awards.pdf

United States Department of Justice. Office of Juvenile Justice and Delinquency Prevention. (2020). OJJDP News @ a glance. Retrieved on January 18, 2021 from https://ojjdp.ojp.gov/newsletter/ojjdp-news-glance-novemberdecember-2020/top-story-ojjdp-awards-nearly-370-million-fiscal-year-2020-grants#:~:text=from%20the%20Administrator-,Top%20Story%3A%20OJJDP%20Awards%20Nearly%20%24370%20Million%20in%20Fiscal%20Year,productive%2C%20crime-free%20lives

United States Department of Justice. Office of Juvenile Justice and Delinquency Prevention. Office of Justice Programs. (2019). Juvenile Justice and Delinquency Prevention Act Reauthorization 2018. Retrieved on January 18, 2021 from https://ojjdp.ojp.gov/sites/g/files/xyckuh176/files/media/document/jjdpa-as-amended_0.pdf

Voisin, D. R., Kim, D., Takahashi, L., Morotta, P. and Bocanegra K. (2017). Involvement in the Juvenile Justice System for African American Adolescents: Examining Associations with Behavioral Health Problems. National Institutes of Health. National Center for Biotechnology Information. U.S. National Library of Medicine. Retrieved on December 17, 2020 from https://www.ncbi.nlm.nih.gov/pmc/articles/PMC5616175/

Vote Smart. (2016). Black Lives Matter and/or All Lives Matter? *Vote Smart*. Retrieved on January 18, 2021 from https://votesmart.org/blog-archive/2016/nov/14/black-lives-matter-andor-all-lives-matter/#.YD62qNWSnhn

Wilson, D. B. Wilson, Olaghere, A. and Kimbrell, C. S. (2017). Effectiveness of restorative justice principles in juvenile justice: A meta-analysis. U.S. Department of Justice. Resource funded by Department of Criminology, Law and Society George Mason University. Retrieved on December 17, 2020 from https://www.ojp.gov/pdffiles1/ojjdp/grants/250872.pdf

Chapter 14

General Conclusion

Abdul Karim Bangura

After reading the preceding chapters many times during the editing process, I came to the general conclusion that the underlying notion in all of them is the Ancient Kemetian/Egyptian *neb ānkh iw neter khe-t* (meaning in English "every life is sacred"), which can also be found in the tenets of the Abrahamic faiths—that is, Judaism, Christianity, and Islam—as the precept to guide human relations across the globe. This Kemetian belief denotes (a) *neb*— everyone; (b) *ankh*—life, to live, to live upon something, all prosperity, all health, joy of heart, a formula of good wishes, which follows each mention of the king's name in documents: for example, "life and content forever"; (c) *inAxy*—revered, revered one, reverence; (d) *neter khe-t* or *akh-t neter*— sacrosanct, the property of God, sacred book, book of temple services; (e) *āa sheps*—most holy, most august; (f) *uāb*—holy, to be innocent, guiltless, to be clean, to be purified, to be ceremonially pure and clean, to purify, to purify oneself, a cleansing, clean, to wash clean, pure; (g) *shepsi*—holy, to be noble, venerable, honored; (h) *s-tcheser*—to sanctify, to beautify (for the English translations of these terms, see Budge, 1978, passim).

In addition, among the forty-two "Ideals of Ma'at of the Temple of Isis: A Positive Confession for the Present Day" is the fifth Ideal that "I affirm that every life is sacred" (for this and the other ideals, see Elgabry, 2019, p. 1). Also, Hany Elgabry informs us about Ma'at as follows:

> Ma'at is the ancient Kemetian goddess of truth, justice, harmony, and balance ... who first appeared during the period known as the Old Kingdom (2613–2181 BCE) but no doubt existed in some form earlier. She is depicted in anthropomorphic form as a winged woman, often in profile with an ostrich feather on her head, or simply as a white ostrich feather. The feather of Ma'at was an integral part of the Weighing of the Heart of the Soul ceremony in the afterlife where the

heart of the soul of the dead person was weighed in the scales of justice against the feather. (Elgabry, 2019, p. 1)

Furthermore, as Asa G. Hilliard III, Larry Williams, and Nia Damali enlighten us, Ma'at, depicted as the woman who personifies order of the universe, was established at creation. She was regarded as the daughter of the god of creation Re, had an extensive sect, and doubled as the "two Ma'ats" from a prior epoch (Hilliard III et al., 1987).

Hilliard and his colleagues also recount that in the temple and tombs designated for the dead, there was worry about what a dead person would say on Judgment Day about whether he or she followed the will of God. This concern led to the development of inscriptions of "Declarations of Virtues" or "Negative Confessions" in the New Kingdom of the Eighteenth Dynasty. These declarations numbered 42 (Hilliard III et al., 1987).

We are, in addition, apprised by Hilliard III and his coeditors that biblical history relays the account of Moses being an Egyptian priest who was well educated in all of the Kemetian wisdom literature. This body of knowledge included the *Perem-Hru* (the *Book of Coming Forth From Darkness Into Light*), also popularly referred to as *The Book of the Dead*. This book has, in addition to plenty other information, the 42 "Declarations of Virtues" or "Negative Confessions" that have a noticeable similarity with the much shorter list of the "Commandments" in the Old Testament (Hilliard III et al., 1987). For more information on *The Book of the Dead*, see E. A. Wallis Budge's 1895 transliteration and transcription of it (the Dover edition was published in 1967).

Moreover, as I point out in my book titled *Branches of Asanteism* (Bangura, 2019), Mahmoud Ezzamel states that Kemetians had a great expectation of their Pharaoh to provide for their basic human needs, security, and social justice, and protect them from outside transgression. This expectation was firmly grounded on Ma'at—that is, the ideal implying "truth, righteousness and order among humans and between them and their gods" (Ezzamel, 2004, p. 501). The ideal of Ma'at influenced every aspect of Ancient Kemet. In his doctoral dissertation later published into a book with the same title, *Maat, The Moral Ideal in Ancient Egypt: A Study in Classical African Ethics* (2003), Maulana Karenga characterizes the paragon as follows:

> Maat in its most expansive sense as rightness in and of the world is the philosophical locus in which all the critical questions in ancient Maatian and modern Maatian thought converge and ground themselves. Maat insists on a holistic view of the moral ideal, one that gives rightful and adequate attention to self, society and the world as component parts of an interrelated order of rightness. The ongoing quest, then, is to maintain, renew, repair, and enhance this order as

self-conscious creators and bringers of the good in the world in a process and practice called *serudj ta*—restoring, repairing and renewing the world. Such a world-encompassing concept of moral practice invites us to move beyond narrow notions of self, national and even species interest and understand and assert ourselves as members of an interrelated order of existence in the world. At this juncture, Maatian discourse offers a contribution to modern moral deliberation about human fragmentation and the ongoing quest to return to an integrity and wholeness of human life that ends division of the social and natural world, mind and body, the past, present and future. (Karenga, 2003, p. 408)

The question that arises here then is: How is, as mentioned earlier, *neb ānkh iw neter khe-t* manifested in the Abrahamic faiths? The ensuing three sections address this question. Of course, a complete discussion of this aspect would require a book, if not several volumes. But for the sake of brevity, after introducing the notion as it appears in the sacred text of each faith, I discuss five instances in which it has been employed to explain a particular phenomenon.

JUDAIC RENDERING

From the Holy Torah, we learn in Genesis 9:8–10 that "every life is sacred" and that human life is especially so. Protecting it is of utmost importance to God, for God takes this so seriously and personally because God made humanity to reflect Him. We are God's earthly representatives, made in His image. To murder another person is to mount an attack on God who created that person.

Involvement as a Response to Hunger

To start with, according to Richard Schwartz, Judaism engenders adherents to care about and be engaged with the predicament of their fellow humans. Thus, adherents are engrained with the belief that "every life is sacred," and that it is incumbent upon adherents to do what is necessary to assist others. To buttress this point, he cites the Holy Torah as stating in Leviticus 19:16: "Thou shalt not stand idly by the blood of thy brother" (Schwartz, 2020, p. 1).

Next, Schwartz states that when adherents of the faith speak out validly against the quietude of the world when six million Jews and five million other people were massacred in the Holocaust, they must also speak out when millions suffer excruciating deaths due to lack of food. He argues that adherents must not tolerate the indifference of the world to the nemesis of starving people. He mentions that Elie Wiesel (Auschwitz survivor and recipient of the Nobel Peace Prize) asserted that there can be no parallelisms to the Holocaust, but that it can be employed as a reference. Thus, adherents must take into account both the eight million infants who die each year from malnutrition and the six million Jews who were murdered by the Nazis. Schwartz points out that the victims of hunger are not being singled out because of their religion, race, or nationality; but that, like the Holocaust victims, they die while others go about their business, complaining about "high taxes" and personal inconveniences while ignoring the predicament of those who starve. He then quotes the Talmud as teaching adherents that "If one saves a single human life, it is as if one has saved a whole world" and asks: What then if one permits a single life to perish? Or 10 million?" (Schwartz, 2020, p. 1).

Also, we glean from Schwartz that the Hebrew prophets rebuked those who were gratified and contended while others were in great anguish. He quotes the following verses from the Holy Torah to support the point: (a) Isaiah 32:11: "Tremble you women who are at ease, Shudder you complacent ones; Strip and make yourselves bare, Gird sackcloth upon your loins" and (b) Amos 1, 4, 6: "Woe to those who are at ease in Zion . . . . Woe to those who lie upon beds of ivory And stretch themselves upon their couches . . . . Who drink wine from bowls And anoint themselves with the finest oils But are not grieved at the ruin of Joseph" (Schwartz, 2020, p. 1).

In addition, Schwartz points out that similar to other peoples, Jews also have had a history of hunger. He mentions the following examples in the Holy Torah: (a) Genesis 12:10: as a consequence of famines, Abraham was compelled to go to Egypt; (b) Genesis 26:1: Isaac went to the land of Avimelech, king of the Philistine, in Gerar to escape famine; (c) Genesis 42:1–3: the children of Jacob went to Egypt to buy grain because of a shortage that resulted from famine; (d) Ruth 1:1–2: Naomi and her family moved from Israel to Moab due to famine; (e) 2 Samuel 21:1: there was a famines in the reign of King David; and (f) 1 Kings 18:1–2: during King Ahab's rule, there was also a famine (Schwartz, 2020).

Furthermore, as Schwartz apprises us, the sadness of considerable hunger is well known by Jews. He quotes the Holy Torah's Lamentations 1:9 in which Prophet Jeremiah said: "Happier were the victims of the sword than the victims of hunger, who pined away, stricken by want of the yield of the field" (Schwartz, 2020, p. 1).

Given the preceding evidence, Schwartz calls upon adherents of Judaism to empathize with the huge number of starving people across the globe. Adherents must do so by speaking out against and engaging in actions that will bring greater attention to the issue. As he puts it, "traditional Jewish ways of pursuing justice, practicing charity, showing compassion, sharing resources, and simplifying lifestyles" are imperative for helping people in need (Schwartz, 2020, p. 1).

Becoming too Individualistic

Rabbi Irwin Huberman makes a number of salient points about the pitfalls of some adherents of Judaism becoming too "individualistic" (i.e., excessively independent and self-reliant). First, during the past seven decades, Judaism has metamorphosed in many countries. For instance, while the faith has been "nationalized" (i.e., made distinctively to relate to a large body of people united by common descent, history, culture, or language, inhabiting the country) in Israel, it has been "privatized" (i.e., transferred from public to personal ownership and control) in the United States. Before the twentieth century, adherents of the faith had a general awareness of and adhered to communal life, traditional standards, and an established collection of precepts and regulations. Beginning in 1948, however, Israel has exhibited the banner of the Torah in a country where Jews, Baha'is, Christians, Muslims, and adherents of other faiths can worship freely. In the United States, a country that was established on the principle of "individuality and personal freedom," a Jew can and does observe Judaism in accordance with what is feasible for him or her (Huberman, 2021).

Second, just about every day Judaic rituals are reframed. While some adherents consider themselves orthodox, others perceive themselves as secular. And, while some observe the rituals, many do not. In the United States, just as the American Dream itself, Judaism has become individually focused. Even more, results from a Google search of practicing Rabbis revealed that there is a religious leader that will assist a person to make his or her belief a reality, whether it is about who to love, with whom to affiliate, whether to be spiritual than structured, and so on. (Huberman, 2021).

Third, the Vayakhel section of the Holy Torah—that is, "And Moses Assembled the Community"—challenges adherents of Judaism to assess the equilibrium between community and individuality. The teaching is about Moses inviting Israelites to engage in the establishment of the community's sacred space in the aftermath of the Golden Calf (Huberman, 2021). Nonetheless, Huberman contends as follows:

> To be sure, Judaism attaches tremendous significance to each individual. Each of us carries Tzelem Elohim, a spark of God, and every life is sacred, irreplaceable. This spark is what makes us unique. But we're also cautioned that we risk isolation when we focus too exclusively on our own individuality, that we must balance this with the role we each play in humankind's universal and collective mission. We are here, say our Sages, to work with God to complete creation. (Huberman, 2021, p. 1)

Fourth, in the first book of the Holy Torah, Genesis 2:18 states that God said, "It is not good for man to be alone" after creating Adam. God then created

Eve. The lesson here is that even though we can value our individuality, we must also recognize that collective power is also sacred in Judaism. Thus, some Rabbis value the individual, albeit not individualism. It is therefore not accidental that some research findings have revealed that people seem to adopt characteristics of those with whom they associate. Judaism comprehends this and puts a high premium not only on study and discussion but also on argumentation and disagreement, which it encourages us not to dodge but in which we must engage (Huberman, 2021).

Stand against the Death Penalty

Oliver Morrison recounts the debate that ensued about the death penalty vis-à-vis the principle of "every life is sacred" among adherents of Judaism when forty-six-year-old Robert D. Bowers on October 27, 2018, shot and killed eleven and injured six congregants at the Or L'Simcha—Tree of Life Congregation at Squirrel Hill in Pittsburgh, Pennsylvania. To begin with, at the end of Shiva (i.e., the seven days of traditional Jewish community mourning) and many were still grieving the dead, attention shifted to the issue of obtaining justice (Morrison, 2018).

Next, the legal system was in gear with forty-four counts against Bowers for his heinous crime. He pleaded not guilty and requested a trial by jury. The crime carries the death penalty, which had to be approved by the then U.S. Attorney General Jeff Sessions. But either because of principle or how unfairly it is perceived to be implemented, all of the major Jewish denominations in the United States are against the death penalty. This is because adherents of Judaism strongly subscribe to the teaching that "every life is sacred." Concomitantly, every Jewish denomination in the country has condemned the death penalty because of the manner it has been applied to black convicts and others who have been put to death and later discovered that they were not guilty (Morrison, 2018).

Nonetheless, Bowers's crime put the "every life is sacred" precept to the test as some congregants at the Tree of Life Synagogue argued that there should be certain cases in which the death penalty should be applied, and the massacre committed by Bowers qualifies for that. Jewish scholars, however, insisted that the precept cannot be discarded even in the face of heinous crimes, as doing so would undermine the fundamental teachings of the faith (Morrison, 2018).

Working Harder for Justice and Righteousness

Based on the teaching that "every life is sacred," a call for adherents of Judaism to work harder for justice and righteousness was made by Rabbi

Mark Kula and Rabbi Ed Stafman (2020) of the Temple of Beth Shalom in Bozeman, Montana, after the murders of Ahmaud Arbery, Breonna Taylor, George Floyd, and many other blacks by law enforcement officers in the United States. The Rabbis provide several reasons for making the call.

First, adherents of Judaism must support the pursuit by people of color and indigenous populations to get equal justice under the law. Compassionate Jewish teachings compel adherents to not stand by idly and watch the blood of their fellow brothers and sisters being shed. Not to adhere to such teachings would be to neglect the principle that everyone is created in the image of God (Kula and Stafman, 2020).

Second, reenacted each year during the Passover Seders is the developmental history of the Jews under bondage of the Egyptian Pharaoh and their attendant liberation struggle (Kula and Stafman, 2020). Thus, Kula and Stafman explain the essence of the ordeal and its nexus with the murder of George Floyd as follows:

> In Hebrew, Egypt means a "narrow place," a place of constriction, and the slavery experience is often described as one where we could not breathe. The Hebrew word for Pharaoh is related to the word "neck," so we empathize with the experience of neck-breaking pressure choking off the ability to breathe. The very purpose of our slavery was to teach us what that feels like so that we would stand up to the oppression of others. We also remember that breath—of which George Floyd was robbed—is sacred: Our stories teach that God created the first human being by breathing into him, and one of the Hebrew names for God is "the Breath of Life." (Kula and Stafman, 2020, p. 1)

Third, the Talmud instructs adherents of Judaism that to save or to destroy a single life is equivalent to saving or destroying the entire world. The lesson of this principle is that, as stated earlier, "every life is sacred"; when one precious life is lost, all of God's children are hurt by it; and we are all bound by a common humanity (Kula and Stafman, 2020).

Life Cycle Events

Temple Kol Ami (2021) explicates how the significance of the principle of "every life is sacred" is steeped in the following four events that are of major importance to believers of Judaism: (1) B'nai Mitzvah—a Jewish coming of age ritual for a mixed sex group, (2) affirmation, (3) weddings, and (4) end of life. These occasions are believed to connect adherents of the faith intimately and allow Rabbis to patiently give their time, modify the ceremonies, and guide congregants. The four events are discussed separately in the rest of this subsection for lucidity.

B'nai Mitzvah, which encompasses Bar Mitzvah (a Jewish coming of age ritual for boys) and Bat Mitzvah (a Jewish coming of age for girls) is quite significant to adherents of Judaism. When organized very well, no child would have to share a date with another child, so that he or she is guaranteed the significance of the ceremony by the entire community. Children learn from the ritual how to lead a prayer, give a teaching to the congregation the portion of the Torah that is assigned to them, and engage in mitzvah (good deeds done from religious duty) projects. All this gives the children a deeper denotation of the ritual (Temple Kol Ami, 2021).

Affirmation involves attesting Jewish children's identity and their own distinct connections to the land of Israel and Judaism. The children are encouraged to interrogate suppositions and to tailor their own services based on a major mitzvah group project. The affirmation ceremony is scheduled to coincide with the Shavuot (Temple Kol Ami, 2021): a major Jewish festival held on the sixth (and usually the seventh) of Sivan, fifty days after the second day of Passover. It was originally a harvest festival, but now also commemorates the giving of the Law (the Torah).

Weddings that are among the most sacred events in the lives of couples require officiants that are caring listeners who will hear couples and treat them with honor and esteem. Rabbis who act as officiants in these ceremonies should be expert pastors who are well known in the community and have strong personnel links with couples. The Rabbis should also be flexible so that they could offer options to non-traditional and interfaith couples (Temple Kol Ami, 2021).

End of life ceremonies are to affirm the major Judaic ethic that "every life is sacred" and, thus, every deceased person deserves honor. Accordingly, it is imperative that Rabbis provide the best end-of-life pastoral care and funeral officiating to the dead and their surviving families (Temple Kol Ami, 2021).

CHRISTIAN RENDERING

As in the Holy Torah, we also glean from Genesis 9:8–10 in the Holy Bible that "Every life is sacred." In addition, Christians cite the following verses as articulating the notion: (a) Genesis 1:27: "God created mankind in his own image" to say that all creation was good in God's eyes, but only humans were made in the loving image of their Creator; (b) Genesis 9:5: "And surely your blood of your lives will I require; at the hand of every beast will I require it, and at the hand of man; at the hand of every man's brother will I require the life of man" to explain that when God made a covenant with Noah, it is because humans are made in the image of God and, thus, are accountable to protect one another; (c) Psalm 8:4–8: 4 "What is man, that thou art mindful of him? and the son of man, that thou visitest him?; 5 For thou hast made him a little lower than the angels, and hast crowned him with glory and honor; 6 Thou madest him to have dominion over the works of thy hands; thou hast put all things under his feet; 7 All sheep and oxen, yea, and the beasts of the field; 8 The fowl of the air, and the fish of the sea, and whatsoever passeth through the paths of the seas" to say that humans are valued above all creation; and (d) Proverbs 24:10–11: "If you falter in a time of trouble, how small is your strength! Rescue those being led away to death; hold back those staggering toward slaughter" to implore humans to protect those who are vulnerable.

Dealing with Suicide

Don Morgan broaches the nexus between the notion of "every life is sacred" and how Christians feel deeply about suicide. He begins by looking at how the issue of suicide is discussed in pro-life circles, which is done generally in terms of the cultural matter of physician-assisted suicide. Nonetheless, when it comes to abortion and euthanasia, pro-life Christians see no "death with dignity" about them; therefore, they always push for legislation at the U.S. Congress that would eliminate the practices (Morgan, 2017).

Next, as it pertains to the issue of suicide in general, Morgan quotes Christian counselor Tim Clinton of stating the following as representative of the common perspective among Christians:

> Suicide as an act that is pursued in order to eliminate what is experienced as unrelenting pain . . . . Someone who commits suicide often cannot see any hope that the future will be different than the painful past or present. People who end their lives are generally burdened by a number of unresolved events or problems that are mostly, if not always, resolvable. (Morgan, 2017, p. 1)

The major identified "unresolved events or problems" that lead to suicide are as follows: "depression, financial distress, broken relationships, personal protest, gender confusion, religious ritual or the desire to escape punishment or pain" (Morgan, 2017, p. 1).

Also, it is imperative for Christians to be concerned about suicide because they support the tenet that "every life is sacred and created by God," even though the underlying causes and contributing factors to the act differs greatly among those who commit it. Morgan provides the following sobering statistics to underscore why Christians must care about the issue: approximately "500,000 people attempt suicide each year in the United States. About 29,000 of these attempts result in death, compared to 19,000 murders and 13,000 AIDS-related deaths. In fact, suicide is the third leading cause of death for people aged 15 to 25" (Morgan, 2017, p. 1). Vis-à-vis the reason for this high number of suicides, Morgan cites Clinton again of saying this: "Without coping skills and without the help of friends, professional assistance, or loved ones, unresolved burdens grow heavier until the weight becomes unbearable and the individual is weakened to the point of despair. The problem is not that such despairing people want to die; it is that they do not know how to live" (Morgan, 2017, p. 1).

Despite the aforementioned realities of this tragedy, Morgan asserts that while the church is a consummate venue for dealing with people contemplating suicide, Christians must, however, also be cognizant of the fact that it takes more than just Christian disciplines and prayer to deal with the matter. To be included in the work to dissuade people who want to commit suicide are professional counseling and other resources. With this in mind, the church has a great potential to play a significant "role in embracing those who are despairing and helping them understand their inestimable value as image bearers of God . . . and help point them toward the promise of John 10:10: The thief comes only to steal and kill and destroy. I came that they may have life and have it abundantly" (Morgan, 2017, p. 1).

Respect Life Program

The Respect Life Program of St. Joseph Catholic Church of Youngstown, Ohio (SJCCYO) advances the notion that Catholics are entrenched in the precept that "every life is sacred" from the moment one is conceived until he or she dies. This is because everyone is made in "the image and likeness of God" and, therefore, everyone has inherent dignity. Concomitantly, in October of each year, the program encourages church members to participate in the countrywide activities designed to emphasize the value of and respect for human life organized by the U.S. Conference of Catholic Bishops (SJCCYO, 2021).

In the belief that assisting to establish the circumstances that will make people live better lives in the universe and a better life for the universe, which is crucial to all life is what being pro-life connotes in the twenty-first century, the program addresses the following wide range of issues and their connotations (SJCCYO, 2021):

(a) *Contraception* prevents new human beings from coming into existence.
(b) *Abortion* ends the life of a child, offends God, and deeply wounds the women and men involved.
(c) *Rights of the Disabled* are ensured when the disabled are integrated into all activities while recognizing not only their "sameness" but also their "differentness."
(d) *Human Trafficking* is a contemporary form of slavery that consists of the illegal trade of human beings through force, fraud, or coercion for the

purposes of commercial sexual exploitation or forced labor that should be condemned and prevented by every Christian.
(e) *Domestic Abuse* is violence against women, inside or outside the home, which should never be justified. It is sinful and criminal to subject a woman to any form of physical, sexual, psychological, or verbal abuse.
(f) *Access to Healthcare* requires that society helps children to attain living conditions that would make it possible for them to grow and reach maturity. Paramount for these living conditions are food and clothing, housing, healthcare, basic education, employment, and social assistance.
(g) *End of Life Care* requires Christians not to promote "vitalism" (i.e., preserving physical life at all costs) but to support the goodness of "fidelity" (i.e., faithfulness to those in need), "compassion" (i.e., suffering with those who are suffering), and individual "dignity" (i.e., the state or quality of being worthy of honor or respect).
(h) *Death Penalty* is perceived as an attack on the inviolability and dignity of the person; consequently, Christians must champion the effort to end capital punishment across the globe.

Promoting Human Dignity

Discussed here is the pastoral letter titled "Living in the Image and Likeness of God: Human Dignity and the Divine Designs," which focuses on human sexuality, marriage, and family, written by the Bishops of Alaska in 2018 to explain their capacity as instructors in regard to how to convalesce an affirmative grasp of the human being. The letter was inspired by the Christian comprehension of a person being situated at the core of the tenets that "every life is sacred" and "everyone possesses an inherent dignity" (Archbishop Etienne, 2018). The bishops make several points to elucidate their undertaking discussed in the remainder of this subsection.

First, a faith point of view and a substantive knowledge of theological precepts that underscore the perceptions and tenets of Christians are needed to deal with the many social issues confronting humanity today. In addition, a genuine comprehension of the human being is requisite for Christians to deal with these issues (Archbishop Etienne, 2018).

Second, the biblical principle that "everyone is created in the image and likeness of God" is also paramount for Christians to make substantive contributions to the many social dialogues of today. With this precept as a backdrop in their conversations on social issues, Christians will be able to get others to connect to the Christian understanding of the sanctity of every life from conception to natural death (Archbishop Etienne, 2018).

Third, since God created every human being, everyone should therefore be able to exercise his or her religious freedom to know and worship God without compulsion or constraint. The profundity of God's love and the genuine selfhood and possibilities of the humanity of Christians are embedded in their connection to God and, more specifically, to Jesus Christ (Archbishop Etienne, 2018).

Fourth, in order for Christians to live in the image and likeness of God, they must also be ready to take on the responsibilities that go with knowing God who created everyone and to live in right connection with the Creator and with one another. Given the growing individualism and secularism that are engulfing the world, Christians must be particularly cognizant of "God's Design" for humanity. Correspondingly, "Truth is something to be discovered by reason—not defined by choice" (Archbishop Etienne, 2018).

Need for Compassionate Care

Narrated here is the urging by the Most Reverend James F. Checchio, Bishop of Metuchen, New Jersey, for Catholics to be imbued by the principle of "every life is sacred" and provide compassionate care for people infected by the COVID-19 in that state. For starters, Checchio notes that for quite some time now, there has been plenty talk about the "precious souls," especially in nursing homes, that have been lost to the disease in the state. This situation has led to calls for every person to sacrifice and do all that he or she can to help moderate the proliferation of the virus (Checchio, 2013).

Next, Checchio points out that in the effort to save lives, people are advised, and even required, to wear masks, obey lockdowns, and practice "social distancing" (this last aspect is oxymoronic in that "social" means needing companionship and "distancing" denotes staying far off). All this coincides with the first anniversary of New Jersey's Medical Aid in Dying for the Terminally Ill Act, which allows some patients to end their own lives. For Catholics, however, any suicide, even the state-sanctioned variety, is painful and they are therefore averse to the practice. Adherents base their position on suicide vis-à-vis the teaching in the Catechism of the Catholic Church, 2280: "We are stewards, not owners, of the life God has entrusted to us. It is not ours to dispose of" (quoted by Checchio, 2013, p. 1).

Also, according to Checchio, since everyone is created in the image and likeness of God, all of us are a gift from the Creator and have inherent and inalienable dignity. Therefore, every life is precious, whether healthy or ill, young or old. Hence, the devaluation of all human life is advanced when society devalues even one human life, particularly the weakest. It is, thus, incumbent on Catholics to also apply the foundational precept of "every life is sacred" in the struggle to end racism in society (Checchio, 2013).

In addition, as Checchio posits, Christians are obligated to provide compassionate care for the sick and dying, but the intrinsic perversion of legislation such as physician-assisted suicide makes the aged and the sick to feel that it is their duty to die. This is happening more so with the COVID-19 pandemic, which has introduced a series of novel stressors like social isolation and loss of community that are adversely affecting the aged and the sick and their families. These factors have led to an increase in the number of suicides and the number of people requesting physician-assisted death (Checchio, 2013).

Furthermore, says Checchio, Christians are needed very much in these challenging times to provide compassionate care. Thus, in order to dissuade those who are ill or are near death from opting for physician-assisted deaths, it behooves Christians to come up with innovative ways to provide "tender accompaniment" for them. In essence, Christians should not be complacent and simply accept physician-assisted death as the law. Instead, they should provide patients "love, support, and companionship, whether in-person or virtually, providing the assistance needed to ease their physical, emotional, and spiritual suffering, always anchored in an unconditional respect for all human life" (Checchio, 2013, p. 1).

Checchio ends on a positive note of Christians in New Jersey rising to meet the challenges of the COVID-19 pandemic by providing the following resources:

> Since the pandemic started, our Catholic Charities has given out $1.3 million in rental assistance and more than $100,000 worth of food assistance. In Unity Square in New Brunswick, it has helped more than 900 households with more than 2,000 bags of food, while the Food Pantry we run in Phillipsburg has given out more than 3,800 bags of food serving almost 1,500 people who have come for assistance. This is in addition to what our parishes and St. Vincent de Paul Societies have done through our parishes. (Checchio, 2013, p. 1)

Indeed, the preceding response is an indication that compassionate care requires more than just prayers. It must also include an economic component given the needs of the people who are suffering from the financial impact of the COVID-19 pandemic.

Building a Culture of Life

Los Angeles Catholics make two principal points for why the tenet of "every life is sacred" is paramount for building a culture of life. The first point is that all societies would be remolded if the entire world believes Jesus Christ's declaration that "God is our Father, and we are created in his image, with God-given dignity and a transcendent destiny" (Los Angeles Catholics, 2021, p. 1). Since this perspective is "spiritual," not "political," Catholics belong first to the "City of God." Nonetheless, they are obligated to rectify unjust acts and help to develop the earthly city. Their precepts compel them "to work for justice and the common good, to protect the vulnerable, to promote freedom and human dignity, and to prefer remedies that are personal, local and small-scale" (Los Angeles Catholics, 2021, p. 1).

The second point is in reference to the verity that we live in a globalized world that permits a number of unjust acts that include "abortion, euthanasia, birth control policies targeting the poor, racial discrimination, a widening gap between poor and rich, pollution, porn and drug addictions, the death penalty and overcrowded prisons, the erosion of religious liberty, a broken immigration system" (Los Angeles Catholics, 2021, p. 1). While the Catholic Church addresses all of these matters, it, nonetheless, treats abortion and euthanasia differently. These latter two issues are perceived to be direct, personal assaults on guiltless and endangered human life. As such Catholics cannot claim to speak for the disenfranchised if they permit millions of children to be killed each year in the womb. The perspective of Catholics must therefore be whole and never partial, since, "for God, every life is sacred, beautiful, and filled with possibility"; consequently, "respect for life means there are no exceptions to our love" (Los Angeles Catholics, 2021, p. 1).

ISLAMIC RENDERING

In the Holy Qur'an, we learn from Surah Al-Isra 17:70 that Allah (SWT) said: "We have certainly dignified the children of Adam and carried them on the land and sea and provided for them of the good things and preferred them over much of what We have created with definite preference." Thus, Islam guarantees the right of life for every human being, whether the person is a Muslim (meaning simply a believer in the one Almighty God) or non-Muslim (non-believer in God). Every human life is sacred in Islam and every person has been granted God-given fundamental and universal rights at the time of his/her birth.

Black Lives Matter

The Iman Center of Kirkland (2020) in Seattle, Washington, also referred to as the Ithna-asheri Muslim Association of the Northwest, urges Muslims to support the peaceful aspects of the Black Lives Matter movement, which are congruent with the notion of "every life is sacred" as represented in the following verse of the Holy Qur'an 49:13: "People, We created you all from a single man and a single woman, and made you into races and tribes so that you should recognize one another. In God's eyes, the most honored of you are the ones most mindful of Him: God is all knowing, all aware." The Center then goes on to discuss some elements that serve as justification for doing so.

To commence with, the Center expresses sorrow over the killing of George Floyd by a police officer while the victim was crying "I can't breathe." Floyd's murder reminds the Center about the many other black victims such as Ahmaud Arbery, Breonna Taylor, and Christian Cooper who have been killed or harassed by law enforcement officers because of their racism and hatred. The Center finds these heinous acts unacceptable because they are not isolated, distinctive instances; instead, they are instances of the long-term, ubiquitous, continuing, systemic brutality, and persecution of blacks that infect the American way of life, government, and systems of power (Iman Center of Kirkland, 2020).

Next, according to the Center, a black person in present-day America faces significant chances to be affected by deadly bias at every point of his/her life. The prejudice against blacks commences at schools where the school-to-prison pipeline is manifested, to the community where police harassment is a common practice, to the healthcare systems where inequities lead to many premature deaths. It is therefore not surprising to the Center that very large numbers of blacks of all ages are dying from the COVID-19 pandemic (Iman Center of Kirkland, 2020).

Also, as the Center points out, blacks put their lives in danger whenever they leave their homes. There is even a high probability of blacks to be gunned down in their homes for no good reason. Blacks who protest peacefully against these unfair practices are condemned, and those who do so loudly could also face violence in addition to being condemned. Many observers pay attention to the violence that often follows the protests while ignoring the unfairness that provoked the protests in the first place. The entire society is infected by racial discrimination. This is evident in "the xenophobic hatred aimed at Asian Americans, the high numbers of COVID-2019 infections among Pacific Islanders and Latino/Latina people, many of whom are doing the essential work of care-giving and food service, the skyrocketing deaths in Native American communities—all of these are part of the unfairness that is embedded into American life" (Iman Center of Kirkland, 2020, p. 1).

In addition, the Center supports every effort geared toward fighting against the existing injustices directed toward blacks in the United States. It agrees that everyone is a part of the system that gives certain people unearned privileges while it marginalizes others. And, while everyone says "all lives mater," we continue to see blacks being discriminated against more than any other racial group. The Center therefore urges everyone to affirm that Black Lives Matter just like other lives because "every life is sacred" (Iman Center of Kirkland, 2020).

Furthermore, the Center concludes that everyone must take a stand against any form of racial or other injustice and to also engage in peaceful protests against it. We must join the many organizations across the United States that are working toward bringing the necessary change. The change is possible if we can work with our colleagues, family members, and neighbors to attain a critical mass on the matter (Iman Center of Kirkland, 2020).

Healthcare for Everyone

The Orange County Register discusses how Muslims seek to establish a nexus between the belief that "every life is sacred" and the provision of healthcare for everyone as a desired outcome. It begins by asking: "How should people of faith respond to the growth in the number of people without adequate healthcare coverage?" It provides the following answer: "Spiraling medical costs and a growing uninsured population require that religious leaders join the healthcare debate and offer a solution" (Orange County Register, 2006, p. 1). The Register then proceeds by delineating a number of aspects that reflect the connection between the belief and the desired outcome by Muslims.

First, many children, elderly and families are being dropped by health insurance companies and deprived of much needed medical care due to continuously increasing costs. The skyrocketing costs have left more than forty-six million U.S citizens without health insurance. Since Islam instructs its adherents to struggle in their societies in order to set duties and rights for everyone, to safeguard the public good, and to advance compassion and justice, it is imperative for Muslims to challenge laws drafted by interest groups that increasingly lack ethical and moral principles (Orange County Register, 2006).

Second, Muslims are commanded to advocate for the economically and politically weak who are victimized by the advantaged. As the Holy Qur'an teaches in verse 16:90, "Verily, God enjoins the doing of justice and compassion to others." Muslims must also advocate for adequate healthcare for everyone because Allah (SWT) commands that "every life is sacred" and "every person has dignity." And, concomitantly, Allah (SWT) says in the Holy Qur'an 5:32: "anyone who saves a life, it shall be as if he had saved the life of all humankind" (cited in Orange County Register, 2006, p. 1).

Third, Islam inculcates that life, particularly a good quality of life, is a basic human right for everyone. Thus, Muslims believe that it is the responsibility of everyone to carry the burden when people are unable to receive adequate medical care. In essence, a society is only as strong as its weakest citizens. It is therefore necessary to make it obligatory for the United States, which has the most powerful economy and most advanced medical technology in the world to provide adequate medical care for all of its children, aged, poor, and sick. If the United States can spend many billions of dollars in warfare, it should provide the needed money to save lives at home (Orange County Register, 2006). This perspective is often buttressed by the following two sayings of the Prophet Muhammad (PBUH): (1) "None of you truly believes until he loves for his brethren (fellow human beings) what he loves for himself" and (2) "The most beloved of people to God is the one who is most helpful and beneficial to people" (quoted by the Orange County Register, 2006, p. 1).

Fourth, Muslims are well aware that similar tenets constitute the kernel of most religions, especially the Abrahamic ones. Therefore, Muslims believe that it is necessary for adherents of all faiths to work together to present and lobby for an all-inclusive national healthcare solution for the United States (Orange County Register, 2006).

Protecting Kenyan Christians in Terror Attack

Will Worley (2016) retells the tale of a Kenyan Muslim named Salah Farah who died while protecting Christians in a terror attack and was posthumously awarded the country's top honor because he believed in the Islamic teaching that people have a right to freedom of worship and that "every life is sacred." The narrative is summarized in the following paragraphs.

To commence with, Kenyan President Uhuru Kenyatta at the 2016 State of Nation address lauded and awarded Farah the Order of the Grand Warrior of Kenya for his extraordinary act of bravery in defending his fellow citizens. Farah died from his injuries in January of 2016 after being shot on a bus, which was attacked by al-Shabaab militants in December of 2015. As is usually the case in al-Shabaab attacks, Muslims were offered the chance to escape. But, Salah refused to get off the bus and instead stated that the militants can kill everyone in it if that was their wish. He was hit by a bullet during the mayhem that followed (Worley, 2016).

Next, in recognizing that by Farah being a Muslim his gallantry was driven by the tenet that "every life is sacred," Kenyatta said this:

> He died defending people who he did not know. This is because he believed in their right to freedom of worship and he knew that every single life—irrespective of faith—is sacred . . . . He is a powerful symbol of our country's ambition to attain the full expression of secure and cohesive nationhood, and he is a costly reminder that we all have a role to play in protecting our freedoms. I want to tell his children that their father's sacrifice will never be forgotten—and will be long admired. (quoted by Worley, 2016, p. 1)

Also, the award was prompted by a social media campaign advocating that Farah's brave act be officially recognized by the Kenyan government and money be raised for the surviving members of his family. Abudallahi Derow who led the effort used the hashtag #HeroSalah. The campaign raised approximately 600,000 Kenyan shillings (about £4,150 or US$5,600.00) to be used to build a house for his family. In an interview with Al-Jazeera, Derow stated that "Salah died serving the country, defending his Christian brothers. He chose to die and save the lives of his countrymen. He is a symbol of unity and strength and his action is an inspiration to many" (cited by Worley, 2016, p. 1). And, while in his hospital bed suffering from the gun-shot wounds, Farah is reported by Voice of America to have said: "People should live peacefully together. We are brothers. It's only the religion that is the difference, so I ask my brother Muslims to take care of the Christians so that the Christians also take care of us . . . and let us help one another and let us live together peacefully" (cited by Worley, 2016, p. 1).

In addition, al-Shabaab is a militant group connected to al-Qaeda. It has been engaged in an insurgency aimed at toppling the regime and launching an Islamic rule in Somalia. Some of its activities have often spilled over the southern parts of the country into Kenya. In April of 2015, al-Shabaab attacked Garissa University in Kenya, leaving 148 people dead. Also, in January of 2016, in the militant group's attack on an African Union military base in Somalia, scores of Kenyan soldiers were killed (Worley, 2016).

Celebrating Holy Week

Presented in this subsection is the perspective of a nineteen-year-old Muslim student named Reem Suleiman, who attends the high school of the Notre Dame Church in San Jose, California (NDCSJC) (2019), as it pertains to what the principle of "every life is sacred" means to the celebration of Holy Week at the school. Reem proffers a number of aspects for the association between the principle and the commemoration.

First, Reem believes that in our current fragmented world, it is inevitable that one should feel disoriented. Society appears to be engulfed by an inescapable vicious cycle as we hear and read headlines highlighting death tolls, victims' names, and details of hate crimes. Soon after one act of violence is reported, another one is perpetrated. In our world today, the age-old aphorism that "time heals all wounds" appears inadequate. Violence today has become timeless (NDCSJC, 2019).

Second, as Reem reminds us, Jesus carried the cross on his back as he approached his crucifixion. The heavy cross conveyed the denotation of dignity, faith, and love. Nonetheless, what brought Jesus to his knees were the discrimination and intolerance of those who condemned him. The effect of the hate was so strong that Jesus stumbled and fell. Yet still, he mustered the courage and strength to get up and face his prosecutors. While courage manifests differently for each person (NDCSJC, 2019), Reem explains hers as follows:

> In my experience, as someone who wears their faith so visibly, courage is an essential part of my everyday attire. It's a virtue I need every time I step out of my house, and as we have all been reminded on March 15, it's a virtue that I—and others like me—need when we enter our houses of worship. March 15th marks the day of the New Zealand massacre at the Christchurch Mosques, October 27th marks the day of the mass shooting at the Tree of Life Synagogue, and the list is endless. I will take New Zealand Prime Minister Jacinda Ardern's approach and shift the conversation away from the nameless perpetrators of such hate and instead direct it to the acts of courage that came about in response. (NDCSJC, 2019)

Third, according to Reem, her mother is a teacher at a school close to a mosque in Santa Clara, California. After the shootings at the two mosques in New Zealand that left forty-nine Muslims dead, as a security measure, police cars were placed at each of the school's entrance and the mosque. The fear in the school children's eyes had a negative effect on Reem as they did not comprehend what was happening. She was particularly disturbed when her young cousin who heard about the shootings asked her "What did we do?" The grim outlook and fear were exacerbated by the thought of the insecurity in the American society and Muslims being a targeted religious community. Reem's perturbation was eased when her mother shared the heartwarming story of how the Rabbis with their congregants at a nearby Synagogue in the community attended the Friday prayer at the mosque to show their solidarity with Muslims. These adherents of Judaism explicated that it is their version of "the human shield" that compels them to protect the religious rights of their Muslim brothers and sisters. The act of solidarity healed Reem of her "emotional paralysis." As she poignantly puts it, "I had let my anger, my horror, and my fear override any form of a meaningful response. I was paralyzed into hopelessness and inaction. This demonstration of kinship and love between two often-targeted faith groups allowed me to appreciate the courage of standing in solidarity and the importance of religious dialogue" (NDCSJC, 2019).

Fourth, Reem purports that in a diverse community such as her school, it is salient for students to cherish the capacity of education to empower them to determine verity and challenge conventional images. Fallacies about others can be quite menacing and depriving of positive human qualities. Hence, for Reem to hear and read the mangled depictions of Islam is quite painful. On many occasions, she could not even recognize the Islam she grew up learning. By looking at the personhood of the individual instead of the labels being ascribed to the person, Reem is able to appreciate the values of Islam and dismiss the distortions that birth divisions among people. This strategy also allows her to appreciate even more the Islamic tenet that "every life is sacred" and, thus, "for every life harmed, it is as though all of humanity and creation is harmed with it" (NDCSJC, 2019, p. 1).

Islamic Case for Religious Freedom

The Centre for Public and Contextual Theology (PACT) at Charles Sturt University in Australia apprises us about how the notion of "every life is sacred" was manifested at the seventh International Islam and Liberty Conference geared toward making an Islamic case for religious freedom convened in Jakarta, Indonesia, from November 11 to 12, 2019. The conference, whose theme was accordingly titled "The Islamic Case for Religious Freedom," was cosponsored by the Islam and Liberty Network; Fatayat—the young women's section of the Nahdlatul Ulama, Indonesia's largest Muslim organization; the International Institute of Advanced Islamic Studies in Malaysia; and the Religious Freedom Institute (PACT, 2019).

For starters, the conference emphasized the fact that given the following verse from the Holy Qur'an 2:256: "There shall be no compulsion in religion," Islam acknowledges religious freedom for everyone. This tenet was later declared and established via the Charter of Medina that ensured religious liberty for every Jew, Christian, and Muslim and was signed by Prophet Muhammad (PBUH) and other citizens of Medina (PACT, 2019).

In addition, the conference noted that the title of its theme was timely in light of the expansion of "illiberalism" at all levels—economic, political, and social—not only in majority Muslim countries but in others as well. The conference believed that the major shift toward national security in international relations has propelled the curtailing of religious and other civil liberties. Therefore, the conference sought to advocate for the advancement of equality and human rights, and their implementation in majority Muslim countries. It also attempted to establish a common comprehension about the discerned aperture between Islam and religious liberty (PACT, 2019).

Finally, the conference highlighted a paper titled "The Concept of Freedom (*Hurriyya*) and Natural Rights in Classical Islamic Jurisprudence" presented by PACT fellow Hakan Coruh. In it, he analyzed the concept of "freedom" (*hurriyyah*) in the classical Islamic scholarship from ethics to law. He also articulated the concept of "fundamental natural human rights" (or inherent rights, God given rights) in some Muslim jurists' sources. These traditional Islamic sources and legal traditions are all concerned with the following three fundamental rights: (1) the Right of Inviolability (*haqq al-ismah*, "every life is sacred"); (2) the Right of Freedom *(haqq al-hurriyya)*; and (3) the Right of Property *(haqq al-milkiyyah)* (PACT, 2019).

REFERENCES

Archbishop Etienne. (February 14, 2018). Bishops of Alaska issue pastoral letter on human dignity and sanctity of life. *Truth in Love*. Retrieved on January 9, 2021 from https://www.archbishopetienne.com/bishops-of-alaska-issue-pastoral-letter-on-human-dignity-and-sanctity-of-life

Bangura, A. K. (2019). *Branches of Asanteism*. Lanham, MD: Lexington Books.

Budge, E. A. W. (1967).*The Egyptian Book of the Dead*. Mineola, NY: Dover Publications, Inc.

Budge, E. A. W. (1978). *An Egyptian Hieroglyphic Dictionary* (Vols. I & II.). Mineola, NY: Dover Publications, Inc.

Centre for Public and Contextual Theology (PACT). (2019). Islamic cases for religious freedom. Retrieved on January 9, 2021 from https://www.csu.edu.au/pact/news/news-items/2019-news/islamic-cases-for-religious-freedom

Checchio, J. F. (2013). Need for compassionate care more important than ever. *The Catholic Spirit*. Retrieved on January 9, 2021 from https://catholicspirit.com/blog/need-for-compassionate-care-more-important-than-ever

Elgabry, H. (March 24, 2019). The 42 ideals of Ma'at. *Kemet Experience*. Retrieved on August 26, 2020 from https://kemetexperience.com/the-42-ideals-of-maat/

Evangelical Immigrant Table. (July 30, 2019). Respecting the God-given dignity of every immigrant: Why God demands it. *Crosswalm.com*. Retrieved on January 9, 2021 from https://www.crosswalk.com/special-coverage/immigration/how-to-respect-the-god-given-dignity-of-every-immigrant.html

Ezzamel, M. (2004). Work organization in the Middle Kingdom, Ancient Egypt. *Organization* 11(4):497–537. Retrieved on August 11, 2018 from https://www.researchgate.net/publication/247747153_Work_Organization_in_the_Middle_Kingdom_Ancient_Egypt

Hilliard III, A. G., Williams, L. and Damali, N., eds. (1987). *The Teachings of Ptahhotep: The Oldest Book in the World*. Atlanta, GA: Blackwood Press.

Holy Bible (King James Version). (2002 edition). Grand Rapids, MI: Zondervan.

Holy Qur'an (text, translation and commentary by Abdullah Yusuf Ali). (1998 edition). Elmhurst, NY: Tahrike Tarsile Quran, Inc.

Holy Torah (edited by Dr. J. H. Hertz). (1981 edition). London, UK: The Soncino Press.

Huberman, I. (2021). Are we becoming too individualistic. *Congregation Tifereth Israel*. Retrieved on January 1, 2021 from https://www.ctionline.org/blog/are-we-becoming-too-individualistic-443

Iman Center of Kirkland. (June 23, 2020). Black Live Matter: Every life is sacred! Retrieved on January 9, 2021 from https://www.iman-wa.org/post/black_lives_matter

Karenga, M. (2003). *Maat, The Moral Ideal in Ancient Egypt: A Study in Classical African Ethics*. Los Angeles, CA: The University of Sankore Press; reprinted in 2012 by Routledge, Abingdon-on-Thames, UK and New York, NY.

Kula, M. and Stafman, E. (June 14, 2020). We must all work toward justice, righteousness. *Gallatin County Democrats*. Retrieved on January 1, 2021 from https://gallatindemocrats.com/we-must-all-work-toward-justice-righteousness/

Los Angeles Catholics. (2021). Building a culture of life. Retrieved on January 11, 2021 from https://lacatholics.org/priorities/life/

Morgan, D. (September 21, 2017). Suicide: Every life is sacred. *Focus on the Family*. Retrieved on January 9, 2021 from https://www.focusonthefamily.com/pro-life/suicide-every-life-is-sacred/

Morrison, O. (November 7, 2018). Jewish tradition frequently stands against the death penalty; synagogue shooter's case may put it to the test. *PaywallProject*. Retrieved on January 1, 2021 from https://www.100daysinappalachia.com/2018/11/jewish-tradition-frequently-stands-against-the-death-penalty-synagogue-shooters-case-may-put-it-to-the-test/

Notre Dame High School in San Jose, California (NDHSSJC). (April 18, 2019). Celebrating holy week. Retrieved on January 9, 2021 from https://www.ndsj.org/news-events/news/1657940/celebrating-holy-week

Orange County Register. (May 13, 2006). Healthcare not only for privileged. *The Orange County Register*. Retrieved on January 9, 2021 from https://www.ocregister.com/2006/05/13/health-care-not-only-for-privileged/

Schwartz, R. (2020). Issues in Jewish ethics: The Jewish response to hunger. *Jewish Virtual Library*. Retrieved on January 1, 2021 from https://www.jewishvirtuallibrary.org/the-jewish-response-to-hunger

St. Joseph Catholic Church of Youngstown, Ohio (SJCCYO). (2021). Respect life. Retrieved on January 9, 2021 from https://stjosephmantua.com/respect-life

Temple Kol Ami. (2021). Life cycle events. Retrieves on January 8, 2021 from https://www.tkolami.org/prayerritual/life-cycle-events/

Worley, W. (April 2, 2016). Kenyan Muslim man who died protecting Christians in terror attack awarded top honour. *Independent*. Retrieved on January 9, 2021 from https://www.independent.co.uk/news/world/africa/kenyan-muslim-man-who-died-protecting-christians-terror-attack-awarded-top-honour-a6964936.html

Bibliography

Acemoglu, D. & Robinson, J. A. (2010). Why is Africa poor? *Economic History of Developing Regions* 25(1):21–50.
Achankeng, F. (2013). Conflict and conflict resolution in Africa: Engaging the colonial factor. *African Journal on Conflict Resolution* 13(2):11–38.
Achebe, C. (1958 & 1959). *Things Fall Apart*. Lagos, Nigeria: William Heinemann ltd.
Ackah, C. A. (1988). *Akan Ethics: A Study of the Moral Ideas and the Moral Behaviour of the Akan Tribes of Ghana*. Accra, Ghana: Ghana University Press.
Adegible, D. P. (2017). Policing through an American prism. *Yale Law Journal* 126(7):2222–2259.
Advocates for Human Rights. (2015). Liberia's compliance with the convention on the elimination of all forms of discrimination against women. Report for the Pre-Sessional Working Group of the Committee on the Elimination of Discrimination against Women. Retrieved on February 28, 2021 from https://tbInternet.ohchr.org/LBR/int_cedaw_lbr_19364_e.pdf
Afreh, E. (2015). The metonymic and metaphorical conceptualizations of the heart in Akan and English. *Legon Journal of the Humanities* 26:38–57.
African Research Bulletin (July 20, 2020). Kenya: Police brutality protests. Retrieved on January 20, 2021 from www.doi.org/10.1111/j.1467-825X.2020.09528.x
Agility. (August 2020). Top 10 U.S. newspapers by circulation. *PR Solutions*. Retrieved on December 24, 2020 from https://www.agilitypr.com/resources/top-media-outlets/top-10-daily-american-newspapers/
Agozino, B. (2018). Black Lives Matter otherwise all lives do not matter. *African Journal of Criminology and Justice Studies* 11(1):1–11. Retrieved on October 28, 2020 from https://www.umes.edu/uploadedFiles/_WEBSITES/AJCJS/Content/AJCJS%20VOL11.%20Agozino.pdf
Akers, R. L. & Sellers, C. S. (2012). *Criminological Theories: Introduction, Evaluation, and Application*, 6th ed. New York, NY: Oxford University Press.
Al-Amoudi, K. (2018). The conceptual structure of 'hand' idioms in Arabic. *Internet Journal of Language Culture and Society* 37:30–41.

Al-Heeti, A. (July 7, 2020). Black Lives Matter: Netflix movies, TV shows and books that touch on systemic racism. *CNET*. Retrieved on October 28, 2020 from https://www.cnet.com/news/black-lives-matter-movies-tv-shows-and-books-on-systemic-racism/

Alba, R. (2018). What majority-minority society? A critical analysis of the Census Bureau's projections of America's demographic future. *Sociological Research for a Dynamic World* 4:1–10.

Aldrich, M. W. (2021). Tennessee teachers could seek to remove unruly students under bill approved by legislature. *Chalkbeat Tennessee*. Retrieved on March 13, 2021 from https://tn.chalkbeat.org/2021/3/11/22326158/tennessee-teachers-could-seek-to-remove-unruly-students-under-bill-approved-by-legislature

Alexander, M. (2010). *The New Jim Crow: Mass Incarceration in the Age of Colorblindness*. New York, NY: The New Press.

Alimentarium. (2021). Eggs as a symbol of life. Retrieved on January 11, 2021 from http://www.alimentation.org/en/knowledge/egg-symbol-life

All Top Everything. (2020). The 10 most watched TV networks in the USA 2020. *The Best of Everything*. Retrieved on December 24, 2020 from https://www.alltopeverything.com/top-10-most-watched-tv-networks-in-the-usa/

Alliance for Safety and Justice. (2016). Crime survivors speak: The first-ever national survey of victims' views on safety and justice. Retrieved on December 8, 2020 from https://allianceforsafetyandjustice.org/crimesurvivorsspeak/

Allison, S. (January 6, 2020). Conflict is still African's biggest Challenge in 2020. *Relief Web*. Retrieved on January 9, 2021 from https://reliefweb.int/report/world/conflict-still-africa-sbiggest-challenge-2020

Altman, A. (June 4, 2020). Why the killing of George Floyd sparked an American uprising. *Time*. Retrieved on January 9, 2021 from https://time.com/5847967/george-floyd proteststrump/

American Psychological Association. (2002). Developing adolescents: A reference for professionals. Retrieved December 7, 2020 from https://www.apa.org/pi/families/resources/develop.pdf

American Psychological Association (APA). (2011). Conceptualizing psychological concepts. *Journal of Theoretical and Philosophical Psychology* 31(2):73–125.

American Psychological Association (APA). (2020). *APA Dictionary of Psychology*. Washington, DC: APA Publications.

Amnesty International, Nigeria. (June 7, 2017). Submission to the United Nations Committee on the elimination of discrimination against women 67th session, July 3–21, 2017. Retrieved on February 25 2021 from https://primarysources.brillonline.com/browse/human-rights-documents-online/submission-to-the-united-nations-committee-on-the-elimination-of-discrimination-against-women;hrdhrd92112016111

Anazodo, R. O., Igbokwe-Ibeto, C. J. & Nkah, B. C. (2015). Leadership, corruption and governance in Nigeria: Issues and categorical imperatives. *African Research Review* 9(2):41–58.

Andersen, M. & Collins, P. (2004). *Race, Class, and Gender*, 5th ed. Belmont, CA: Wadsworth.

Anderson, C. (2016). *White Rage: The Unspoken Truth of Our Racial Divide.* New York: Bloomsbury Press.

Anderson, M. & Hitlin, P. (2016). The Hashtag #BlackLivesMatter emerges: Social activism on twitter. *Pew Research Report.* Retrieved from http://www.pewinternet.org/2016/08/15/thehashtag-blacklivesmatter-emerges-social-activism-on-twitter/

Anderson, M., Toor, S. R. & Smith, A. (July 11, 2018). 2. An analysis of #BlackLivesMatter and other Twitter hashtags related to political or social issues. *Pew Research Center.* Retrieved on December 8, 2020 from https://www.pewresearch.org/internet/2018/07/11/an-analysis-of-blacklivesmatter-and-other-twitter-hashtags-related-to-political-or-social-issues/

Anja, P. (September 7, 2017). Gender-based violence against women: Both cause for migration and risk along the journey. Retrieved on February 25, 2021 from https://www.migrationpolicy.org/article/gender-based-violence-against-women-both-cause-migration-and-risk-along-journey

Annan-Yao, E. (2004). Analysis of gender relations in the family, formal education and health. *Gender Economies and Entitlements in Africa: CODESRIA* 1–17. Retrieved on March 2, 2021 from https://www.codesria.org/IMG/pdf/GE-Chapter-1-annan.pdf

Apfelbaum, E., Sommer, S. & Norton, M. (2008). Seeing race and seeming racist? Evaluating strategic color-blindness in social interaction. *Journal of Personality and Social Psychology* 95(4):918–932.

Applewhite, D. (2018). Founders and venture capital: Racism is costing us billions. *Forbes.* Retrieved on March 19, 2021 from https://www.forbes.com/sites/forbesnonprofitcouncil/2018/02/15/founders-and-venture-capital-racism-is-costing-us-billions/?sh=3b805f862e4a

Aquinas, T. (1964). Summa theologiae. Trans. Blackfriars. Vol. 39: *Religion and Worship.* New York, NY: McGraw Hill.

Archbishop Etienne. (February 14, 2018). Bishops of Alaska issue pastoral letter on human dignity and sanctity of life. *Truth in Love.* Retrieved on January 9, 2021 from https://www.archbishopetienne.com/bishops-of-alaska-issue-pastoral-letter-on-human-dignity-and-sanctity-of-life

Aremu, J. O. (2010). Conflicts in Africa: Meaning, causes, impact and solution. *African Research Review* 4(4):549–560.

Arendt, H. (1958). *The Human Condition.* Chicago, IL: The University of Chicago Press.

Arif, A., Stewart, G. L. & Starbird, K. (2018). Acting the part: Examining information operations within #BlackLivesMatter discourse. In Proceedings of the ACM on Human-Computer Interaction, 2 (CSCW):1–27. Retrieved on February 15, 2021 from https://faculty.washington.edu/kstarbi/BLM-IRA-Camera-Ready.pdf

Awolalu, J. O. & Dopamu, P. A (2005). *West African Traditional Religion.* Lagos, Nigeria: Macmillan Publishers, 26–27.

Bâ, M. (1981). *So Long a Letter.* Oxford, UK: Heinemann Publisher.

Bailey, G. A. (1994). Rebirth of the non-western world. *Anthropology News* 35(9):1–5.

Baker, P. K. (June 23, 2020). Why saying 'All lives matter' misses the big picture. *CNN*. Retrieved on November 4, 2020 from https://www.cnn.com/2020/06/23/opinions/all-lives-matter-misses-the-big-picture-baker/index.html

Balko, R. (June 10, 2020). There's overwhelming evidence that the criminal justice system is racist. Here's the proof. Retrieved on January 14, 2021 from https://www.washingtonpost.com/graphics/2020/opinions/systemic-racism-police-evidence-criminal-justice-system/

Bambabele, P. (December 19, 2019). Hashtag activism finds a home in social media sites. Retrieved on February 22, 2021 from https://www.sowetanlive.co.za/news/south-africa/2019-12-19-hashtag-activism-finds-a-home-in-social-media-sites/

Bangura, A. K. (2019). *Branches of Asanteism*. Lanham, MD: Lexington Books.

Bangura, A. K. (2020). *The African Mother Tongue and Mathematical Ideas: A Diopian Pluridisciplinary Approach*. Wilmington, DE: Vernon Press.

Bangura, A. K., Obando, J. A., Munene, I. I. & Shisanya, C. (2019). *Conducting Research and Mentoring Students in Africa: CODESRIA College of Mentors Handbook*. Dakar, Senegal: CODESRIA Publications.

Bangura, S. (November 8, 2020). The sunrise of a new dawn: A poem written by me.

Barron-Lopez, Laura. (2020). Why the Black Lives Matter movement doesn't want a singular leader. *Politico*. Retrieved on November 20, 2020 from https://www.politico.com/news/2020/07/22/black-lives-matter-movement-leader-377369

Battle, M. (2000). A theology of community: The ubuntu theology of Desmond Tutu. *Interpretation* 54(2):173–182.

Baumann, H. (1964). *Schofung und Urszeit des Menschen in Mythus der afrikanishen Volker*. Berlin, Germany: Dietrich Reimer.

Beauchamp, B. (April 10, 2014). Rwanda's genocide—What happened, why it happened, and how it still matters. *Vox*. Retrieved on February 27, 2021 from https://www.vox.com/2014/4/10/5590646/rwandan-genocide-anniversary

Bell, C. (2015). The hidden side of zero tolerance policies: The African American perspective. *Sociology Compass* 9(1):14–22.

Berk, C., Ezgi, T., Pamir, K., Deniz, C. & Fatih, I. (2020). Black Lives Matter movement - A comprehensive study on institutionalized racism, sexism and its approach towards intersectionality. Conference Paper.

Berkenpas, J. R. (2016). The behavioral revolution in contemporary political science: Narrative, identity, practice (doctoral dissertation, Western Michigan University, Michigan, USA). Retrieved on March, 7, 2021 from https://scholarworks.wmich.edu/cgi/viewcontent.cgi?article=2404&context=dissertations

Berman, B. J. (1998). Ethnicity, patronage and the African state: The politics of uncivil nationalism. *African Affairs* 97(388):305–341.

Bertuccelli, P. M. (2013). Idiomatic and figurative uses of 'hand' in English and mano in Italian: Embodiment and cultural filters. *Rassegna di Linguistica Applicata* 1:17–38.

Bjornstrom, E., Kaufman, R., Peterson, D. & Slater, M. (2010). Race and ethnic representations of lawbreakers and victims in crime news: A National study of television coverage. *Social Problems* 57(2):269–293.

Black Lives Matter. (2018). Black Lives Matter 13 guiding principles (a project of teaching for change by the DC area educator for social justice). Retrieved on

October 31, 2020 from https://www.dcareaeducators4socialjustice.org/black-lives-matter/13-guiding-principles

Black Lives Matter. (2020). BLM's #WHATMATTERS2020 resources. Retrieved on October 27, 2020 from https://blacklivesmatter.com/

Black, M. (1962). *Models and Metaphors*. Ithaca, NY: Cornell University Press.

Blake-Beard, S., Murrell, A. & Thomas, D. A. (2006). *Unfinished Business: The Impact of Race on Understanding Mentoring Relationships*. Working Paper No. 06-060.

Bonilla, T. & Tillery Jr., A. B. (2020). Which identity frames boost support for and mobilization in the #BlackLivesMatter movement? An experimental test. *American Political Science Review* 114(4):947–962.

Bonilla-Silva, E. (2003). *Racism without Racists*. New York, NY: Rowman & Littlefield Publishers, Inc.

Bonilla-Silva, E. (2014). *Racism without Racists: Color-blind Racism and the Persistence of Racial Inequality in the United States*. Lanham, MD: Rowman & Littlefield.

Bonilla-Silva, E., Moon-Kie, J. & Vargas, J. (2011). *State of White Supremacy: Racism, Governance, and the United States*. Stanford, CA: Stanford University Press.

Borch, M. (2001). Rethinking the origins of terra nullius. *Australian Historical Studies* 32(117):222–239.

Braithwaite, T. (June 2020). How companies decided that Black Lives Matter. Retrieved on July 30, 2020 from https://www.ft.com/companies/the-top-line

Bouie, J. (September 30, 2015). Elizabeth Warren just gave the best response to Black Lives Matter. *Slate*. Retrieved on November 1, 2020 from https://slate.com/news-and-politics/2015/09/elizabeth-warrens-black-lives-matter-speech-was-the-best-one-yet-its-still-not-enough.html

Bozeman, A. B. (1976). *Conflict in Africa: Concepts and Realities*. Princeton, NJ: Princeton University Press.

Brewer, M. B. & Campel, D. T. (1976). *Ethnocentrism and Intergroup Attitudes: East African Evidence*. New York, NY: John Wiley and Sons.

Bridge, K. (December 4, 2015). What's the harm? Prof. Khiara M. Bridges on the poverty of privacy rights. Retrieved on January 16, 2021 from https://lawprofessors.typepad.com/reproductive_rights/2015/12/whats-the-harm-prof-khiara-m-bridges-on-the-poverty-of-privacy-rights.html

Britannica Online Encyclopedia (October, 2020). Business organization. Retrieved on March 17, 2021 from https://www.britannica.com/topic/business-organization

British Broadcasting Corporation (BBC) News. (September17, 2018). Rwanda country profile. *BBC News*. Retrieved on February 27, 2021 from https://www.bbc.com/news/world-africa-14093238

British Broadcasting Corporation (BBC) Africa. (December 16, 2019). Nigerian university lecturer sacked over sexual harassment. Retrieved on February 19, 2021 from https://www.bbc.com/news/world-africa-50817098?intlink_from_url=https://www.bbc.com/news/world&link_location=live-reporting-story

British Broadcasting Corporation (BBC) Africa. (June 5, 2020). #WeAreTired: Nigerian women speak out over wave of violence. *BBC News*. Retrieved on January 12, 2021 from https://www.bbc.com/news/world-africa-52889965

British Broadcasting Corporation. (2020). George Floyd: What happened in the final moments of his life. Retrieved on June 20, 2021 from https://www.bbc.com/news/world-us-canada-52861726

Brown, C. & Ainley, K. (2005). *Understanding International Relations*, 3rd ed. Basingoke, UK: Palgrave Macmillan.

Brown, G. (2016). *The Universal Declaration of Human Rights in the 21st Century*. Cambridge, UK: Open Book Publishers. Retrieved on February 26, 2021 from https://www.equalrightstrust.org/ertdocumentbank/Brown-Universal-Declaration-Human-Rights21C.pdf

Brown, W. (2015). An intersectional approach to criminological theory: Incorporating the intersectionality of race and gender into Agnew's General Strain Theory. *Ralph Bunche Journal of Public Affairs* 4(1), Article 6:229–243.

Bryant-Davis, T., Ullman, S. E., Tsong, Y., Tillman, S. & Smith, K. (2010). Struggling to survive: Sexual assault, poverty, and mental health outcomes of African American women. *The American Journal of Orthopsychiatry* 80(1): 61–70.

Buchanan, L., Bui, Q. & Patel, J. K. (July 3, 2020). Black Lives Matter may be the largest movement in U.S. history. *The New York Times*. Retrieved on October 28, 2020 from https://www.nytimes.com/interactive/2020/07/03/us/george-floyd-protests-crowd-size.html

Budge, E. A. W. (1967). *The Egyptian Book of the Dead*. Mineola, NY: Dover Publications, Inc.

Budge, E. A. W. (1978). *An Egyptian Hieroglyphic Dictionary*, vols. I & II. Mineola, NY: Dover Publications, Inc.

Buettner, R. & Buettner, K. (2016). A systematic literature review of twitter research from a socio-political revolution perspective. In *2016 49th Hawaii International Conference on System Sciences (HICSS)* (pp. 2206–2215). IEEE. Retrieved on February 20, 2021 from https://www.researchgate.net/publication/282150020_A_Systematic_Literature_Review_of_Twitter_Research_from_a_Socio-Political_Revolution_Perspective

Bujo, B. (2006). *African Theology in its Social Context*. Eugene, OR: Wipf and Stock Publishers.

Burt, C., Simons, R. & Gibbons, F. (2012). Racial discrimination, ethnic-racial socialization, and crime: A micro-sociological model of risk and resilience. *American Sociological Review* 77(4):648–677.

California Department of Education (CDE). (April 9, 2020). Literary genres. Retrieved on January 20, 2021 from https://www.cde.ca.gov/ci/cr/rl/litrlgenres.asp

Caproni, P. J. (2005). *Managing Cultural Diversity: Management Skills for Everyday Life: The Practical Coach*, 2nd ed. Upper Saddle River, NJ: Pearson Prentice Hall.

Centre for Public and Contextual Theology (PACT). (2019). Islamic cases for religious freedom. Retrieved on January 9, 2021 from https://www.csu.edu.au/pact/news/news-items/2019-news/islamic-cases-for-religious-freedom

Chanin, J. (2017). Police reform through an administrative lens: Revisiting the Justice Department's pattern or practice initiative. *Administrative Theory & Praxis* 39(4):257–274.

Chanthamith, B., Wu, M., Yusufzada, S. & Rasel, M. (2019). Interdisciplinary relationship between sociology, politics and public administration: Perspective of theory and practice. *Sociology International Journal* 3(4):353–357.

Chapel, R. (October 7, 2020). Opposed to Black Lives Matter. Retrieved on January 12, 2021 from https://www.telegram.com/story/lifestyle/2020/10/07/opinionfirst-person-opposed-to-Black-lives-matter/114235446/

Chapman-Hilliard, C. & Adams-Bass, V. (2016). A conceptual framework for utilizing Black history knowledge as a path to psychological liberation for Black youth. *Journal of Black Psychology* 42(6):479–507.

Checchio, J. F. (2013). Need for compassionate care more important than ever. *The Catholic Spirit*. Retrieved on January 9, 2021 from https://catholicspirit.com/blog/need-for-compassionate-care-more-important-than-ever

Chelwa, G. (May 22, 2013). The scramble for Africa, fractionalization and open borders. Retrieved on March 9, 2021 from https://openborders.info/blog/the-scramble-for-africa-fractionalization-and-open-borders/

Christensen, H. S. (2011). Political activities on the Internet: Slacktivism or political participation by other means? *Peer-reviewed Journal on the Internet*. Retrieved on February 25, 2021 from https://firstmonday.org/article/view/3336/2767

CNN Editorial Research. (October 19, 2020). Trayvon Martin shooting fast facts. Retrieved on January 12, 2021 from https://edition.cnn.com/2013/06/05/us/trayvon-martin-shooting-fast-facts/index.html

Coalition for Juvenile Justice. (2018). Summary of the Juvenile Justice Reform Act of 2018. Retrieved on December 9, 2020 from https://www.juvjustice.org/sites/default/files/resource-files/Summary%20of%20the%20Juvenile%20Justice%20Reform%20Act%20of%202018.pdf

Coates, T. N. (July 15, 2013). Trayvon Martin and the irony of American justice. *The Atlantic*. Retrieved on January 15, 2021 from www.theatlantic.com/national/archive/2013/07/trayvon-martin-and-the-irony-of-american-justice/277782/

Cocodia, J. (2008). Exhuming trends in ethnic conflict and cooperation in Africa: Some selected states. *African Journal on Conflict Resolution* 8(3):9–26.

Cohen, H. J. (1995). What should we do when nations get angry? *Nexus Africa* 1(2):11–14.

Cohen, J. (2004). Deviance as resistance: A new research agenda for the study of Black politics. *Du Bois Review* 1(1):27–45.

Cohn, N. & Quealy, K. (June 10, 2020). How public opinion has moved on Black Lives Matter. *The New York Times*. Retrieved on October 28, 2020 from https://www.nytimes.com/interactive/2020/06/10/upshot/black-lives-matter-attitudes.html

Cole, C. (June, 2020). Black Lives Matter—and that applies in the corporate world too! Retrieved on March 21 from https://diversityq.com/blacklivesmatterandthatappliesinthecorporateworldtoo

Collins, C., Hamilton, D., Asante-Muhammed, D. & Hoxie, J. (April 2019). Ten solutions to bridge the racial wealth divide. *Institute for Policy Studies*. Retrieved on October 28, 2020 from https://ips-dc.org/report-racial-wealth-divide-solutions/

Colson, E. (1969). African society at the time of the scramble. In Gann, L. & Duignan, P. (eds.). *Colonialism in Africa 1870–1960*. Cambridge, UK: Cambridge University.

Communications Workers of America—CWA. (2020). Black Lives Matter, All Lives Matter: Resolution 75A-15-9. Retrieved on August 30, 2020 from https://cwa-uni on.org/pages/black_lives_matter_all_lives_matter

Condevillamar, J. (July 2, 2020). Black Lives matter countermovement abd criticism. *The Thunderbolt*. Retrieved on November 4, 2020 from https://millsthunderbolt.com/black-lives-matter-countermovement-and-criticisms/

Cone, J. H. (July 1, 1975). The story context of Black theology. Retrieved on February 17, 2021 from www://doi.org/10.1177/004057367503200203

Cornelius, N. (September 4, 2020). From slavery and colonialism to Black Lives Matter: New mood music or more fundamental change? Retrieved on February 10, 2021 from www://doi.org/10.1108/EDI-07-2020-0199

Cowell, A. (April 10, 2014). Colonialism, bloodshed and blame for Rwanda. *The New York Times*. Retrieved on February 27, 2021 from https://www.nytimes.com/2014/04/11/world/europe/colonialism-bloodshed-and-blame-forrwanda.html

Crenshaw, K. (1995). Mapping the margins: Intersectionality, identity politics, and violence against women of color. In Crenshaw, K., Gotanda, N., Peller, G. & Thomas, K. (eds.). *Critical Race Theory: The Key Writings that Formed the Movement*. New York, NY: New Press.

Crenshaw, K., Ocen, P. & Nanda, J. (2015). *Black Girls Matter: Pushed Out, Overpoliced, and Underprotected*. New York, NY: African American Policy Forum, Centre for Intersectionality and Social Policy Studies.

Croft, W. & Cruse, A. (2004). *Cognitive Linguistics*. Cambridge, UK: Cambridge University Press.

Day, E. (July 19, 2015). #BlackLivesMatter: The birth of a new civil rights movement. *The Observer*. Retrieved on October 28, 2020 from https://www.theguardian.com/world/2015/jul/19/blacklivesmatter-birth-civil-rights-movement

Dangarembga, T. (1988). *Nervous Conditions*. New York, NY: Seal Press.

De Bortoli, M. & Maroto, J. (2001). Translating colors in website localization. *Proceeding of the European Language and Implementation of Communication and Information Technologies conference*. University of Paisley.

De Choudhury, M., Jhaver, S., Sugar, B. & Weber, I. (May 2016). Social media participation in an activist movement for racial equality. Paper presented at the 10th International AAAI Conference on Web and Social Media, Cologne, Germany. Retrieved on March 15, 2021 from http://www.munmund.net/pubs/BLM_ICWSM16.pdf

De Kosnik, A. & Feldman, K. (2019). *#Identity: Hashtagging Race, Gender, Sexuality, and Nation*. Ann Arbor, MN: University of Michigan Press.

Dedmon, R. (2017). Roles of Family and School in Preventing Juvenile Delinquency. *Operation 10-8*. Retrieved on November 29, 2020 from http://operation8.com/roles-of-family-and-school-in-preventing-juvenile-delinquency

Definitions.net. (2020). Television station. *Definitions & Translations*. Retrieved on December 24, 2020 from https://www.definitions.net/definition/television+station

DefundThePolice.org. (2020). Defund The Police. Retrieved on October 28, 2020 from https://defundthepolice.org/

DeJong, P., Trupe, E. & Zwingel, E. (n.d.). Motivating students positively through restorative justice discipline. *Empowering Research for Educators* 4(1) Article 2.

Denney, L. & Ibrahim, A. F. (2012). Violence against women in Sierra Leone. How women seek redress. *Overseas Development Institute*. Retrieved on January 12, 2020 from https://www.refworld.org/pdfid/523ac7a94.pdf

Department of Justice. (December, 2020). President's Commission on Law enforcement and the administration of justice. Retrieved on January 15, 2021 from https://www.justice.gov/file/1347866/download

Devlin, K. (2000). *The Language of Mathematics: Making the Invisible Visible*. New York, NY: W. H. Freeman Henry Holt and Company.

DiAngelo, R. (2018). *White Fragility: Why It's So Hard for White People to Talk about Racism*. Boston, MA: Beacon Press.

Dickey, J. (May 31, 2016). The revolution on America's campuses. Retrieved on February 18, 2021 from https://time.com/4347099/college-campus-protests/

Donne, John. (2021). The first anniversary: A poem. *Poetry Foundation*. Retrieved on January 20, 2021 from https://www.poetryfoundation.org/poems/50336/the-anniversary-56d22d56d635f

Dressel, J. & Farid, H. (2018). The accuracy, fairness, and limits of predicting recidivism. *Science Advances* 4(1) from doi:10.1126/sciadv.aao5580

Dur, B, İ. U. (2015). Hand Image as metaphor and is usage in poster design. *Global Journal of Arts Humanities and Social Sciences* 3:19–28.

Durkheim, E. (1915). *The Elementary Forms of The Religious Life*. London, UK: George Alien Unwin.

Durmaz, M. (April 5, 2019). It's time to accept the west failed Rwanda during genocide. *TRT World*. Retrieved on February 27, 2021 from https://www.trtworld.com/opinion/it-s-time-to-accept-the-west-failed-rwanda-during-genocide25593

DW (n.d). EU-Africa free trade will create more imbalances, say critics. Retrieved on February 28, 2021 from https://www.dw.com/en/eu-africa-free-trade-will-create-more-imbalances-say-critics/a-45018168

Dzobo, N. K. (1992). Knowledge and truth: Ewe and Akan conceptions. In Gyekye, K. & Wiredu, K. (eds.). *Person and Community: Ghanaian Philosophical Studies*. Washington, DC: The Council for Research in Values and Philosophy.

Edgar, A. N. & Johnson, A. E. (2018). *The Struggle over Black Lives Matter and All Lives Matter*. Lanham, MD: Lexington Books.

Editors of the *Encyclopedia Britannica*. (2020). Newspaper. *Encyclopedia Britannica*. Retrieved on December 24, 2020 from https://www.britannica.com/biography/Nikolay-Rimsky-Korsakov

Elgabry, H. (March 24, 2019). The 42 ideals of Ma'at. *Kemet Experience*. Retrieved on August 26, 2020 from https://kemetexperience.com/the-42-ideals-of-maat/

Esteban, J. & Ray. D (2011). A model of ethnic conflict. *Journal of the European Economic Association* 9(3):496–521.

Evangelical Immigrant Table. (July 30, 2019). Respecting the God-given dignity of every immigrant: Why God demands it. *Crosswalm.com*. Retrieved on January 9, 2021 from https://www.crosswalk.com/special-coverage/immigration/how-to-respect-the-god-given-dignity-of-every-immigrant.html

Evans, V. & Green, M. (2006). *Cognitive Linguistics: An Introduction.* Edinburg, UK: Edinburg University.

Executive Order No. 13896, 84 F.R. 58595 (2019). Retrieved on January 15, 2021 from https://www.federalregister.gov/documents/2019/11/01/2019-24040/commission-on-law-enforcement-and-the-administration-of-justice

Ezekwugo, C. U. M. (1987). *Chi, the True God in Igbo Religion.* Muvattupuzha Kerala, India: Mar Matthew Press.

Ezorsky, G. (1991). *Racism and Justice: The Case for Affirmative Action.* Ithaca, NY: Cornell University Press.

Ezzamel, M. (2004). Work organization in the Middle Kingdom, Ancient Egypt. *Organization* 11(4):497–537. Retrieved on August 11, 2018 from https://www.researchgate.net/publication/247747153_Work_Organization_in_the_Middle_Kingdom_Ancient_Egypt

Faal, C. (February 21, 2019). The partition of Africa. *Blackpast.* Retrieved on February 23, 2021 from https://www.blackpast.org/global-african-history/partition-africa/#:~:text=This%20conference%20was%20called%20by,were%20invited%20to%20the%20conference

Fakhoury, L. (2017, November). Restorative justice [Video file]. Retrieved on January 11, 2021 from https://www.youtube.com/watch?v=MSy-qOiYjrA

Fair, J. (1995). *Remembering the Revolution: Behaviorism in American Political Science: Political Science in History.* Cambridge, UK: Cambridge University Press.

Fairchild, H. H. & Fairchild, H. F. (2017). *Reflections on Black Lives Matter: Lifespan Perspectives.* Delhi, India: Indo American Books.

Fan, H. (2017). A study of "Hand" metaphor in English and Chinese: Cognitive and cultural perspective. *Advanced Literary Studies* 5(4):84–93. Retrieved on October 28, 2020 from https://m.scirp.org/papers/79776

Fang-fang, W. (2009). Metaphorical and metonymical expressions including face and eye in everyday language. Retrieved on December 12, 2021 from http://hkr.diva-portal.org/smasg/get/diva2:292843/FULLTEXT01.pdf

Feagin, J. E. & Imani, N. (1994). *Racial Barriers to African American Entrepreneurship: An Exploratory Study.* Omaha, NE: Black Studies Faculty Publications.

Fearon, J. D. & Laitin, D. D. (2003). Ethnicity, insurgency, and civil war. *American Political Science Review* 97(1):75–90.

Forceville, C. (1996). *Pictorial Metaphor in Advertising.* London, UK; New York, NY: Routledge.

Foreman, C. H. (2000). Facing up to racial disparity. *The Brookings Review* 8(2):29–30.

Forsey, C. (2020). The top 7 search engines, ranked by popularity. *Hub Spot.* Retrieved on December 24, 2020 from https://blog.hubspot.com/marketing/top-search-engines

Foxworth, D. (July 26, 2016). Richard Sherman: As human beings, All Lives Matter. *The Undefeated.* Retrieved on August 30, 2020 from https://theundefeated.com/features/richard-sherman-as-human-beings-all-lives-matter/

Francis, E. K. (1976). *Inter-Ethnic Relations: An Essay in Sociological Theory*. New York, NY: Elsevier.

Frankfort-Nachmias, F. & Nachmias, D. (1996). *Research Methods in the Social Sciences*. New York, America: St. Martin's Press.

Freedman, J. L. (1982). *Introductory Psychology*. Boston, MA: Addison-Wesley Publishing Company, Inc.

Freelon, D., McIlwain, C. D. & Clark, M. D. (2016a). *Beyond the Hashtags: #Ferguson, #BlackLivesMatter, and the Online Struggle for Offline Justice*. Washington, DC: American University, Center for Media and Social Impact. Retrieved on March 15, 2021 from http://cmsimpact.org/wp-content/uploads/2016/03/beyond_the_hashtags_2016.pdf

Freelon, D., McIlwain, C. D. & Clark, M. D. (2016b). Quantifying the power and consequences of social media protest. *New Media & Society*. Advance online publication. doi:10.1177/1461444816676646

French, B. H., Lewis, J. A., Mosley, D. V., Adames, H. Y., Chavez-Dueñas, N. Y., Chen, G. A. & Neville, H. A. (2020). Toward a psychological framework of radical healing in communities of color. *The Counseling Psychologist* 48(1):14–46.

Frey, W. H. (2018). Diversity explosion: How new racial demographics are remaking America. Retrieved on March 5, 2021 from https://www.brookings.edu/blog/the-avenue/2018/03/14/the-us-will-become-minority-white-in-2045-census-projects/

Friedman, G. (August, 2020). Here's what companies are promising to do to fight racism. *The New York Times*. Retrieved on March 19, 2021 from https://www.nytimes.com/article/companies-racism-george-floyd-protests.html

Funk, A. (June 22, 2020). How domestic spying tools undermine racial justice protests. Retrieved on January 18, 2021 from https://freedomhouse.org/article/how-domestic-spying-tools-undermine-racial-justice-protests

Galderisi, S., Heinz, A., Kastrup, M., Beezhold, J. & Sartorius, N. (2015). Toward a new definition of mental health. *World Psychiatry: Official Journal of the World Psychiatric Association (WPA)* 14(2):231–233.

Gale. (2020). Black Lives Matter topic overview: Black Lives Matter. *Gale Opposing Viewpoints Online Collection*. Retrieved on January 14, 2021 from https://www.gale.com/open-access/Black-lives-matter

Gallagher, R. J., Reagan, A. J., Danforth, C. M. & Dodds, P. S. (2018). Divergent discourse between protests and counter-protests: #BlackLivesMatter and #AllLivesMatter. *PloS One* 13(4): 1–23.

Garza, A. (2014). A history of the #BlackLivesMatter movement. Retrieved on March 15, 2021 from http://blacklivesmatter.com/herstory/

Gates Jr., H. L. & McKay, N. Y., general editors. (1997). *The Norton Anthology of African American Literature*. New York, NY: W. W. Norton and Company.

Gehman, R. J. (1999). *Who Are the Living Dead? A Theology of Death, Life after Death, and the Living Dead*. Nairobi, Kenya: Evangel Publishing House.

Gehman, R. J. (2000). *African Traditional Religion in Biblical Perspective*. Nairobi, Kenya: East African Educational Publishers.

Geller, A., Fagan, J., Tyler, T. & Link, B. G. (2014). Aggressive policing and the mental health of young urban men. *American Journal of Public Health*. Retrieved on December 08, 2020 from https://www.ncbi.nlm.nih.gov/pmc/articles/PMC 4232139/

Genovese, D. (June, 2020). How are big tech companies responding to George Floyd killing? From public sentiments to multi-million donations big tech is responding in big ways. *Fox News*. Retrieved on June 10, 2020 from https://www.foxbusiness.com/howarebigtechcompaniesrespondingtogeorgefloydilling

German, M. (June 26, 2020). The FBI targets a new generation of Black activists. Retrieved on February 24, 2021 from https://www.brennancenter.org/our-work/analysis-opinion/fbi-targets-new-generation-Black-activists

Ghafel, B. & Mirzaie, A. (2014). Colors in everyday metaphoric language of Persian speakers. *Procedia-Social and Behavioral Sciences* 136:133–143.

Ghandnoosh, N. (2015). Black Lives Matter: Eliminating racial inequity in the criminal justice system. *The Sentencing Project*. Retrieved on December 02, 2020 from https://sentencingproject.org/wp-content/uploads/2015/11/Black-Lives-Matter.pdf

Gillborn, D. (2015). Intersectionality, critical race theory, and the primacy of racism, class, gender, and disability in education. *Qualitative Inquiry* 21(3):277–287.

Gillborn, D., Rollock, N., Vincent, C. & Ball, S. J. (2012). You got a pass, so what more do you want? Race, class and gender intersections in the educational experiences of the Black middle class. *Race Ethnicity and Education* 15:121–139.

Gilman, M. (2013). The return of the welfare aueen. *Journal of Gender, Social Policy & the Law* 22:247–79.

Gjelten, E. (February 5, 2019). What are zero tolerance policies in schools? Retrieved on January 4, 2021 from https://www.lawyers.com/legal-info/research/education-law/whats-a-zero-tolerance-policy.html

Gladwell, M. (2010). Small change. *The New Yorker* 4:42–49. Retrieved on February 22, 2021 from https://www.newyorker.com/magazine/2010/10/04/small-change-malcolm-gladwell

Goffman, A. (2009). On the run: Wanted men in a Philadelphia ghetto. *American Sociological Review* 74(3):339–357.

Goffman, A. (2014). *On the Run: Fugitive Life in an American City*. Chicago, IL: The University of Chicago Press.

Goldberg, D. T. (September 25, 2016). Why 'Black Lives Matter' because all lives don't matter in America. *Huftpost*. Retrieved on November 5, 2020 from https://www.huffpost.com/entry/why-black-lives-matter_b_8191424

Gospel Light Society. (2020). All Lives Matter to God. #*alllivesmatter*. Retrieved on October 31, 2020 from http://gospellightsociety.com/glmx/all-lives-matter-to-god/

Gottfried, M. H. & Eccher, M. (October 3, 2015). Black Lives Matter's Twin Cities Marathon protest peaceful. *St. Paul Pioneer Press*. Retrieved on October 30, 2020 from https://www.twincities.com/2015/10/03/black-lives-matters-twin-cities-marathon-protest-peaceful/

Graham, M. (2020). The right way for companies to weigh in on racism, according to experts. Retrieved on July 31, 2020 from https://www.cnbc.com/technology/

Greenberg, J. & Kosloff, S. (2008). Terror management theory: Implications for understanding prejudice, stereotyping, intergroup conflict, and political attitudes. *Social and Personality Psychology Compass* 2(5):1881–1894.

Greenberg, J., Pyszczynski, T. & Solomon, S. (1986). The causes and consequences of a need for self-esteem: A terror management theory. In R. F. Baumeister (ed.). *Public Self and Private Self.* New York, NY: Springer-Verlag.

Griffith, J. W. & Frey, C. H. (1981). *Classics of Children's Literature.* New York, NY: Macmillan Publishing Company, Inc.

Gusman, J. (2015). The concept of human rights: Political and moral approaches. (Master's thesis, Radboud University, Nijmegen, The Netherlands). Retrieved on January 6, 2021 from https://theses.ubn.ru.nl/bitstream/handle/123456789/1160/Gusman%2C_Jesse_1.pdf?sequence=1

Hagopian, J. (December 1, 2020). Making Black Lives Matter: The national movement has four key demands to eliminate racism in education. Retrieved from February 15, 2021 from https://progressive.org/magazine/making-Black-lives-matter-hagopian/

Hait, A. (January, 2021). What is a small business? Retrieved on March 18, 2021 from https://www.census.gov/library/stories/2021/01/what-is-a-small-business.html

Hardy. W (September 25, 2020). Riches & misery: The consequences of the Atlantic slave trade. *OpenLearn.* Retrieved on March 17, 2021 from https://www.open.edu/openlearn/history-the-arts/history/riches-misery-the-consequences-the-atlantic-slave-trade

Harlow, C. (2003). Education and correctional populations. Bureau of Justice Statistics Special Report. Retrieved on January 20, 2021 from https://files.eric.ed.gov/fulltext/ED543577.pdf

Hayes, A. (July, 2020). Business. *Investopedia.* Retrieved on March 17, 2021 from https://www.investopedia.com/Business%20Definition.html

Herr, K. (2017). A Black African feminist theory to examine female genital mutilation (FGM) within African immigrant families, in the United States, Mame Kani Diop, Doctoral Candidate Pearl Stewart, PhD Retrieved on January 22, 2021 from https://www.ncfr.org/sites/default/files/2017-08/TCRM%204%20-%20A%20Black%20African%20Feminist%20Theory.pdf

Hill, E., Tiefenthäler, A., Triebert, C., Jordan, D., Willis, H. & Stein, R. (May 31, 2020). How George Floyd was killed in police custody. Retrieved on January 12, 2021 from https://www.nytimes.com/2020/05/31/us/george-floyd-investigation.html

Hill, J. (2008). *Everyday Language of White Racism.* Oxford. UK: Blackwell Publishing.

Hill, M. (September 4, 2020). You can't talk about Black Lives Matter and ignore black on black crimes. *NJ Spotlight News.* Retrieved on November 5, 2020 from https://www.njspotlight.com/news/video/you-cant-talk-about-black-lives-matter-and-ignore-black-on-black-crime/

Hilliard III, A. G., Williams, L. & Damali, N. (eds.) (1987). *The Teachings of Ptahhotep: The Oldest Book in the World.* Atlanta, GA: Blackwood Press.

Hines, D., Carter, A. & Dorinda, J. (2020). The effects of zero tolerance policies on Black girls: Using critical race feminism and figured worlds to examine school discipline. *Urban Education* 55(10):1419–1440.
Hinson, S., Healey, R. & Bester, D. (2012). *Race, Power and Policy: Dismantling Structural Racism*. Berkeley, CA: National People's Action by the Grassroots Policy Project.
Hiribarren, V. (2018). Scramble for and partition of West Africa. In N. Achebe, S. Adu-Gyamfi, J. Alie, et al. (eds.). *History Textbook: West African Senior School Certificate Examination*. Retrieved on February 23, 2021 from https://wasscehistorytextbook.com/wpcontent/uploads/sites/334/2018/06/WASSCE_History_Textbook.pdf
Hirschfield, P. J. (2008). The declining significance of delinquent labels in disadvantaged urban communities. *Sociological Forum* 23(3):575–601.
Hoffman, L., Granger, N., Vallejos, L. & Moats, M. (2016). An existential-humanistic perspective on Black Lives Matter and contemporary protest movements. *Journal of Humanistic Psychology* 56(6):595–611.
Holt, L. & Sweitzer, M. (2020). More than a black and white issue: Ethnic identity, social dominance orientation, and support for the black lives matter movement. *Self and Identity* 19(1):16–31.
Holy Bible (King James Version). (2002 edition). Grand Rapids, MI: Zondervan.
Holy Qur'an (text, translation and commentary by Abdullah Yusuf Ali). (1998 edition). Elmhurst, NY: Tahrike Tarsile Quran, Inc.
Holy Torah (edited by Dr. J. H. Hertz). (1981 edition). London, UK: The Soncino Press.
Holt, L. F. & Sweitzer, M. D. (2018). More than a black and white issue: Ethnic identity, social dominance orientation, and support for the black lives matter movement. *Self and Identity* 2018:1–15.
hooks, b. (2010). *Feminism Is for Everybody: Passionate Politics*. Cambridge, MA: South End Press. Retrieved on February 12, 2021 from https://excoradfeminisms.files.wordpress.com/2010/03/bell_hooks-feminism_is_for_everybody.pdf
Hordge-Freeman, E. & Loblack, A. (2020). "Cops only see the Brown skin, they could care less where it originated": Afro-Latino perceptions of the #BlackLivesMatter Movement. *Sociological Perspectives* 1–18.
Horowitz, J. M. & Livingston, G. (2016). How Americans view the Black Lives Matter Movement. *Pew Research Center*. Retrieved on December 03, 2020 from https://www.pewsocialtrends.org/2020/06/12/amid-protests-majorities-across-racial-and-ethnic-groups-express-support-for-the-black-lives-matter-movement/
Horowitz, J. M. & Thomas, D. (2020). Support for Black Lives Matter has decreased since June but remains strong among Black Americans. *Pew Research Center*. Retrieved on December 03, 2020 from https://www.pewresearch.org/fact-tank/2020/09/16/support-for-black-lives-matter-has-decreased-since-june-but-remains-strong-among-black-americans/
Horowitz, J. M., Parker, K. & Anderson, M. (2020). Amid protests, majorities across racial and ethnic groups express support for the Black Lives Matter movement: Deep partisan divides over factors underlying George Floyd demonstrations. *Pew Research Center*. Retrieved on December 03, 2020 from https://www.pewsocia

ltrends.org/2020/06/12/amid-protests-majorities-across-racial-and-ethnic-groups-express-support-for-the-black-lives-matter-movement/

Hoston, W. (June 24, 2020). Revealing a cultural truth: Not all Black Lives Matter. Retrieved on January 12, 2021 from https://www.pvamu.edu/blog/opinion-revealing-a-cultural-truth-not-all-Black-lives-matter/

Huber, J. D. & Mayoral, L. (2014). *Inequality Ethnicity and Civil Conflict*. New York, NY: Columbia University Press.

Huberman, I. (2021). Are we becoming too individualistic. *Congregation Tifereth Israel*. Retrieved on January 1, 2021 from https://www.ctionline.org/blog/are-we-becoming-too-individualistic-443

Hughes, C. (2018). From the long Arm of the state to eyes on the street: How poor African American mothers navigate surveillance in the social safety net. *Journal of Contemporary Ethnography* 48(3):339–376.

Human Right Campaign Foundation. (2020). An epidemic of violence: Fatal violence against transgender and gender nonconforming people in the United States in 2020. Retrieved on January 25, 2021 from https://www.hrc.org/resources/an-epidemic-of-violence-fatal-violence-against-transgender-and-gender-non-conforming-people-in-the-u-s-in-2020

Hymowitz, K. (Spring 2005). What's holding Black kids back? Bill Cosby is right: The problem is the parents. Retrieved on January 23, 2021 from https://www.city-journal.org/html/what%E2%80%99s-holding-Black-kids-back-12863.html

Ighobor. K (2014). Trade between two unequal partners. *Africa Renewal*. Retrieved on February 28, 2021 from https://www.un.org/africarenewal/magazine/august-2014/trade-between-two-unequal-partners

Iheukwumere, E. O. & Iheukwumere, C. A. (2003). Colonial rapacity and political corruption: Roots of African underdevelopment and misery. *Chi.-Kent J. Int'l & Comp. L.* 3:1.

Iman Center of Kirkland. (June 23, 2020). Black Live Matter: Every life is sacred! Retrieved on January 9, 2021 from https://www.iman-wa.org/post/black_lives_matter

Independent Advisory Group on Country Information (IAGCI). (2015). Country information and guidance Nigeria: Gender-based discrimination/harm/violence against women. Retrieved on February 28, 2021 from https://www.refworld.org/pdfid/55dda9204.pdf

Ingraham, C. (November 16, 2017). Black men sentenced to more time for committing the exact same crime as a White person, study finds. Retrieved on February 11, 2021 from https://www.washingtonpost.com/news/wonk/wp/2017/11/16/Black-men-sentenced-to-more-time-for-committing-the-exact-same-crime-as-a-white-person-study-finds/

Ipas. (August 6, 2020). As sexual violence continues to rise in Nigeria, Ipas and partners advocate for state-level protections. Retrieved on February 24, 2021 from https://www.ipas.org/news/as-sexual-violence-continues-to-rise-in-nigeria-ipas-and-partners-advocate-for-state-level-protections/

Isabirye, S. B. & Mahmoudi, K. M. (2000). Rwanda, Burundi, and their "ethnic" conflicts. *Ethnic Studies Review* 23(1):62–80.

Islam, G. (2014). Social dominance theory. *Encyclopedia of Critical Psychology* 28(1):1779–1781.
Jennings, A. (October 30, 2015). Longtime L.A. civil rights leaders dismayed by the in-your-face tactics of new crop of activists. *Los Angeles Times*. Retrieved on November 4, 2020 from https://www.latimes.com/local/california/la-me-black-lives-matter-20151030-story.html
Johnson, D, Tress T, Burkel, N, Taylor, C. & Cesario, J. (2019). Officer characteristics and racial disparities in fatal officer-involved shootings *PNAS*.116 (32):15877–15882.
Johnson, J. B. & Joslyn, R. A. (1991). *Political Science Research Methods*. Washington, DC: America: Congressional Quarterly Press, Inc.
Johnson-Ahorlu, R. (2012). The academic opportunity gap: How racism and stereotypes disrupt the education of African American undergraduates. *Race Ethnicity and Education* 15(5):633–652.
Juby, H. L. (2005). Racial ambivalence, racial identity and defense mechanisms in white counselor trainees. *Dissertation Abstracts International: Section B: The Sciences and Engineering* 66(5–B):2855.
Kahn, R. (2020). Internet computer network. *Encyclopedia Britannica*. Retrieved on December 24, 2020 from https://www.britannica.com/technology/Internet
Kamaloni, S. (2019). *Understanding Racism in a Post-racial World: Visible Invisibilities*. New York, NY: Palgrave Macmillan.
Kamara, G. (2001). The feminist struggle in the Senegalese novel: Mariama Ba and Sembene Ousmane. *Journal of Black Studies* 32(2):212–228.
Kamaara, E. K. (2012). *(Re)constructing Gender: A Holistic Strategy to Controlling HIV/AIDS in Kenya. Moi University Inaugural Lecture 15 Series No. 2012*. Eldoret, Kenya: Moi University Press.
Karenga, M. (2003). *Maat, The Moral Ideal in Ancient Egypt: A Study in Classical African Ethics*. Los Angeles, CA: The University of Sankore Press; reprinted in 2012 by Routledge, Abingdon-on-Thames, UK and New York, NY.
Kasomo, D. (2009). An investigation of sin and evil in African cosmology. *International Journal of Sociology and Anthropology* 1(8):145–155.
Kauffman, M. E. (2016). Kauffman compilation: Research on race and entrepreneurship. Retrieved on July 31, 2020 from www.kauffman.org
Kellaway, M. & Brydum, S. (January 12, 2016). The 21 trans women killed in 2015. *The Advocate*. Retrieved on January 11, 2020 from http://www.advocate.com/transgender/2015/07/27/
Ketels, C. (July 6, 2020). Black Lives Matter protests under aerial surveillance. Retrieved on January 19, 2021 from https://natoassociation.ca/Black-lives-matter-protests-under-aerial-surveillance/
Kim, C., Losen, D. & Hewitt, D. (2010). *The School-to-Prison Pipeline: Structuring Legal Reform*. New York, NY: New York University Press.
Kim, G. J-S. & Jackson, J. (December 18, 2014). 'I Can't Breathe': Eric Garner's last words symbolize our predicament. *HuffPost*. Retrieved on October 30, 2020 from https://www.huffpost.com/entry/i-cant-breathe-eric-garne_b_6341634
Kinoti, H. W. (2003). The integrity of creation: An African perspective. In Theuri, M. M. & Grace, W. (eds.). *Quests for Integrity in Africa*. Nairobi, Kenya: Acton Publishers.

Kolawole, M. M. (2002). Transcending Incongruities: Rethinking feminism and the dynamics of identity in Africa, *Agenda* 17(54):92–98. Retrieved on February 12, 2021 from https://researchgate.net

Korgen, K., White, J. &White, S. (2013). *Sociologists in Action: Sociology, Social Change, and Social Justice*, 2nd ed. Los Angeles, CA: Sage Publications.

Kövesces, Z. (2006). *Language, Mind and Culture: A Practical Introduction.* Oxford, UK: Oxford University Press.

Krige, J. D. & Krige, E. J. (1954). The Lovedu of Transvaal. In Forde, D. (ed.). *African Worlds: Studies in the Cosmological Ideas and Social Values of African Peoples.* London, UK: Oxford University Press.

Krohn, M. D. & Massey, J. L. (1980). Social control and delinquent behavior: An examination of the elements of the social bond. *Sociological Quarterly* 21(4):529–544. Retrieved on December 15, 2020 from https://www.ojp.gov/ncjrs/virtual-library/abstracts/social-control-and-delinquent-behavior-examination-elements-social

Kula, M. & Stafman, E. (June 14, 2020). We must all work toward justice, righteousness. *Gallatin County Democrats.* Retrieved on January 1, 2021 from https://gallatindemocrats.com/we-must-all-work-toward-justice-righteousness/

Kwasi, G. A. (August 14, 2019). Internet clicktivism. Retrieved on February 24, 2021 from https://www.dandc.eu/en/article/ghanaian-feminists-are-using-social-media-change-public-discourse

Lakoff, G. & Johnson, M. (1980). Conceptual metaphor in everyday language. *The Journal of Philosophy* 77(8):453–486.

Lakoff, G. (1987). *Women, Fire and Dangerous Things: What Categories Reveal about the Human Mind.* Chicago, IL: The University of Chicago Press.

Lakoff, G. & Johnson, M. (2003). *Metaphors We Live By.* Chicago, IL: The University of Chicago Press.

Lanyer, A. Salve Deus Rex Judaeorum*: A poem. Press Books.* Retrieved on January 20. 2021 from https://earlybritishlit.pressbooks.com/chapter/aemilia-lanyar-salve-deus-rex-judaeorum/

Le Masson, V., Benoudji, C., Reyes, S. S. & Bernard, G. (2018). Violence against women and girls and resilience links, impacts and perspectives from the Chadian context working and discussion papers. Retrieved on January 12, 2021 from https://www.odi.org/publications/11026-violence-against-women-and-girls-and-resilience

Leach, C. W. & Allen, A. M. (2017). The social psychology of the Black Lives Matter meme and movement. *Current Directions in Psychological Science* 26(6):543–547.

Leiber, N. (July, 2009). The anatomy of an entrepreneur. *Bloomberg Business Week.* Retrieved on March 18, 2021 from www.BusinessWeek.com/smallbiz/running_small_business/archives/2009/07/anatomy_of_an_e.html

Lerman, A. & Vesla, W. (2014). Staying out of sight? Concentrated policing and local political action. *Annals of the American Academy of Political and Social Science* 651(1):202–219.

Li, T. (2020). The metaphorical expressions of basic color words in English and Chinese. *English Language Teaching* 3(13):84–91.

Liberman, A. M., Kirk, D. S. & KiDuek, K. (2014). Labeling effects of first juvenile arrests: Secondary deviance and secondary sanctioning. *Urban Institute.* Retrieved on December 12, 2020 from https://www.urban.org/sites/default/files/publication/

33701/413274-Labeling-Effects-of-First-Juvenile-Arrests-Secondary-Deviance-and-Secondary-Sanctioning.PDF

Linda, S. & Silvio, W. (2017). *News of Baltimore: Race, Rage and the City.* New York, NY: Routledge Taylor & Francis.

Lindblom, C. E. (1977). *Politics and Markets.* New York, NY: Basic Books.

Lindsey, T. B. (2015). Post-Ferguson: A Herstorical' approach to Black violability. *Feminist Studies* 41(1):232–237.

Loadenthal, M. (2013). Jah People: The culture hybridity of White Rastafarians. Glocalism. *Journal of Culture, Politics and Innovation.* Retrieved on January 3, 2021 from https://glocalismjournal.org/wp-content/uploads/2020/03/loadenthal_gjcpi_2013_1.pdf

Loiaconi, S. (June 15, 2020). As Black Lives Matter donations surge, some want to know where the money goes. *abc6.* Retrieved on November 4, 2020 from https://abc6onyourside.com/news/nation-world/as-black-lives-matter-donations-surge-some-want-to-know-where-the-money-goes

Los Angeles Catholics. (2021). Building a culture of life. Retrieved on January 11, 2021 from https://lacatholics.org/priorities/life/

Lubin, J. (2016). How Sociology can support Black Lives Matter. Retrieved on January 19. 2021 from https://www.asanet.org/news-events/footnotes/dec-2016/features/how-sociology-can-support-Black-lives-matter

Lum, C. & Nagin, D. (2017). Reinventing American criminal justice. *Crime and Justice* 46. Retrieved on October 28, 2020 from https://www.journals.uchicago.edu/doi/10.1086/688462

Lumumba-Kasongo, T. (2017). Contemporary theories of conflict and their social and political implications. In Lumumba-Kasongo, T. & Gahama, J. (eds.). *Peace, Security and Post-Conflict Reconstruction in the Great lake Region of Africa. Dakar.* Senegal: CODESRIA.

Luttrell, C. (2019). *White People and Black Lives Matter: Ignorance, Empathy, and Justice.* New York, NY: Palgrave Macmillan.

M4BL. (2020). Reparations. Retrieved on October 30, 2020 from https://m4bl.org/policy-platforms/reparations/

McCord, S-W. & Crowell, N. A. (eds.) (2001). Juvenile Crime, Juvenile Justice. National Academies of Sciences. *National Academies Press.* Retrieved on December 03, 2020 from https://www.nap.edu/read/9747/chapter/7

MacDonald, J., Stokes, R. J., Ridgeway, G. & Riley, K. J. (2007). Race, neighbourhood context and perceptions of injustice by the police in Cincinnati. *Urban Studies* 44(13):2567–2585.

Maddocks, K. G. (June 26, 2020). What is political science all about? South New Hampshire University. Retrieved on March 9, 2021 from https://www.snhu.edu/about-us/newsroom/2018/08/what-is-political-science

Magesa, L. (1977). *African Religion.* New York, NY: Maryknoll.

Magesa, L. (1997). *African Religion: The Moral Tradition of Abundant Life.* New York, NY: Orbis Books, Maryknoll.

Magonya, A, L. (2017). Cross cultural variations of HIV/AIDS IS DEATH PICTORIAL metaphor. *Linguistics and Literature Studies* 5(5):375–389.

Makaryk, I. R., general editor and compiler. (1993). *Encyclopedia of Contemporary Literary Theory: Approaches, Scholars, Terms*. Toronto, Canada: University of Toronto Press.

Maloney, A. (September 29, 2015). When police turn violent, activists Brittany Packnett and Johnetta Elzie push back. *The New York Times*. Retrieved on October 28, 2020 from https://web.archive.org/web/20161219043331/http://nytlive.nytimes.com/womenintheworld/2015/09/29/when-police-turn-violent-activists-brittany-packnett-and-johnetta-elzie-push-back/

Mark, J. J. (November 14, 2016). Ancient Egyptian literature. *Ancient History Encyclopedia*. Retrieved on January 19, 2021 from https://www.ancient.eu/Egyptian_Literature/

Mårup, E. (2016). Eye to Eye a contrastive view of metaphorical use of Eye in English and Japanese. Center for Language and Literature-Japanese Studies. Lund University, Sweden.

Masolo, D. A. (1994). *African Philosophy in Search of Identity*. Bloomington, IN: Indiana University Press.

MATLAB. (2020). What is MATLAB? *Math Works*. Retrieved on December 26, 2020 from https://www.mathworks.com/discovery/what-is-matlab.html

Maurice, S. C., Phillips, O. R. & Ferguson, C. E. (1986). *Economic Analysis: Theory and Application*. Homewood, IL: Richard D. Irwin, Inc.

May, A. & USA Today. (July 13, 2016). #AllLivesMatter hashtag is racist, critic say. *The Gazette*. Retrieved on November 6, 2020 from https://gazette.com/news/alllivesmatter-hashtag-is-racist-critics-say/article_ce21318a-a6d4-5dbf-b918-6426ed55b95d.html

Mbiti, J. S. (1975). *The Prayers of African Religion*. New York, NY: Orbis Books.

Mbiti, J. S. (1975). *African Religions and Philosophy*, 15: *Introduction to African Religion*, 2nd ed., Nairobi, Kenya: East African Educational Publishers Ltd.

Mbiti, J. S. (1982). *African Religions and Philosophy*. London, UK: Heinemann.

Mbiti, J. S. (1990). *African Religions and Philosophy*, 2nd ed. New York, NY: Heinemann.

Mbiti, J. S. (2012). *Concepts of God in Africa*. Nairobi, Kenya: Acton Publishers.

McCall, A. (2019). Resident assistance, police chief learning, and the persistence of aggressive policing tactics in Black neighborhoods. *Journal of Politics* 81(3):1133–1142.

McCulloch, A. (2020). Global businesses embrace Black Lives Matter movement. Retrieved on July 31, 2020 from https://www.personneltoday.com

McDonald, S. N. (July 14, 2016). President Obama clarifies his definition of 'Black Lives Matter.' *The Undefeated*. Retrieved on November 1, 2020 from https://theundefeated.com/features/president-obamas-clarifies-his-definition-of-black-lives-matter/

McGirt, E. (August 8, 2016). raceAhead: Why Ford Foundation is underwriting Black Lives Matter. *Fortune*. Retrieved on October 30, 2020 from https://fortune.com/2016/08/08/raceahead-why-ford-foundation-is-underwriting-black-lives-matter/

McLeod, S. A. (2019). Social identity theory. *Simply Psychology*. Retrieved on October 7, 2020 from www.simplypsychology.org/social-identity-theory.html

Medie, P. A. (2013). Fighting gender-based violence: The women's movement and the enforcement of rape law in Liberia. *African Affairs* 112(448):377–397. Retrieved on February 24, 2021 from https://doi.org/10.1093/afraf/adt040

Mekoa, I. (2019). How Africa got into a mess: Colonial legacy, underdevelopment, corruption and human rights violations in Africa. *Journal of Reviews on Global Economics* 8:43–52.

Melber, H. (October 29, 2020). #ShutItAllDown in Namibia – the fight against gender-based violence. Retrieved on February 24, 2021 from https://theconversation.com/shutitalldown-in-namibia-the-fight-against-gender-based-violence-148809

Mende, J. (2019). Are human rights western—And why does it matter? A perspective from international political theory. *Journal of International Political Theory*. Retrieved on January 25, 2021 from https://journals.sagepub.com/doi/10.1177/1755088219832992

Merwe, W. J. (1957). *The Shona Idea of God*. Fort Victoria, Zimbabwe: Morgenster Mission Press.

Michalopoulos, S. & Papaioannou, E. (2013). Pre-colonial ethnic institutions and contemporary African development. *Econometrica* 81(1):113–152.

Michalopoulos, S. & Papaioannou, E. (2016). The long-run effects of the scramble for Africa. *American Economic Review* 106(7):1802–1848.

Mills Communication Group. (July 2009). Entrepreneur vs. small business owner: What's the difference? Retrieved on March 19, 2021 from www.millscommgroup.com/blog/2009/06/entrepreneur-vs-small-business-owner-whats-the-difference

Milton, J. (1989). *Paradise Lost*. London, UK: Penguin Classics.

Mofarrej, O. B. & Rabab'ah, G. (2020). Conceptualization of the heart in Jordanian Arabic: A cognitive perspective. *International Journal of Linguistics* 12(4):65–80.

Mogul, J., Ritchie, A. & Whitlock, K. (2011). *Queer Injustice: The Criminalization of LGBT People in the United States*. Boston, MA: Beacon Press.

Mohan, P. (2020). How the end of the white majority could change office dynamics in 2040. Retrieved on March 5, 2021 from https://www.fastcompany.com/90450018/how-the-end-of-the-white-majority-could-change-office-dynamics-in-2040

Moore, R. & Bellamy, J. (December 7, 2020). The Biden Administration must prioritize reversing Trump's damage to racial justice policy. Retrieved on January 4, 2021 from https://www.aclu.org/news/racial-justice/the-biden-administration-must-prioritize-reversing-trumps-damage-to-racial-justice-policy

Morgan, D. (September 21, 2017). Suicide: Every life is sacred. *Focus on the Family*. Retrieved on January 9, 2021 from https://www.focusonthefamily.com/pro-life/suicide-every-life-is-sacred/

Morris, M. (2016). *Pushout: The Criminalization of Black Girls in Schools*. New York, NY: The New Press.

Morrison, O. (November 7, 2018). Jewish tradition frequently stands against the death penalty; synagogue shooter's case may put it to the test. *PaywallProject*. Retrieved on January 1, 2021 from https://www.100daysinappalachia.com/2018/11/jewish-tradition-frequently-stands-against-the-death-penalty-synagogue-shooters-case-may-put-it-to-the-test/

Mosley, T. & Hagan, A. (June 19, 2020). 'An extraordinary moment': Angela Davis says protests recognize long overdue anti-racist work. *WBUR Here and Now*. Retrieved on November 1, 2020 from https://www.wbur.org/hereandnow/2020/06/19/angela-davis-protests-anti-racism

Mudimbe, V. Y. (1994). *Invention of Africa: Gnosis, Philosophy, and the Order of Knowledge*. Bloomington. IN: Indiana University Press.

Mugambi, J. & Kirima, N. (1976). *The African Religious Heritage* (a textbook based on Syllabus 224 of the East African Certificate Education). Nairobi, Kenya: Oxford University Press.

Mugambi, J. N. K. & Magesa, L. (eds.) (1990). *The Church in African Christianity: Innovative Essays in Ecclesiology*. Nairobi, Kenya: Initiatives.

Muluneh, D. M., Stulz, V., Francis, L. & Agho, K. (2020). Gender-based violence against women in Sub-Saharan Africa: A systematic review and meta-analysis of cross-sectional studies. *International Journal of Environment and Public Health*. Retrieved on January 12, 2021 from https://www.mdpi.com/1660-4601/17/3/903

Mummolo, J. (2018). Modern police tactics, police-citizen interactions, and the prospects for reform. *Journal of Politics* 80(1):1–15.

Murphy, G. (2007). E(a)vesdropping in *Paradise Lost*: Knowledge and disobedience. MA Thesis, Acadia University. Library and Archives Canada.

National Center for Education Statistics. (2019). Condition of education: Students with disabilities. Institute of Education Sciences. Retrieved on December 13, 2020 from https://nces.ed.gov/programs/coe/indicator_cgg.asp?referer=raceindicators

National Center for Education Statistics. (2019). Status and trends in the education of racial and ethnic groups. Institute of Education Sciences. Retrieved on December 15, 2020 from https://nces.ed.gov/programs/raceindicators/indicator_RDA.asp

National Institute of Health. (2020). Black Lives Matter and the Hatch Act. U.S. Office of Special Counsel. Retrieved on November 20, 2020 from https://www.training.nih.gov/assets/Black_Lives_Matter_Opinion.pdf

National Juvenile Justice Network. (2012). Using adolescent brain research to inform policy: A guide for juvenile justice advocates. Retrieved on December 19, 2020 from http://www.njjn.org/uploads/digital-library/Brain-Development-Policy-Paper_Updated_FINAL-9-27-12.pdf

National Reentry Resource Center. (2017). Collateral consequences of a juvenile adjudication: How juvenile records can affect youth even after the case is over. Retrieved on December 12, 2020 from https://nationalreentryresourcecenter.org/

National Research Council and Institute of Medicine. (2000). Education and delinquency: Summary of a workshop. *National Academy of Sciences*. Retrieved on December 10, 2020 from https://www.nap.edu/read/9972/chapter/1

Negro, I. (2019). Metaphor and metonymy in food idioms. *Languages* 4(3):2–8.

Nell Edgar, A. & Johnson, A. (2019). *The Struggle Over Black Lives Matter and All Lives Matter*. Lanham, MD: Lexington Books.

New World Wealth. (2018). The AfrAsia Bank: Africa wealth report. Retrieved on February 18, 2021 from https://enterprise.press/wp-content/uploads/2018/09/africa-wealth-report-2018.pdf

Newman, B. M. & Newman, P. R. (2017). *Development through Life: A Psychological Approach*, 13th ed. Homewood, IL: The Dorsey Press.

Nguyen-Phuong-Mai, M. (2017). *Intercultural Communication: An Interdisciplinary Approach: When Neurons, Genes and Evolution Joined the Discourse*. Amsterdam, The Netherlands: Amsterdam University Press.

Niemeier, S. (2003). Straight from the heart: Metonymic and metaphorical explorations. In Barcelona, A. (ed.). *Metaphor and Metonymy at Crossroads: A Cognitive Perspective*. Berlin, Germany: Mouton de Gruyter.

Nitisha. (n.d). Behaviouralism in politics: Definition, origin and credo. *Political Science*. Retrieved on March 8, 2021 from https://www.politicalsciencenotes.com/behaviouralism/behaviouralism-in-politics-definition-origin-and-credo/717

Nkealah, N. (2006). Conceptualizing feminism(s) in Africa: The challenges facing African women writers and critics. *English Academy Review*:133–141. Retrieved on February 16, 2021 from https://www.researchgate.net/publication/232977377_Conceptualizing_feminisms_in_Africa_The_challenges_facing_African_women_writers_and_critics

Noam, G., Warner, L. & Dyken, L. (2001). Beyond the rhetoric of zero tolerance: Long-term solutions for at-risk youth. *New Directions for Youth Development* 92:155–182.

Norton, W. (2009). Racial inequality in contemporary American society. Retrieved on July 31, 2020 from https://www.ssc.wisc.edu/~wright/ContemporaryAmericanSociety/Chapter%2014%20--%20Racial%20inequality--Norton%20August.pdf

Notre Dame High School in San Jose, California (NDHSSJC). (April 18, 2019). Celebrating holy week. Retrieved on January 9, 2021 from https://www.ndsj.org/news-events/news/1657940/celebrating-holy-week

Nyerere, J. K. (1971). *Ujamaa: The Basis of African Socialism*. Dar es Salaam, Tanzania: Jihad Productions.

Nyerere, J. K. (1976). *Socialism and Rural Development*. Dar es Salaam, Tanzania: Government Printer.

Obia, V. A. (November 11, 2020). ENDSARS, a unique Twittersphere and social media regulation in Nigeria. Retrieved on February 26, 2021 from https://blogs.lse.ac.uk/medialse/2020/11/11/endsars-a-unique-twittersphere-and-social-media-regulation-in-nigeria/

Ocen, P. (2012). Punishing pregnancy: Race, incarceration, and the shackling of pregnant prisoners. *California Law Review* 100(5):1239–1311.

Ocheni, S. & Nwankwo, B. C. (2012). Analysis of colonialism and its impact in Africa. *Cross-Cultural Communication* 8(3):46–54.

O'Donovan, W. (1996). *Biblical Christianity in African Perspective*. Carlisle, PA: Paternoster.

Oduah, C. (December 9, 2020). Rest of the world. The revolution will be hashtagged. Retrieved on February 25, 2021 from https://restofworld.org/2020/the-revolution-will-be-hashtagged/

Ogot, B. A. (1986). *Kenya before 1900*. Nairobi, Kenya: East African Publishing House.

Ogundipe-Leslie, O. (1983). African women, culture and another development. *Journal of African Marxist* 5:77–92.

Okechi, O. S. (2018). The indigenous concept of sexuality in African tradition and globalization. *Global Journal of Reproductive Medicine* 6(1):1–5. Retrieved on March 2, 2021 from https://www.researchgate.net/publication/328192431_Glob alization_and_the_Indigenous_Concept_of_Sexuality_in_African_Tradition_Char ting_a_New_Course_for_Sexual_Right_and_Safe_Society

Olanrewaju, A. (December 9, 2020). In the wake of tumultuous #EndSARS demonstrations, Nigerian artists tell a story of hope and determination through photos— *CNN Style*. Retrieved on 12 December 2020 from https://edition.cnn.com/style/ article/new-nigeria-studios-end-sars-protest-photo-exhibit/index.html

Olaoluwa, A. (December 1, 2020). EndSars protests: The Nigerian women leading the fight for change. *BBC News 2020*. Retrieved on February 20, 2021 from https:// www.bbc.com/news/world-africa-55104025

Omare, S. G. (2015). *Witchcraft Scapegoat: Abagusii Beliefs and Violence against 'Witches.'* Saarbrücken, Germany: Lambert Academic Publishing.

Oneworldnationsonline. (n.d). Rwanda. Retrieved on February 27, 2021 from https:// www.nationsonline.org/oneworld/rwanda.htm#:~:text=Population%3A%2011.5 %20million%20(2016%3B,1.7%25%20claim%20no%20religious%20beliefs.

Onyeani, C. (2012). *Capitalist Nigger: The Road to Success, A Spider Web Doctrine.* London, UK: Timbuktu Publishers.

Opoku, K. A. (1978). *West African Traditional Religion.* Islamabad, Pakistan: FEP International Private Limited.

Orange County Register. (May 13, 2006). Healthcare not only for privileged. *The Orange County Register*. Retrieved on January 9, 2021 from https://www.ocregist er.com/2006/05/13/health-care-not-only-for-privileged/

Page, G. (July 2, 2020). "All Lives Matter," niece of MLK tells VT radio audience. *The Newport Daily Express*. Retrieved on November 1, 2020 from https://newport vermontdailyexpress.com/content/all-lives-matter-niece-mlk-tells-vt-radio-au dience

Pager, D. (2003). The mark of a criminal record. *Harvard University*. Retrieved on December 18, 2020 from https://scholar.harvard.edu/files/pager/files/pager_ajs.pdf

Parker, K., Horowitz, J. M. & Anderson, M. (June 12, 2020). Majorities across racial, ethnic groups express support for the Black Lives Matter Movement. *Pew Research Center's Social and Demographic Trends Project*. Retrieved on October 28, 2020 from https://www.pewsocialtrends.org/2020/06/12/amid-protests-majoriti es-across-racial-and-ethnic-groups-express-support-for-the-black-lives-matter- movement/

Parrinder, E. G. (1970). *African Traditional Religion*. Boulder, CO: Greenwood Press.

Participedia. (2020). All Lives Matter. Retrieved on October 29, 2020 from https:// participedia.net/case/5563

Pennock, R. J. & Smith, D. G. (1964). *Political Science: An Introduction*. New York, NY: The Macmillan Company.

Pereira, L. M. (2014). Intercultural exodus: From Jamaica to the world. *Centro de Estudos Interculturais.* Retrieved on December 3, 2020 from https://core.ac.uk/download/pdf/47142906.pdf

Perrine, L. (1993). *Literature: Structure, Sound, and Sense*, 6th ed. San Diego, CA: Harcourt Brace Jovanovich College Publishers.

Petersen-Smith, K. (2015). Black Lives Matter. *International Socialist Review* 96. Retrieved on March 15, 2021 from https://isreview.org/issue/96/black-lives-matter

Pew Research Center. (2016). On views of race and inequality, Blacks and Whites are worlds apart: About four-in-ten Blacks are doubtful that the U.S. will ever achieve racial equality. Retrieved on December 12, 2020 from https://www.pewresearch.org/social-trends/2016/06/27/on-views-of-race-and-inequality-blacks-and-whites-are-worlds-apart/

Pfarrer, M. (2020). Content analysis. Resource by the Department of Management at the Terry College of Business, University of Georgia. Retrieved on December 28, 2020 from https://www.terry.uga.edu/contentanalysis/index.php

Phelps, M. S. (2011). Rehabilitation in the Punitive Era: The Gap between Rhetoric and Reality in U.S. Prison Programs. National Institutes of Health. National Center for Biotechnology Information. *U.S. National Library of Medicine.* Retrieved on December 18, 2020 from https://www.ncbi.nlm.nih.gov/pmc/articles/PMC3762476/

PolicyLink. (April 2019). How companies can advance racial equity and create business growth. Retrieved on July 31, 2020 from https://www.policylink.org/

Pondy, L. R. (1967). Organizational conflict: Concepts and models. *Administrative Science Quarterly* 12:296–320.

Pratto, F., Sidanius, J. & Levin, S. (2006). Social dominance theory and the dynamics of intergroup relations: Taking stock and looking forward. *European Review of Social Psychology* 17(1):271–320.

Price, J. & Payton, E. (2017). Implicit racial bias and police use of lethal force: Justifiable homicide or potential discrimination? *Journal of African American Studies* 21(4):674–683.

Prilleltensky, I. & Fox, D. (1997). Introducing critical psychology: Values, assumptions, and the status quo. In Fox, D. & Prilleltensky, I. (eds.). *Critical Psychology: An Introduction.* Thousand Oaks, CA: Sage Publications.

Qiang, H. (2011). The study of the metaphor "Red" in the Chinese Culture. *American International Journal of Contemporary Research* 1(3):99–102.

QuickMBA. (2010). A definition of entrepreneurship. Retrieved on March 18, 2021 from http://www.quickmba.com/entre/definition/

Radice, J. (2018). The juvenile record myth. *The Georgetown Law Journal.* Retrieved on December 12, 2020 from https://www.law.georgetown.edu/georgetown-law-journal/wp-content/uploads/sites/26/2018/02/zt100218000365.pdf

Ralph, R. O. & Corrigan, P. W. (2005). *Recovery in Mental Illness: Broadening Our Understanding of Wellness.* Washington, DC: American Psychological Association.

Rasmussen Reports. (August 20, 2015). Black Lives Matter or All Lives Matter? *Rasmussen Reports.* Retrieved on October 29, 2020 from https://www.rasmusse

nreports.com/public_content/politics/general_politics/august_2015/black_lives_matter_or_all_lives_matter

Ray, R. (2020). Setting the record straight on the Movement for Black Lives. *Ethnic and Racial Studies* 3(8): 1–9.

Rasekh, E. & Ghafel, B. (2011). Basic colors and their metaphoric expressions in English and Persian. In the proceedings of the first *International Conference on Foreign Language Teaching and Applied Linguistics*. 211–224.

Rattansi, A. (2007). *Racism: A Very short Introduction*. Oxford, UK: Oxford University Press.

Remster, B. & Kramer, R. (2018). Race, space, and surveillance: Understanding the relationship between criminal justice contact and institutional involvement. *Sociological Research for a Dynamic World* 4:1–16.

Republic of Namibia Ministry of Gender Equality and Child Welfare. (2012–2016). National plan of action on gender-based violence. Retrieved on February 28, 2021 from www.undp.org.dam.docs

Reuters. (August 2, 2016).Slavery reparations sought in first Black Lives Matter agenda. *Reuters*. Retrieved on October 30, 2020 from https://www.reuters.com/article/us-usa-politics-race-idUSKCN10C3E1

Reynolds, L. G. (1985). *Macroeconomics: Analysis and Policy*. Homewood, IL: Richard D. Irwin, Inc.

Richardson, S. (2020). What is Easter: Understanding the history and symbols. Retrieved on January 11, 2021 from http://www.crosswalk.com/faith/spiritual-life/understanding-the-history-and-symbol-of-easter-1256039.html

Richmond, Y. & Gestrin, P. (1988). *Into Africa: Intercultural Insights*. Boston, MA: Nicholas Brealey Publishing.

Riddle, T. & Sinclair, S. (2019). Racial disparities in school-based disciplinary actions are associated with county-level rates of racial bias. Retrieved on December 15, 2020 from https://www.pnas.org/content/116/17/8255/tab-figures-data

Roberts, J. (January 24, 2011). How western environmental policies are stunting economic growth in developing countries. *The Heritage Foundation*. Retrieved on February 13 from https://www.heritage.org/global-politics/report/how-western-environmental-policies-are-stunting-economic-growth-developing

Routley, N. (January 12, 2018). Map: All of the world's borders by age. Retrieved on February 22, 2021 from https://www.visualcapitalist.com/map-worlds-borders-by-age/

Ruane, J. M. (2017). Re(searching) the truth about our criminal justice system: Some challenges. *Sociological Forum* 32:1127–1139.

Ruffin II, H. G. (2020). Working together to survive and thrive: The struggle for Black lives past and present. *Leadership* 17(1):1–15.

Sakpa, D. (September 7, 2020). In Africa, concerns rising over police brutality. Retrieved on December 11, 2020 from www.dw.com/en/in-africa-concerns-over-rising-police-brutality/a-54845922

Salami, M. (September 2018). Feminism in Nigeria – By and for who? Retrieved on February 15, 2021 from https://www.zeitschrift-luxemburg.de/feminism-in-nigeria-by-and-for-who/

Salomon, H. (February 24, 2015). Exclusive: Erica Garner slams "Fraudulent Claims" in O'Keefe video, announces foundation. *NewsOne*. Retrieved on October 26, 2020 from https://newsone.com/3093518/erica-garner-sharpton/

Salter, P. S., Adams, G. & Perez, M. J. (2018). Racism in the structure of everyday worlds: A cultural-psychological perspective. *Current Directions in Psychological Science* 27(3):150–155.

Samuelson, P. A. & Nordhaus, W. (2010). *Economics*, 19th ed. New York, NY: McGraw-Hill Book Company.

Sānchez, T. M. (2012). Grasping metaphor and metonymic processes in Terminology. *Journal of Specialised Translation* 18:1–19.

Sawyer, J. & Gampa, A. (2018). Implicit and explicit racial attitudes changed during Black Lives Matter. *Personality & Social Psychology Bulletin* 44(7):1039–1059.

Saxena, N. (2011). Political science: A conceptual analysis. *The Indian Journal of Political Science* 129–134.

Schmidt, S. M. & Kochan, T. A. (1972). Conflict: Toward conceptual clarity. *Administrative Science Quarterly* 17:359–371.

Schwartz, R. (2020). Issues in Jewish ethics: The Jewish response to hunger. *Jewish Virtual Library*. Retrieved on January 1, 2021 from https://www.jewishvirtuallibrary.org/the-jewish-response-to-hunger

Scott, E. (September 3, 2015). Tim Scott defends use of 'all lives matter.' *CNN Politics*. Retrieved on November 3, 2020 from https://www.cnn.com/2015/09/03/politics/tim-scott-all-lives-matter/index.html

Scott, M. S. (2009). Progress in American policing? Reviewing the national reviews. *Law & Social Inquiry* 34(1):169–185.

Seery, E. & Caistor, A. A. (2014). Even it up: Time to end extreme inequality. *Oxfam*. Retrieved on February 28, 2021 from http://policy-practice.oxfam.org.uk/publications/even-it-up-time-to-end-extreme-inequality-333012

Senghor, L. S. (1959). *African Socialism*. New York, NY: Mercer Cook.

Shantel, B., Cassi, C., San, G., Onoso, I., Verna, K., Hadi, K., Catherine, L., Sarah, M., Victor, R. & Wendy, R. (2020). Systemic anti-Black racism must be dismantled: Statement by the American Sociological Association Section on Racial and Ethnic Minorities. *Sociology of Race and Ethnicity* 6(3):289–291.

Shebesta, P. I. (1936). *My Pygmy and Negro Hosts*. London, UK: Hutchinson and Company.

Sherfinski, D. (October 15, 2015). Ben Carson: Of course all lives matter—and all lives include Black lives. *The Washington Times*. Retrieved on November 2, 2020 from https://www.washingtontimes.com/news/2015/oct/15/ben-carson-course-all-lives-matter-and-all-lives-i/

Shiffman, K. (n.d.). Scream bloody murder. *CNN*. Retrieved on March 9, 2021 from https://edition.cnn.com/2008/WORLD/africa/11/13/sbm.dallaire.profile/

Shulman, S. W. (2004). The Internet still might (but probably won't) change everything. *Journal of Law and Policy* 1(1). Retrieved on February 24, 2021 from https://core.ac.uk/download/pdf/159565779.pdf

Silverman, R. M. (2000). *Doing Business in Minority Markets: Black and Korean Entrepreneurs in Chicago's Ethnic Beauty Aids Industry.* New York, NY: Garland Publishing, Inc.

Simmons, K. C. (1998). The politics of policing: Ensuring stakeholder collaboration in the federal reform of local law enforcement agencies. *The Journal of Criminal Law & Criminology* 98(2):489–546.

Simmons-Horton, S. (2020). Ending anti-Black racism in child welfare and juvenile justice systems. *University of Texas at San Antonio.* Retrieved on December 03, 2020 from https://www.utsa.edu/today/2020/07/story/ending-anti-black-racism.html

Simonson, J. (November 16, 2020). Police reform through a power lens. *Social Science Research Network.* Retrieved on January 15, 2021 from https://ssrn.com/abstracts=3731173

Sisay, H. (2012). Ode to my cultural heritage: A poem. Retrieved on February 21, 2021 from http://thepatrioticvanguard.com/ode-to-my-cultural-heritage

Škara, D. (2004). Reading the body in contemporary culture. *Coll Arthropol* 28(1):183–189.

Skiba, R. (2014). The failure of zero tolerance. *Reclaiming Children and Youth* 22(4):27–33.

Smith, E. & Dale, A. M. (1920). *The Illa-Speaking Peoples of Northern Rhodesia.* London, UK: Macmillan.

Solotaro, L. J. & Pande, P. R. (2014). Violence Against Women and Girls: Lessons from South Asia. World Bank, Washington, DC, ISBN 978-1-4648-0171-6. Retrieved on January 12, 2021 from https://openknowledge.worldbank.org/handle/10986/20153

Southern Poverty Law Center. (2016). White Lives Matter. Retrieved on August 21, 2020 from https://www.splcenter.org/fighting-hate/extremist-files/group/white-lives-matter

Soyinka, W. (1963). *The Lion and the Jewel.* Oxford, UK: Oxford University Press.

St. Joseph Catholic Church of Youngstown, Ohio (SJCCYO). (2021). Respect life. Retrieved on January 9, 2021 from https://stjosephmantua.com/respect-life

Steinvall, A. (2007). 'Colors and Emotions.' In MacLaury, R., Paramei, G. & Dedrick, D. (eds.). *Anthropology of Color: Interdisciplinary Multilevel Modeling.* Amsterdam, The Netherlands: John Benjamins Publishers.

Steven, F. (1988). Explaining and blaming: Racism and sociology. *Patterns of Prejudice* 22(1):21–30.

Strong, K. (December 21, 2017). Do African lives matter to Black Lives Matter? Youth uprisings and the borders of solidarity. Retrieved on December 25, 2020 from www.doi.org/10.1177/0042085917747097

Strutton, F. (1994). *Contemporary African Literature and the Politics of Gender.* New York, NY: Routledge.

Sullivan, T. M. (2006). Small business by the numbers. *National Small Business Administration.* Retrieved on March 18, 2011 from www.nsba.biz/docs/bythenumbers.pdf

Swan, T. (2009). Metaphors of body and mind in the history of English. *English Studies* 90(4):460–475.

Swartz, O. (2019). The struggle over Black Lives Matter and All Lives Matter. *Rhetoric Review* 38(4):489–492.

Tabak, R. (1986). The death of fairness: The arbitrary and capricious imposition of the death penalty in the 1980s. *Review of Law & Social Change* 14(4):797–848.

Taibbi, M. (2017). *I Can't Breathe: A Killing on Bay Street*. New York, NY: Spiegel and Grau.

Tajfel, H. (1970). Experiments in intergroup discrimination. *Scientific American* 223:96–102.

Tajfel, H. (1978). The achievement of inter-group differentiation. In Tajfel, H. (ed.). *Differentiation between Social Groups*. London, UK: Academic Press.

Tajfel, H. & Turner, J. C. (1979). An integrative theory of inter-group conflict. In Austin, W. G. & Worchel, S. (eds.). *The Social Psychology of Inter-group Relations*. Monterey, CA: Brooks/Cole.

Tawa, J., Ma, R. & Katsumoto, S. (2016). "All Lives Matter": The cost of color-blind racial attitudes in diverse social networks. *Race and Social Problems* 8(2):196–208.

Temple Kol Ami. (2021). Life cycle events. Retrieves on January 8, 2021 from https://www.tkolami.org/prayerritual/life-cycle-events/

Terborg, P. R. (1995). Through an African feminist theoretical lens: Viewing Caribbean women's history cross-culturally. In Sheperd, V., Brereton, B. & Bailey, B. (eds.). *Engendering History: Caribbean Women in Historical Perspective*. Retrieved on February 22, 2021 from https://link.springer.com/chapter/10.1007/978-1-137-07302-0_1

Terrell, K. (August 1, 2016). Black Lives Matter releases policy demands, includes reparations and abolishing the death penalty. *HelloBeautiful*. Retrieved on October 30, 2020 from https://hellobeautiful.com/2891207/black-lives-matter-releases-demands/

The Civil Rights Project, Advancement Project. (June 01, 2000). Opportunities suspended: The devastating consequences of zero tolerance and school discipline policies. Retrieved on January 4, 2021 from https://www.civilrightsproject.ucla.edu/research/k-12-education/school-discipline/opportunities-suspended-the-devastating-consequences-of-zero-tolerance-and-school-discipline-policies

The Guardian. (June 9, 2013). Edward Snowden: The whistle-blower behind the NSA surveillance revelations. Retrieved on January 16, 2021 from https://www.theguardian.com/world/2013/jun/09/edward-snowden-nsa-whistleblower-surveillance

The Guardian. (September 5, 2019). Thousands protest in South Africa over rising violence against women. Retrieved on February 24, 2021 from https://www.theguardian.com/world/2019/sep/05/thousands-protest-in-south-africa-over-rising-violence-against-women

The National News. (2021). Transcript: President Joe Biden's inauguration speech in full. Retrieved on January 24, 2021 from www.thenationalnews.com/world/the-americas/transcript-president-joe-biden-s-inauguration-speech-in-full

The Rachel Maddow Show. (August 10, 2015). Black Lives Matter builds power through protest. Retrieved on October 30, 2020 from https://www.msnbc.com/rachel-maddow/watch/-black-lives-matter--presses-equality-demands-501828675508

Thomas, D. & Zuckerman, A. (2018). Black Lives Matter in community psychology. *Community Psychology in Global Perspective* 4(2):1–10.

Thompson, C. (June 17, 2020). Abolish the (Tone) Police. Retrieved on January 12, 2020 from https://540westmain.org/2020/06/17/abolish-the-tone-police-by-chris-thompson/

Thompson, N. J., McGee, R. E. & Mays, D. (2012). Race, ethnicity, substance use, and unwanted sexual intercourse among adolescent females in the United States. *The Western Journal of Emergency Medicine* 13(3):283–288.

Thornhill, T. (2019). We want Black students, just not you: How White admissions counselors screen Black prospective students. *Sociology of Race and Ethnicity* 5(4):456–470.

Tucker, B. & Hegg, S. (October 22, 2015). Tactics of Black Lives Matter. IN Close. Episode 216. KCTS-TV. Archived from the original on November 2, 2015. Retrieved on October 30, 2020 from https://web.archive.org/web/20151102024356/http://kcts9.org/programs/in-close/tactics-black-lives-matter

Tutu, D. (1999). *No Future Without Forgiveness.* New York, NY: Image Books.

Uhlmann, T. (1978). Black elite decision making: The case of trial judges. *American Journal of Political Science* 22:884–895.

Umamaheswar, J. (2020). Policing and racial (in)justice in the media: Newspaper portrayals of the 'Black Lives Matter' movement. *Civic Sociology* 1(1):1–13.

United Nations. (1948). Universal declaration of human rights. Retrieved on January 7, 2021 from https://www.un.org/en/universal-declaration-human-rights/

United Nations Educational, Scientific and Cultural Organization (UNESCO). (2003). UNESCO's gender mainstreaming implementation framework baseline definitions of key concepts and terms. Retrieved on March 2, 2021 from http://www.unesco.org/new/fileadmin/MULTIMEDIA/HQ/BSP/GENDER/PDF/1.%20Baseline%20Definitions%20of%20key%20gender-related%20concepts.pdf

United Nations International Children Emergency Fund (UNICEF). (2018). Child marriage in West and Central Africa at a Glance. Retrieved on February 22, 2021 from https://www.unicef.org/wca/media/2596/file#:~:text=The%20prevalence%20of%20child%20marriage

United Nations Office of the High Commissioner for Human Rights (UNOHCHR). (2001). Gender dimensions of racial discrimination. Retrieved on January 12, 2021 from https://digitallibrary.un.org

United Nations (UN) Women. (2002). Gender mainstreaming: An overview. United Nations, New York, 2002. Retrieved on March 2, 2021 from https://www.un.org/womenwatch/osagi/conceptsandefinitions.htm

United Nations (UN) Women (December 2020). In focus: 16 days of activism against gender-based violence. Retrieved on February 12, 2021 from https://www.unwomen.org/en/news/in-focus/end-violence-against-women

United States Census Bureau. (March 2021). Business formation statistics by state. Retrieved on March 18, 2021 from https://www.census.gov/library/visualizations/interactive/bfs-by-state.html

United States Department of Education Office for Civil Rights. (2014). Civil rights data collection data snapshot: School discipline. Retrieved on January 15, 2021 from https://eric.ed.gov/?q=source%3A%22Office+for+Civil+Rights%2C+US+Department+of+Education%22&id=ED577231

United States Department of Justice—USDOJ. (March 4, 2015). Department of justice report regarding the criminal investigation into the shooting death of Michael Brown by Ferguson, Missouri Police Officer Darren Wilson. Retrieved on October 30, 2020 from https://www.justice.gov/sites/default/files/opa/press-releases/attachments/2015/03/04/doj_report_on_shooting_of_michael_brown_1.pdf

United States Department of Justice. (2020). Criminal resource manual. U.S. Department of Justice Archives. Retrieved on November 08, 2020 from https://www.justice.gov/archives/jm/criminal-resource-manual

United States Department of Justice. (July 2020). Office of Juvenile Justice and Delinquency Prevention. 2019 annual report. Retrieved on January 18, 2021 from https://www.ojjdp.ojp.gov/sites/g/files/xyckuh176/files/media/document/253179.pdf

United States Department of Justice. (July 2020). Office of Juvenile Justice and Delinquency. OJJDP Fiscal Year 2020 Awards at a Glance. Retrieved on January 18, 2021 from https://ojjdp.ojp.gov/publications/fy-2020-awards.pdf

United States Department of Justice. Office of Juvenile Justice and Delinquency Prevention. (2020). OJJDP News @ a glance. Retrieved on January 18, 2021 from https://ojjdp.ojp.gov/newsletter/ojjdp-news-glance-novemberdecember-2020/top-story-ojjdp-awards-nearly-370-million-fiscal-year-2020-grants#:~:text=from%20the%20Administrator-,Top%20Story%3A%20OJJDP%20Awards%20Nearly%20%24370%20Million%20in%20Fiscal%20Year,productive%2C%20crime-free%20lives

United States Department of Justice. Office of Juvenile Justice and Delinquency Prevention. Office of Justice Programs. (2019). Juvenile Justice and Delinquency Prevention Act Reauthorization 2018. Retrieved on January 18, 2021 from https://ojjdp.ojp.gov/sites/g/files/xyckuh176/files/media/document/jjdpa-as-amended_0.pdf

United States Federal Bureau of Investigation—FBI. (2020). 2016 crime in the United States. Retrieved on November 5, 2020 from https://ucr.fbi.gov/crime-in-the-u.s/2016/crime-in-the-u.s.-2016/tables/expanded-homicide-data-table-3.xls

U.S. News & World Reports. (August 1963). A Negro businessman speaks his mind. *U.S. News & World Reports* 58.

Utsey, S. & Gernat, A. (2002). White racial identity attitudes and the ego defense mechanisms used by White counselor trainees in racially provocative counseling situations. *Journal of Counseling & Development* 80(4): 475–483.

van Dijk, T. (1987). *Communicating Racism: Ethnic Prejudice in Thought and Talk*. London, UK: Sage publications.

van Dijk, T. (1993a). *Elite Discourse and Racism*. Center of Discourse Studies, Madrid, Spain: Sage Publications.

van Dijk, T. (1993b). Political discourse and racism. Describing others in Western parliament. In Riggins, S. H. (ed.). *The Language and Politics of Exclusion: Others in Discourse*. Thousand Oaks, CA: Sage Publishers.

van Dijk, T. (ed.) (1997). *Discourse Studies: A Multidisciplinary Introduction.* London, UK: Sage Publishers.
van Dijk, T. (2001). Critical discourse analysis. In Schiffin, D., Tannen, D. & Heidi, E. (eds.). *The Handbook of Discourse.* Boston, MA: Blackwell Publishers.
van Dijk, T. (2005). *Racism and Discourse in Spain and Latin America.* Amsterdam, The Netherlands: John Benjamin Publishers.
Villemez, W. J. & Beggs, J. J. (1984). Black capitalism and Black inequality: Some sociological considerations. *Social Forces* 63(1):117–144.
Voisin, D. R., Kim, D., Takahashi, L., Morotta, P. & Bocanegra, K. (2017). Involvement in the Juvenile Justice System for African American adolescents: Examining associations with behavioral health problems. National Institutes of Health. National Center for Biotechnology Information. U.S. National Library of Medicine. Retrieved on December 17, 2020 from https://www.ncbi.nlm.nih.gov/pmc/articles/PMC5616175/
Vote Smart. (2016). Black Lives Matter and/or All Lives Matter? *Vote Smart.* Retrieved on January 18, 2021 from https://votesmart.org/blog-archive/2016/nov/14/black-lives-matter-andor-all-lives-matter/#.YD62qNWSnhn
Wagner, G. (1954). The Abaluyia of Kavirondo. In Forde, D. (ed.). *Africa Worlds: Studies in the Cosmological and Social Values of African Peoples.* London, UK: Oxford University Press.
Wallis, A. (2006). Rwanda rift in La Francafrique. *Open Democracy.* Retrieved on February 27, 2021 from https://www.opendemocracy.net/en/rwanda_france_4183jsp/
Wang, C. (2015). Symbolism of colors and color meanings around the world. Retrieved on July 2, 2020 from https://colourofcity.files.wordpress.com/2018/03/symbolism-of-colors-and-color-meanings-around-the-world.pdf
Ward, J. (2013). Violence against women in conflict, post-conflict and emergency settings. *UN Women.* Retrieved on February 22, 2021 from https://www.endvawnow.org/uploads/modules/pdf/1405612658.pdf
Watson, A. (January 13, 2020). Leading ad supported broadcast and cable networks in the United States in 2019, by average number of viewers. *Statista.* Retrieved on December 28, 2020 from https://www.statista.com/statistics/530119/tv-networks-viewers-usa/
Watson-Singleton, N. N., Mekawi, Y., Wilkins, K. V. & Jatta, I. F. (2021). Racism's effect on depressive symptoms: Examining perseverative cognition and Black Lives Matter activism as moderators. *Journal of Counseling Psychology* 68(1):27–37.
Weisberg, H. F. (1986). *Political Science: The Science of Politics.* New York, NY: Agathon Company.
Weissinger, S., Mack, D. & Watson, E. (2017). *Violence against Black Bodies: An Intersectional Analysis of How Black Lives Continue to Matter.* New York, NY: Routledge Taylor and Francis Group.
Williams, E. J. (2003). Structuring in community policing: Institutionalizing innovative change. *Police Practice & Research* 4(2):119–129.
Wilson, D. B. Wilson, Olaghere, A. & Kimbrell, C. S. (2017). Effectiveness of restorative justice principles in juvenile justice: A meta-analysis. U.S. Department of

Justice. Resource funded by Department of Criminology, Law and Society George Mason University. Retrieved on December 17, 2020 from https://www.ojp.gov/pdffiles1/ojjdp/grants/250872.pdf

Wimmer, A. (2004). Toward a new realism. *Facing Ethnic Conflicts: Toward a New Realism* vii:333–359.

Wiredu, K. (2004). Truth and an African language. In Brown, L. M. (ed.). *African Philosophy: New and Traditional Perspectives*. New York, NY: Oxford University Press.

Wodak, R. & Reisigil, M. (2001). Discourse and racism. In Schiffrin, D., Tannen, D. & Hamillton, H. (eds.). *Handbook of Discourse Analysis*. Boston, MA: Blackwell Publishers.

Wogu, I. A. P. (2013). Behaviouralism as an approach to contemporary political analysis: An appraisal. *International Journal of Education and Research* 1(12):1–12.

World Economic Forum (WEF). (2020). Global gender gap report 2020. Retrieved on February 12, 2021 from http://www3.weforum.org/docs/WEF_GGGR_2020.pdf

World Health Organization (WHO). (2004). *Promoting Mental Health: Concepts, Emerging Evidence, Practice* (Summary Report). Geneva, Switzerland: WHO Publications.

World Health Organization (WHO). (2013). Global and regional estimates of violence against women: Prevalence and health effects of intimate partner violence and non-partner sexual violence. Retrieved on February 12, 2021 from https://apps.who.int/iris/bitstream/handle/10665/85239/9789241564625_eng.pdf;jsessionid=26C5EE024F9574130FAC506880560355?sequence=1

World Health Organization (WHO). (2021). Sexual health. Retrieved on March 3, 2021 from https://www.who.int/health-topics/sexual-health#tab=tab_2

Worldometer. (February 27, 2021). Rwanda population (LIVE). Retrieved on February 27, 2021 from https://www.worldometers.info/world-population/rwanda-population/

Worley, W. (April 2, 2016). Kenyan Muslim man who died protecting Christians in terror attack awarded top honour. *Independent*. Retrieved on January 9, 2021 from https://www.independent.co.uk/news/world/africa/kenyan-muslim-man-who-died-protecting-christians-terror-attack-awarded-top-honour-a6964936.html

Yew, L. K. (2000). *From Third World to First World: Singapore Story (1965–2000)*. New York, NY: Harper Publishing.

Yu, Hui-Chich. (2014). A cross-cultural analysis of symbolic meanings of color. *Chang Gang Journal of Humanities and Social Sciences* 7(1):49–74.

Zimring, F. E. (2020). Police killings as a problem of governance. *The Annals of the American Academy* 687:114–123.

Index

Abrahamic faiths, xiv, 45, 299, 301, 315
Achebe, Chinua, 33, 49–50, 65
Adam and Eve, 4, 45, 185
Afghanistan, 176
African Charter on the Rights of Women in Africa, 174
African Union, 248, 316
American Broadcasting Company (ABC), 69–70
American Dream, 303
American Psychological Association (APA), 199, 284–85, 291–92
Amnesty International, 164, 174–75
Ancient Kemet/Egypt, xiv, 42, 182, 185, 299–300
Angola, 262
Aquinas, Thomas, 19
Aristotle, 252
Armed Conflict Location & Event Data Project, 248
Asian American, 190, 313
Australia, 2, 318

Bâ, Mariama, 55–58
Bantu, 25
behavioral approach, 200, 253
bivariate, xi, 62–63, 68, 70
black capitalism, 191, 193, 195
Black Codes, 291

Black History Knowledge (BHK), 209
Black Liberation Psychology, 209
black nationalism, 118
Black Panther Party, 7
Blue Lives Matter, ix, 6
Boyd, Rekia, 10
Bring Back Our Girls, 176
Burundi, 162, 163, 262, 264

California, 13, 43, 316–17
California Department of Education (CDE), 43
Canada, 2
Carson, Ben, 8
Center for Global Policy Solutions, 228
Central Africa, 167, 259
Chad, 163, 167, 262
Chicago, 182, 187, 225, 230–31
Chicago Tribune, 67–68
Civil Rights Movement, 187, 190, 230
Civil Rights Project at Harvard University, 135
Civil War in the United States, 185
cognitive approach, 200
COINTELPRO, 142
Cold War, 261
Columbia Broadcasting System (CBS), 69–70

Commission on the Social Status of
    Black Men and Boys Act, 76, 101
Communications Workers of America
    (CWA), 11
Community Action Programs, 224
Community Reinvestment Act, 224
content analysis, 72, 85, 251, 254, 268
Coronavirus/COVID-2019, 7
Correctional Offender Management
    Profiling for Alternative Sanctions
    (COMPAS), 142
Côte d'Ivoire, 248
Cullors, Patrisse, 1, 138, 153
Cup Foods, 108
Curse of Ham, 185

Dangarembga, Tsitsi, xi, 50, 57
Davis, Angela, 7, 142
Democratic National Committee (DNC),
    10
Democratic Party, 275, 278, 293
Democratic Republic of the Congo,
    163
Denmark, 2
dichlorodiphenyltrichloroethane (DDT),
    256
Dieng, Daouda, 57–58
Du Bois, W. E. B., 215
Durkheim, Emile, 19

Easton, David, 252–53
Economic Partnership Agreements
    (EPAs), 267
END SARS, 170–71, 173
Ethiopia, 260
Europe, 238, 251, 258–60, 265–66

Fatima (hand of), 117
fiction, 42–44
Financial Institutions Reform, Recovery,
    and Enforcement Act (FIRREA), 191
Fox Broadcasting (FOX), 70
Fox News Channel (Fox News), 70
France, 2, 56, 176, 260, 264
Freud, Sigmund, 20

Garza, Alicia, 1, 18, 138. 153, 171, 203
Germany, 2, 22, 67, 260, 263–64
Google, 66, 186, 303
Great Depression, 230–31, 261
Great Migration, 230

Hijra, 19
Hispanic, 190, 226–27, 231, 286
Holy Bible, 4, 8, 185, 306
Holy Qur'an, 185, 312, 314, 318
Holy Torah, 185, 301–3, 306
humanistic approach, 200

Ibn Khaldun, 252
India, 107, 176
Individuals with Disabilities Act
    (IDEA), 287
Indonesia, 108, 318
Industrial Revolution, 252, 260
Iran, 226
Iraq, 226

Japan, 2
Jesus Christ, 19, 122, 310–11, 316
Juvenile Justice and Delinquency
    Prevention Act (JJDPA), 273–74
Juvenile Justice Reform Act, 274

Kagame, Paul, 264–65
Kennedy, John F., 7
Kenya, 24, 33, 315–16
Kenyatta, Jomo, 33
Kenyatta, Uhuru, 315
King, Alveda, 7
King Jr., Martin Luther, 7–8

Latino/Latina, 134, 137, 223–24, 227,
    229, 234–35, 286, 313
Liberia, 175, 260, 262

Ma'at, 299–300
Malaysia, 318
Mali, 248
Mapping Police Violence, 247
Martin, Michael, 10

Martin, Trayvon, 10, 18, 75, 138, 153, 171
Marx, Karl, 26, 257
Mary (hand of), 117
Matrix Laboratory (MATLAB), 63
mean ($\bar{X}$ or m), 62–63, 68, 70
Medina, 318
metaphonymy, 110–13
metaphoricity, 113
Middle East, 265
Milton, John, 45
Minneapolis, Minnesota, ix, 108, 138, 247
Mitterrand, Francois, 264
Moore, Kayla, 10
Museveni, Yoweri, 265

Namibia, 164–66, 171–73
National Broadcasting Company (NBC), 69–70
National Center for Education Statistics (NCES), 287
Native American, 8, 190, 223, 234, 286, 313
New York Post, 67–68
The New York Times, 67–68
New Zealand, 2, 317
Nigeria, 24, 48, 52, 163–67, 169–76, 226, 248, 257, 262
nonfiction, 42–45

Obama, Barack, 6, 82, 96, 187, 190–91
Office of Juvenile Justice and Delinquency Prevention (OJJDP), 274

Pacific Islander, 220, 313
paired sample t-test (t), 63, 68, 70–71
part-whole metonymic relations, 110, 121
patterns of meaning, 199
percentage, 62, 86, 91, 218
physiological-biological approach, 200
powernomics, xii, 181
pro-life Christians, 307
Prophet Muhammad (PBUH), 19, 315, 318

race-based economic inequities, 191, 218
range (Rang(x)), 62–63, 68, 70
Rasmussen Reports, 3
Rastafarian, 118
Reconstruction Racial Order, 224
Republican Party, 2, 275, 278, 293
Rwanda, 22, 163, 248, 262–65

Scales, Kailee, 188
Scott, Tim, 9, 276
Senegal, 55–56
Sessions, Jeff, 304
Shutterstock.com, 107
Siddhartha Gautama, 19
Sierra Leone, 162, 170, 262
Small Business Administration, 217
South Africa, 164–65, 172, 226
Soyinka, Wole, 53–55
standard deviation (σ or sd), 62–63, 67–68, 70
The Sudan, 248, 261–62

Talent x Opportunity, 234
Taylor, Breonna, 305, 313
Tillich, Paul, 20
Tometi, Opal, 1–2, 138, 153
Trans-Atlantic Slave Trade, 259
Tutu, Desmond, 32

Ubuntu, 32, 37
Uganda, 226, 265
Undungu, 32
Union of Soviet Socialist Republics (USSR), 261
United Kingdom, 171, 238, 260
United Nations Convention on the Elimination of All Forms of Discrimination Against Women (CEDAW), 174–75
United Nations Office of the High Commissioner for Human Rights (UNOHCHR), 161–62, 164, 167–68
United States Census Bureau, 190
univariate, xi, 62, 66–67, 69

Universal Declaration of Human Rights, 261, 266
University of Memphis in Tennessee, x
Utu, 32–33, 37

venture capital, 191, 228
Voting Rights Act, 7

The Wall Street Journal, 67–68
Warren, Elizabeth, 7
The Washington Post, 67–68, 187, 247
White Lives Matter, ix
White Student Union Facebook Groups, ix
World Trade Organization (WTO), 256
World Wide Web (WWW), 66, 186, 289

Yugoslavia, 22

Zamani, 27
zero tolerance policy (ZTP), 131–36
Zimbabwe, 50–51, 171
Zimmerman, George, 18, 22, 138, 153, 171, 203

About the Contributors

Lilian Achieng' Magonya holds a PhD in linguistics. She is a lecturer in the Department of Linguistics at Maseno University in Kenya. She has published scientific articles in thirteen peer-reviewed journals and several book chapters in press. Her research interests are in the fields of pragmatics and cognitive linguistics.

Cecy Edijala Balogun is a PhD candidate in rural sociology at University of Ibadan in Nigeria. She is also a research fellow in the Nigerian Institute of Social and Economic Research (NISER), Ibadan, Nigeria. She is a coauthor in the following book projects: *Theoretical Grounding in African Research*, *Corohysteria*, and *Great Books by Africans across the Disciplines* (in press). She is a prestigious Scholar of the CODESRIA College of Mentors. She has also worked with a nongovernment organization where she coordinated youth empowerment programs for youth development and is highly interested in youth development and rural sociology studies.

Abdul Karim Bangura has five PhDs in political science, development economics, linguistics, computer science, and mathematics. He is a researcher-in-residence of Abrahamic connections and Islamic peace studies at American University's Center for Global Peace in Washington, D.C.. He is the author and editor of 105 other books and 708 scholarly articles, some of which have won major scholarly awards. He is the recipient of more than fifty other prestigious national and international scholarly and community service awards. In addition to serving on many national and international organizations' committees, he also has lectured and done television and newspaper interviews in many countries across the globe.

About the Contributors

Saidu Bangura holds a PhD in translation, communication and culture, with a specialty in English sociolinguistics, from the University of Las Palmas, Canary Islands, Spain. He is an assistant professor of English at the University of Cape Verde, where he directs the M.A. in English studies, a program he helped to build. He has coauthored book chapters and articles around the Cape Verdean linguistic situation and regional integration. He has published several poems and has an anthology of poems published in June 2021. He has won several academic fellowship awards in Portugal, University of Coimbra (2011); Brazil, State University of Campinas (2014); and Spain, University of Las Palmas (2015).

Gerald K. Fosten is a research associate at the African Institution in Washington D.C.. His focus is on American government, international relations, and public policy issues pertaining to African Americans. He is the author of the book *Social Inequality, Race, and Criminal Justice in Tennessee: 1960–2014*. He also has coauthored several book chapters and published many articles in several journals, including those at Temple University and California State University. He received his B.Sc. in business administration from Fisk University, master in public administration from the College of Public of Service (formerly the Institute of Government) at Tennessee State University, and PhD in political science from Howard University.

Abdul Amin Kamara is the principal of Nashirr Islamic Secondary School in Freetown, Sierra Leone. He holds a B.A. degree (history and sociology) and a postgraduate diploma in education from Fourah Bay College of the University of Sierra Leone. He is currently a MPhil candidate in the same school and university. He is the author of another book chapter in press.

Benson Waiganjo Kanyingi is a doctoral candidate at Karatina University. He is also a lecturer at Egerton University and an emerging researcher who has put his expertise in history and sociology to fruitful use. He has published two scholarly articles on land allocation, contestations, war of independence memories, and entitlements related to Mau Mau discourses. He is a laureate of the CODESRIA Gender Institute, where he presented a paper on gender, diseases and governance, a clear illustration that he appreciates what is happening in Africa.

Olumuyiwa Adekunle Kehinde is a PhD candidate at University of Zululand in South Africa with interest in English and communication disorders. He is a trained journalist with a main focus on education, health, and business. He has authored several scholarly articles. He is one of the 2019 CODESRIA doctoral mentees, and he has won several awards as a student member of the

International Society of Autism Research. He has also lectured on a part-time basis at some institutions in Nigeria and served as Tutor Champion at the University of Zululand.

Lilian Anyango Olick is a PhD candidate in business administration and finance at the University of Nairobi in Kenya. She is a communication and grants officer at Columbia Global Centers in Nairobi, Kenya, and the author of another book chapter and more than three scholarly articles. She also has lectured at Jomo Kenyatta University of Agriculture and Technology and worked for International Rescue Committee (United States) as a scale design consultant/field researcher, at Women Fighting Aids in Kenya as a program director, at Transparency International Kenya and LVCT Health as a grant officer, and at Wimssy Limited as a strategic management consultant. She has a great passion for project design and development and a keen interest in social enterprise modeling, sustainability finance, youth empowerment, and education.

Pamela Anyango Oloo holds a PhD in linguistics. She is senior lecturer and chairperson of the Department of Linguistics at Maseno University, Kenya, and also a German Academic Exchange Service (Deutscher Akademischer Austausch Dienst—DAAD) scholar. She is the author of one book, twenty scholarly articles in recognized peer-reviewed journals, and several book chapters in press. She also holds various postgraduate professional development certificates. Her research interests include discourse analysis, language and gender, and health communication. Her most recent research activity entailed investigating the role of leadership in the use of innovative pedagogies for learning and research outputs in Kenyan public universities.

Simon Gisege Omare holds a PhD in religious studies. His area of interest is sociology of religion. He is a senior lecturer at Moi University, Kenya. He is the author of *Witchcraft Scapegoat: Abagusii Beliefs and Violence against "Witches."* and *Religion and Environment Conservation: The Role of Isukha Religious Beliefs and Practices in the Conservation of Kakamega Forest, Kenya*. He also has written five chapters and more than ten scholarly articles. He enjoys reading works and writing on topics dealing with the sociology of religion.

Omosefe Oyekanmi is a PhD candidate of political science at the University of Ibadan, Nigeria. She is a research fellow at the Nigerian Institute of Social and Economic Research (NISER), Ibadan. She has published several book chapters and several scholarly articles. As a fellow at the Ibadan School of Government and Public Policy (ISGPP) and a 2019 CODESRIA College of

Mentors Scholar, she is a recipient of both national and international scholarly awards. She has lectured in the University of Ibadan Distant Learning Centre and supervised over thirty students in political science. Her works span peace and conflict, development, federalism, and women and gender studies.

Rachael M. Rudolph holds a PhD in political science. She is an assistant professor for a joint program between Bryant University and the Beijing Institute of Technology, Zhuhai, China. She also serves as an advisory board member for the New York Center for Foreign Policy Analysis, which is headquartered in New York and has an office in Washington D.C. She is the author of four books, more than ten scholarly articles, and numerous media articles. She has lived in the Indo-Asia Pacific region for eight years and traveled for field work to Africa, Central America, Europe, and the Middle East.